# On Goodness

# On Goodness

DAVID CONAN WOLFSDORF

OXFORD
UNIVERSITY PRESS

# OXFORD
### UNIVERSITY PRESS

Oxford University Press is a department of the University of Oxford. It furthers
the University's objective of excellence in research, scholarship, and education
by publishing worldwide. Oxford is a registered trade mark of Oxford University
Press in the UK and certain other countries.

Published in the United States of America by Oxford University Press
198 Madison Avenue, New York, NY 10016, United States of America.

© Oxford University Press 2019

Library of Congress Cataloging-in-Publication Data
Names: Wolfsdorf, David, 1969– author.
Title: On goodness / David Conan Wolfsdorf.
Description: New York : Oxford University Press, 2019. |
Includes bibliographical references and index. | Description based on print version
record and CIP data provided by publisher; resource not viewed.
Identifiers: LCCN 2019981553 | ISBN 9780190688509 (cloth : alk. paper)
Subjects: LCSH: Good and evil. | Semantics (Philosophy) | Virtue.
Classification: LCC BJ1401 | DDC 111/.84—dc23
LC record available at https://lccn.loc.gov/2019981553

1 3 5 7 9 8 6 4 2

Printed by Sheridan Books, Inc., United States of America

*for Janet*

# Contents

# Acknowledgments

Research for this book began in earnest during a sabbatical in 2013–14. I would like to thank the American Council of Learned Societies for a fellowship and Temple University for financial support which made the sabbatical possible.

In the last five years, I have contacted many linguists from around the world to request copies of their works in progress or published but difficult to obtain, to ask questions, and to exchange ideas. With few exceptions, they have been generous and encouraging. I especially want to thank Muffy Siegel for offering me advice at an early stage in the project and for occasional discussions of my work. I want to thank Jessica Rett for sharing her manuscript, *The Semantics of Evaluativity*, then in progress, since published; and for her generosity in welcoming my questions, tolerating my muddled ideas, and patiently attempting to steer me toward clarity.

Two philosophers who have recently studied the semantics or syntax of "good" are Robert Shanklin and Stephen Finlay. I want to thank Robert for sharing his dissertation *On "Good" and Good*, and for occasional exchanges. I want to thank Stephen for sharing his work *Confusion of Tongues*, then in progress, since published; for occasional exchanges; and for his comments on a draft of my manuscript.

It is customary for academic authors to append to their acknowledgments of gratitude to other scholars the claim that these other scholars bear no responsibility for the author's failings and misunderstandings. In the past, such claims have seemed to me mere formalities. But I fully appreciate the need to make such a claim here.

For the last five odd years, I have been teaching portions of the material that has become this book, in various phases of its development, to an undergraduate class at Temple University called Good and Bad, Right and Wrong. I am grateful to the students for giving me the opportunity to present and develop my ideas, and for their interest in the subject and helpful questions and criticisms. I recall with particular fondness the bright and engaged class of spring semester 2018.

I want to thank Lucy Randall, my editor at Oxford University Press, for originally inviting submission of my work and for her efficient and kind support through the review and publication process. I want to thank Hannah Doyle, Lucy's editorial assistant, for her kind support. I want to thank Rajesh Kathamuthu for overseeing the copyediting process. I also want to thank two external reviewers for Oxford University Press, for their thoughtful and constructive criticisms.

I want to thank the Visual Artists and Galleries Association at the Artists Rights Society for permission to reproduce the cover image, Wayne Thiebaud's 1969 oil painting *Candy Counter*.

The goodness of Thiebaud's painting and the goodies it depicts should indicate to the reader that the following is not intended as work of ethical philosophy. To be sure, it is not a work of aesthetics either. As I state in the introduction that follows, I regard this as a work of metaphysics, precisely at the foundations of value theory.

# On Goodness

# 1
# Introduction

> A thorough examination of this opinion belongs to a different field
> of study, one that inevitably, in many ways is more akin to logic and
> language.[1]

The goal of this study is to answer the question "What is goodness?"[2] It is natural to associate this question with ethics. But goodness is not confined to ethics. Water and wine, a strategy for streamlining maintenance operations, a proof or disproof of the null hypothesis, and a rendering of a candy counter in oil may all be good and in non-ethical ways. Goodness figures prominently in ethics. So the study serves ethics. But it serves other domains as well. And it offers a variety of services.

This study is a contribution to the foundations of value theory. It is also a metaphysical inquiry, for two related reasons. As the preceding examples indicate, the entity under investigation is extremely general. Goodness occurs in potables, plans, proofs, and paintings, among countless other kinds of things. Second, it is particularly obscure what sort of being the entity is. Besides the description "good," is there a single thing that good drinks, strategies, arguments, and artworks share? Is their goodness related in a more complex way? Is goodness in some cases unrelated to goodness in others? If so, why? And regardless of these relations, in any instance, just what is that goodness?

For these reasons, I will speak of "What is goodness?" as a metaphysical question, a metaphysical question at the foundations of value theory. This question has been central to philosophy since Socrates and Plato made it their polestar. The distinctive contribution of this study lies in its methodology. The method

---

[1] Aristotle, *Eudemian Ethics*, 1217b17–18. My phrase "logic and language" corresponds to the single Greek word *logikē*. Cp. Jonathan Barnes' remark: "*logikē* was the science which studies *logos* in all its manifestations." *The Cambridge History of Hellenistic Philosophy*, K. Algra, J. Barnes, J. Mansfeld, and M. Schofield, eds., Cambridge University Press, 1999, 67.

[2] Throughout this study, I follow the standard philosophical practice of employing quotation marks when mentioning linguistic expressions, more precisely when mentioning linguistic expressions within the main text. (I employ a different convention when mentioning linguistic expressions set off from the main text; see footnote 5.) In linguistics, the standard practice is instead to italicize such expressions. In this study, such employment of italics is confined to quotations from others who follow that practice. Otherwise, I use italics for emphasis and to represent certain logical and linguistic symbols.

of pursuing the metaphysical question will be linguistic. The basic proposal is that achieving the answer depends on clarifying the meaning (sense or denotation)[3] and use of the words "good" and "goodness." Consequently, the study will be pervasively informed by and critically engaged with theories and ideas in contemporary semantics and pragmatics as well as syntax, on which both crucially depend.[4]

Many aspects of contemporary linguistics grew out of the philosophical study of language that dominated the first three-quarters of the twentieth century. Contemporary philosophers in turn have benefited from the kinds of contemporary linguistic work that I will be recruiting here. A good example is work on deontic modality. Compare the occurrences of "must," one among several modal auxiliary verbs, in the following two sentences:

1. You must treat him more respectfully.
2. The train must be arriving soon.[5]

Assume that in (1) "must" is being used deontically. In (2), the use is epistemic. Reconsider both sentences after replacing "must" with the weaker "might":

1w. You might treat him more respectfully.
2w. The train might be arriving soon.

So the meanings that modal auxiliary constructions are used to convey vary according to at least two parameters: the kind of modality (here, deontic versus epistemic) and the strength of modality (here, "must" versus "might"). This result

---

[3] Throughout this study, I use the terms "meaning," "sense," and "denotation" interchangeably. There are subtle distinctions between these terms in ordinary language. But I ignore them here and employ the terms in a regimented way conforming to their usage in semantic theory.

[4] The sense of "metaphysics" in which I am employing this term here conforms to one of several common senses according to which this term is employed in contemporary philosophy. According to the sense in which I am using the term, concern with the general and fundamental nature of things is at least a significant part of metaphysics. Granted this, note that my primary goal in this work is not to make existential claims, but rather definitional or at least identity claims: "Goodness $=_{df}$ X" or "Goodness = X." Contrast: "Goodness exists." Beyond this, the reader should feel free to treat my use of "metaphysics" in as robust or as deflationary a way as it suits his or her metasemantics. On matters of metasemantics, I myself am silent here. Securing substantive metasemantic claims belongs to a weighty enterprise different from the one that I am pursuing. That said, consider finally the following argument: "Goodness" means "M." Assume that meanings are intensions. (The weaker claim, that synonymous terms are cointensional, would serve just as well in this case.) Since cointensional terms are coextensional, if "goodness" and "M" refer to anything, then they refer to the same entity or entities. This much suffices for my purposes.

[5] Throughout the study, I use Gill Sans MT font for examples of linguistic expressions set off from the main text.

derives from formal semantic theory originally developed in the seventies by Angelika Kratzer.[6]

G. E. Moore famously ushered philosophical work on goodness into the twentieth century with the leading questions of his *Principia Ethica*: "What, then, is good? How is good to be defined?"[7] Much of that work came to turn on the century's governing metaethical debate: cognitivist versus non-cognitivist interpretations of ethical thought and language. For instance, can the content of the sentence "Pleasure is good" be the content of a belief? Accordingly, does the sentence have truth-value? Must the content of the sentence instead be the content of a non-cognitive state such as an attitude of approbation? And in that case, is the sentence itself not evaluable for truth or falsity?

Philosophers vigorously debated such questions, and some continue to do so. But since the rise of formal semantics in the seventies, there has been little work by philosophers on the meaning of "good" that is well informed by and critically engaged with pertinent linguistic literature. Chapter 2 of Stephen Finlay's 2014 *Confusion of Tongues* is exceptional in being a recent semantic analysis of "good" by a philosopher.[8] Robert Shanklin's 2011 dissertation *On "Good" and Good*, written partly under Finlay's guidance and critically engaged with some of his ideas, is another exception.[9] When I began the research that has eventuated in this book, both Finlay's and Shanklin's contributions served as valuable sources of information and inspiration.

Since the sixties, there has been sporadic work in linguistics on the semantics of "good"—in all cases, as part of, if not tangential to, broader agendas. In Muffy Siegel's seminal 1976 dissertation *Capturing the Adjective*, "good" is one example of what she argues are doublets, that is, adjectives with two semantic and syntactic profiles. In a section of a lengthy chapter published in 1987,[10] Manfred Bierwisch argues that "good" and "bad" are members of a subset of gradable adjectives whose antonymy differs from that of ordinary gradable adjectives insofar as "good" and "bad" are each associated with a distinct gradable property. Another incisive discussion of "good" occurs in Zoltán Szabó's 2001 paper "Adjectives in Context."[11] Szabó argues that "good" exemplifies a class of adjectives whose context sensitivity conforms to the principle of compositionality. The adjective "good" is analyzed as an incomplete unary

---

[6] "What 'Must' and 'Can' Must and Can Mean," *Linguistics and Philosophy* 1 (1977) 337–55.
[7] *Principia Ethica*, Cambridge University Press, 1903, §2.
[8] Oxford University Press.
[9] University of Southern California, dissertation in philosophy.
[10] "The Semantics of Gradation," in *Dimensional Adjectives*, M. Bierwisch and E. Lang, eds., Springer, 1987, 71–262.
[11] *Perspectives on Semantics, Pragmatics, and Discourse*, I. Kenesei and R. M. Harnish, eds., John Benjamins, 2001, 119–46.

predicate, which contains a variable whose contextually determined values specify ways of being good.

With respect to "goodness," there has been no philosophical work that is well informed by and critically engaged with the pertinent linguistic literature. In fact, I know of no work by linguists or philosophers on "goodness" that is informed by the relevant linguistic literature. "Goodness" is a noun, hence a nominal expression. It is formed from an adjective; so it is an adjectival nominalization. The adjective itself is gradable. For instance, consider the three grades of comparison of traditional grammar: "good," "better," "best." So "goodness" is a gradable adjectival nominalization.

Almost all nominalizations formed with the suffix "-ness" are mass as opposed to count nouns. The standard interpretation of the semantics of mass nouns appeals to an algebraic structure called a "lattice." The seminal source of the lattice theory of mass nouns is Godehard Link's 1983 paper "The Logical Analysis of Plural and Mass Terms."[12] As the title of Link's paper suggests, the denotation of mass nouns is akin to that of plural count nouns. For example, consider the following quantifier phrases:

a lot of kindness
a lot of cats
* a lot of cat.

(Throughout this study, I follow the linguistic convention of affixing an asterisk to the beginning of an expression to indicate that it is syntactically ill formed.) The fact that the singular mass noun "kindness" and the plural count noun "cats" admit the vague quantifier "a lot of," whereas the singular count noun "cat" does not, suggests that the denotations of "kindness" and "cats" share something that the denotation of "cat" lacks. This something is a type of lattice structure.

In addition, since "kindness," like "goodness," is a gradable adjectival mass nominalization, a phrase such as "a lot of kindness" is ambiguous between "many instances of kindness" and "a high degree of kindness in a single instance"; for example:

Janet's action demonstrated a lot of kindness.
Janet encountered a lot of kindness during her trip to Croatia.

---

[12] *Meaning, Use, and Interpretation of Language*, R. Bäuerle, C. Schwarze, and A. von Stechow, eds., de Gruyter, 1983, 127–46.

Frederike Moltmann's recent book, *Abstract Objects and the Semantics of Natural Language*, examines the semantics and metaphysical implications of the semantics of adjectival nominalizations, including gradable adjectival nominalizations.[13] Moltmann's work has significantly influenced my thinking on these topics. Central to her account is the view that natural language has a prevailing nominalistic tendency. Accordingly, she argues that nouns of the form "*F*-ness" such as "tallness," "kindness," and "goodness" are not property-denoting terms, according to any robust metaphysical conception of properties. Rather, their denotations consist of tropes and more precisely quantitative tropes.

Tropes are property instances.[14] In other words, tropes are unique features of particulars. Quantitative tropes are unique quantitative features of particulars. For example, consider the phrase

Paolo's height.

This phrase denotes a particular quantitative feature of Paolo, precisely the (maximal) degree of his vertical extension. Support for the view that such a phrase denotes a quantitative trope and so a particular quantitative feature derives from the fact that such entities can play causal roles; for example:

Paolo's height disabled him from standing fully upright in the cabin.

Granted this, the meaning of a term such as "height" differs from the meaning of a term such as "tallness." Insofar as nominalizations of the form "*F*-ness" derive from gradable adjectives, they denote entities consisting of ordered pairs of quantitative tropes. Adapting Kit Fine's notion of qua objects, Moltmann suggests that such entities are qua tropes; precisely, one quantitative trope qua exceeding another quantitative trope. For instance, the phrase

Paolo's tallness

denotes the quantitative trope of Paolo's height qua exceeding another quantitative trope, in the latter case an abstract quantitative trope consisting of a contextually determined standard of comparison. Likewise:

The goodness of Thiebaud's 1969 *Candy Counter*.

---

[13] Oxford University Press, 2013.
[14] The mention of "property" here is heuristic. A commitment to tropes does not require a commitment to properties. On the contrary, trope theory tends to be nominalistic.

Finally, the meaning of mass nouns and so "goodness" is further complicated by the fact that they can occur in a syntactic configuration called a "bare noun phrase." That is, they can occur in argument positions, for example, as the subject of a declarative sentence, without a so-called determiner such as the indefinite or definite article; for example:

Goodness is rare.
Goodness is a measure of value.

Contrast the ungrammaticality of an ordinary singular count noun such as "dog" or "house" without a determiner in such a position:

* Dog is barking.
* House has three bedrooms.

Since Gregory Carlson first systematically studied them in his 1977 dissertation *Reference to Kinds in English*,[15] it has been recognized that bare noun phrases may be at least four ways ambiguous, admitting universally quantified, generically quantified, existentially quantified, and so-called kind-denoting readings. The principles that explain these readings remain elusive.

In short, there is a sizable gap in the philosophical literature. On the one hand, there is a deep and long-standing interest in understanding the nature of goodness. On the other, there are rich, highly sophisticated bodies of linguistic literature that bear on that understanding. This gap is curious. Contemporary linguistics and its various subfields, especially syntactic theory and formal semantics, have reached a level of maturity including a level of technicality that impedes access by non-specialists. But technical linguistic contributions have informed other areas of contemporary philosophical research. Work on modality previously mentioned is a case in point. Indexical or relativistic interpretations of philosophically important and contested terms such as "true," "know," and even "cause" as well as predicate expressions of personal taste such as "fun" and "tasty" are others. For whatever reason, philosophers have overlooked or underappreciated certain properties of "good" and "goodness," properties that linguists have studied, in many cases intensively.

Because philosophers are my target audience, I have been reluctant to incorporate into my discussion the sorts of formalizations that are conventional in the contemporary linguistic, especially semantic literature. One of the reviewers for

---

[15] University of Massachusetts, Amherst, dissertation in linguistics (published by Garland Press, 1980).

the press expressly discouraged doing so. I agree that on balance such formalism would have a discouraging, indeed alienating effect. Some examples should illustrate the point:

3. $[\![A_{\text{nom-pos}}]\!]^{c,w,i} = \{<t,x> | \exists t'(B(x,t')\&t' \in c(A)(w,i)\&t=f(t',\lambda y[y \geq_A \text{std}(c(A),c)],w,i))\}$

4. $[\![A(\mathcal{P}')_{\text{AP}}]\!] = \lambda x.\exists P[P \in \mathcal{D}ist(\text{Cons},\mathcal{U}p(\mathcal{A}vg(\mathcal{P}'),[\![A_A]\!]))\&P(x)]$

5. $[\![\text{pos}]\!]^c = \lambda C \in D_{\langle x,t \rangle}.\lambda f \in D_{\langle x,r \rangle}.\lambda x \in D_x.f(x) \geq \text{norm}_c(f,C)$

Item (3) is Moltmann's interpretation of the denotation of a gradable adjectival nominalization such as "kindness."[16] Item (4) is Ad Neeleman, Hans van de Koot, and Jenny Doetjes's interpretation of the denotation of a gradable adjectival phrase composed of a gradable adjective in the morphologically basic form and an adjunctive comparison class prepositional phrase, for example, "tall for a five-year old."[17] And item (5) is Robert van Rooij and Galit Sassoon's interpretation of the denotation of the covert degree morpheme, called *pos*, that is standardly taken to be a part of the semantics of constructions of the form "*x* is *a*,"[18] where *a* stands for a gradable adjective in the morphologically basic form, for example, "*x* is good."[19]

So all three formalizations pertain to core expressions and ideas within the formal semantic literature on gradable adjectives and adjectival nominalizations. Such formalizations are not occasional within this literature; they are the default mode of representing meanings and meaning derivations. Although it may appear ungainly, item (5) is in fact very simple. The authors do not and would not pause to provide a natural language paraphrase, let alone to explain the symbols employed. Or rather, the symbols C, f, and x are explained, but within the formula itself, in the terms of the lambda-categorical language and semantic type theoretic notation standard in the discipline.

Of course, such formalism can be learned, and likely with particular facility by philosophers comfortable with formal logic. However, I see no compelling reason to attempt a tutorial here and then to impose such expressions on my audience—especially in the context of introducing all of the informal, but unfamiliar, complex, sometimes abstruse linguistic ideas. The result is that the following chapters assume no background in linguistics; and the limited formal expressions I do employ are either explained when they occur or should be

---

[16] "Degree Structure as Trope Structure," *Linguistics and Philosophy* 32 (2009) 51–94, at 83.

[17] "Degree Expressions," *Linguistic Review* 21 (2004) 1–66, at 39.

[18] Robert Van Rooij and Galit W. Sassoon, "The Semantics of *for* Phrases and Its Implications," unpublished, 13.

[19] For convenience, throughout I follow the practice of using symbols such as *a* as names for themselves.

readily intelligible to anyone with basic logic. In general, all technical linguistic terminology and ideas are explained when they are first introduced.

Beyond having told the truth, my hopes for this study are twofold. I hope that the results will provide clearer and more secure foundations for value theory generally and for various particular inquiries that crucially involve the terms "good" and "goodness." Second, I hope that the method I have employed to pursue my governing question will encourage other philosophers who have not already been impressed by the linguistic developments of recent decades to consider these contributions and their applicability. There is much to be gained philosophically by attending to topics central to this study such as ambiguity and polysemy, gradability and multidimensionality, indexicalism (which I call syntactic "determinism") and free pragmaticism (which constitutes a large part of what I call "compatibilism"), mass nouns and count nouns, adjectival nominalization and bare noun phrases; and to the works of those who have thought deeply about them.

Finally, the structures of the chapters and their central claims and arguments are signposted and summarized all along the way. Consequently, at this point the reader should feel free to turn to chapter 2. However, for those who would like a quick overview of the remainder, I conclude this introduction by offering one.

The study may be viewed as divisible into two parts. Chapters 2 through 5 focus on the meaning and use of the adjective "good." Chapters 6 and 7 focus on the meaning and use of the adjectival nominalization "goodness."

Chapter 2 argues that "good" is three ways ambiguous. I call the three senses of "good" "evaluative," "quantitative," and "operational." I suggest that evaluative "good" and operational "good" are two polysemous senses of a single word, and that quantitative "good" is a distinct word, whose sense stands in the relation of homonymy to the former two.

Evaluative "good" is the sense of "good" that has been of principal philosophical interest and that is the focus of chapters 3 through 5. Consequently, in the remainder of this introduction, I will drop the modifier "evaluative" when referring to this sense of "good."

As suggested above, "good" is a gradable adjective. With the aim of clarifying the meaning of "good," chapter 3 elaborates on the semantics of gradable adjectives, especially so-called relative gradable adjectives.

Gradable adjectives are associated with gradable properties. For example, "tall" is associated with the gradable property of height. "Good" is associated with the gradable property of value. Chapter 4 examines the nature of value, and does so by linguistic means. The central thesis of the chapter is that value is purpose serving. Consequently, if something has value, it serves or is serving a purpose; and so if something is good, it serves or is serving a purpose. "Purpose" itself is at least two ways ambiguous; and in the relevant so-called modal sense of "purpose," there are at least four fundamentally distinct kinds of purpose and so value and so ways of being good.

Some gradable adjectives are specifiable by kind; others are not. For example, there are not kinds of height; but there are kinds of value. As just noted, there are at least four basic kinds. But within each kind, there are countless sub-kinds. In the formal semantic literature, gradable properties are called "dimensions." Accordingly, I characterize "tall" as a unidimensional gradable adjective, and "good" as a multidimensional gradable adjective. Chapter 5 examines how the dimension of value with which "good" is associated is specified on occasions of use. In pursuing this question, I consider two broad types of explanation: syntactic determinism—exemplified by, among others, Szabó's position previously mentioned—and compatibilism. According to the latter, dimensional specification is compatible with, but not mandated by, the syntax of "good." In other words, dimensional specification is syntactically optional. The linguistic operation responsible for its occurrence is what I call "supplementation," the crux of which is adverbial modification of "good."

Having clarified the meaning and use of "good," I turn to the meaning and use of the adjectival nominalization. As noted previously, "goodness" is a mass as opposed to count noun. Chapter 6 explains the distinction between mass and count nouns and argues that, semantically, the distinction rests on a pair of correlative properties, which I call "semantic cumulativity" and "semantic divisibility." I then explain the standard lattice theoretic account of the denotation of mass nouns, and finally clarify the metaphysical implications of the preceding linguistic results for the nature of goodness.

At the conclusion of chapter 6, the governing metaphysical question "What is goodness?" has been answered. Consequently, chapter 7 might be viewed as a coda to the study. However, the topic that it introduces is crucial to any adequate understanding of how "goodness" is used. As previously mentioned, "goodness" and other mass nouns, as well as plural count nouns, can occur as bare noun phrases; and in such cases, they are subject to various readings. I consider two principal theories that have been proposed to explain the variety of readings: the kind-denoting theory, which ultimately derives from Carlson, and the ambiguity theory, various versions of which arose in response to Carlson. While I incline to accept some neo-Carlsonian explanation of the phenomena, the aim of the chapter is merely to introduce the problem of the ambiguity of bare noun phrases and the principal responses to it.

# 2

# Ambiguity

Then if we cannot capture the good with one form, let us grasp it with three.[1]

## 1. The Fundamental Ambiguity of "Good"

Compare the instances of "good" in the following three sentences:

1. That is a good painting.
2. It's a good distance from here to City Hall by foot.
3. The light bulb is good; it's the wiring in the switch that's frayed.

Throughout this study, I will refer to tokens of and the meaning of "good" as it occurs in sentence (1) as "evaluative."

In using the term "evaluative" to characterize "good" in sentences such as (1), I intend to convey that in such cases "good" is associated with value. For example, the phrase "a good painting" denotes a painting that has value, in typical instances precisely aesthetic value. Likewise, the phrase "a good person" denotes a person who has value, in some instances precisely moral value.[2]

Granted this, the claim that a word such as "good" is associated with a thing such as value is vague. The nature of the association can be precisified in terms of semantic and metaphysical entailments. A sentence of the form "$x$ is good"— where evaluative "good" occurs in the predicate—semantically entails "$x$ has value." Likewise, where $N$ stands for a nominal expression, a sentence of the form "$x$ is a good $N$" entails "$x$ is an $N$ that has value." The semantic entailments in turn suggest the following metaphysical entailments. That $x$ is good metaphysically entails that $x$ has value; and that $x$ is a good $N$ metaphysically entails that $x$ is an $N$ that has value.[3]

---

[1] Plato, *Philebus* 65a1–2.
[2] Cp. Shanklin (2011) 145–91.
[3] One exception to the preceding semantic and consequently metaphysical entailments relates to certain agentive nominal expressions insofar as they denote temporary or so-called stage-level properties of individuals. This point is discussed in section 3.6.1 of chapter 5.

I will refer to tokens of and the meaning of "good" as it occurs in sentence (2) as "quantitative." In (2), "good" modifies the expression "distance," which denotes a kind of quantity or magnitude; and, crucially, "good" itself describes the quantity or magnitude expression it modifies in quantitative terms.[4] A "good distance" is here equivalent to a "long distance."[5]

I will refer to tokens of and the meaning of "good" as it occurs in sentence (3) as "operational." Assume the following context for this sentence. The speaker has tried to turn on a lamp, but the lamp has not come on, and the speaker is offering an explanation. In claiming that the bulb is good, the speaker is claiming that the bulb is operational, functional, in working order.

This chapter will clarify and corroborate the fundamental three-way ambiguity of "good."[6] It will do so by identifying and explaining several distinguishing semantic properties of evaluative, quantitative, and operational "good" as well as several distinguishing syntactic and phonological properties.

Section 2.1 begins by elaborating on quantitative "good" and precisely on the kinds of quantity it may describe. Section 2.2 distinguishes quantitative and evaluative "good" on the basis of eight linguistic properties: gradability, association with value, antonymy, sensitivity to definiteness effects, modification of mass nouns, predicativity, and two kinds of stress patterns in modified nominal expressions. Section 2.3 concludes the discussion of quantitative "good" by considering quantitative "good" modification of measure phrases. I argue that the properties of such constructions conform to the properties of quantitative "good," thereby also corroborating the results of section 2.2.

Section 3 discusses operational "good" and focuses on the relation between operational "good" and evaluative "good" in terms of the eight linguistic properties discussed in section 2.2.

Section 4 applies pro-form replacement tests to corroborate the central thesis of the chapter that "good" is fundamentally three ways ambiguous.

---

[4] The term "modification" may be understood informally here and elsewhere, unless otherwise stated. But "modification" has the following precise meaning in contemporary syntactic theory. Modification is a syntactic complex consisting of two constituents: a modifier and a modificand, where the modificand does not syntactically require the modifier, and the phrasal category to which the complex belongs is the same as the phrasal category to which the modificand belongs. This definition is discussed in section 3.7 of chapter 5.

[5] There are semantic and syntactic differences between the terms "quantity" and "magnitude," which I will discuss in section 2.5 of chapter 4; in particular, see footnote 40 of chapter 4. It would have been possible, perhaps preferable, to use the expression "magnitudinal 'good'" instead of "quantitative 'good'"; but in this context, I will use the terms "quantity" and "quantitative."

[6] Here and throughout this study, by "ambiguity" I intend "linguistic ambiguity."

Section 5 concludes the chapter by canvasing various kinds of ambiguity and then specifying the kinds of ambiguity that quantitative, evaluative, and operational "good" exhibit. The central conclusion is that there are two lexemes that have the same orthographic form "good." The meanings of these two lexemes are distally, if at all, related. One of these lexemes is quantitative "good." The other lexeme has two meanings: that of evaluative "good" and operational "good." These two meanings stand in a relation of polysemy, more precisely irregular polysemy.

## 2.1. Quantitative "Good" and Kinds of Quantity

There are many kinds of quantity; for example: height, weight, and depth. So it is questionable whether there are restrictions on the kinds of quantity that tokens of quantitative "good" may be used to denote.

Consider the following sentences, which employ quantitative "good":

4. That's a good load you're hauling on your truck.
5. We've had a few good snowfalls up in Saskatchewan already.

It is natural to gloss "good" in (4) and (5) by "large":

That's a large load you're hauling on your truck.
We've had a few large snowfalls up in Saskatchewan already.

In (2), I glossed "good" as "long" rather than "large." "Distance" admits modification by "large"; but in (2) "long" is more natural:

? It's a large distance from here to City Hall by foot.

(Throughout this study I follow the convention in linguistics of affixing one or more question marks to the beginning of a sentence or expression to indicate that it is to a lesser [?] or greater [?? or ???] degree semantically unacceptable.) This fact is significant, for otherwise one might think that quantitative "good" simply means "large."

Consider the following examples:

6. I was laid up in bed with pneumonia for a good spell.
7. For a good while, I feared we would not make it out of the country.

In these cases, "large" is not an acceptable gloss of "good":

> \# I was laid up in bed with pneumonia for a large spell.
> \# For a large while, I feared we would not make it out of the country.

(Throughout this study I follow the convention in linguistics of affixing the pound symbol to the beginning of a sentence or expression to indicate that it is semantically unacceptable.) However, "long" is an acceptable gloss:

> I was laid up in bed with pneumonia for a long spell.
> For a long while, I feared we would not make it out of the country.

So in (6) and (7), "good" modifies an expression that denotes a kind of temporal quantity. Temporal quantity is often described in terms of length.

The preceding examples might encourage the thought that quantitative "good" only modifies expressions that denote kinds of spatial quantity and temporal quantity. But consider the following examples:

8.   Dax gave the rope a good tug.
9.   Jett gave the machine a good whack.
10.  Adam gave the handle a good pull.

The nominal expressions that "good" modifies here—"tug," "whack," and "pull"—denote events, specifically actions. Quantitative "good" modifies a quantitative aspect of the events, but not a temporal or spatial aspect. In (8)–(10), "good" cannot be glossed by "long":

> \# Dax gave the rope a long tug.
> \# Jett gave the machine a long whack.
> \# Adam gave the handle a long pull.

Rather, "good" describes the events in terms of strength or force:

> Dax gave the rope a strong / forceful tug.
> Jett gave the machine a forceful / hard whack.
> Adam gave the handle a strong / forceful pull.

Consider the following example:

11.  A good number of subscribers wrote in to complain about the editorial.

Here "good" can be glossed by "large":

> A large number of subscribers wrote in to complain about the editorial.

However, in describing the number of subscribers, "large" describes neither spatial quantity nor temporal quantity, nor quantity of force or strength. Rather, it describes the magnitude of the cardinality of a set.

These considerations encourage the hypothesis that there are no restrictions on the kinds of quantity that quantitative "good" may describe in quantitative terms. For instance, consider the following examples of quantitative "good" modification of expressions relating to the classical sense modalities:

> A good light emanated from the torch.[7]
> The explosion produced a good bang.
> The plumes of smoke emitted a good stench.
> The chili gives that marinade a good kick.
> That bug bite caused a good itch.

In these cases, "good" can be glossed as

> A strong / powerful light emanated from the torch.
> The explosion produced a loud / intense bang.
> The plumes of smoke emitted a strong stench.
> The chili gives that marinade a strong / intense kick.
> That bug bite caused a strong / intense itch.

Quantitative "good" can also modify expressions denoting algesic sensations:

> Kneeling in the pew for so long gave her a good backache.
> The vaccination caused a good pain in his shoulder.

There are, however, restrictions on quantitative "good" modification of expressions that can denote quantitative properties of sensory properties. For example, although "flavor" admits modification by "strong" and "intense," the expression "good flavor" can only be read with evaluative "good":

> The chili gives that marinade a good flavor.

---

[7] This sentence can of course also be read with evaluative "good."

Likewise, although "smell" admits modification by "strong" and "intense," the expression "good smell" seems only marginally acceptable with quantitative "good":

> ? The plumes of smoke emitted a good smell.

Finally, although "sound" admits modification by "loud" and "intense," the expression "good sound" likewise seems only marginally acceptable with quantitative "good":

> ? The explosion produced a good sound.

I have no explanation for these seemingly idiosyncratic restrictions on quantitative "good" modification of expressions that denote entities that have quantitative properties and that clearly do admit other quantitatively descriptive modifiers. Even so, the range of kinds of quantity that quantitative "good" may describe is evidently very broad. Granting the idiosyncratic exceptions, I will offer one principle that explains the nature of the quantity or magnitude that quantitative "good" denotes in the following section.

## 2.2. Quantitative and Evaluative "Good"

Consider again sentence (2):

> It's a good distance from here to City Hall by foot.

Previously, I glossed quantitative "good" in (2) as "long." Observe that the phrase "long distance" per se is non-evaluative. In other words, a long distance per se has no value. So, the quantitative description of "distance" that quantitative "good" provides is non-evaluative. In fact, a speaker may use sentence (2) in an effort to dissuade the audience from doing the walk:

> It's a good distance from here to City Hall by foot. So I suggest taking a taxi rather than walking.

There are instances of evaluative "good" that are associated with properties that are partly constituted by non-evaluative kinds of quantity. For example, consider the following dialogue between two theater managers who are discussing their audience numbers:

A: Our numbers this season are good. How are yours?

B: Better than last season, but since the actors' strike still not very good.

I underscore that these instances of "good" are not instances of quantitative "good." They are instances of evaluative "good." These instances of evaluative "good" are associated with a non-evaluative kind of quantity. Number of audience members per se is non-evaluative. But because evaluative, rather than quantitative, "good" is here employed, the cardinality of the set of audience members is value laden. The greater the number of audience members, the better.

Contrast this with example (11) of quantitative "good," repeated here:

11.  A good number of subscribers wrote in to complain about the editorial.

A newspaper editor may utter this sentence in dismay: the greater the number of subscribers writing in to complain, the worse for the newspaper. So here "good number" means "large number." A large number, like a long distance, per se has no value. In lamenting the fact that the number of subscribers who have complained is large, the editor is expressing a negative evaluation of the number.

In short, evaluative "good" is associated with value. And in some contexts, value is associated with a non-evaluative kind of quantity; for example:

Ronan earns a good salary.

Inga got a good score on her GRE.

Paolo clocked a good time in the half marathon.

In contrast, quantitative "good" denotes quantity independently of any value.

While value and quantity are different properties, they share an attribute that will be a focal topic of this study and that will be useful to introduce here. Value and quantity are gradable properties. Clarification of this point will also serve to clarify a crucial restriction on the range of kinds of quantity that quantitative "good" can be used to denote.

A gradable property, in contrast to a non-gradable property, is a property that an entity can have various degrees, extents, or amounts of. For example, one painting can have more or less value than another. Again, one length or distance can be greater or smaller than another. Contrast gradable properties with non-gradable properties. For example, being pregnant is a non-gradable property. Although one woman can be more or less far along in a pregnancy than another, one woman cannot be more or less pregnant than another. Likewise, mathematical evenness is a non-gradable property of numbers. One number cannot be more or less even than another.

The claim that an entity can have various degrees or extents of a gradable property might be misinterpreted. Consider the property of height. One entity can have more or less height than another. So height is a gradable property. Granted this, entities either have height or they do not. For example, Isabella's desire to study environmental design, the Second Amendment, and the number eleven do not have height. So while height is a gradable property, the state of having height is not gradable. There are not degrees of having height. Rather, an entity that has height has some degree of height, and in principle may have various degrees of height. So a height-possessing entity in principle may have more or less height, in other words may have a greater or lesser degree of height, than another.

Since degrees, amounts, and extents themselves are quantities, it follows that one painting may have a greater or lesser quantity of value than another. Analogously, we are bound to speak of degrees, amounts, extents, and so quantities of kinds of quantity (or of kinds of magnitude or of kinds of quantitative properties). For example, height is a gradable property; so there are degrees and so quantities of height. But height is a kind of quantity (or magnitude or quantitative property). So various quantities of height are quantities of the quantitative kind height.

Observe now that since degrees are quantities, all gradable properties are kinds of quantity. Consequently, value itself is a kind of quantity. So one crucial restriction on the denotation of quantitative "good" is that it excludes the quantity of value. Put in positive terms, and ignoring the few seemingly idiosyncratic exclusions observed toward the end of the preceding section, quantitative "good" is associated with non-evaluative quantity. Note that I understand the association relation here in the same way that I explained it previously with respect to evaluative "good" and value. That is, I understand the association relation in terms of semantic and correlative metaphysical entailments.

Having introduced the point that value and non-evaluative quantity are both gradable properties, I return to clarifying the differences between evaluative "good" and quantitative "good." Arguably, the most important semantic difference between evaluative and quantitative "good" is precisely the fact that evaluative and quantitative "good" are associated with different kinds of gradable properties: value and non-evaluative quantity respectively.

A second semantic difference between evaluative and quantitative "good" relates to the range of so-called degree expressions that they license. Adjectives associated with gradable properties are called "gradable adjectives."[8] So evaluative "good" and quantitative "good" are gradable adjectives. All gradable adjectives license certain degree expressions. There are different classes of degree expressions. Classification of degree expressions depends on substantive and often contested semantic, syntactic, and morphological considerations.[9] Rather than engage such considerations, I will simply introduce several kinds of degree expressions.

Some degree expressions have the semantic function of raising or intensifying the degree associated with a gradable adjective. "Very" is a paradigmatic case; for example:

Paolo is very tall.

Accordingly, "very" is a so-called degree intensifier.

Contrast "very" with "fairly" and "somewhat," which are so-called degree diminishers or hedges:

Isabella is fairly tall.
Jett is somewhat competent.

A different kind of degree expression is a so-called measure phrase. A measure phrase is a nominal expression composed of a numeral and a so-called measure noun, that is, a noun that denotes a standard of measurement; for example "six feet" and "two miles."[10] A small subset of gradable adjectives, called "measure adjectives," admit measure phrases; for example:

Paolo is six feet tall.
The trail is two miles long.

---

[8] Cp. Christopher Kennedy: "A defining characteristic of gradable adjectives is that there is some gradient property associated with their meaning with respect to which the [individuals] in their domains can be ordered." *Projecting the Adjective*, University of Southern California, dissertation in linguistics, 1997; published by Garland Press, 1999, 4.

[9] Grammar is standardly divided into two fields: morphology and syntax. Morphology is the study of the internal structure of words. Syntax is the study of the structural relations between words.

[10] The term "measure phrase" is introduced in Christopher Kennedy and Peter Svenonius, "Northern Norwegian Degree Questions and the Syntax of Measurement," in *Phases of Interpretation*, M. Frascarelli, ed., Mouton de Gruyter, 2006, 129–57. Cp. Jessica Rett, *The Semantics of Evaluativity*, Oxford University Press, 2015, 14.

Other kinds of degree expressions relate to the traditional grammatical distinction called "grades of comparison." Consider "tall," "taller," and "tallest." Traditionally, "tall" is referred to as the "positive" form of the adjective"; "taller" as the comparative form; and "tallest" as the superlative form. Observe here that the comparative and superlative forms are constructed using the suffixes "-er" and "-est." The expressions "-er" and "-est" are morphemes, precisely degree morphemes. A morpheme is a minimal grammatical unit with meaning. Morphemes are distinguished as free and bound. A free morpheme can appear as an independent word, for example the adjective "tall" itself. A bound morpheme, for example "-er," cannot. So the word "taller" consists of two morphemes, one free and one bound.

The comparative and superlative bound morphemes "-er" and "-est" are semantically akin to the free morphemes "more" and "most."[11] For example, consider the gradable adjectives "flexible" and "sensitive," whose comparative and superlative forms are constructed using "more" and "most":

Gail is more flexible than Wendy.
Ronan is the most sensitive of Joe's sons.

Note that the comparative and superlative forms semantically related to "good" employ the bound morphemes "-er" and "-est," but suffixed to a distinct root, "bet-." So the comparative and superlative forms "better" and "best" are, in this respect, morphologically irregular—although semantically they are regular.

In short, "-er" and "more" are degree expressions and figure in comparative constructions. And "-est" and "most" are degree expressions of a different kind that figure in superlative constructions.

As noted, in traditional grammatical terms, the gradable adjectives occurring in the predicates in the sentences

Paolo is tall.
Thiebaud's 1969 *Candy Counter* is good.

as well as those in attributive position in the sentences

Paolo is a tall boy.
Thiebaud's 1969 *Candy Counter* is a good painting.

---

[11] Given a gradable adjective whose positive form is *a*, the expressions "*a*-er" and "*a*-est" are referred to as "suppletive" or "synthetic" forms, while the expressions "more *a*" and "most *a*" are referred to as "periphrastic" or "analytic" forms.

are said to be of the "positive" form. In these instances, the positive form of the gradable adjective occurs without a degree expression.[12] In the context of theories of gradability, the term "positive" is used in numerous ways. To avoid confusion, I will hereafter refer to the positive (in grade) form of a gradable adjective as the "basic" form. The basic form is morphologically basic.

As we will see shortly and in chapter 3, there are numerous other degree expressions. Presently, having clarified the term "degree expression" by example, I can now clarify the point that while, semantically speaking, evaluative "good" is regularly gradable, quantitative "good" is not.[13] By "regularly gradable" here, I mean that evaluative "good" licenses an ordinary range of degree expressions. In contrast, the range of degree expressions that quantitative "good" licenses is restricted.

For example, quantitative "good" does not consistently admit comparative or superlative forms. Contrast

> It's a good distance from here to City Hall.

with

> # It's a good distance from here to City Hall. But the distance from here to Independence Mall is better [in the sense of "longer"].
> # The best [in the sense of "longest"] distance is from here to the Delaware River.

Quantitative "good" does, however, admit certain degree intensifiers and hedges:

> It's a very good distance from here to City Hall.
> It's a rather good distance from here to City Hall.
> It's quite a good distance from here to City Hall.

Quantitative "good" can also occur in so-called equative constructions, that is, in constructions of the form "$x$ is as $a$ as $y$" (where $a$ stands for a gradable adjective in the basic form); for example:

---

[12] In fact, as I will discuss in chapter 3, this claim is controversial. More cautiously, I should say that in these instances, the positive form of the gradable adjective *ostensibly* occurs without a degree expression.

[13] This is not to be confused with the morphological irregularity of "good" in the comparative and superlative forms, "better" and "best."

It's as good a distance from here to the Delaware River as from here to the Schuylkill River.

This encourages the hypothesis that quantitative "good" only admits degree expressions when such constructions consist of the morphologically basic form "good," as opposed to "better" and "best." I will return to this hypothesis later.

One exception to the hypothesis is that "extremely" modification is unacceptable:

# It's an extremely good distance from here to City Hall.

In contrast, evaluative "good" does admit "extremely" modification:

He's extremely good at chess.

In short, although quantitative "good" is a gradable adjective, it appears not to be regularly gradable.[14]

A third semantic difference between quantitative and evaluative "good" is that quantitative "good" does not have an antonym. Precisely, quantitative "good" does not have an antonym quantitative "bad." There is no quantitative "bad." Moreover, there is no single other antonym that is consistently felicitous. Contrast this with evaluative "good," whose antonym is evaluative "bad"; for example:

Cassius Marcellus Coolidge's *A Friend in Need* is a bad painting.

This sentence means something like: the painting in question is lacking in aesthetic value. But again in the case of quantitative "good," there is no quantitative "bad"; for example:

# It's a bad [in the sense of "short"] distance from here to City Hall.
# That's a bad [in the sense of "small"] load you're hauling on your truck.
# It's a worse [in the sense of "shorter"] distance from here to City Hall than to the Post Office.

---

[14] Cp. Aimo Seppänen, "Lexical Integrity or Semantic Diversity: *Good, Great,* and *Well,*" *English Studies* 65 (1984) 534–49, at 536–37, examples (5b), (10b), who focuses on quantitative "good" modification of measure phrases, a topic that I discuss later. (I thank Christopher Langston for drawing my attention to Seppänen's article, which he did after reading an earlier version of my chapter. A number of my conclusions regarding these two adjectives are consistent with those of Seppänen.)

This lack of an antonym may be distinguished from the former two semantic properties of quantitative "good" insofar as it is an extrinsic rather than intrinsic semantic property.

A fourth difference between evaluative and quantitative "good" is syntactic: quantitative "good" is sensitive to so-called definiteness effects.[15] In particular, in the case of quantitative "good," shifting from the indefinite article to the definite article is rarely permissible. In considering this point, observe first that all of the nominal expressions consisting of quantitative "good" in the examples I gave when I originally introduced quantitative "good" are preceded by the indefinite article. I repeat several of those examples here, with the indefinite article italicized:

> It's *a* good distance from here to City Hall by foot.
> That's *a* good load you're hauling on your truck.
> We've had *a* few good snowfalls up in Saskatchewan already.
> *A* good number of subscribers wrote in to complain about the editorial.

None of these examples permits a shift from the indefinite article to the definite article:

> * It's the good distance from here to City Hall by foot.
> * That's the good load you're hauling on your truck.
> * We've had the few good snowfalls up in Saskatchewan already.
> * The good number of subscribers wrote in to complain about the editorial.[16]

In certain cases where a shift to the definite article may seem permissible, the shift in fact requires a non-quantitative sense of "good." I will adapt the second example to illustrate this point. Consider the following dialogue between two truckers. Assume that each trucker is preparing to haul a load of provisions and that one of the two loads is tainted:

> A: I've forgotten now which load I'm hauling.
> B: You're hauling the good load.
> A (pointing to one load): Is that it?
> B (pointing to the other load): No, that's the good load.[17]

---

[15] Cp. Barbara Abbott, "Definite and Indefinite," in *Encyclopedia of Language and Linguistics*, K. Brown, ed., Elsevier, 2006².

[16] Recall the linguistic convention of affixing the asterisk symbol to the beginning of an expression to indicate that it is syntactically ill-formed.

[17] The instances of "good" here are in fact operational.

However, there are marginally acceptable cases of quantitative "good" with the definite article. I offer one here. Assume that a married couple lives in the urban capital of a country. The woman has been hired to supervise construction of a medical facility in a remote part of the country. Travel to that area is only by means of poor roads, and these are often impassable. She says:

? Due to the good distance and the poor road conditions, it is likely I will see my husband only sporadically over the next few months.

Still, I think it would be more natural here to drop the word "good."[18]

Tangentially related to the preceding point is another syntactic distinction between quantitative and evaluative "good." The fact that quantitative "good" almost exclusively modifies nouns that take the indefinite article suggests that quantitative "good" may resist modification of mass nouns. Mass and count nouns are complementary and exhaustive kinds of common nouns. I discuss the distinction between mass and count nouns in section 3 of chapter 4 and more thoroughly in section 3.1 of chapter 6. For the present purpose, it suffices to note that only count nouns admit the indefinite article. For example, "idea" is a count noun and "endurance" is a mass noun:

Adam has an idea.
* Adam has an endurance.

Evaluative "good" can modify both count nouns and mass nouns. For example, consider evaluative "good" modification of the count noun "engine" and the mass noun "mileage" in the following sentences:

Ronan's new truck has a good engine.
Ronan's new truck gets good mileage.

But quantitative "good" can only modify count nouns. In other words, quantitative "good" cannot modify mass nouns. For example, "height" and "distance" can occur as mass nouns. For example, assume Inga is practicing long jumping; and her coach says:

She gets good height, but not good distance.

The instances of "good" here can only be read evaluatively.

[18] Cp. Seppänen (1984) 536, example (8b), who observes that quantitative "good" is infelicitous when not preceded by the indefinite article.

A sixth difference between quantitative and evaluative "good" is also syntactic: quantitative "good" generally cannot occur in predicate position.[19] For example, the following sentences are only acceptable if they are not read in terms of quantitative "good":

> The walk from here to City Hall is good.
> That load you're hauling on your truck is good.
> The snowfalls up in Saskatchewan have been good.
> The number of subscribers who wrote in to complain about the editorial is good.

To my knowledge, one exception to the inadmissibility of quantitative "good" in predicate position is when the subject is a term such as "chances," "odds," "probability," or "likelihood"; for example:

> The chances / odds / probability / likelihood that you will hurt yourself if you use the equipment while intoxicated are / is good.

The reason for the acceptability of quantitative "good" in predicate position in this type of context is difficult to understand. But one condition that appears to support this construction is that the sentence does not admit substitution with evaluative "good." So the absence of the potential for ambiguity here seems to support the predicative use of quantitative "good."

With these results in hand, I return to the topic of the irregular gradability of quantitative "good." The fact that quantitative "good" is generally not predicative may explain why the second clause in the following sentence is unacceptable:

> It's a good distance from here to City Hall; # and the distance from here to Independence Mall is even better.

Contrast this with the more acceptable:

> It's a good distance from here to City Hall; and it's an even better distance from here to Independence Mall.

Compare the use of quantitative "better" in the following sort of example, which also happens to be a rare case where the use of the definite article is acceptable:

---

[19]  Cp. Seppänen (1984) 536, example (7b).

Joe spent the better part of Sunday afternoon cleaning up the garage.

Consequently, the hypothesis that quantitative "good" constructions only admit degree expressions when such constructions are composed of the morphologically basic form "good" is false.

The unacceptability of the superlative form of quantitative "good" can also, at least partly, be explained on different grounds, namely the sensitivity of quantitative "good" to definiteness effects. Again, quantitative "good" rarely admits the definite article. But the superlative "best" typically requires the definite article.[20]

In short, the irregularity of the gradability of quantitative "good" is explicable in terms of these other semantic and syntactic properties. These results naturally invite the question why quantitative "good" is sensitive to definiteness effects. I note the desirability of an explanation, but cannot provide one.

A seventh and final difference between evaluative and quantitative "good" is phonological.[21] As Aimo Seppänen notes, in a phrase of the form "good $N$" (where "good" is evaluative and $N$ stands for a noun) the normal stress pattern involves stress on both words:

a góod knífe.

Furthermore, a single heavy stress on only one word "leads to a contrastive interpretation":

a góod knife        (as opposed to a bad knife)
a good knífe        (as opposed to some other good thing).

In the case of quantitative "good," the normal stress pattern consists of a stress only on the noun, for example:

a good dístance.

It is possible to stress both the adjective and noun:

a góod dístance.

In this case, the largeness of the quantity seems to be emphasized.

---

[20]   One exception is the expression "a personal best."
[21]   I owe the following point to Seppänen (1984) 536–37.

In contrast, it is unnatural to express the phrase "good N" (using quantitative "good") with a stress on "good" and with no stress on the noun:

* a góod distance.[22]

In sum, I suggest that there are considerable semantic, syntactic, and phonological differences between quantitative and evaluative "good." These differences encourage the thesis that quantitative "good" and evaluative "good" are two different adjectives rather than a single adjective with two different senses. In other words, the semantic, syntactic, and phonological differences encourage the thesis that quantitative "good" and evaluative "good" stand in a relation of homonymy rather than polysemy.[23]

## 2.3. Quantitative "Good" Modification of Measure Phrases

Before leaving the discussion of quantitative "good," I want to consider the ostensibly peculiar phenomenon of quantitative "good" modification of measure phrases.[24] Note that when I introduced measure phrases as a kind of degree expression, I was concerned with measure phrases preceding gradable adjectives; for example "six feet tall" and "two miles long." Here, I am concerned with "good," precisely quantitative "good" modification of measure phrases; for example:

It's a good two miles from here to the Post Office.
Inga practiced the piano for a good hour and a half.
A good twenty-five students showed up for the first Philosophy Club meeting.

In the analysis of "good" that concludes his *Semantic Analysis*, Paul Ziff cites two examples of quantitative "good" modifying a measure phrase.[25] Ziff cites these examples as failing to conform to his otherwise allegedly unified analysis of

---

[22] In this instance, the asterisk is used to indicate phonological infelicity.

[23] I elaborate on the distinction between homonymy and polysemy in section 5 of this chapter. Note that Louise McNally and Christopher Kennedy, "Degree v. Manner *Well*: A Case Study in Selective Binding," in *Advances in Generative Lexicon Theory*, J. Pustejovsky et al., eds. Spring, 2013, 247–62, have argued that the relation between quantitative and evaluative "good" and "well" is one of polysemy rather than homonymy. My grounds for thinking that quantitative and evaluative "good" are homonyms will ultimately be clarified in section 2.2 of chapter 4.

[24] There is very little linguistic work on this topic. But cp. Seppänen (1984).

[25] *Semantic Analysis*, Cornell University Press, 1960, 247. I have adapted these in my examples. Ziff in fact cites three examples. But the third, "He's looking pretty good in there today," is just a case of evaluative "good" with "pretty" functioning as a degree diminisher.

"good." According to that analysis, "good" means "answering to certain interests." I will discuss this thesis in section 2.1 of chapter 4. Presently, since I am arguing that "good" has three meanings, I reject Ziff's view that "good" admits a unified analysis. With regard to the measure phrase examples, Ziff writes:

> That the analysis [of "good" as answering to certain interests] will not easily fit this or that case [of "good" modification of measure phrase], what does that prove? For it does fit the other cases cited and so one can always construe the cases that don't fit as special cases. Only one thing will upset the analysis presented here: a better one.[26]

I suggest that quantitative "good" modification of measure phrases is not a special case. In other words, the semantics of quantitative "good" modification of measure phrases largely conforms to the preceding analysis of quantitative "good."

In explaining quantitative "good" modification of measure phrases, it is necessary to clarify one further point regarding gradable adjectives. Many constructions composed of the basic form of a gradable adjective denote a significant degree of the gradable property associated with the adjective. For example, consider the following sentences:

> Thiebaud's 1969 *Candy Counter* is good.
> Paolo is tall.

These two sentences may be glossed as

> Thiebaud's 1969 *Candy Counter* has a significant degree of value.
> Paolo has a significant degree of height.

Compare the uses of quantitative "good" in the following sentences:

> It's a good distance from here to City Hall by foot.
> We've had a few good snowfalls up in Saskatchewan already.

These two sentences may be glossed as

> The distance from here to City Hall by foot is a significant length.
> We've had a few snowfalls up in Saskatchewan already that have been of significant size.

---

[26]  Ziff (1960) 247.

Precisely what "significance" of degree means here and why certain constructions with the basic form have this meaning will be focal topics of chapter 3. But this much suffices here to explain quantitative "good" modification of measure phrases.

Observe now that the measure phrase that quantitative "good" modifies can be replaced with a quantity expression that denotes the quantitative type of the measure phrase:

> A good *twenty-five students* attended the first Philosophy Club meeting.
> A good *number of students* attended the first Philosophy Club meeting.

> It's a good *two miles* from here to the Post Office.
> It's a good *distance* from here to the Post Office.

> She spent a good *three-quarters of an hour* trying to unclog the disposal.
> She spent a good *length of time* trying to unclog the disposal.

Consequently, just as quantitative "good" modification of a quantity expression $Q$ that is not a measure phrase requires that $Q$ be a significant quantity, quantitative "good" modification of a measure phrase $M$ requires that $M$ be a significant quantity. For example, just as

> It's a good distance from here to the Post Office.

entails

> The distance from here to the Post Office is a significant quantity.

so

> It's a good two miles from here to the Post Office.

entails

> The two miles from here to the Post Office is a significant quantity.

Contrast this interpretation with the following hypothesis: quantitative "good" modification of a measure phrase $M$ has the semantic effect of making $M$ imprecise.[27] According to this hypothesis, "It's a good two miles from here to the Post Office" means something like

---

[27] This hypothesis was suggested to me by Muffy Siegel (p.c.).

It's more or less two miles from here to the Post Office.

A diagnostic for testing this alternative is that the addition of "exactly" would yield a contradiction. But it doesn't:

It's a good two miles from here to the Post Office exactly.

Compare the felicity of quantitative "good" modification of an unusually precise measure phrase:

A good 87.3% of the population cast their votes in the referendum today.

Further evidence that quantitative "good" modification of a measure phrase $M$ entails that $M$ is a significant quantity derives from the following consideration. If the quantity is extreme, then the use of "good" is awkward; for example:

?? The United States beat Fiji by the greatest margin of victory in the history of international basketball, obliterating their rivals by a good 152 points.

In contrast, measure phrase modification by a so-called extreme adjective such as "mammoth," "monstrous," or "extraordinary" is preferable:

The United States beat Fiji by the greatest margin of victory in the history of international basketball, obliterating their rivals by a whopping / mammoth / monstrous / extraordinary 152 points.[28]

Finally, constructions consisting of quantitative "good" modification of a measure phrase do not permit comparative or superlative forms. Indeed, they are even more irregular in the range of degree expressions they admit than quantitative "good" constructions without a measure phrase; for example:

# It's a better two miles from here to City Hall than to the Post Office.
# It's a very good two miles from here to City Hall.

In addition, there is no antonym of quantitative "good" when it modifies a measure phrase; for example:

# It's a bad [in the sense of "short"] two miles from here to City Hall.

---

[28] In this context, it also worth recalling that while evaluative "good" admits "extremely" modification, quantitative "good" without a measure phrase does not.

And constructions in which quantitative "good" modifies a measure phrase cannot be reconstructed so that "good" occurs in predicate position.

> * The two miles from here to the Post Office is good [in the sense of "long"].[29]

When quantitative "good" modifies a measure phrase, in some cases it permits the definite article. For example, the following is impossible:

> * It's the good two miles from here to City Hall.

However, the following seems marginally acceptable:

> ? The good twelve miles they spent on the trail today, with no tree cover and in full sun, left the hikers woozy and dehydrated.

In short, there is reason to believe that quantitative "good" modification of measure phrases is not idiomatic or a special case, but that in such constructions quantitative "good" largely conforms to the semantics and syntax of quantitative "good" without measure phrases.

## 3. Operational "Good"

I turn now from quantitative "good" to what I suggest is a third fundamental meaning of "good." Consider the following sentence:

> This wine is good.

One might express this sentence in the context of sampling wines to determine which to buy for a dinner party and upon discovering one of high quality. In that case, evaluative "good" is being used. Alternatively, one might express this sentence in the context of tasting wines to determine whether they have turned and upon finding that one hasn't. In that case, I suggest, a meaning of "good" is being employed that is neither evaluative nor quantitative.

Compare the following sentence:

> These batteries are good.

---

[29] The example is well-formed with an evaluative "good" reading.

One might express this sentence in the context of recommending durable batteries to a customer at a hardware store. In that case, evaluative "good" is being used. Alternatively, one might express this sentence in the context of testing batteries to determine whether they still have life and upon finding some that do. In that case, I suggest, a meaning of "good" is being employed that is neither evaluative nor quantitative.

Compare the following sentences, all of which employ this third meaning of "good":

> The tires are still good for another 20,000 miles.
> The bulb is good; it's the switch that needs rewiring.
> The warranty is good for the life of the product.

In the preceding examples, "good" seems to convey that the nominal expression it modifies or of which it is predicated is working, functional, in effect, or usable in its characteristic way. Consequently, I refer to this sense of "good" as "operational."

Operational "good" differs from evaluative and quantitative "good" in that it is not gradable. Consider the following dialogues:

> A: This coffee tastes funny. Is the milk good?
> B: Yes, it's good. # But there's some other milk in the fridge that's better.

> A: This coffee tastes funny. Is the milk good?
> B: # Yes, it's very good.

> A: This coffee tastes funny. Is the milk good?
> B: # It's quite good, but here's some even better milk.

> A: This coffee tastes funny. Is the milk good?
> B: # It's somewhat good; but if you want some better milk, check the
>     fridge.

Observe that it is possible to use comparative forms and other degree expressions in similar sentences. However, such usage triggers evaluative "good":

> These batteries are good. But if you're planning to use the device regularly for over six hours at a time, then these other batteries are better. The best batteries however are the ones behind the counter, but they're also the most expensive.

A: Without refrigeration pasteurized milk stays fresh longer than unpasteurized milk; and ultra-pasteurized milk stays fresh even longer. So if you're going to be hiking for several days and you're not bringing a cooler, pasteurized milk is good, and ultra-pasteurized milk is even better.

B: Yes, if you're set on taking cow's milk, ultra-pasteurized milk is the best milk. But soymilk and almond milk are much better. Almond milk is especially good. It lasts for months unopened and weeks after opening.

Like evaluative "good" and in contrast to quantitative "good," operational "good" has an antonym, operational "bad":

A: The coffee tastes funny. Is the milk still good?
B: I'm sorry, I forgot to throw it out. That milk is bad.

This wine is bad. Someone must have left it uncorked over the weekend.

We had a power outage over the weekend. The fish in the refrigerator has gone bad.[30]

Like operational "good," operational "bad" is not gradable:

A: This coffee tastes funny. Is the milk good?
B: No, it's bad.
C: # And this milk is even worse.

A: These batteries are dead. Do you have any good ones?
B: # Unfortunately these others are even worse.

As some of the examples above indicate, like evaluative "good" and in contrast to quantitative "good," operational "good" can appear in predicate position.

Again like evaluative "good" and in contrast to quantitative "good," operational "good" does not appear to be sensitive to definiteness effects; for example:

A: This milk is bad. Do you have any other milk?
B: There's a good milk in the fridge.
A (holding up a carton): Is this the good milk?
B: No, that carton contains the bad milk. The good milk is in a plastic container.[31]

---

[30] Note however that not all felicitous instances of operational "good" admit the antonym. For example, "That warranty is still good"; but # "That warranty is now bad."

[31] Operational "good" does not admit measure phrases: * "This milk is two weeks good / bad"; * "The warranty is ten years good." The former sentence is naturally read as trying to convey that a

Like evaluative "good," operational "good" can modify mass as well as count nouns. In the exchange above, "milk" in "a good milk" occurs as a count noun. However, in B's reply in the following exchange, "milk" occurs, as it typically does, as a mass noun:

A: The milk in the plastic container has gone bad.
B: There's good milk in the jug on the bottom shelf.

Finally, with respect to stress patterns, it seems that operational "good" again conforms to evaluative "good." At least, the normal stress pattern for operational "good $N$" phrases involves stress on both "good" and the noun:

a góod wárranty.

On the other hand, the phonology of operational "good" seems to differ from evaluative "good" in the following way. If "good" is stressed and the noun is un-stressed, this seems to trigger evaluative "good":

a góod warranty          (in contrast to an evaluatively, not operationally, bad warranty).

To my knowledge no prior philosopher or linguist has recognized operational "good" as such, let alone attempted to analyze it. Surely many have stumbled over it or conflated it with evaluative "good."

I am aware of one particular case where a philosopher has stumbled over op-erational "bad" in the context of analyzing "good." The example occurs in Peter Geach's seminal 1956 paper "Good and Evil."[32] One of the claims Geach makes about "bad" is that it, in contrast to "good," is what medieval philosophers call an *alienans* adjective.[33] The *Oxford Dictionary of Philosophy* offers the following def-inition of an *alienans* adjective:

An adjective that appears to be qualifying a subsequent description, but in fact functions to deny or leave open the question of whether the description applies: a fake parrot, an alleged criminal, a near victory.[34]

carton of milk is good for two weeks or went bad two weeks ago; the latter that a certain warranty is good for ten years.

[32] "Good and Evil," *Analysis* 17 (1956) 33–42. Incidentally, the title is in fact a misnomer; nowhere in the paper is the word "evil" discussed. Moreover, Geach's silence with respect to "evil" is not expli-cable on the grounds that his analysis of "good" can simply be transposed to its antonym. "Evil" is not the antonym of "good."

[33] Geach (1956) 33.

[34] Simon Blackburn, ed., Oxford University Press, 2008[2].

Accordingly, an *alienans* adjective *A* is an adjective used to modify a nominal expression *N* with the following entailment property:

"*x* is an *A N*" does not entail "*x* is an *N*."

For example, "Eddie is an alleged criminal" does not entail "Eddie is a criminal."

The meaning of "good" that Geach in effect analyzes in his paper is evaluative "good." But in making his claim about "bad" as "something like" an *alienans* adjective, Geach is in effect speaking of operational "bad." So in fact the meaning of "bad" that he discusses is not the antonym of the meaning of "good" that he discusses. Nonetheless, Geach is correct to claim that (operational) "bad" is "something like" an *alienans* adjective rather than that it is an *alienans* adjective. One example he gives is "bad food," by which I take him to mean spoiled or rotten food.[35] Food has a characteristic functional property, namely to be edible. Bad food lacks this property. So operational "bad" has the following entailment property that is arguably akin to the entailment property of an *alienans* adjective:

"*x* is an *A N*" entails "*x* lacks the characteristic functional property of an *N*."

So much for operational "good."

## 4. Ambiguity and Pro-form Replacement Tests

For convenience, I here summarize the principal preceding results regarding the semantic, syntactic, and phonological differences between evaluative, quantitative, and operational "good":

|  | Evaluative | Quantitative | Operational |
|---|---|---|---|
| Is gradable | ✓ | *Irregularly* | × |
| Is associated with non-evaluative quantity | × | ✓ | ×[36] |
| Has an antonym | ✓ | × | ✓ |

---

[35] "We cannot infer e.g. that because food supports life bad food supports life" (Geach, 1956, 33).
[36] This claim will be further clarified and justified in section 2.2 of chapter 4.

|                                                      | Evaluative | Quantitative  | Operational |
|------------------------------------------------------|:----------:|:-------------:|:-----------:|
| Is sensitive to definiteness effects                 |     ×      |      ✓        |      ×      |
| Can modify a mass noun                                |     ✓      |      ×        |      ✓      |
| Is predicative                                        |     ✓      | *Generally not* |    ✓      |
| Normally stresses both adjective and modified noun    |     ✓      |      ×        |      ✓      |
| Admits stress on adjective alone                      |     ✓      |      ×        |      ×      |

A standard test for ambiguity involves an appeal to anaphoric processes.[37] For instance, consider the following sentence:

Paolo bought an iPhone and Isabella did so too.

The phrase "did so too" entails that Isabella also bought an iPhone. Generalizing, the use of "did so too" replacement and other so-called pro-form expressions requires identity of meaning of the relevant phrases. A pro-form is "any form, such as a pronoun, that is treated as 'standing for' another form whose meaning can be understood."[38] Consequently, if a phrase is two ways ambiguous, then when the phrase is conjoined to a pro-form expression, the entire sentence will be two ways ambiguous.[39] Consider the following example:

Ronan saw her duck, and Adam did too.[40]

This sentence can mean two things:

Ronan saw the duck that belonged to her, and Adam saw the duck that belonged to her.

Ronan saw her quickly lower her head, and Adam saw her quickly lower her head.

---

[37] The test is introduced and discussed in Ruth Kempson, *Semantic Theory*, Cambridge University Press, 1977, 128–35. Cp. Arnold Zwicky and Jerrold Sadock, "Ambiguity Tests and How to Fail Them," in *Syntax and Semantics*, J. Kimball, ed., vol. 3, Academic Press, 1975, 1–36.

[38] P. H. Matthews, *Oxford Concise Dictionary of Linguistics*, Oxford University Press, 2007².

[39] Kempson (1977) 130.

[40] The example is adapted from Kempson (1977).

In each of the two representations of the original sentence's meaning, the meaning of the pro-form expression—here "did too"—must be identical to its antecedent.

We can employ an anaphoric replacement test using the pro-form "so" to confirm that the relation between operational and evaluative "good" is one of ambiguity. Assume that a person is remarking on the fact that some milk is still potable (as opposed to turned) and that the jug holding the milk is suitably attractive for a table setting:

> The milk is good and so is the jug.

"So" replacement fails to produce the desired meaning. The second clause is nonsensical; or it suggests something like: the jug can perform its characteristic function.

A replacement test involving quantitative "good" is more difficult to engineer. Consider evaluative and quantitative "good" in the following sentence:

> The scenery between here and City Hall is good and so is the distance.

If the test were admissible, "so" replacement would fail to produce the desired meaning. In the second clause, the distance must be read as having significant value rather than simply being of significant quantity. But the test as formulated is problematic because it requires that "good" be predicative, and quantitative "good" is rarely predicative. The same problem occurs in the following test relating to operational and quantitative "good." Assume that a trucker is hauling a large load and that the contents of the load are provisions that are unspoiled:

> The contents are good and so is the load he's hauling.

Again, if the test were admissible, "so" replacement would fail to produce the desired meaning. In the second clause, the load must be read as having its characteristic functional property—whatever that might be.

The fact that quantitative "good" is generally not predicative is itself indicative of the fact that its meaning differs from those of evaluative and operational "good." Nonetheless, an alternative "so" replacement test can be devised that respects the syntactic properties of quantitative "good" as follows. Assume that there are two loads of provisions and that we are trying to convey of one that it is large and of the other that its contents are usable in their characteristic way or that the load has significant value. In other words, we are trying to convey that one load is quantitatively "good" and that the other is operationally or evaluatively "good." We use the following sentence in an effort to convey this content:

This is a good load, and so is that one.

The test fails to convey the intended meaning. In the second clause, "so" replacement requires that the demonstrative phrase "that one" denote a large load.

I conclude that evaluative, quantitative, and operational "good" are distinct meanings of "good."

## 5. Kinds of Ambiguity

There are various kinds of ambiguity. In arguing that "good" is three ways ambiguous, I have not specified the kind of ambiguity. I will conclude this chapter by doing so.

Consider the following definition of the ambiguity of a word:

A word is ambiguous if it has more than one meaning.

Now consider the following definition of a word in terms of orthographic form:

A word is a meaningful string of letters that can occur independently in a sentence.

So understood, a word can be contrasted with a bound morpheme. For example, "good" can appear independently in a sentence, but "-ness" cannot.

Although the definition of a word in terms of orthographic form is highly intuitive and especially so for a language such as English, it is theoretically inadequate. Some written languages do not use spaces to separate words. But more fundamentally, the use of spaces to distinguish words presupposes the individuated words themselves. So the definition of a word in terms of orthographic form is question-begging.[41]

---

[41] Cp. M. Lynne Murphy, *Lexical Meaning*, Cambridge University Press, 2010, 12.

An alternative definition of a word appeals to grammatical properties:

A word belongs to a basic syntactic category and is distinguishable from a meaningful expression that is not a word in virtue of the respective phrase distribution and morphological inflection properties of the word and non-word.[42]

Evidently, this definition does not specify the distinctive phrase distribution and morphological inflection properties of words. However, that a specification of the distinctive grammatical properties is available suffices for our present purposes.

Granted the grammatical definition of a word, it will be useful here to recognize a distinction between a word and its orthographic form. I will call the latter a "word form." Correspondingly, I note the following distinct kind of ambiguity in terms of word form:

A word form is ambiguous if it has more than one meaning.

In light of this, compare the following two claims:

W   The word "good" is ambiguous.
F    The word form "good" is ambiguous.

W entails F, but F does not entail W. For example, if there are exactly two words with the same word form "good" and these two words have different meanings, then F is true, but W is false and falsely presupposes that there is a single word "good."

According to the definition of word form ambiguity, the word form "good" is three ways ambiguous. On the other hand, it is questionable whether there is one word "good" in English or rather two or three words that share the word form "good." Before addressing this question directly, I want to introduce some further distinctions that are relevant to specifying several other kinds of ambiguity.

By "lexicon" is meant the inventory of words that constitutes a language at a given time in its history.[43] A comprehensive dictionary aims to capture this inventory. Compare the mental lexicon, which is the inventory of lexical concepts, that is, concepts corresponding to words, that individual language users possess.

---

[42]   Cp. Murphy (2010) 13; and John I. Saeed, *Semantics*, Wiley Blackwell, 2009[3], 55–58.
[43]   The lexicon includes idiomatic phrases. But, for the sake of simplicity, I ignore this point.

A lexeme is a word as it occurs in the lexicon.[44] Accordingly, we can distinguish words that are lexemes from words that are their derivative grammatical forms. For example, the lexical form of nouns is, in most cases, singular in number; for instance "apple." Contrast the derived plural "apples." So "apple" is a lexeme, and "apples" is a derived grammatical form of this lexeme. Again, the lexical form of a verb is, in most cases, the present active infinitive without the preposition "to." So "eat" is a lexeme, and words such as "ate" and "eats" are among its derived grammatical forms.

As the preceding examples illustrate, the derived grammatical forms of lexemes often involve morphological inflection of the lexemes from which they are derived. But there are many instances in which lexemes and some of their derived grammatical forms share the same word form. For example, the noun "fish" and its derived plural have the same word form:

Paolo caught one fish.          [LEXICAL FORM]
Paolo caught two fish.          [DERIVED GRAMMATICAL FORM]

The meanings of "fish" in turn depend on this morphological fact. For example, the following sentence admits two readings depending on whether "fish" is singular or plural:

Isabella photographed the fish.

In short, this example illustrates a kind of word form ambiguity: a lexeme and one of its derived grammatical forms have the same word form, but distinct meanings.

A second kind of word form ambiguity owes to the fact that there are many instances of cognate lexemes or derived grammatical forms that belong to distinct syntactic categories, but that have the same word form. By "cognate" here, I mean sharing a single etymology. For instance, consider "her" and "fish" in the following sentence:

12.  Ronan saw her fish.

In (12), "her" may be a possessive adjective or a pronoun. Correlatively, "fish" may be a noun or a verb. If "her" is a possessive adjective, then "fish" is a noun; and the noun phrase "her fish" is the direct object of the only verb in the sentence, "saw." On this reading, the syntactic structure of (12) may be represented as

$[_N \text{Ronan} [_V \text{saw} [_{NP} [_A \text{her} [_N \text{fish}]]]]]$.

---

[44] Lexemes also include idiomatic phrases. But again I ignore this point.

If instead "her" is a pronoun, then "fish" is a verb; and "her fish" is a clause, a so-called small clause.[45] On this reading, the syntactic structure of (12) may be represented as

$$[_N \text{Ronan} [_V \text{saw} [_{CP} [_{Pro} \text{her} [_V \text{fish}]]]]].^{46}$$

In short, "her" and "fish" here exemplify another kind of word form ambiguity: two cognate lexemes or derived grammatical forms that belong to distinct syntactic categories and that have the same word form, but distinct meanings.

A third kind of word form ambiguity consists of two non-cognate lexemes belonging to the same syntactic category and having the same word form, but distinct meanings. This is an especially salient kind of ambiguity—albeit not in these terms. However, it is in fact rare. The noun "bark" is an example:

Dax pealed the bark off the branch.
Adam listened for the dog's bark.

A different kind of ambiguity relates to the distinction between word types and word tokens; for example:

13.  Gail ate an apple and Joe ate an apple.

In (13), there are two word tokens of the word type "apple." Word tokens and word types by definition have the same word form. I will call the meaning of a word type its "lexical" meaning.[47] The meaning of a word token may be identical to the lexical meaning of the word type. For example, if the word type "apple" has only one lexical meaning, namely the fruit, then since each of the tokens of "apple" in (13) denotes that fruit, each of the tokens of "apple" in (13) has the same meaning as the lexical meaning of the word type "apple."

I will call the meaning of a word token its "literal" meaning. As in (13), the literal meaning of a word token is often the same as the lexical meaning of the word type. But a word token can have a literal meaning that differs from the lexical meaning of the word type. For example, consider the token of "money" in the following sentence:

14.  To buy a house in Brookline, you need money.

---

[45] A small clause consists of a subject and a predicate, but the predicate is untensed. Cp. "He fell" with "She saw him fall"; and "She was naked" with "He saw her naked."

[46] In this representation, "CP" stands for complementizer phrase, of which a small clause is a form.

[47] Some lexemes have more than one meaning, a point I discuss below in terms of polysemy.

This sentence does not state the trivial truth that in order to buy something, one needs some amount of money. Brookline is an affluent suburb of Boston. The token of "money" in (14) has a meaning akin to "a large amount of money." So, as it occurs in (14), the token of "money" has a narrower meaning than the lexical meaning of the word type "money." Consequently, in (14), the literal meaning of the token of "money" differs from the lexical meaning of the word type "money." Here then is a kind of ambiguity involving a single word rather than merely a single word form: a word type and a word token with distinct meanings.

Most of the preceding kinds of ambiguity will figure in the ensuing study. However, the three-way ambiguity of "good" does not exemplify any of them. Rather, I propose to explain the three-way ambiguity of "good" in terms of the following two kinds of ambiguity:

- One lexeme with two meanings
- Two cognate lexemes of the same syntactic category with the same word form but distinct meanings.

To appreciate how these kinds of ambiguity explain the three-way ambiguity of "good," it is necessary to recognize a different way of distinguishing kinds of ambiguity, one which cuts across all of the preceding kinds. This distinction is between homonymy and polysemy. Homonymy consists of a single word form with two or more meanings that are distally related or wholly unrelated. Among the preceding examples, "bark" is the only instance of homonymy.

Homonymy tends to occur when two lexemes with the same word form have unrelated etymologies. For example, tree "bark" derives from Old Norse *börkr*; dog's "bark" derives from Anglo-Saxon *beorcan*. However, homonymy arguably does not require etymological distinction. An example of homonymous word forms with a common etymology are the two nouns with the word form "cardinal." The name of the North American finch derives from the red cassock of the church official. But some linguists—and I incline to agree with them—regard ornithological "cardinal" and ecclesiastical "cardinal" as homonyms on the ground that their meanings are remote.

Polysemy consists of a single word or word form with two or more meanings that are closely related.[48] Excepting "bark" and "cardinal," all of the other examples of ambiguity that I have discussed in this section are

---

[48] Cp. Gergely Pethö, "What Is Polysemy?—a Survey of Current Research and Results," in *Pragmatics and Flexibility of Word Meaning*, E. T. Németh and K. Bibok, eds., Elsevier, 2001, 175–224.

cases of polysemy. Indeed, polysemy is rife in natural language; and it will feature prominently in this study. I will refer to polysemous meanings as "polysemes."[49]

Different kinds of polysemy are distinguishable. One kind is between cognate words of different syntactic categories. An example is the noun and the verb "fish." Another kind is in terms of a single word. A polysemous word has two or more closely related meanings.

A different distinction between kinds of polysemy, which cuts across the preceding two kinds of polysemy, is between regular and irregular polysemy. For instance, consider the polysemy of the word "healthy" in

healthy diet
healthy body.

A healthy diet is one that causes or causally contributes to a state of health. A healthy body is a body that is in a state of health.

Cause-effect or producer-product is one among several forms of polysemous meaning relation that is regular or systematic in the sense that it occurs widely through the language. In other words, there are numerous adjectives, as well as other parts of speech, that exhibit the kind of meaning relation exhibited by "healthy" in the preceding examples. Compare the adjectives "sad" and "abstract" and the noun "newspaper" in the following pairs of phrases:

sad film
sad person

abstract painter
abstract painting

The newspaper is going out of business.
The newspaper is missing the arts and entertainment section.

---

[49] Insofar as proximity and distance are vague, the definitions of homonymy and polysemy are. Depending on how one interprets vagueness, there may be cognitive or metaphysical limits on the determinability of the border between homonymy and polysemy. But the problem is more complicated than the vagueness of proximity and distance. We know what we mean, for example, by spatial or temporal proximity. But how are we to understand semantic proximity? Assume that we did a study in which we asked subjects to array several words with respect to their intuitive semantic

Contrast regular polysemy with irregular or non-systematic polysemy.[50] In this case, the meaning relation between the polysemes is limited to one word form or word; or at least, the meaning relation is not widespread through the language. Some examples include "true," "running," and "responsible," as in

true love
true belief.

The horse / his nose / her stocking is running.

15a. The virus is responsible for the death of the chickens.
15b. The janitor is responsible for emptying the trash cans in the offices.
15c. She is a responsible employee.


In sentences such as (15a), "$x$ is responsible" means that $x$ is the cause of some event. In (15b), it means that $x$ has an obligation to do something. And in (15c), it means that $x$ is a normatively competent agent and characteristically does what $x$ ought to do.

I suggest that evaluative "good" and operational "good" exemplify a kind of ambiguity in which one lexeme and so one word has two meanings. In such cases, the two meanings are closely related and so polysemous. More precisely, evaluative and operational "good" are irregular polysemes.

I will not here present an argument for the polysemy of evaluative and operational "good." I will defend the claim in section 2.2 of chapter 4. But I will here note that evaluative "good" and operational "good" share the three syntactic properties I have cited in comparing them: neither is sensitive to definiteness effects, both can modify mass nouns, and both are predicative.

With respect to these syntactic properties, contrast evaluative and operational "good" with quantitative "good." Quantitative "good" is rarely predicative; it is sensitive to definiteness effects; and it cannot modify a mass noun. These considerations encourage the view that quantitative "good" is a distinct lexeme and so word. Moreover, I suggest that quantitative "good" stands in a relation of homonymy to the lexeme "good" whose irregular polysemes are evaluative and operational "good." Again, I will not argue for this claim further here; but I will provide a defense of it in section 2.2 of chapter 4.

---

proximity; and assume that the subjects' answers were wholly uniform. We might then conclude that the study had confirmed a set of relative semantic proximities of the items. But it would remain obscure what the study had confirmed. What is a judgment or appearance of semantic proximity a judgment or appearance of?

[50] Cp. Gergely Pethö, "On Irregular Polysemy," in *The Cognitive Basis of Polysemy: New Sources of Evidence for Theories of Meaning*, M. Rakova, G. Pethö, and C. Rákosi, eds., Peter Lang, 2007, 123–56.

In short, I suggest that the three-way ambiguity of "good" is explicable as follows. There are two lexemes that have the same word form "good." These two lexemes are cognate. On the other hand, the meanings of these two lexemes are distally, if at all, related. So they stand in a relation of homonymy. Furthermore, one of these lexemes is itself two ways polysemous. Finally, this polysemy is irregular.

# 3

# Gradability

## 1. The Basic Sentence

The previous chapter introduced the semantic property of gradability. I claimed that evaluative "good" and quantitative "good" are gradable adjectives, whereas operational "good" is a non-gradable adjective. The present chapter elaborates on the semantics of gradable adjectives, with the principal aim of advancing the interpretation of evaluative "good." Given the focus on evaluative "good," I will hereafter drop the modifier "evaluative," except when needed for disambiguation.

The study of gradable adjectives has been central to formal semantic analyses of adjectives since the seventies.[1] Among these analyses, two main approaches have been developed: so-called inherent vagueness and degree-based.[2] Today, although some prominent linguists advocate inherent vagueness theories,[3] degree-based theories are the most widely accepted.[4] Continuous with the

---

[1] Marcin Morzycki, *Modification*, Cambridge University Press, 2016, 97–148, provides an excellent contemporary overview of semantic theories of gradable adjectives. Arnim von Stechow, "Comparing Theories of Comparison," *Journal of Semantics* 3 (1984) 1–77, is a major, but demanding, review of theories from the seventies and early eighties. Some noteworthy early contributions in non-formal linguistics include Edward Sapir, "Grading: A Study in Semantics," *Philosophy of Science* 11 (1944) 93–116; Herbert Pilch, "Comparative Constructions in English," *Language* 41 (1965) 37–58; Rodney Huddleston, "More on the English Comparative," *Journal of Linguistics* 3 (1967) 91–102; Dwight Bolinger, *Degree Words*, Mouton, 1972.

[2] Inherent vagueness theories have been referred to by various other names, including "superevaluation," "delineation," and "extension gap" theories. Cp. Morzycki (2016) 97.

[3] For example, Ewan Klein, "A Semantics for Positive and Comparative Adjectives," *Linguistics and Philosophy* 4 (1980) 1–45; Ewan Klein, "The Interpretation of Adjectival Comparatives," *Journal of Linguistics* 18 (1982) 113–36; Jenny Doetjes, Camelia Constantinescu, and Katerina Souckova, "A Neo-Kleinian Approach to Comparatives," *SALT* 19 (2011) 124–43; Robert van Rooij, "Vagueness and Linguistics," in *Vagueness: A Guide*, G. Ronzitti, ed., Springer, 2011, 123–70; Heather Burnett, *Gradability in Natural Language*, Oxford University Press, 2017.

[4] Cp. Frederike Moltmann: "what has come to be the current standard approach to the semantics of positive and comparative adjectives, namely the degree-based approach" (2009, 52); Stephanie Solt, "This approach could be described as the current standard in the analysis of gradability and vagueness" ("Notes on the Comparison Class," in *Vagueness in Communication: Lectures Notes in Computer Science*, R. Nouwen et al., eds., vol. 6517, Spring 2011, 189–206, at 190); Lisa Bylinina and Stas Zadorozhny: "We will use the mainstream semantics for gradable adjectives that treats them as measure functions of type $\langle e,d \rangle$ from the domain of individuals to degrees" ("Evaluative Adjectives, Scale Structure, and Ways of Being Polite," in M. Aloni et al., eds., *Language, Logic, and Meaning*, The 18th Amsterdam Colloquium, 2012, 133–42, at 134). Max Creswell, "The Semantics of Degree," in *Montague Grammar*, B. Partee, ed., Academic Press, 1976, 261–92, is responsible for introducing degree-based theories into formal semantics. Creswell's account builds on Renate Bartsch and Theo Vennemann, "The Grammar of Relative Adjectives and Comparison," *Linguistische Berichte* 20 (1972) 19–32, which provides a good historical point of departure. Rett (2015, 3–37) provides a helpful review of degree-based theories from the seventies to the present.

discussion in the last chapter, I restrict my focus here to a degree-based framework.[5]

Recall that I refer to the morphologically basic form of a gradable adjective—for example, those italicized in the following sentences—as the "basic" form:

1. Paolo is *tall*.
2. This painting is *good*.
3. The glass is *full*.
4. The stove is *hot*.

Observe that in sentences (1)–(4), the gradable adjective occurs without any degree expression. More cautiously, as I suggested in the previous chapter, in sentences (1)–(4) the gradable adjective occurs without any overt degree expression. As we will see, it is questionable whether some covert—that is, not lexicalized or phonologically expressed—degree expression is in fact present in such constructions.

Note that sentences (1)–(4) share the following form:

*x* is *a*.

That is, they consist of a grammatically singular subject *x*, a copula, and a predicate expression, the last of which (at least ostensibly) solely consists of a gradable adjective *a* in the basic form. Such sentences will be central to the ensuing discussion. I will hereafter refer to them as "basic sentences." Likewise, I will refer to the gradable adjectival phrase that constitutes the predicate expression in the basic sentence as the "basic predicate expression." So, for example,

The painting is good.

is itself a basic sentence. Therefore, its predicate expression is a basic predicate expression; and the gradable adjective "good" that, at least ostensibly, is the only constituent of the basic predicate expression, is the basic form of this adjective.

The chapter is structured in four parts. The first part, section 2, introduces a distinction between two kinds of gradable adjectives, so-called relative and absolute gradable adjectives. Clarification of this distinction requires the introduction

---

[5] However, I make some further remarks on the inherent vagueness theory in section 3.4.

of several additional semantic entities associated with gradable adjectives, in particular scales and scale structures.

In discussing the scalar properties associated with gradable adjectives, I incorporate and elaborate on the topic of antonymy, which was also introduced in the previous chapter. The central results of section 2 are the following two. First, a gradable adjective is associated with a degree on a scale, which is open or closed, which has a particular orientation, and which is based on the gradable property with which the adjective is associated. Second, "good" is a relative gradable adjective, and more precisely the unmarked member of the antonym pair "good"/ "bad."

The second part of the chapter constitutes the bulk of the discussion. Section 3 focuses on the degree associated with a relative gradable adjective. In certain relative gradable adjectival constructions, most saliently in the basic sentence, the degree associated with a relative gradable adjective has what I call a "significant" value. Note that I am using "value" here in the sense of "semantic value." Compare the mathematical and logical uses of "value" as in "the value of a variable" or "the value of a function." Accordingly, sentence (1) is naturally read as

1s.   Paolo has a significant degree of height.

or simply

1s′.   Paolo has significant height.

However, in other contexts, the degree associated with a relative gradable adjective has no significant value. For example,

Paolo is taller than Isabella.

is naturally read to mean

Paolo's degree of height is greater than Isabella's degree of height.

or simply

Paolo has more height than Isabella has.

It does not follow from these sentences that Paolo, let alone Isabella, has a significant degree of height.

In short, significant value occurs in the basic sentence, but not in certain more complex constructions. So the distribution of significant and non-significant values for the degree associated with a gradable adjective presents a problem for the principle of semantic compositionality. Resolution of this problem has been central to analyses of gradable adjectival constructions.

The standard solution to the compositionality problem is that the lexical meaning of a relative gradable adjective is associated with a degree of non-significant value. This facilitates compositionality in the case of complex constructions. However, it does not resolve the source of significant value of the degree associated with the adjective in the basic construction. I call this aspect of the compositionality problem the "significance problem."

Section 3.1 introduces the problem of compositionality and the problem of significance that is an aspect of the former. Sections 3.2 and 3.3 discuss two solutions to the significance problem. Section 3.2 focuses on the principal solution in the literature. This consists of positing a covert degree morpheme, called *pos*, in the basic predicate expression. According to one implementation of this theory, *pos* binds the degree associated with the relative gradable adjective in the basic predicate expression and orders it in relation to a second degree, called a "standard of comparison," which *pos* also introduces, and whose value is based on a contextually determined comparison class.

Section 3.3 discusses an alternative solution to the problem of significance, advanced by Jessica Rett. Rett rejects the appeal to *pos*. She argues that in the basic sentence, but also in select other gradable adjectival constructions, the significant value of the degree associated with the relative gradable adjective results from two sequential factors: first, existential binding of a degree variable associated with the lexical meaning of the relative gradable adjective, and then an uninformativity-based quantity implicature.

Section 3.4 concludes the second part of the chapter by summarizing the account of the meaning of relative gradable adjectives and specifically by clarifying the relation between relative gradable adjectives, degrees, scales, and gradable properties.

The third part of the chapter, section 4, focuses on the nature, in contrast to the source, of significant value. Precisely, what is a *significant* degree of a given gradable property? Here, I entertain a statistically based proposal by Stephanie Solt, according to which significance of degree is a function involving a median absolute derivation.

Part four of the chapter, section 5, concludes the discussion with a historical reflection on the importance of the thesis that "good" is a gradable adjective.

## 2. Scales and Antonyms

A distinction is drawn between two kinds of gradable adjectives: so-called rel-ative and absolute.[6] The grounds for the terms "relative" and "absolute" will be clarified in section 3.2. Presently, note that the distinction between relative and absolute gradable adjectives correlates with the types of degree expressions that these two kinds of gradable adjectives admit. For example, only absolute grad-able adjectives admit so-called totality modifiers such as "totally" itself as well as "100%," "completely," and "fully." Compare the following two sets of examples:

> The room was totally empty.
> The class is 100% full.
> The room is completely quiet.
> The cruise is fully booked.

> # The painting is totally good.[7]
> # Paolo is 100% tall.
> # Janet is completely beautiful.
> # Toby is fully young.

Likewise, although not all absolute gradable adjectives admit fraction phrases such as "half," "three-quarters," and "a third," the only gradable adjectives that do admit fraction phrases are absolute:

> The room was half empty.
> The class is a third full.
> The cruise is three-quarters booked.

> # The painting is half beautiful.
> # Paolo is a third tall.
> # Toby is three-quarters young.[8]

---

[6] Cp. Carmen Rotstein and Yoad Winter, "Total Adjectives versus Partial Adjectives: Scale Structure and Higher-Order Modifiers," *Natural Language Semantics* 12 (2004) 259–88; Christopher Kennedy, "Vagueness and Grammar: The Semantics of Relative and Absolute Gradable Adjectives," *Linguistics and Philosophy* 30 (2007) 1–45.

[7] There is a slang use of "totally," which means "very" or "extremely"; and on that reading the sentence is acceptable.

[8] Contrast "quiet," which does not accept fraction phrases: # "The room is half / two-thirds quiet." (Contrast this with felicitous expressions such as "Half of the students were quiet"; "Two-thirds of the room was quiet.")

This difference in the licensing of totality modifiers and fraction phrases is indicative of a further fundamental semantic property of gradable adjectives: the degrees with which they are associated are themselves constituents of scales. A scale is an ordered set of degrees. More precisely, scales are understood to be ordered by the greater-than relation ($>$), totally ordered, and dense. By "totally ordered" is meant that every degree that is a constituent of a scale is ordered in relation to every other degree that is a constituent of that scale and that no two degrees have the same value in the order. By "dense" is meant that for any two degrees $d$ and $d'$ where $d > d'$, there is a third degree $d''$ such that $d > d'' > d'$.[9]

Typically, degrees are conceived as points. An alternative is that degrees are intervals, in other words extents consisting of sets of degrees. I will assume that degrees are points.[10] Presently, I conclude that the degrees associated with gradable adjectives are constituents of scales and that these scales are based on the gradable properties associated with the gradable adjectives.

So a gradable adjective is associated with a degree on a scale based on a gradable property. At the beginning of chapter 2, I clarified the claim that gradable adjectives are associated with gradable properties. I did so in terms of semantic and correlative metaphysical entailments. For example, "$x$ is tall" entails "$x$ has height"; and that $x$ is tall entails that $x$ has height. Likewise, it is desirable to clarify the relation of association between gradable adjectives, on the one hand, and degrees and scales, on the other. I note this desideratum, but, for reasons that will become clear, postpone precisification of the relation until section 3.4 of the chapter.

Presently, I return to the distinction between relative and absolute gradable adjectives. The admissibility of totality modifiers or fraction phrases indicates that the scale associated with the adjective is bounded or closed. Precisely, the scale is bounded at the degree denoted by the phrase "totally / 100% / fully / completely $a$." By "bounded" at this point, I mean that the scale does not admit a

---

[9] Evidence for the density of scales can be adduced in various ways. For example, that Paolo is six feet tall entails that for any degree $d'$ less than the degree denoted by "six feet tall" (and down to the minimum degree on the associated scale), Paolo is at least as tall as $d'$. Cp. Irene Heim, "Degree Operators and Scope," in *Audiatur Vox Sapientiae*, C. Féry and W. Sternefeld, eds., *Studia Grammatica* 52 (2001) 214–39, at 216. (I note in passing that in the linguistics literature on gradability, the mathematical property of density tends to be conflated with the mathematical property of continuity. A clear example of the conflation is Morzycki (2016) 111, who writes: "It is also common to suppose that scales are perfectly gradient rather than granular; that is, the scale has a DENSE ordering relation." Density, as defined, does not in fact entail perfect gradience. Granted this, the conflation of density and continuity will not affect the ensuing discussion; and I will assume that scales are both dense and continuous. [Thanks to Peter Epstein for confirming the mathematical point.])

[10] An argument for identifying degrees with intervals can be found in Christopher Kennedy, "Polar Opposition and the Ontology of 'Degrees,'" *Linguistics and Philosophy* 24 (2001) 33–70.

degree beyond this point. In other words, "$x$ is totally / 100% / fully / completely $a$, but it could be more $a$" is contradictory; for example:

# The room is completely quiet; but it could be quieter.
# The class is 100% full; but it could be more full.
# The cruise is fully booked; but there is still one cabin available.

Note that in the case of absolute gradable adjectives, the meaning of "$x$ is totally / 100% / fully / completely $a$" is equivalent to "$x$ is $a$"; for example:

The room is completely quiet. ≡ The room is quiet.
The cruise is fully booked. ≡ The cruise is booked.

Consequently, a gradable adjective $a$'s admission of a totality modifier or fraction phrase indicates that at the degree denoted by sentences of the form "$x$ is $a$," the scale associated with $a$ is bounded. Consequently, the scales associated with absolute gradable adjectives are bounded at the degree denoted by sentences of the form "$x$ is $a$."

In contrast, since relative gradable adjectives do not admit totality modifiers or fraction phrases, the scales associated with this class of gradable adjectives are unbounded or open at the degree denoted by sentences of the form "$x$ is $a$." For example, the following sentences are semantically acceptable:

The building is tall; but it could be taller.
The painting is beautiful; but it could be more beautiful.

The properties of boundedness and unboundedness of scales are referred to as properties of "scale structure" or "scale type."[11] I underscore that these claims about scale structure are semantic rather than metaphysical. For example, in a world where individuals had a maximum height, an individual with that height might truly be called "tall"—even though "tall" is a relative gradable adjective, is associated with an open scale, and so does not admit a totality modifier. For example, physical conditions might make it impossible for a tall building to be taller. In that case, the sentence "The building is tall, but it could be taller" would be false. But it remains a semantically felicitous sentence.

Below, I will elaborate on the topic of scales. The elaboration requires reference to another topic associated with gradable adjectives: antonymy. Several types of semantic relations have been discussed under the rubric of antonymy. Examples

---

[11] Cp. Christopher Kennedy and Louis McNally, "Scale Structure, Degree Modification, and the Semantics of Gradable Predicates," *Language* 81 (2005) 345–81.

include logical contradiction, as in "red" and "not red"; so-called conversivity, as in "buy" and "sell"; and so-called reversivity, as in "tie" and "untie."[12] Here, I am concerned with so-called "gradable" antonymy, in particular antonymy as it pertains to pairs of gradable adjectives.

Many, although not all, gradable adjectives are members of antonym pairs, for example:

tall/short, deep/shallow, expensive/cheap

full/empty, open/closed, opaque/transparent.

The first set here consists of pairs both of whose members are relative gradable adjectives. The second set consists of pairs both of whose members are absolute gradable adjectives. Antonym pairs may also consist of one absolute and one relative gradable adjective; for example:

certain/uncertain, clean/dirty, pure/impure, quiet/loud.

In these examples, the first member of each pair is an absolute gradable adjective and the second is a relative gradable adjective.[13]

It has been suggested that the following two conditions are required for gradable antonymy. First, for an antonym pair of gradable adjectives *a* and *b*, the scales that are associated with *a* and *b* are based on the same gradable property. For example, scales of height are associated with "tall" and "short."[14] Second, within a given context, those entities that are *a* are not *b*, and those entities that are *b* are not *a*. For example, those entities that are clean are not dirty, and those entities that are dirty are not clean. In other words, the set of entities that are *a* and the set of entities that are *b* are disjoint.

In the case of antonym pairs exactly one of whose members is an absolute gradable adjective, the individuals in the domain of these adjectives are exhaustively either *a* or *b*. For example, in the case of "pure"/"impure," every individual is either pure or impure. In contrast, in the case of antonym pairs both of whose members are relative or absolute gradable adjectives, individuals may be neither *a* or *b*. For example, some individuals may have a degree of height such that they are neither tall nor short or a degree of value such that they are neither good nor

---

[12] These examples are drawn from Adrienne Lehrer and Keith Lehrer, "Antonymy," *Linguistics and Philosophy* 5 (1982) 483–501, at 483. Cp. Adrienne Lehrer, "Markedness and Antonymy," *Journal of Linguistics* 21 (1985) 397–429, which discusses over 150 pairs of gradable antonyms.

[13] These examples are drawn from Kennedy (2007) 34.

[14] We will revisit this condition in section 2.5 of chapter 4, specifically as it pertains to the antonym pair "good"/"bad."

bad. Again, some individuals may have a degree of fullness of content such that they are neither full nor empty.

The members of an antonym pair of gradable adjectives are widely believed to be divisible into distinct classes, one of which is typically called "positive" or "unmarked," the other "negative" or "marked." This is a second way in which the term "positive" is used in the context of theories of gradable adjectives. Hereafter, I will use only the terms "marked" and "unmarked" in this context.

Various criteria have been adduced to support the distinction between the marked and unmarked members of an antonym pair of gradable adjectives. The criterion with the strongest evidential support is that in questions of the form "How *a* is *x*?" only one member of the antonym pair, namely the marked member, presupposes that *x* is *a*.[15] For example, consider the pair "wide"/"narrow" in the following two questions:

How wide is the river?
How narrow is the river?

The first question does not presuppose that the river is wide. The second question presupposes that the river is narrow. Accordingly, "narrow" is the marked member of the antonym pair.

Other criteria that have been proposed for distinguishing marked and unmarked members of antonym pairs of gradable adjectives are more problematic.[16] I will discuss four of them. Christopher Kennedy appeals to one criterion in the following remark:

> [Unmarked gradable] adjectives like "tall," "full," and "wet" measure increasing amounts of a [gradable] property (if *x* is taller than *y*, then *x* has more height than *y*), while [marked gradable] adjectives [in this case "short," "empty," and "dry"] measure decreasing amounts of [the same gradable] property (if *x* is shorter than *y*, then *x* has less height than *y*).[17]

The problem here is that the principle does not seem applicable to many gradable antonyms. Consider "peaceful"/"violent," "impulsive"/"restrained," and "compact"/"diffuse." Which member of these pairs measures increasing amounts of the relevant gradable property? Relatedly, what justifies the claim that "full" rather than "empty," or "dry" rather than "wet," measures increasing amounts

---

[15] Cp. Lehrer (1985) 401–2.
[16] Lehrer (1985) provides a good critique.
[17] Kennedy (2007) 33.

of the relevant gradable property? The answer seems to vary according to context. For example, in a context where the goal is to create a vacuum or to create a moistureless environment, it would seem that "empty" and "dry" would denote increasing amounts of the gradable property.

Another criterion for distinguishing unmarked and marked members of an antonym pair of gradable adjectives pertains to measure phrases. Recall that a measure phrase is a nominal expression consisting of a numeral and a noun that denotes a standard of measurement; for example "six feet" and "ten kilometers." In the context of the discussion of quantitative "good" in chapter 2, I focused on "good" modification of measure phrases; for example:

> He played the cello for a good two hours.
> She earned a good $25,000 bonus.

But here, I am referring to gradable adjectives themselves licensing measure phrases; for example:

> Paolo is six feet tall.
> The race is ten kilometers long.[18]

In cases where a gradable adjective admits a measure phrase, the member of an antonym pair that admits the measure phrase is said to be unmarked, for example:

> Paolo is six feet tall.
> # Paolo is six feet short.

> The pool is five feet deep.
> # The pool is five feet shallow.

> The canyon is one and a half miles wide.
> # The canyon is one and a half miles narrow.

The problem here is that the principle cannot be extended to most antonym pairs because, as noted earlier, only a small number of gradable adjectives admit measure phrases.

---

[18] Precisely what syntactic role measure phrases play in relation to the gradable adjectives that license them is questionable. For example, Roger Schwarzschild argues that they are modifiers. ("Measure Phrases as Modifiers of Adjectives," *Recherches Linguistiques de Vincennes* 34 (2005) 207–28) But cp. Rett (2015) 14–18.

Finally, Kennedy, drawing on the work of Pieter Seuren, endorses the following two criteria, which he subsumes under the category of monotonicity properties.[19] The first involves the use of so-called positive and negative polarity items. A positive polarity item is an expression that can only occur in a context of affirmation, for example in the clausal complement of an affirmation.[20] A negative polarity item is an expression that can occur only in a context of negation or denial. For example, consider the uses of the negative polarity item "anyone" in the following sentences (note that the complement clauses here are demarcated by straight lines):

He denied | that anyone had been prosecuted |.
* He affirmed | that anyone had been prosecuted |.

He disliked / did not like | that anyone had been prosecuted |.
* He liked | that anyone had been prosecuted |.

The criterion then is that the member of the antonym pair that licenses negative polarity items in a clausal complement is unmarked, whereas the member that does not license negative polarity items in a clausal complement is marked. In the following examples, the negative polarity items within the complement clauses are italicized:

It's difficult | for Tim to admit that he has *ever* been wrong |.
It's terrible | that you have to talk to *any* of these people at all |.
It would be foolish | of her to *even bother to lift a finger* to help |.

* It's easy | for Tim to admit that he has *ever* been wrong |.
* It's great | that you have to talk to *any* of these people at all |.
* It would be clever | of her to *even bother to lift a finger* to help |.[21]

---

[19] Kennedy (1999) 17–19; Pieter A. M. Seuren, "The Structure and Selection of Positive and Negative Gradable Adjectives," in *Papers from the Parasession on the Lexicon*, Chicago Linguistics Society, vol. 14, 1979, 336–46.

[20] Note that "complement" is a syntactic term. A complement *C* is a syntactic constituent of a larger expression *E*, and where *E* syntactically requires *C*. For example, in "Ronan loves Katie," "Katie" is the direct object complement of the transitive verb "love." Since "love" is transitive, it syntactically requires a direct object. Since "love" also syntactically requires a subject, "Ronan" is also a complement of "love." Complements are to be distinguished from adjuncts, where an adjunct *A* is a syntactic constituent of a larger expression *E*, but where *E* does not syntactically require *A*. For example, in "Ronan deeply loves Katie," the adverb "deeply" is not syntactically required by "love" or any other part of the expression.

[21] Kennedy (1999) 18.

According to this criterion, then, "difficult," "terrible," and "foolish" are the marked, and "easy," "great," and "clever" the unmarked members of the antonym pairs.

Second, Kennedy maintains that those members of antonym pairs that license upward entailments in clausal complements are unmarked, whereas those members that license downward entailments in clausal complements are marked. The first set of examples consists of upward entailments:

It is safe | to drive fast in Rome |. →
It is safe | to drive in Rome |.

It is common | to see Frances playing electric guitar poorly |. →
It is common | to see Frances playing electric guitar |.

The second set of examples consists of downward entailments:

It is dangerous | to drive in Rome |. →
It is dangerous | to drive fast in Rome |.

It is strange | to see Frances playing electric guitar |. →
It is strange | to see Frances playing electric guitar poorly |.[22]

According to this principle, "safe" and "common" are unmarked, and "dangerous" and "strange" are marked.

For all their interest, however, it is not clear that these two monotonicity criteria for distinguishing unmarked and marked members can be extended to most, let alone all, antonym pairs of gradable adjectives. For example, I see no way to construct diagnostic sentences using pairs such as "tall"/"short," "fast"/"slow," "deep"/"shallow."

The upshot of this discussion of the distinction between unmarked and marked members of antonym pairs of gradable adjectives is then somewhat negative and inconclusive: the distinction between unmarked and marked members rests on a disparate set of principles, each of which in most cases holds for a limited set of gradable adjectives. To be clear, the problem is not that various criteria are being used and may have to be used to diagnose unmarked and marked members. Rather, it is that unless the various criteria depend on a set of unified principles, then the distinction that one criterion reveals may not be the same property as the distinction that another criterion reveals. In other words, there may not be a single

---

[22] Kennedy (1999) 18.

property of unmarkedness or of markedness, but several. But we won't know this unless we know that the various criteria do depend on unified principles.

Granted this, consider now the antonym pair of relative gradable adjectives "tall"/"short." Both adjectives are associated with degrees on open scales based on the gradable property of height. But "tall" and "short" clearly have different meanings. Consequently, the scales associated with these adjectives must consist of some additional feature. One proposal is that the scales of tallness and shortness have distinct and more precisely inverse scalar orientations. To clarify this point, I will first consider two standard comparative constructions, one incorporating "tall," the other "short":

y is taller than x.

This sentence compares the degrees of y and x on a single scale of tallness. The sentence states that on this scale, y's degree is greater than x's degree. What does it mean for y's degree on the scale of tallness to be greater than x's degree on that scale? It means that y has more height than x. So the scale of tallness is structured in terms of increasing height, which may be represented as follows:

TALLNESS

The arrow here indicates the scalar orientation of the scale of tallness.

Now consider a standard comparative construction involving "short":

y is shorter than x.

This sentence compares the degrees of y and x on a single scale of shortness. The sentence states that on this scale, y's degree is greater than x's degree. What does it mean for y's degree on the scale of shortness to be greater than x's degree on that scale? It means that y has less height than x. So the scale of shortness is structured in terms of decreasing height, which may be represented as follows:

SHORTNESS

The arrow here indicates the scalar orientation of the scale of shortness. Consequently, the scales of tallness and shortness have inverse orientations: $0 \Leftrightarrow \infty$ for tallness; $\infty \Leftrightarrow 0$ for shortness.

In light of these points, consider the following sentence:

If $x$ is taller than $y$, then $y$ is shorter than $x$.

This sentence states that if, on a scale of tallness, $x$'s position is greater than $y$'s position, then, on a scale of shortness, $y$'s position is greater than $x$'s position. The explanation of the truth of this sentence is that if $x$ has more height than $y$, then $y$ has less height than $x$; and the scales of tallness and shortness have inverse scalar orientations.

Consider now the phenomenon Kennedy calls "cross-polar anomaly."[23] Cross-polar anomaly results from comparison that incorporates both members of a pair of gradable antonyms:

? $x$ is taller than $y$ is short.

As Kennedy writes: "such sentences demonstrate that comparatives formed out of [polarly antonymous gradable] adjectives are semantically anomalous."[24] I suggest that for felicitous comparison to occur, the degrees associated with the relata ($x$ and $y$) must be located on a single scale. Consequently, insofar as the sentence here is semantically anomalous, the anomaly is explicable on the grounds that degrees on two different scales are being compared. On this reading, the sentence states, anomalously, that $x$'s position on the scale of tallness is greater than $y$'s position on the scale of shortness.[25]

Granted this, consider the sentence once again, but now in terms of what Kennedy calls "comparison of divergence."[26] Like cross-polar anomaly, comparison of divergence incorporates both members of a pair of gradable antonyms. However, comparison of divergence felicitously consists in comparison of the relata on a common scale. Precisely, this common scale measures degree of divergence from a common point. For convenience, I repeat the example sentence:

$x$ is taller than $y$ is short.

We can represent this sentence according to its interpretation as a comparison of divergence by means of the following diagram:

---

[23] Cp. Christopher Kennedy, "Comparison and Polar Opposition," in *The Proceedings of Semantics and Linguistic Theory*, vol. 7, A. Lawson, ed., Cornell Linguistics Club Publications, 1997, 240–57; Kennedy (2001).
[24] Kennedy (2001) 36.
[25] Kennedy offers a different view, which depends on the claim that degrees are intervals.
[26] Kennedy (2001) 40.

DIVERGENCE FROM C

$$0 \longleftarrow \quad \underset{y}{\bullet} \quad \underset{C}{|} \quad \underset{x}{\bullet} \quad \longrightarrow \infty \text{ degrees of height}$$

Observe here that the common scale, divergence from C, is constructed on the basis of the distinct scales, including distinct scalar orientations, associated with "tall" and "short." This fact at least provides the beginning of an answer to the following question. Since the felicity of comparison of divergence may be based on the same sentence that yields cross-polar anomaly when interpreted in terms of two distinct scales, what determines the common scale that makes the comparison of divergence felicitous? I will not pursue the answer to this question further here, save to note the following. Comparison consisting of two different gradable adjectives triggers a psychological attempt to construct a common scale on the basis of the two distinct scales. I underscore that the two gradable adjectives needn't be antonyms; they need only be different. For example, compare the following two sentences:

The river is wider than it is deep.
The tree is taller than its flowers are beautiful.

To the extent that construction of a common scale is psychologically unachievable, semantic anomaly prevails. To the extent that common scale construction is achieved, comparison of divergence or some other semantically acceptable, but non-standard comparison results.[27]

I have introduced the preceding considerations to support the claim that a gradable adjective *a* is associated with a degree on a scale, which is open or closed, which has a particular orientation, and which is based on a gradable property. I conclude these introductory remarks concerning the semantics of gradable adjectives by considering their implications for "good."

"Good" is a relative gradable adjective. Accordingly, "good" does not admit totality modifiers or fraction phrases:

# Isabella is completely good at chess.
# Ronan is a fully good with children.
# The painting is half good.
# The meal was three-quarters good.[28]

---

[27]  I have in mind here Kennedy's so-called "comparison of deviation" (2001, 40).
[28]  Contrast these last two sentences with the following two, with which they are not to be confused: "Half of the painting is good"; "Three-quarters of the meal was good."

Consequently, the scale associated with "good" is unbounded at the degree denoted by "$x$ is good."[29] For example, the following sentences are felicitous:

> Isabella is good at chess; but she could be better.
> The essay is good; but it could be better.

Likewise, the gradable antonym of "good," namely "bad," is a relative gradable adjective:

> # Isabella is completely bad at chess.
> # Ronan is fully bad with children.
> # The painting is half bad.[30]
> # The meal was three-quarters bad.

And the scale associated with "bad" is unbounded at the degree denoted by "$x$ is bad":

> The meal was bad; but it could have been worse.
> The essay is bad; but it could be worse.

With respect to the criteria for distinguishing unmarkedness and markedness—inconclusive and problematic as they are—consider the following observations. First, compare the following questions:

> How good is the film?
> How bad is the film?

The presuppositions of these questions differ. The second question presupposes that the film is bad. The first question does not presuppose or only weakly presupposes that the film is good. The fact that questions of the form "How good is $x$?" may weakly presuppose that $x$ is good is perhaps explicable on the grounds that questions of the form "How is $x$?"—that is, without the adjective "good"— can be used to inquire into the value of $x$; for example:

> How is the book?
> How was the restaurant?

---

[29]  A referee questioned the expression "$x$ is perfectly good." But I take "perfectly" here to function as a so-called discourse adverb. It underscores the veracity of the claim that $x$ is good. Compare: "$x$ is absolutely good," which, I think, would be more accurately represented with commas, viz.: "$x$ is, absolutely, good"; and which means "It is absolutely the case that $x$ is good."

[30]  I note in passing the colloquial use of "half bad" in a negation: "The meal was not half bad." The intuitive meaning of this sentence is that the meal was, for the most part, good.

In that case, "good" is somewhat anomalous with respect to this diagnostic for un/markedness.

Second, "x is good" seems to entail "x has value," while "x is bad" seems to entail "x lacks value."[31] The better x is, the more value x has. The worse x is, the less value x has. In that case, the scales associated with "good" and "bad" have inverse scalar orientations.[32]

Third, recall that the measure phrase licensing criterion is not applicable here since "good" and "bad" do not license measure phrases. We simply lack *general* standards of measurement for value. "General" here is emphasized because we do have standards of measurement for some types of value, for example financial value. However, it is noteworthy that even in such cases measure phrases are unacceptable:

# He's earning a six-figure good salary.
# She received a ninety-one-point good score on her exam.[33]

Fourth, "good" does not license negative polarity items in clausal complements, whereas evaluative "bad" does:

* It's good | that you have to talk to *any* of these people at all |.
It's bad | that you have to talk to *any* of these people at all |.

Finally, Kennedy's second set of monotonicity properties is not effectively applicable to "good" and "bad." "Good" does not consistently license upward entailments in clausal complements; for example:

It's good | to drive fast in Rome |. →
# It's good | to drive in Rome |.

It's good | to see Frances playing electric guitar poorly |. →
# It's good | to see Frances playing electric guitar |.

---

[31] To be clear, the suggested entailments here differ from the entailment I cited in chapter 2 in clarifying the claim that there is a sense of "good," namely evaluative "good" that is associated with value. In the present context, "good and "bad" being associated with having and lacking value respectively is analogous to "tall" and "short" being associated with having and lacking height respectively. See footnote 32.

[32] I return to this point in section 2.5 of chapter 4, where I argue that matters are more complicated and problematic.

[33] I note in passing that "better" does admit some measure phrases: "My score on the first exam was two points better than on the second one." "The salary they're offering is three times better than what I'm getting paid now." Compare factor phrases with an equative phrase with "good": "My score on the first exam was twice as good as my score on the second exam."

And "bad" does not consistently license downward entailments in clausal complements; for example:

It's bad | to drive in Rome |. →
It's bad | to drive fast in Rome |.

It's bad | to see Frances playing electric guitar |. →
# It's bad | to see Frances playing electric guitar poorly |.

In sum, although the diagnostics for un/markedness are generally problematic, the evidence still supports the view that "good" is the unmarked and "bad" the marked member of the antonym pair.

## 3.1. The Problems of Compositionality and Significance

To this point I have suggested that a gradable adjective is associated with a degree on a scale, which is open or closed, which has a particular orientation, and which is based on a gradable property, precisely the gradable property associated with the gradable adjective. For example, "tall" is associated with a degree on a scale, which is open, whose orientation is the inverse of that of "short," and which is based on the gradable property of height; and "good" is associated with a degree on a scale, which is open, whose orientation is the inverse of that of "bad," and which is based on the gradable property of value.

In the present section, I further refine this view by focusing on the degree associated with the gradable adjective. To begin, consider again the following basic sentence:

1. Paolo is tall.

Sentence (1) entails

1d. Paolo has a degree of height.

(Note that here and often hereafter I elide mention of the scale of which the degree is a constituent.)[34]

---

[34] I do this for two reasons: one trivial, one substantive. With respect to the semantics of gradable adjectives, my decision not to mention the associated scales is a convenience and merely for the sake of brevity. But with respect to the metaphysical implications of gradable adjectival expressions, my

Now, it is true that sentence (1) entails sentence (1d). But this itself does not entail that sentence (1) has the same meaning as sentence (1d). Indeed, "Paolo is tall" does *not* mean "Paolo has a degree of height." Every vertically extended entity has a degree of height. But not every vertically extended entity is tall. More precisely, as I suggested in the previous chapter and above in this chapter, "Paolo is tall" means:

1s. Paolo has a significant degree of height.

We may gloss this sentence more simply as

1s'. Paolo has significant height.

Generalizing, I will hereafter assume that when a relative gradable adjective constitutes the predicate expression in a basic sentence, that sentence can be glossed as

*x* has a significant degree of the *a*-associated gradable property.

or more simply as

*x* has significant G (where G stands for the *a*-associated gradable property).

In short, significance of degree is a semantic feature of the basic sentence when a relative gradable adjective constitutes the predicate expression. For this reason, the property of significance of degree requires scrutiny. But it requires scrutiny for at least two additional reasons. One is that "significant" itself is a gradable adjective, indeed a relative gradable adjective. So, strictly speaking, the claim that the basic sentence means that *x* has a significant degree of the *a*-associated gradable property entails a regress. I will return to this problem in section 4.

Presently, the property of significance of degree requires scrutiny because the sense of significance in the basic sentence seems to contradict a foundational principle of semantic theory: the principle of compositionality. According to one version of the principle of compositionality, the literal, that is, truth-conditional, meaning of a complex expression depends on the literal meanings of its constituents and the syntactic structure of those constituents. For example, the literal meaning of

Adam loves Inga.

decision not to mention the associated scales owes to the fact that the metaphysical implications are questionable. I introduce this point in section 3.4; and I return to it in section 4.2 of chapter 6.

depends on the literal meanings of its constituents, "Adam," "loves," and "Inga," as well as on the syntactic structure of those constituents. If we substitute one constituent, "Adam," with another, "Dax,"

Dax loves Inga.

then the literal meaning of the sentence changes. And if we alter the syntactic structure of the constituents, for example by inverting the order of the subject and object of "loves,"

Inga loves Adam.

the literal meaning of the sentence changes.

The basic sentence is a complex expression. Again, it consists of a subject $x$, a copula, and a gradable adjective $a$. So the meaning of the complex should depend on the meanings of these constituents and their syntactic structure. The problem is that, in the case of relative gradable adjectives, the property of significance of degree does not seem to derive from the meanings of any of the constituents, let alone from the syntax of the basic sentence.

To appreciate this claim, consider again sentence (1): "Paolo is tall." I maintain that this sentence means what sentence (1s') means: "Paolo has significant height." Consequently, it appears that "tall" in (1) is associated with a significant degree of height. After all, for any $x$, "$x$ is tall" means "$x$ has significant height." But now assume that Paolo is a full-grown man whose height measures five feet exactly; and consider the following measure phrase construction:

Paolo is five feet tall.

Here "tall" appears not to be associated with a significant degree of height. On the contrary, if Paolo is a full-grown man and he is five feet tall, then he is short. Yet "Paolo is five feet tall" is true; "tall" is associated with a degree, which is a semantic constituent of the sentence; and again, according to the principle of compositionality, the literal meaning of the sentence depends on the literal meanings of its constituents and their syntax.

In contrast to the significant degree associated with a relative gradable adjective $a$ in the basic sentence, in the measure phrase construction the degree associated with $a$ does not have a significant value. Accordingly, I will speak of the sense or value of the degree associated with the gradable adjective in the measure phrase construction as "non-significant."[35] The non-significant sense occurs in a wide range of constructions. For example, consider the following dialogue:

| A: | How *tall* is Paolo? | [NON-SIGNIFICANT] |
| B: | He's five feet *tall*. | [NON-SIGNIFICANT] |
| A: | That's not *tall*. | [SIGNIFICANT] |
| | In fact, five feet *tall* | [NON-SIGNIFICANT] |
| | is *short*. | [SIGNIFICANT] |
| B: | True. But he is *tall*er | [NON-SIGNIFICANT] |
| | than he was last year. | |

Compare "good." To be sure, "good" does not admit measure phrases. Also, as I noted, the interrogative "How good is $x$?" may weakly presuppose that $x$ is good. Nonetheless, consider the comparatives "better" and "best" in the following, semantically felicitous sentences:

This cell phone may be better than that one, but neither is good.
This is the best solvent the hardware store sells, but it's not good.

Compare:

Dax is taller than Jett, but neither is tall.
Dax is the tallest of Adam's sons, but none of them is tall.

The point here is that the meanings of the comparatives and superlatives derive from the meaning of the basic form. But, more precisely, the degree associated with the basic form from which they derive has a non-significant value. So if, as the basic sentence indicates, the meaning of the basic form is associated with a degree that has a significant value, then a problem of compositionality follows.

## 3.2. The Standard Solutions to the Compositionality and Significance Problems

The standard solution to the compositionality problem is to maintain that the degree associated with the lexical—I underscore lexical, as opposed to

---

[35] Compare Morzycki (2016) 183–86, who uses the term "neutral(ized)" for the same purpose.

literal—meaning of a relative gradable adjective has a non-significant value. Contrast this view with a view according to which the degree associated with the lexical meaning of a relative gradable adjective has a significant value. In this latter case, compositionality becomes problematic. For example,

Paolo is five feet tall.

must then mean something like

Paolo has a significant five feet of height.

Instead, assuming that the degree associated with the lexical meaning of a relative gradable adjective has a non-significant value facilitates compositionality as follows. In complex degree constructions, that is, constructions that consist of degree expressions modifying or ordering or quantifying over the degree associated with the basic form of the relative gradable adjective, the degree expression values or orders or binds the associated degree. It is such valuing, ordering, or binding that endows the sentences with their intuitive meanings. For example, consider again the measure phrase sentence

Paolo is five feet tall.

Here, the measure phrase "five feet" values the degree associated with "tall," and thereby yields the intuitive meaning that the degree to which Paolo has height has the value of five feet.

Compare the following comparative construction:

Paolo is taller than Isabella.

In this case, the comparative morpheme "-er" introduces a complement clause "than Isabella." Assume that the complement clause involves syntactic ellipsis:[36]

Paolo is taller than Isabella ~~is tall~~.

So both the main clause "Paolo is tall" and the complement clause "than Isabella is tall" introduce degrees: the degree $d$ to which Paolo is tall and the degree $d'$ to which Isabella is tall. Assume that the comparative morpheme "-er" that is suffixed to "tall" in the main clause takes two degrees and orders them according

---

[36] On this subject, cp. section 3.4 of chapter 5.

to the greater-than (>) relation. In that case, "Paolo is taller than Isabella" is interpreted, as intuitively, to mean that the degree $d$ of height that Paolo has is greater than the degree $d'$ of height that Isabella has.

Similarly, consider the following example of an equative construction:

Paolo is as tall as Ronan.

Here the equative degree expression "as" (the first "as" in the sentence) introduces a complement clause, "as Ronan." Here too the complement clause involves syntactic ellipsis:

Paolo is as tall as Ronan is tall.

Again, assume that the equative "as," which precedes "tall" in the main clause, takes two degrees and orders them, in this case according to the at-least-as-great-as ($\geq$) relation. In that case, "Paolo is as tall as Ronan" is interpreted, as intuitively, to mean that the degree $d$ of height that Paolo has is at least as great as the degree $d'$ of height that Ronan has.[37]

These considerations provide support for the view that the degree associated with the lexical meaning of a relative gradable adjective has a non-significant value. Granted this, the problem of the significant value of the degree in the basic sentence has not been addressed. Again, since the gradable adjective in the basic predicate expression ostensibly occurs without a degree expression, the meaning of the basic sentence is predicted to be: $x$ has a non-significant degree of the $a$-associated gradable property $G$. This result is clearly unsatisfactory since, intuitively, the basic sentence means that $x$ has a significant degree of the $a$-associated gradable property $G$. What then explains the sense of significance of degree in the basic sentence? I will call this aspect of the compositionality problem "the significance problem."

The earliest and most common solution to the significance problem is the postulation of a covert degree morpheme in the basic predicate expression, which overtly lacks any degree expression. Recall that by "covert" (or "hidden" or "phonologically or orthographically null") is meant that the degree morpheme does not appear in the surface syntax; hence, it is not pronounced or written. This covert morpheme is standardly called *pos*, short for "positively" or "positive form."[38] On this view, the constituency of the basic sentence may, more revealingly, be represented as

$x$ is *pos* $a$.

---

[37] For a more thorough and formal analysis of these constructions, cp. Morzycki (2016) 152–74.

[38] The name derives from the term "positive" first mentioned with respect to grades of comparison, and which I am calling "basic." The term *pos* was first proposed by Bartsch and Venneman (1972, 175).

Since *pos* was introduced precisely to explain the sense of significance in the basic sentence, the semantic function of *pos* is to endow the degree associated with the relative gradable adjective with significant value. In principle, there are various ways that *pos* could achieve this result. One way is analogous to the operation of the comparative and equative degree morphemes, that is, by ordering two degrees. So consider the following implementation of this idea.

In the case of the basic sentence, one degree derives from the subject of which the gradable adjective is predicated. For example, in "Paolo is tall," it is the degree of height that Paolo has. In contrast to the comparative and equative constructions, however, the basic sentence lacks a complement clause. *Pos* then is the source of the second degree. *Pos* introduces a second degree and orders the two degrees according to, say, the greater-than or at-least-as-great-as relation.

I will refer to the second degree, which *pos* introduces, as the "standard of comparison" or "standard degree."[39] The intuitive idea is that for $x$ to be $a$, for example, for Paolo to be tall, $x$ must exceed, that is, be greater than, or at least meet, that is, be at least as great as, a standard.

The standard of comparison is based on a so-called comparison class. A comparison class is a subset of the universe of discourse specified by the context in which $a$ is tokened.[40] For example, in one context "Paolo is tall" may mean that Paolo is tall relative to his siblings; in another context, that Paolo is tall relative to his classmates. In the former case, Paolo's siblings constitute the comparison class; in the latter case, Paolo's classmates do.

Observe that comparison class specification can be overtly lexicalized by an adjoined "for" prepositional phrase:

Paolo is tall for a twelve-year-old boy.
Paolo is tall for his class.

---

[39] Note that in the literature the term "standard of comparison" or "standard degree" is used more broadly to include, for example, the degrees denoted by complement clauses in comparative and equative constructions.

[40] Cp. Ewan Klein: "A comparison class is a subset of the universe of discourse which is picked out relative to the context of use. A similar idea is involved in restricting the range of quantifier phrases. The truth, in a context [C], of *everybody is having a good time*, depends on the domain of quantification, and this will typically be a small subset of all things that could possibly be talked about in [C]" (1980, 13). Klein notes that the term "comparison class" is used as early as R. M. Hare, *The Language of Morals*, Clarendon Press, 1952. Precisely, Hare introduces the phrase "class of comparison" at 133.

Consider also cases where the gradable adjective modifies a noun phrase, for example:

Paolo is a tall sixteen-year-old boy.

The nominal expression, here "sixteen-year-old boy," typically makes salient a property that determines the comparison class. Once again, however, no such overt lexical specification or indication of the comparison class is required for an instance of the basic sentence to be felicitous.[41]

Granted this, it is contested how the standard of comparison is determined on the basis of the comparison class. For the sake of simplicity, assume for now that the standard of comparison is derived through an average function. (I will revisit this claim in section 4.) Consequently, in a context where the sentence "Paolo is tall" means that Paolo is tall relative to his classmates, the standard of comparison derives from the average of the set of degrees of height of Paolo's classmates. In that case, we may assume, *pos* relates Paolo's degree of height $d$ to the degree $d'$ that is the standard of comparison according to the greater-than relation. Consequently, in this context "Paolo is tall" is interpreted to mean that the degree $d$ of height that Paolo has is greater than the standard of comparison $d'$, which is the average of the degrees of height that his classmates have.

In short, *pos* denotes a context-sensitive function that relates one degree, namely the degree to which the subject of which the gradable adjective is predicated, to another degree, namely the standard of comparison, where the standard of comparison is determined through some algorithm, perhaps the average function, based on the members of a comparison class. Compare Kennedy's remark:

> *pos* is a context-sensitive function that chooses a standard of comparison in such a way as to ensure that the objects that the [gradable adjective] is true of [for example, Paolo] "stand out" in the context of utterance, relative to the kind of measurement [for example, height] that the adjective encodes.[42]

I will return to Kennedy's remark subsequently, and in particular to the idea of "standing out." Presently, I presume that to "stand out" in the context of utterance is equivalent to having a significant degree of the *a*-associated gradable property $G$.[43]

---

[41] On the semantics of "for" prepositional phrases and modified nominals, cp. Kennedy (2007) 7–21.

[42] Kennedy (2007) 17.

[43] An alternative solution, noted by Kennedy, is that in the basic sentence, *a* undergoes a type shift that is semantically equivalent to *pos a*: "the content of my proposals and argumentation remains the

In concluding this standard account of the compositionality problem for complex constructions that incorporate relative gradable adjectives, including the significance problem for basic sentences, I can now clarify the terminology "relative" and "absolute" employed to distinguish the two classes of gradable adjectives. A *relative* gradable adjective is so-called precisely insofar as the value of the degree with which it is associated in the basic sentence varies in relation to a contextually sensitive standard of comparison. In contrast, as I have explained, the degree associated with an absolute gradable adjective in the basic sentence is fixed. Precisely, it is fixed to the degree at which the scale associated with the adjective is bounded. In other words, it invariably denotes the maximum degree on that scale.

### 3.3. Rett's Implicature Theory

Among degree-based theories, appeal to *pos*, or at least to some such covert degree morpheme, is the standard solution to the problem of significance. Recently, however, Jessica Rett has adduced several reasons for rejecting *pos*. In doing so, she has also advanced an ingenious alternative, which I will explain here.[44]

The most important reason Rett endorses for rejecting *pos* as a solution to the significance problem is that the sense of significance is not restricted to the basic sentence.[45] For example, consider:

Paolo is as short as Ronan.

This sentence entails "Paolo is short"; hence, it entails "Paolo has a significant lack of height." Generalizing, the sense of significance of degree occurs with the marked member of a pair of gradable antonyms in equative constructions. In addition, as I have shown, the sense of significance of degree is presupposed in degree questions with the marked antonym. For example, the question

How short is Toby?

presupposes that Toby is short.

---

same if we assume instead that 'the positive degree morpheme *pos*' is really 'the positive type-shifting rule *pos*'" (2007, 7). However, cp. Rett's critical response at (2015, 31).

[44]   Rett (2015).
[45]   The property I am calling "significance of degree," Rett calls "evaluativity" (2015, 1).

The sense of significance of degree also occurs in degree demonstratives that employ the marked antonym.[46] For example, imagine that the speaker is pointing to a height:

Toby is that short.

This sentence entails "Toby is short."

In sum, the *pos* theory cannot explain and, more damagingly, is inconsistent with this distribution of, that is, this range of, contexts exhibiting the sense of significance of degree.

Another reason that appeal to *pos* is untenable is that the sense of significance of degree is a universal property of certain gradable constructions. By "universal" property here is meant that the sense of significance of degree is a property of certain gradable constructions throughout the world's languages.[47] Consequently, if *pos* existed, we would expect it "to be (overtly) lexicalized in at least some languages."[48] But there is no compelling evidence that it is.[49]

How then is the sense of significance of degree and its peculiar distribution—for example, in "*x* is as short as *y*," but not "*x* is as tall as *y*"—to be explained? Rett's solution is inspired and informed by the theory of implicature. As Grice, who first introduced the theory,[50] understands it, an implicature is the content of an expression, for example of a sentence, that is non-deductively inferable from the use of that expression, where the inferred content differs from the literal meaning of the expression, which Grice calls "what is said." For example, consider the following sentence:

Joe ate lunch and took a walk.

This sentence implicates

Joe took a walk shortly after eating lunch.

---

[46] Rett (2015) 97–123.

[47] Cp. Leon Stassen, *Comparison and Universal Grammar*, Blackwell, 1985; Leon Stassen, "Comparative Constructions," in *World Atlas of Language Structures Online*, M. Haspelmath et al., eds., chap. 121, Max Planck Digital Library, 2008; Jonathan D. Bobaljik, *Universals in Comparative Morphology*, MIT Press, 2012.

[48] Rett (2015) 31.

[49] Kennedy and McNally (2005, n. 5) had in fact suggested that the Mandarin word *hen* is an example. But the claim has been criticized by Thomas Grano, "Mandarin *Hen* and Universal Markedness in Gradable Adjectives," *Natural Language and Linguistic Theory* 30 (2012) 513–65; cp. Rett (2015) 31–32.

[50] Paul Grice, "Logic and Conversation," in *Syntax and Semantics*, vol. 3: *Speech Acts*, P. Cole and J. Morgan, eds., Academic Press, 1975, 41–58.

However, the truth-conditions of "Joe ate lunch and took a walk" merely require that Joe performed each of the acts, eating lunch and taking a walk, and not necessarily in that order.

Grice further distinguishes conventional from conversational implicatures. In the former case, the implicature is lexically encoded and is never cancelable. For example, consider the following sentence:

Helen is taking Chinese cooking lessons, so Ron bought her a wok.

Here, "so" conventionally implicates that the second clause explains the first.[51] Consequently, the following continuation is unacceptable:

Helen is taking Chinese cooking lessons, so Ron bought her a wok.
# But Ron did not buy Helen a wok because she is taking Chinese cooking lessons.

As Yan Huang remarks:

a conventional implicature is a non-truth-conditional inference that is not deductive in any general, natural way from the saying of what is said, but arises solely because of the conventional features attached to particular lexical items and/or linguistic constructions.[52]

In contrast to conventional implicatures, conversational implicatures are the "result of a hearer reasoning about the utterance relative to the utterance context or conversation."[53] For example, the following sentence,

Bernie has two children.

conversationally implicates that Bernie has exactly two children. Grice holds that because conversational implicature is not lexicalized, it is cancelable. For example, the following continuation is acceptable:

Bernie has two children. In fact he has four; two are from his former marriage.

---

[51] The example is adapted from Yan Huang, *Pragmatics*, Oxford University Press, 2007, 55.
[52] Huang (2007) 54.
[53] Rett (2015) 70–71.

Here, the cancellation signifier "in fact" that begins the second sentence indicates that the implicature of the first sentence, that Bernie has exactly two children, is being canceled.

Grice further distinguishes between generalized and particularized conversational implicatures. Generalized conversational implicatures do not require any particular contextual conditions, while particularized conversational implicatures do.[54] For instance, the following sentence,

Most of Joe's siblings live in the United States.

implicates that not all of Joe's siblings live in the United States. This is a generalized conversational implicature since any sentence of the form "most Fs are G" implicates that not all Fs are G. One might then wonder why this implicature is not conventional. One reason is that the implicature is cancelable:

Most of Joe's siblings live in the United States. In fact all of them do.

Contrast this with the following exchange:

A: Where is Joe?
B: The light is on in his office.

Here speaker B's statement implicates that Joe is in his office. But this implicature requires particular contextual conditions.

Grice holds that conventional and conversational implicature are categorically distinct in virtue of properties such as cancellability. In contrast, Rett maintains that "there is a continuum from conventionalized to particularized conversational implicature based on the varying extent to which an implicature is grammaticalized ('conventionalized') in a lexical entry or phrase."[55] This point is crucial to Rett's account since she argues that the sense of significance of degree is a conversational implicature, but a non-cancelable one.

More precisely, Rett explains the sense of significance of degree in a basic sentence consisting of a relative gradable adjective as a so-called quantity implicature, and the sense of significance of degree in equative constructions and degree demonstratives and questions consisting of a relative gradable adjective with antonymously marked gradable adjectives as a so-called manner implicature. The terms "quantity implicature" and "manner implicature" derive from Grice's pragmatic maxims of conversation, among which are maxims of

---

[54]   Huang (2007) 31.
[55]   Rett (2015) 71.

quantity and manner. I will limit my discussion here to Rett's account of the sense of significance degree in the basic sentence and so in terms of quantity implicature.

I return to my paradigm sentence (1): "Paolo is tall." Assume that the lexical meaning of the relative gradable adjective "tall" is associated with a degree of non-significant value, such that according to the lexical meanings of the constituents of the sentence, (1) means

Paolo has height to degree $d$.[56]

With respect to the degree variable $d$ here, Rett appeals to a default operation called "existential closure." According to the operation of existential closure, an existential quantifier can bind any unvalued and unbound variable in a clause. For example, assume "eat" is a transitive verb.[57] In other words, it requires a direct object as well as a subject to yield a propositional content. Consider then the sentence

Joe is eating.

Here, no direct object is explicit. Given existential closure, a variable corresponding to the semantic thing-eaten argument that "eat" requires can be bound by an existential quantifier, with the result that "Joe is eating" is interpreted as

Joe is eating something.

Formally:

$\exists x \, [E(x,j)]$.

In the case of "Paolo is tall," existential closure yields the meaning

Paolo has height to some degree.

Formally:

$\exists d \, [H(d,p)]$.

---

[56] This reading will be further explained in section 3.4.
[57] This assumption is debatable, but I am employing it for the sake of illustration.

Observe now that while this result is consistent with the composition of complex constructions derived from the basic form of a relative gradable adjective, such as comparatives and equatives, it is unsatisfactory for the basic sentence itself since every individual that has height will satisfy the description of being tall. With this in mind, consider Grice's first maxim of quantity:

Make your contribution as informative as required for the current purposes of the exchange.[58]

And consider Grice's remark on tautologies:

Extreme examples of a flouting of the first maxim of quantity are provided by utterances of patent tautologies like "Women are women" and "War is war." I would wish to maintain that at the level of what is said, in my favored sense, such remarks are totally uninformative and so, at that level, cannot but infringe the first maxim of Quantity in any conversational context. They are, of course, informative at the level of what is implicated, and the hearer's identification of their informative content at this level is dependent on his ability to explain the speaker's selection of this *particular* patent tautology.[59]

The tautologous meaning of sentences of the form "$x$ is $a$" would flout Grice's first quantity maxim. Consequently, Rett argues, such constructions undergo a further semantic adjustment. The further adjusted sense of "$x$ is $a$" is closer to

$x$ has the $a$-associated gradable property to a significant degree.

Granted this, as Rett observes, an individual $x$ may have a significant degree of the gradable property in one of two ways: by significant excess or significant deficit. The adjusted sense of "$x$ is $a$" is in fact intensified rather than diminished. Rett acknowledges that she cannot explain why the semantic adjustment operates through intensification rather than diminution; however, she cites evidence, originally adduced by Dwight Bolinger, that "degree constructions or other gradable forms systematically receive intensified readings where they are logically compatible with other interpretations."[60] For example, ambivalent degree expressions such as "so" and "how,"[61] that is, expressions that in principle

---

[58]   Grice, cited by Rett (2015) 69. Rett also cites Horn's Q Principle, on which cp. Lawrence Horn, "Toward a New Taxonomy for Pragmatic Inference: Q- and R-based Implicature," in *Meaning, Form, and Use in Context*, D. Shiffrin, ed., Georgetown University Press, 1984, 11–42, at 13.

[59]   Rett (2015) 119, citing Grice (1975, 52).

[60]   Rett (2015) 101.

[61]   The term "ambivalent" here is mine. Rett uses "neutral."

should be able to intensify or diminish, only receive intensifying interpretations; for example:

> She is so smart.
> How handsome he looks.[62]

Compare the interpretations of the indefinite article and the quantifier "some" in the following sentences:

> Now that's a catch.
> What a performance.
> That's some fish you've caught.
> She is some woman.

I will not attempt to explain the intensifications involved in the noun phrases. But the intensification of degree associated with gradable adjectives seems explicable in terms of the property of scalar orientation—rather than the mere gradable property—associated with the adjective. For example, if the semantic adjustment of "$x$ is tall" involved a diminution of degree, then "$x$ is tall" would mean what "$x$ is short" intuitively means; and vice versa. In other words, informally "tall" means "has height to some / to a significant degree," while "short" means "lacks height to some / to a significant degree."

In short, according to Rett's theory, following existential closure, in the basic sentence the degree associated with the relative gradable adjective is semantically intensified or strengthened through a quantity implicature, more precisely through what Rett describes as an "un-informativity-based" quantity implicature. Consequently, Rett achieves a similar result to the *pos* solution, without resorting to *pos*.[63]

---

[62] Other examples are given at Rett (2015) 102. Rett writes: "The relevant observation is that these examples all unambiguously involve intensification despite the fact that they are formed with modifiers that are in principle neutral" (102). Rett discusses additional evidence from Bolinger (1972) at Rett (2015) 102–104.

[63] Rett's interpretation should be also compared to Daniel Lassiter and Noah Goodman, "Context, Scale Structure, and Statistics in the Interpretation of Positive-Form Adjectives," *SALT* 23 (2013) 587–610. Like Rett, Lassiter and Goodman do not subscribe to *pos*. Consequently, they maintain that when a gradable construction contains no degree operator (as in the case of the basic sentence), the degree of the standard of comparison remains unsaturated and pragmatic inference must determine its value. (With respect to compositionality, they suggest that in other gradable constructions the meaning of the unmodified gradable adjective may be "type-shifted to allow composition to proceed.") Their pragmatic solution depends on game-theoretic and Bayesian theories of linguistic coordination. "Speaker and listener share the goal of coordinating utterance and interpretation so as to maximize the probability that the listener" will interpret the utterance correctly. Lassiter and Goodman define the "utility of [an utterance] for a reflective speaker to be proportional to [the] informativity [of the utterance] to the literal listener about the [true content], minus a non-negative

It must also be stressed here that while Grice's theory of implicature is a pragmatic theory, Rett maintains that the adjustment to the meaning of the degree associated with the relative gradable adjective in the basic sentence (and elsewhere)
is truth-conditional. In other words, recall that Grice holds that implicatures do
not affect a sentence's truth-conditions and so are not entailments of the sentence.
However, Rett suggests that this depends on the content *at issue* in the context of
utterance. For example, compare the following two exchanges, derived from Jan
van Kuppevelt's discussion of implicatures as topic-dependent inferences:

A: Who bought four books?
B: Harry bought four books. In fact he bought five.

A: How many books did Harry buy?
B: He bought four books. # In fact he bought five.

In the first exchange, the identity of the buyer is at issue. In the second, it is the
number of books that he bought. Where the number is at issue, the implicature—
that Harry bought exactly four books—is not cancelable. Consequently, as van
Kuppevelt suggests and Rett maintains, in this context "He bought exactly four
books" appears to be an entailment of "He bought four books."[64]

Likewise, Rett maintains, the quantity implicature that occurs with the basic
sentence is an entailment and so is constitutive of truth-conditional content. For
example, it can be embedded under truth-conditional operators such as negation and conditionals:

Paolo is not tall.
If Paolo is tall and Ronan is taller than Paolo, then Ronan is tall.[65]

cost." And they "quantify informativity . . . as surprisal." For example, consider a case such as "Paolo
is tall," where both speaker and listener understand that Paolo is an adult male and share background
knowledge about heights for adult males. If the value of the standard degree were extremely small,
for example, one inch, then, since the utterance would be highly uninformative, the probability that
the speaker would intend to convey such a proposition would be extremely low. "The informativity
of [the sentence, therefore,] increases [as the value of the standard increases]." On the other hand,
informativity does not lead to extremely high values for the standard, since the "low prior probability
of the [sentence's] truth under [very high] values" counterbalances such interpretations. The result
is that the preferred interpretations "make [Paolo] fairly tall, but not implausibly so." In short, "background knowledge . . . interacts with lexical meaning and the pragmatic preference for informativity
to yield a context-sensitive probabilistic meaning." The concept of informativity, understood in terms
of surprisal, is evidently akin to the concept of significance that is central to Rett's account. Moreover,
the pragmatically saturated value of the standard is equivalent to the significant degree.

[64] Rett (2015) 89, citing Jan van Kuppevelt, "Inferring from Topics: Implicatures as Topic-
Dependent Inferences," in *Linguistics and Philosophy* 19 (1996) 393–443, at 412. Cp. Mandy Simons
et al., "What Projects and Why," *SALT* 20 (2011) 309–27.
[65] Rett (2015) 90.

Compare Rett's statement:

> I'm happy to admit, for instance, that [such] implicature differs from other sorts
> in that it occurs in embedded contexts, so must be calculated sub-sententially,
> and, then, is arguably not pragmatic.[66]

## 3.4. The Meaning of Relative Gradable Adjectives

So what is the meaning of a gradable adjective? More precisely, what is the meaning of the basic form of the unmarked member of a relative gradable adjective such as "tall" or "good"? Although in one respect it is uninformative to say so, the answer depends on the way one analyzes these adjectives.

In the mainstream tradition of formal semantics, which descends from Frege, the denotations of predicate expressions, including adjectives, are identified with functions of one kind or another. For example, within an extensionalist framework, the denotation of a non-gradable adjective is identified with a semantic function from individuals to truth-values. And within an intensionalist framework, the denotation of a non-gradable adjective is identified with a semantic function from possible worlds to a function from individuals to truth-values. For convenience, I will here restrict the discussion to an extensionalist framework.

---

[66] Rett (p.c.). I note here a problem for both Rett's theory and the *pos* theory. This problem concerns the interpretation of absolute gradable adjectives. Consider first the *pos* theory, according to which *pos* relates one degree *d* to a standard of comparison *d'* based on a contextually determined comparison class. In an instance of the basic sentence that incorporates an absolute gradable adjective, for example "*x* is full," the absolute gradable adjectival predicate expression cannot covertly consist of *pos*. That is, the basic sentence cannot actually be: "*x* is *pos* full." So, absolute gradable adjectives in the basic sentence require a distinct account. But complex constructions, that is, predicate expressions consisting of the absolute gradable adjective as a proper part, also require a distinct account. For example, consider the comparative sentence "Paolo's cup is fuller / more full than Isabella's cup." If we could apply a non-significance interpretation to the degree associated with an absolute gradable adjective, the meaning of this sentence would be that the degree to which Paolo's cup is full, *d*, is greater than the degree to which Isabella's cup is full, *d'*. However, my account of non-significance of degree applied to relative, not absolute, gradable adjectives. Alternatively, we might propose to extend the non-significance account to include all gradable adjectives. But then we would have to find an alternative to *pos* to explain the reading of absolute gradable adjectives in the basic sentence. In short, if the lexical meanings of absolute gradable adjectives are associated with non-significant degrees, then how do they denote maximal degrees in the basic sentence? For a response to this problem by an advocate of *pos*, cp. Kennedy (2007) 36. Turning to Rett's implicature theory—this theory proposes to explain the semantics of relative gradable adjectives, and does not focus on the semantics of absolute gradable adjectives. As such, the implicature theory is incomplete. This is a limitation of Rett's account. But consider her remarks at Rett (2015) 130–46.

A standard way of representing such denotations employs a simple and, to my mind, highly intuitive notation, which derives from Richard Montague.[67] The notation depends on a small number of primitive so-called semantic types. In the most austere typology, the primitive semantic types are limited to two: individuals, which are typically represented by the symbol $e$; and truth-values, which are represented by the symbol $t$. Functions are represented by placing primitive symbols within angle brackets $\langle\rangle$, and, typically, using a comma to distinguish the argument from the value of the function. For example, a function from individuals to truth-values is represented as

$$\langle e, t \rangle.$$

Compare a truth-functional operator such as conjunction, whose denotation is a function from truth-values to truth-values, and which therefore is represented as

$$\langle t, t \rangle.$$

Recall now that at the beginning of the chapter I distinguished two principal analyses of gradable adjectives: inherent vagueness and degree-based. According to the inherent vagueness analysis, the denotation of a relative gradable adjective is, like that of a non-gradable adjective, identified with a semantic function from individuals to truth-values, in other words, with a unary or monadic semantic function.[68]

---

[67] Cp. Irene Heim and Angelika Kratzer, *Semantics in Generative Grammar*, Blackwell, 1998, 26–29.

[68] According to this theory, what distinguishes gradable adjectives from non-gradable adjectives is that the individuals in the domains of gradable adjectives are, as a primitive metaphysical fact, ordered relative to the gradable properties associated with these adjectives; whereas in the case of non-gradable adjectives there is no such ordering. (Contrast degree-based theories, according to which the meaning of the adjective itself determines the ordering.) Assume that the ordering is linear and from lesser to greater degree of the gradable property possessed. Then those individuals in the upper range of, say, height will satisfy the description "tall," while those in the lower range will satisfy the description "short." In addition, a mid-range, sometimes called an "extension gap," may satisfy the description "neither tall nor short." In that case, when applied to individuals in their domains, gradable adjectives, more precisely, denote partial functions, returning no truth-value as well as true and false. In normal tokenings of a gradable adjective, the speaker does not intend that a given individual is, say, tall relative to the entire domain. If that were the intention, then, for instance, no human being could ever be tall. Instead, tokenings of the gradable adjective normally occur relative to a subset of the domain, namely the comparison class. For example, one may say of a man that he is tall, intending the claim relative to his colleagues. Recall that Klein first referred to this subset as the "comparison class" (1980, 13). In his exposition of the inherent vagueness theory, Klein added the stipulation that the primitive ordering of individuals relative to a gradable property is preserved in the comparison class. Consequently, in a given context, the individuals that fall within the upper range of the subset determined by the comparison class will satisfy the description of the gradable adjective, say "tall." This also explains why the same individual, intrinsically unchanged, can truly be said to be tall in one context and not tall in another. Cp. Christopher Kennedy, "Gradable Adjectives Denote Measure Functions, Not Partial Functions," *Studies in Linguistic Sciences* 29 (1999) 65–80.

According to degree-based analyses, the denotations of relative gradable adjectives differ from the denotations of non-gradable adjectives in that the former are associated with degrees. Degree-based semantic frameworks distinguish degrees from individuals and include degrees as an additional primitive semantic type within their typology. The semantic type of degrees is typically symbolized as $d$.[69]

Different degree-based analyses interpret the association of gradable adjectives with degrees in different ways. According to the so-called measure function analysis, of which Kennedy is a representative, a relative gradable adjective is analyzed as a function from individuals to degrees: $\langle e,d \rangle$. Observe that on this view, if the basic predicate expression merely consisted of a relative gradable adjective, then the basic sentence would not have propositional content.[70] For example, the denotation of "Paolo is tall" would simply be the degree of Paolo's height.[71] Granted this, advocates of the measure function analysis typically here appeal to *pos*. In doing so, they typically interpret *pos* as a function from a measure function to a function from individuals to truth-values.[72] In other words, *pos* takes as its argument a relative gradable adjective (analyzed as a measure function) and returns as its value a unary function.[73]

According to the relational analysis, of which Rett is a representative, relative gradable adjectives are analyzed as functions that take two arguments, in other words as binary functions. One of these arguments is a degree; the other is an individual. More precisely, according to the canonical formulation of the relational analysis, a relative gradable adjective is analyzed as a function from degrees to a function from individuals to truth-values: $\langle d,\langle e,t \rangle \rangle$. Observe that as such the canonical relational analysis of gradable adjectives is similar to that of transitive verbs. The latter also take two arguments, but in this case two individual arguments: $\langle e,\langle e,t \rangle \rangle$.

Granted the similarity between the semantic types of transitive verbs and gradable adjectives according to the relational analysis, it is also noteworthy that gradable adjectives and transitive verbs are syntactically disanalogous in the

---

[69] Note that, unfortunately and confusingly in the literature, the symbol $d$ is also used to stand for a degree variable in syntactic representations.

[70] Indeed, if a predicate expression is a function from individuals to truth-values, then the basic predicate expression would not actually be a predicate expression. It is, as Kennedy calls it, a measure function.

[71] The predicate expression, which ex hypothesi consists solely of the relative gradable adjective "tall," and so of an expression of semantic type $\langle e,d \rangle$, maps the individual denoted by "Paolo" to a degree.

[72] In type theoretic notation, *pos* is then of semantic type $\langle e,d,\langle e,t \rangle \rangle$, more simply $\langle ed,et \rangle$.

[73] For convenience, I here ignore the contribution that a contextually determined comparison class makes to the value of the standard of comparison.

following respect. Consider the following sentence employing the transitive verb "kiss":

Inga kisses Jett.

The direct object of "kiss" here is the so-called internal argument of the verb, whereas the subject of the verb is its so-called external argument.[74] In the semantic type theoretic notation, the first $e$ in the formula $\langle e, \langle e, t \rangle \rangle$ corresponds to the internal argument of "kiss"; and, syntactically, this is the direct object of "kiss." In the case of a gradable adjective, again on the relational analysis, the semantic degree argument also corresponds syntactically to the internal argument of the adjective. However, in contrast to the syntactic structure of a transitive verb phrase, the syntactic position of the degree precedes rather than follows the adjective. Accordingly, strictly, the syntactic form of the basic sentence should be represented as

$x$ is $d$ $a$.

For example:

Paolo is $d$ tall.

Now, in chapter 2 and up to the present point in this chapter, I have used the vague term "associate with" to describe the relation between gradable adjectives, gradable properties, degrees, and scales. The reason for the vague expression can now be explained as due to my desire to remain neutral with respect to the two different degree-based analyses: measure function and relational. According to the relational analysis, degrees are the internal arguments of the adjective; whereas according to the measure function analysis, degrees are values of the unary measure function. In short, the nature of the association between degrees and gradable adjectives differs according to these distinct analyses of gradable adjectives.

Since a degree is a constituent of a scale, the nature of the association between gradable adjectives and scales follows the nature of the association between gradable adjectives and degrees. In the case of the measure function analysis, scales are values of the adjective. In the case of the relational analysis, scales are

---

[74] By "internal" is meant that the argument is a constituent of the so-called maximal projection of, in this case, the verb. In contrast, the other individual argument of the verb phrase is external to the maximal projection of the verb. On the internal-external argument distinction, cp. Edwin Williams, "Predication," *Linguistic Inquiry* 11 (1980) 203–38.

arguments of the adjective. On both analyses, however, properties of the scale associated with the adjective are constrained by that adjective. For example, in the case of the unmarked member of a relative gradable adjective such as "good," on both analyses the associated scale must be a scale of value, and more precisely an open scale with a particular scalar orientation, where this particular orientation corresponds to the idea of having in contrast to lacking or being deficient in value.

Having clarified the association relation between gradable adjectives, degrees, and scales in this respect, I turn to remark on the sorts of semantic and metaphysical entailments in terms of which in chapter 2 I characterized the association relation between gradable adjectives and gradable properties. Where $a$ stands for a relative gradable adjective, a sentence of the form "$x$ is $a$" semantically entails a sentence of the form "$x$ has a significant degree of the $a$-associated gradable property." Moreover, insofar as entities that have gradable properties have various degrees, that is, quantities, of the gradable properties, that $x$ is $a$ metaphysically entails that $x$ has a significant degree of the $a$-associated gradable property.

Finally, I note two important points regarding the metaphysical claim. First, having a significant degree of a gradable property is itself a relational property since it consists of having a degree of a gradable property that meets or exceeds a standard of comparison. Second, there is an ambiguity in the claim that $x$ has a degree of a gradable property. On the one hand, any entity that has a gradable property has a certain degree, in the sense of a certain amount or quantity, of that gradable property. On the other hand, the degrees that are constituents of scales and so the scales themselves are abstract representations of measurement. For convenience, I'll call the former sort of degree a "metaphysical" degree and the latter a "semantic" degree.

Let me also clarify that in claiming that the degrees that are constituents of scales and so the scales themselves are abstract representations of measurement, by "abstract representations of measurement" I here understand the following. I assume that semantic degrees and scales are ultimately, albeit not necessarily occurrently, derived from psychological acts of comparative judgment. Consequently, these degrees and scales derive from mental representations. However, since gradable adjectives—like all other established terms—have established meanings, the semantic degrees and scales associated with gradable adjectival expressions are encoded as constituents of the meanings of these expressions and therefore are abstracted from occurrent psychological comparisons. For example, the truth of a sentence such as "Paolo is tall" entails that on a scale of tallness Paolo's degree exceeds the degree that is the contextually determined standard of comparison—regardless of any speaker's or author's having any occurrent mental state involving comparison of Paolo's height and the height of others.

Granted this, in understanding a claim such as that $x$ has a significant degree of a gradable property, it is necessary to distinguish the metaphysical degree of a gradable property from the semantic degree that is a constituent of a scale and that is therefore an abstract entity. That an individual has a significant degree of a gradable property metaphysically entails that that individual has a certain metaphysical degree of the gradable property. But, without further justification, it does not entail that that individual has a certain semantic degree on a scale—whatever it might mean for a vertically extended individual such as Paolo to *have* an abstract object such as a semantic degree on a scale.

In short, I am drawing attention to an ambiguity in the term "degree" here. And I underscore the need to clarify the metaphysical implications, if any, that follow from an individual, such as Paolo, being associated with a semantic degree. I will return to this point in section 4.2 of chapter 6, where I discuss the metaphysical implications of the semantic results of the study.

## 4.  Significance

The preceding results leave many crucial questions unanswered. One question is what significance of degree consists in. Recall and compare here Kennedy's expression: the degree to which $x$ has the $a$-associated gradable property must "stand out" in the context of utterance. I underscore that while things may stand out or be significant in any number of ways, in the present context the concern is with something's standing out or being significant with respect to the quantity of the degree of the gradable property associated with that thing.

In the discussion of *pos*, I suggested—merely for convenience—that the standard of comparison might be computed through an average function. For example, on this view "Paolo is tall for his class" means that the degree of Paolo's height exceeds the average height of Paolo's classmates. Regardless of *pos*, on this view, significance of degree is equivalent to the degree exceeding an average. But this is untenable. If Paolo's height exceeded the average of his classmates' heights, but only by a tiny amount, it would be false to say: "Paolo is tall for his class."

The phrases "standing out" and "being significant" may encourage the idea that the property of significance of degree should be explained in phenomenal terms, that is, as a mere appearance property. Alternatively, significance of degree might be interpreted in terms of personal interests.[75] A third view, suggested by Kennedy, is that significance of degree is explicable according to a "purely distributional criterion."[76] By this, I take Kennedy to mean that there is an objective fact of the matter as to whether $x$ is $a$, and that this fact is based on the mind-independent values of the metaphysical degrees of the subject and the members of the comparison class as well as their statistical distribution. Consequently, it might appear to one that $x$ is $a$, but that appearance could be misleading. Likewise, whether $x$ is $a$ would not, at least in this respect, owe to the speaker's personal interests.

In support of this third possibility, consider the following example. Assume that in the region where you have always lived the apples tend to be small. If you travel elsewhere and for the first time encounter an apple that, while being of average size, is significantly larger than the apples in your region, you might remark: "This apple is large." In this case, the apple is large compared to your regional apples. But according to the explicit terms of the example, the apple is not in fact large, but of average size. The apple is, then, large to you or for you. But the "to" or "for" prepositional phrases here precisely serve to restrict the comparison class to those that you have encountered. Furthermore, although in the present case "This apple is large to / for you"—in contrast to "This apple is large"—may be true, in general even when the comparison class is restricted to entities that the assessor has experienced, the assessor's judgments of significance may be mistaken.

Granted this, what sort of distribution might significance of degree consist in? The topic has received surprisingly little attention. Among the few treatments it has received, the following statistical proposal by Stephanie Solt seems to me a suggestive, if underdeveloped, line of inquiry.[77] Assume that one is concerned with the unmarked member of the antonym pair $a$, and that $a$, qua unmarked, is associated with measurement of increasing amounts of the relevant gradable property, for example height. Individuals assessable for possession of the gradable property in question, say height, may be neither $a$ nor the antonym of $a$, for example, neither tall nor short. Accordingly, in a given context there is a range of neutral degrees, again degrees whose possession implies that $x$ is neither $a$ nor the antonym of $a$. Let $s+$ symbolize significant excess of the gradable property. So to determine $s+$, one must determine the upper bound of the range. The range depends on the dispersion of values of the members of the comparison class. Solt

---

[75] Cp. Andrzej Boguslawski, "Measures Are Measures: In Defense of the Diversity of Comparatives and Positives," *Linguistische Berichte* 36 (1975) 1–9; Delia Graff, "Shifting Sands: An Interest-Relative Theory of Vagueness," *Philosophical Topics* 20 (2000) 45–81.

[76] Kennedy (2007) 17.

[77] Solt (2011). Cp. Lassiter and Goodman (2013), discussed in footnote 63.

formalizes these ideas using a median and the statistical concept of a median absolute derivation, $MAD$.[78]

Observe that in a symmetric distribution, the central 50% of cases fall within one $MAD$ of the median.[79] Accordingly, an individual that is *a* will belong to the upper quartile relative to the comparison class (while an individual that is the antonym of *a* will belong to the lower quartile). The value of the range can therefore be given as

$$R = MED\big(m(x)\big) \pm n \times MAD\big(m(x)\big).$$

Here $R$ stands for the range relative to a given comparison class; $MED$ stands for a median function; $m$ stands for a function that returns the degree of the scale based on the gradable property at issue for each individual $x$ that is a member of the comparison class. Since I am proposing to determine 1 $MAD$ of the median, assume $n = 1$.[80] Accordingly, this formula states that the range $R$ relative to a given comparison class equals the median value of the gradable property based on the individuals $x$ in the comparison class plus or minus 1 times the median absolute derivation of the gradable property based on the individuals in the comparison class. Let $R_+$ stand for the upper bound of $R$. Then on this view, $s+ > R_+$.

As Solt notes, however, an empirical study on "tall" in fact suggests that this unmarked relative gradable adjective is used to denote approximately the upper third, rather than quartile, of individuals in a given domain.[81] Assuming that this fact is representative of unmarked relative gradable adjectives generally, the value of $n$ must be lowered. Regardless, the gist of Solt's hypothesis, which again is consistent with Kennedy's suggestion that significance is purely distributional, is that significance of degree is a statistical property and in particular based on the property of deviation from a norm.[82]

---

[78]  Solt (2011) 193–95.

[79]  Solt (2011) 194.

[80]  Since $1 \times MAD(m(x)) = MAD(m(x))$, the inclusion of $n$ is unnecessary if its value = 1. However it is included here precisely because the value of $n$ as 1 is questioned subsequently.

[81]  Solt (2011) 194, citing David Barner and Jesse Snedecker, "Compositionality and Statistics in Adjective Acquisition: 4-Year-Olds Interpret *Tall* and *Short* Based on the Size Distributions of Novel Noun Referents," *Child Development* 79 (2008) 594–608.

[82]  A referee for the press expressed skepticism that a formula as mathematically complex as the one that Solt proposes could explain the meaning of "ordinary uses" of relative gradable adjectives in the basic sentence. But observe that in explaining what significance of degree consists in, an attempt is being made here to clarify significance in semantically *externalist* terms. This is why, for example, Barner and Snedecker's empirical results are relevant to the proposal. A helpful analogy might be between hearing distinct musical intervals and knowing the mathematical ratios in terms of which they are related.

Clearly, more empirical work needs to be done on a wider range of gradable adjectives in order to corroborate the core idea as well as to specify the value of $R$ and the statistical operations on which it is based. Moreover, in considering the relevance of such work for the semantics of an adjective such as "good," it must be borne in mind that "good" does not license measure phrases. More fundamentally, as noted above, in contrast, for example, to height, there is no single standard of measurement for value and in most cases no standard of measurement at all.

Finally, recall the problem that the adjective "significant" is itself gradable. Consequently, the claim that the basic sentence means "$x$ has a significant degree of the $a$-associated gradable property $G$" or simply "$x$ has significant $G$" yields a regress. In light of Solt's account of significance, I can skirt the regress problem by simply acknowledging that the terms "significant" and "significance" are here employed for convenience and as heuristics. What it means for a subject $x$ to have a significant degree of the $a$-associated gradable property is for $x$ to have a degree of the gradable property that exceeds $R_+$ (or some such value). Throughout this study, I will continue to use the terms "significant" and "significance," but again for convenience and heuristically.

## 5. A Historical Coda

As a coda to the foregoing discussion of the semantics of gradable adjectives, I offer the following historical reflection on the importance of the thesis that "good" is a gradable adjective.

Throughout the history of Western philosophy, philosophers who have focused on what is good have expressed the concept corresponding to "good" in terms of their written and spoken languages; for example, *agathon, bonum, bon,* and *gut*—all of which are relative gradable adjectives. For example, Plato maintains that the Form of the Good is the supreme Form.[83] But surely the Form of Excellence would be better than the Form of the Good. In fact, in *Gorgias* Plato has the character Socrates explicitly claim that everything that is good is so in virtue of some excellence (*aretē*) that it possesses.[84] But that cannot be true; $x$ may be good simply in virtue of possessing goodness or something good.

---

[83]  *Republic* 504e and following.
[84]  *Gorgias* 506d.

Aristotle begins the *Nicomachean Ethics* with the psychological claim that everything strives for what is good.[85] Setting aside the psychological possibility of desiring what is bad qua bad, some things surely sometimes desire what is best.[86] The Stoics maintain that the only thing that is good is excellence and what depends on excellence.[87] Even if that were true, excellence and what depends on it would be best, not just good.

Spinoza maintains that a thing is objectively good insofar as it is powerful.[88] Assuming so and assuming the existence of a supremely powerful God, such power would be objectively excellent, not merely good. Rousseau claims that in its savage state, humanity was naturally good. But he also maintains that the savage state is a state of human perfection.[89] So he should hold that the savage state is best, not merely good.

Kant claims that the only thing that is unconditionally good is a good will.[90] But for humans at least, such a will is optimal and not merely good. One might attempt to justify Kant's attribution of mere goodness to the optimal human will in view of the contrast that he draws between the conditions of the human will and the divine will. Only the divine and more generally holy will are free from necessitation. Such freedom implies perfection of the will. Insofar as it is necessitated to act in conformity with the law, the human will, even in its optimal condition, would then be merely good. Yet this defense of Kant falters in the face of Kant's own terminology. In drawing the preceding distinction, Kant expressly characterizes the divine and holy will as "perfectly / completely good" (*vollkommen guter*).[91]

In the *Philosophy of Right*, Hegel claims that the ethical life "is the Idea of freedom as the living good which has its knowledge and reason in self-consciousness, and its actuality through self-conscious action."[92] But once again, the condition here described is by Hegel's own lights optimal, not merely good. Indeed, in an earlier passage of the work, Hegel writes: "The good is realized freedom, the absolute and ultimate purpose of the world."[93]

All of these philosophers appear to have conflated words such as *agathon, bonum, bon, gut,* and "good" with other terms. Some seem to have conflated "good" and "excellent." Spinoza in particular probably conflated "good" with

---

[85]   *Nicomachean Ethics* 1094a.
[86]   Or, more egregiously, cp. *Magna Moralia* 1182b: "By 'good' (*agathon*) we may signify either what is best (*ariston*) in each class of things or . . ."
[87]   Stobaeus 2.57.19 (= *SVF* 3.70).
[88]   Cp. *Ethics*, Part 1, Appendix.
[89]   Cp. *Beaumont* 935–36; *Dialogues* III: 934; *Second Discourse* 151; *Emile* II: 92.
[90]   *Groundwork* 393.
[91]   *Groundwork* 414.
[92]   §142.
[93]   §129.

"perfect." Kant probably conflated "good" with "right." But "right" is not a gradable adjective. Nor is "perfect."[94] "Excellent" is a so-called extreme adjective. It is associated with a very high degree on a scale.[95] Compare "huge" and "tiny" with "large" and "small."

Finally, Moore defines ethics as "the general inquiry into what is good."[96] But evidently ethics and value theory in general have been and should continue to be concerned with optimal as well as merely significant value.

---

[94] It has been claimed that "perfect" is an absolute gradable adjective. But observe that, in contrast to "full," "perfect" does not admit degree expressions such as "very" or "more." (The phrase "a more perfect union" seems to be an exception.)

[95] Cp. Morzycki (2016) 140–44.

[96] *Principia Ethica* §2.

# 4

# Value

## 1. The Value Thesis

Gradable adjectives are associated with gradable properties. "Tall" is associated with the gradable property of height, and evaluative "good" is associated with the gradable property of value. Gradable properties such as height are distinguishable from gradable properties such as value in that the former are not specifiable by kind, whereas the latter are. There are not kinds of height, but there are kinds of value. Compare non-evaluative quantity, the gradable property associated with quantitative "good," which is also specifiable by kind.

In formal semantic theories of gradable adjectives, the word "dimension" is often used to refer to the gradable property associated with a gradable adjective.[1] Accordingly, we may say that height is the gradable property or equivalently the dimension associated with "tall" and that value and non-evaluative quantity are the dimensions associated with evaluative "good" and quantitative "good" respectively.

Because there are different kinds or species of value, we may say that evaluative "good" is a multidimensional gradable adjective. Likewise, quantitative "good" is a multidimensional gradable adjective.[2] In contrast, since there are not different kinds or species of height, "tall" is a unidimensional gradable adjective. Hereafter, I will use the expression "dimension-type" to refer to a gradable property that is specifiable by kind. So, more precisely, while "tall" is associated with the dimension of height, evaluative "good" and quantitative "good" are associated with the dimension-types of value and of non-evaluative quantity respectively.

---

[1] Kennedy (1999) employs the term "dimension" and refers its introduction to Bierwisch (1987). But the term is used as early as Siegel (1980), first at 223. Cp. also Lars Hellan, *Towards an Integrated Analysis of Comparatives*, Narr, 1981, who speaks of "quality dimensions."

[2] This is not the only way that the term "multidimensional" is used in the secondary literature. For example, Galit W. Sassoon, "A Typology of Multidimensional Adjectives," *Journal of Semantics* 30 (2013) 335–80, uses the term to characterize gradable adjectives that are associated with multiple dimensions simultaneously. For example, she maintains that "healthy" is multidimensional since the claim that $x$ is healthy means that $x$ is healthy in all respects, where a respect corresponds to a dimension of health.

Chapter 5 will examine how specification of the dimension-type associated with a multidimensional gradable adjective such as evaluative "good" occurs in a context of use. For example, how is it that in the basic sentence "$x$ is good," the basic predicate expression can in one context denote aesthetic value and in another ethical value? The focus of the present chapter is on the dimension-type associated with evaluative "good." Since I will be focusing on evaluative "good," I will hereafter drop the modifier "evaluative," except when needed for disambiguation.

Consider the following claim:

THE VALUE THESIS

Value is the dimension-type associated with "good."

I submit that the value thesis is straightforwardly defensible as follows. Consider the following argument:

$x$ is good.
_____
$x$ has value.

The premise semantically entails the conclusion. Indeed, the entailment is transparent.

Conversely, the following argument is transparently contradictory:

$x$ is good.
_____
$x$ has no value.

Furthermore, value is a gradable property. Something can have more or less value. And the more value $x$ has, the better $x$ is. Finally, value is specifiable by kind. From these considerations, it follows that "good" is associated with the dimension-type of value. So the value thesis is true.

I believe that the value thesis needs no further defense. On the other hand, the value thesis is explanatorily inadequate in several respects. The aim of this chapter is to provide a more adequate explanation of the value thesis. I will pursue this task by considering two points. The first and main point pertains to the fact that the nature of value is obscure. In the context of an inquiry into the nature of goodness, it is inadequate to leave unexplained the claim that "good" is associated with the dimension-type of value.

The second point relates to the term "quality." The term "quality" occurred in passing in chapter 2. In the context of discussing operational "good," I said that the sentence "The wine is good" admits the following two readings:

The wine is potable (it hasn't turned).     [OPERATIONAL]

The wine is of high quality.     [EVALUATIVE]

Mention of "quality" in the context of analyses of evaluative "good" also occurs in the secondary literature. For example, Seppänen, who recognizes a distinction akin to my distinction between evaluative and quantitative "good," claims that "good" is "applicable in the [assessment] of *quality* as well as *quantity*."[3] And Louise McNally and Kennedy, in a discussion of the ambiguity of "well," the adverb semantically akin to the adjective "good," describe what I would call "evaluative 'well'" as "a *quality* reading" of this adverb.[4] For example, the following sentence,

The wagon is well loaded.

admits the following two readings:

The quantity loaded onto the wagon is large.

The quality of the loading of the wagon is high.

In light of this, the relation between value and quality needs clarification. Is quality also a dimension-type? If so, is "good" also associated with the dimension-type of quality? If so, how could "good" be associated with two dimension-types? One possibility is that value and quality are identical. Another possibility is that quality is a type of value. Whatever the case, failure to clarify the relations between evaluative "good," quality, and value would be an explanatory defect of the present account.

The chapter is structured in two parts according to these two points pertaining to the explanatory adequacy of the value thesis. The first part, sections 2.1 through 2.5, clarifies the nature of value. Section 2.1 argues that value is purpose serving. Consequently, insofar as something has value, it serves or is serving a purpose. Granted this, there are at least four basic kinds of purposes and so at least four basic kinds of value: biological, characteristic artificial, ad hoc intentional, and ad hoc desiderative. This fact might suggest that "purpose," "value," and so "good"—that is, evaluative "good"—are correlatively at least four ways ambiguous. I resist this conclusion and maintain that "value" and "good" are univocal, at least in this regard.

---

[3] Seppänen (1984) 535 (with my italics).

[4] For example, at McNally and Kennedy (2013) 247.

Section 2.2 may be viewed as constituting a brief interlude, in which I revisit the claim made in section 5 of chapter 2 that evaluative and operational "good" are irregular polysemes, whereas quantitative "good" stands in a relation of homonymy to the former two. Justification of these claims was deferred. Here, I justify the claims in light of the results of section 2.1.

Section 2.3 returns to the main topic. Here, I examine a pertinent type of adjunctive prepositional "for" phrase that "good" admits;[5] for example:

> This knife is good *for slicing vegetables*.
> That vehicle is good *for driving on mountain roads*.

I call such phrases "purposive 'for'" phrases. Compare them with the following adjunctive "for" phrases that "good" also admits:

> That soil is good *for succulents*.
> The extra discussion sections were good *for the second-year students*.

I call such phrases "beneficiary 'for'" phrases. The interpretation of purposive "for" phrases is both informed by and corroborates the claim that value is purpose serving. In addition, I argue that although purposive and beneficiary "for" phrases are ostensibly syntactically and semantically distinct, in fact the latter are a variant of the former. A beneficiary "for" phrase of the form "$x$ is good for $b$" entails "$x$ makes or $x$ is disposed to make a significant contribution to the realization of the purpose that $b$ serves."

Section 2.4 considers the interpretation of the basic sentence "$x$ is good" in light of the thesis that value is purpose serving. I argue that while $x$'s being good requires that $x$ serve a purpose to a significant degree, "$x$ is good" does not mean "$x$ serves a purpose to a significant degree." The adjectival and verbal predicate expressions are distinct in at least the following two respects. First, the verbal predicate expression admits aspectual distinctions that the adjectival predicate expression does not. Second, the nominal complement of the verbal predicate expression contains an indefinite article, which engenders a scopal ambiguity. The adjectival predicate expression contains no indefinite article and does not exhibit the scopal ambiguity of the verbal predicate expression. Following the discussion of these problems, I consider adjectival glosses of the basic sentence. Given the thesis that value is purpose serving, I focus on the adjectives "purposive" and "useful." After explaining how the

---

[5] On the syntactic term "adjunct," see footnote 20 of chapter 3.

meanings of these terms differ from "good," I conclude that no adjective is synonymous with "good."

Although "purpose" and so "value" and so "good" are not four ways polysemous, section 2.5 notes that, for a different reason, "value" is in fact two ways polysemous. One sense of "value," which I call "generic 'value,'" comprises so-called positive, neutral, and negative value. Another sense, which I call "specific 'value,'" denotes only positive value. This polysemy is clearly consequential for the value thesis, but, less obviously, also for understanding the scales associated with the members of the antonym pair "good"/"bad." In particular, there is reason to think that, consequently, the scales associated with the comparatives "better" and "worse" must differ from the scales associated with the comparatives of ordinary relative gradable adjectives. Whereas the latter are based on a single dimension or dimension-type, the former are bidimensional, that is, based on the concatenation of two dimensions or dimension-types.

The second part of the chapter, section 3, is devoted to explaining the relation between "good," value, and quality. In order to clarify these relations, I begin by clarifying the meaning of "quality." I argue that "quality" is variously polysemous. But in particular, I distinguish two meanings of "quality" relevant to the question at issue. One of these, I call "evaluative 'quality'"; the other, "non-evaluative 'quality.'" For instance, contrast the following two sentences:

> This knife is of good quality.    [EVALUATIVE]
> The sound of the snare drum has a tinny quality.    [NON-EVALUATIVE]

Evaluative and non-evaluative "quality" are syntactically as well as semantically distinct. The former is a mass noun, the latter a count noun.

The question concerning the relation between value and quality is directly concerned with "quality" in the evaluative sense and so with the mass noun. But evaluative quality partly consists of non-evaluative qualities. Precisely, I argue that the evaluative quality of an entity $x$ is the contribution that the aggregate of a certain subset of non-evaluative qualities of $x$ makes to $x$'s characteristic purpose. Consequently, evaluative quality is neither identical to nor a type of value.

## 2.1. Value and Purpose Serving

The question "What is value?" like the question "What is goodness?" is very general and obscure. Accordingly, like the question "What is goodness?" I regard the question "What is value?" as a metaphysical one. Like the question "What is goodness?" I suggest that linguistic considerations can be recruited to advance an answer.[6]

The value thesis states that value is the dimension-type associated with "good." In other words, the basic sentence "*x* is good" makes a claim about the measure of the value of *x*. Consequently, in principle the value thesis can be used to probe the nature of value by examining the meaning of "good." An observation inspired by a discussion in Paul Ziff's *Semantic Analysis* suggests a way of doing this.

The final chapter of Ziff's book presents an interpretation of the meaning of "good."[7] Ziff proposes that " 'good' means 'answering to certain interests.' " Ziff is largely unaware of the fundamental ambiguities of "good."[8] But his de facto focus is on evaluative "good." So his de facto proposal is that evaluative "good" means "answering to certain interests."

Ziff evinces some awareness that his claim concerning the meaning of "good" relates to an earlier tradition,[9] one that arguably culminates with Ralph Barton Perry's 1926 *General Theory of Value: Its Meaning and Basic Principles Construed in Terms of Interest.*[10] Perry begins chapter 5 of his work with the suggestion that "it is characteristic of the living mind to be *for* some things and *against* others." He claims that "to be 'for' or 'against' is to view with favor or disfavor," and that this duality of favoring and disfavoring "appears in many forms, such as liking and disliking, desire and aversion, will and refusal, or seeking and avoiding." Somewhat stipulatively, Perry then defines an interest as a "state, act, attitude or disposition of favor or disfavor." And he claims that interest is the "original source and constant feature of all value. That which is an object of interest is *eo ipso* invested with value."[11]

Compare Perry's view with that of Charles Leslie Stevenson, who in his 1937 paper "The Emotive Meaning of Ethical Terms"[12] distinguishes his own emotive theory of "good"—according to which "good" expresses a positive pleasing emotion—from what he calls traditional, descriptive "interest theories":

> The word "good" has often been defined in terms of *approval* or similar psychological attitudes. We may take as typical examples: "good" means *desired by me* (Hobbes); and "good" means *approved by most people* (Hume, in effect). It will

---

[6] In making this claim, I do not mean to suggest that linguistic considerations alone can wholly resolve the question.

[7] Ziff (1960) 200–247.

[8] Ziff does not recognize operational "good." At the end of his analysis, he notes that the following two sentences do not fit his account: "It is a good two miles off" and "He played a good hour on the cello" (247). These sentences employ quantitative "good."

[9] "Since the word ['interest'] has been used in extraordinary ways by philosophers, it is, I suppose, necessary for me to disassociate myself from that tradition."

[10] Oxford University Press, cited by Ziff (1960, 219).

[11] Perry (1926) 115.

[12] *Mind* 46 (1937) 14–31.

be convenient to refer to definitions of this sort as "interest theories," following Mr. R. B. Perry.[13]

Here, Stevenson's use of "interest" is limited to pro-attitudes rather than the conjunction of pro- and con-attitudes; and so his use is narrower than Perry's use of the term.

Ziff understands the word "interest" in a still narrower sense. He expressly claims that interests are not to be identified with "motives, wants, wishes, hopes, cravings, longings, likings, hankerings, and so on."[14] Rather, Ziff suggests that interests are relatively dispassionate attitudes. However, beyond that, he does little to clarify his understanding of "interest." In fact, he expressly resists clarification:

> I mean to be using [the word "interest"] in an ordinary way. I shall assume that you know what that is, that you are familiar with the word.[15]

Likewise, Ziff does not clarify his use of "answering to" interests. But in this case, he presumably has in mind something like "promoting" or "being conducive to the realization of" interests.

Granted the limitations of Ziff's discussion in this respect, in light of his proposal regarding the meaning of "good," consider the following sentences:

1.  ? That atom is good.
2.  ? That shadow is good.
3.  ? That seven is good.

Ziff would argue that these sentences are semantically peculiar (hence the question marks) precisely insofar as there are no interests associated with atoms, shadows, or sevens. At least, there are no associated interests that readily come to mind and to which an atom, shadow, or seven may intelligibly answer.

But now consider an utterance of (1) in the following context. A physicist and her assistant have access to a scanning electron microscope powerful enough to render images of individual atoms. Assume that it is due to certain intrinsic properties of atoms that they appear more clearly than others. Given a relatively clear image of an atom, the physicist turns the microscope over to the assistant and says: "Have a look; that atom is good."

---

[13]  Stevenson (1937) 15.
[14]  Ziff (1960) 219.
[15]  Ziff (1960) 219.

Similar contexts can be imagined that yield sensible interpretations of sentences (2) and (3). In the case of (2), assume that two sisters are using their hands to make shadows on a wall; one is entertained by a certain shadow and says to the other: "That shadow is good." In the case of (3), assume that a kindergarten teacher is instructing her pupils in rendering the numerals one to ten. As the class moves sequentially through the numerals, the teacher singles out well-wrought renditions. When the children render the numeral seven, the teacher says of one rendition: "That seven is good."

In accordance with Ziff's proposal, we might conclude as follows. The discussion suggests that sentences (1)–(3) are intelligible as long as pertinent interests can be identified to which the referents of the subjects of the sentences answer. Loosely speaking, I believe that this is correct and that the examples provide a helpful probe into both the meaning of "good" and the nature of value. But it is a delicate question precisely what conclusions should be drawn from these cases.

My first suggestion is that in explaining the examples, the expression "answering to an interest" should be replaced with the expression "contributing to the realization of an intention." The physicist and her assistant, the sisters, and the teacher and her students all have intentions. The physicist and assistant are trying to observe individual atoms. This is the intention that they share. The sisters share the intention of entertaining themselves by making shadows on the wall using their hands. And in the kindergarten classroom, the pupils have the intention of accurately rendering numerals.

In turn, the referents of the linguistic subjects of which "good" is predicated in sentences (1)–(3), namely the atom, the shadow, and the seven, are variously contributing to the realization of these intentions. Given the significance condition on the predicate expression in the basic sentence, the contributions that the atom, shadow, and seven make must somehow be significant. More precisely, their contributions must be significant relative to the contributions of members of contextually determined comparison classes. For example, in the context of sentence (1), the comparison class might consist of atoms viewed under the microscope. In context of (2), the comparison class might consist of shadows that the sisters have made with their hands. And in the context of (3), the comparison class might consist of the pupils' renditions of the numeral seven. Clearly, other reasonable construals of the comparison classes are possible. I offer these ones merely to underscore the point that the significance condition requires a comparison class.

Assume that we could generalize from these results to all sentences of the form "x is good," that is, to all instances of the basic sentence with "good" in the predicate. In that case, we might draw the following conclusion:

To be good is to make a significant contribution to the realization
of an intention.

And arguably, this metaphysical claim correlates with the following semantic
one:

"*x* is good" means "*x* makes a significant contribution to the
realization of an intention."

Likewise, with respect to the nature of value, we might conclude that

Value is contribution to the realization of an intention.

Again, a semantic correlate of this claim is arguably that

"Value" means "contribution to the realization of an intention."

However, we cannot generalize from the results of sentences (1)–(3) in this way.
The following example illustrates one reason why we cannot. Assume that the Red
Sox are scheduled to play the Yankees in their next baseball game. Clay is a fan of the
Red Sox. So Clay wants the Red Sox to win. This want or desire is a non-practical
mental state. There is nothing that Clay intends to do or thinks that he can do to
affect the game's outcome. What Clay has is a non-practical desire. So Clay non-
practically desires that the Red Sox win. Now, Clay learns that the Yankees' scheduled pitcher, who is the Yankees' ace, has just come down with the flu and won't in
fact be pitching. So Clay says to a fellow Red Sox fan:

4.  That's good.

Here, the demonstrative "that" refers to the fact that the Yankees' ace won't be
pitching in the game.

Assume now that we could generalize from this account of (4). Consequently, we
might draw the following metaphysical conclusion:

To be good is to make a significant contribution to the realization of a desire.

And, with respect to the nature of value:

Value is contribution to the realization of a desire.

For convenience, I pass over the semantic correlates of these two theses.

Now, if intention were a kind of desire, the initial generalizations concerning intention that I suggested on the basis of sentences (1)–(3) could simply be reconstrued in terms of the new generalizations concerning desire. One reason to resist such reconstruals is that the claim that intention is a kind a desire is controversial.[16] But then if intention is not a kind of desire, it seems to follow that there are two ways of being good and two kinds of value. I note that that consequence might be blocked if there were a superordinate kind of which intention and desire were sub-kinds that could explain sentences (1)–(4). But I am unaware of one.

In that case, a fundamental bipartition of being good and of value seems to follow. In other words, there are two fundamentally distinct kinds of entities called "good" and two fundamentally distinct kinds of entities called "value." Hereafter, I will call these "intentional" and "desiderative" ways of being good and value. Semantically, this bipartition seems to entail that "value" and (evaluative) "good" are each two ways ambiguous and presumably more precisely polysemous. Again, contrast the bipartite view of what it is to be good and of what value is with the view that "good" denotes a single kind that comprises two sub-kinds and that value is single kind that comprises two sub-kinds.

Whether the metaphysical bipartition thesis and its semantic correlates are true, it is worth noting that insofar as the metaphysical bipartition thesis explains being good and value in terms of intention and desire, it is a type of interest theory. Likewise, if we managed to retain a unified account of being good and value, an interest theory would result. In this respect, my present conclusions are continuous with, albeit refinements of, Ziff's and his predecessors' positions.

But now consider a further set of examples. Assume that Sloan has just completed a physical and that the speaker is her doctor:

5. Sloan's heart is good.
6. Sloan's lungs are good.

Assume that in this context the comparison classes pertinent to (5) and (6) are hearts and lungs of females in Sloan's age group. Assume that sentences (5) and (6) are true. What makes sentences such as (5) and (6) true is that biological organs have functions and that significant contribution to the realization of those functions requires the organs to be in a certain condition.

---

[16] For example, cp. Richard Holton, *Willing, Wanting, Waiting*, Oxford University Press, 2009.

It is contestable what biological functions are. It is contestable whether biological functions are to be explained in terms of mental states such as our desires and intentions. I think that biological functions do not depend on our desires or intentions. But I will not undertake to defend that position here. If biological functions must be explained in terms of our intentions and desires, then the position that I am ultimately going to advocate will require an adjustment. However, it will not fundamentally be affected.

If biological functions are not explicable in terms of our interests, then any interest theory of "good" or of "value" is doomed. Indeed, I think that is correct and so I reject interest theories. But, again, I will not undertake to argue for that position here. Rather, I am entertaining now a further partition of being good and of value. Arguably, to intentional and desiderative ways of being good and intentional and desiderative value, we must add what I will call a "biological functional" way of being good and biological functional value. According to such tripartition, once again there is not a single superordinate way of being good with three fundamental sub-ways, and value is not a superordinate kind with three basic sub-kinds. Accordingly, the semantic implications would seem to be that "good" and "value" are three ways polysemous.

Consideration of biological functions prompts one final set of examples:

7. This watch is good.
8. This toaster is good.

What makes sentences such as (7) and (8) true is that the subjects denote entities that have artificial functions, and contribution to the realization of those artificial functions requires the artifacts to be in a certain condition. More precisely, the artificial functions are characteristic artificial functions. By "characteristic function," I mean a function that an entity has in virtue of being a member of a functional kind. Biological functions are then also characteristic functions.

Artificial functions do not depend on intentions and desires, but on collective intentions and desires that constitute a cultural history. As such, contribution to the realization of an artificial function is not reducible to contribution to the realization of the occurrent intention or non-practical desire of an individual.

Notice of characteristic artificial functions therefore suggests one further partition of being good and of value. Accordingly, I add what I will call an "artificial functional" way of being good and artificial functional value to the sets of basic ways of being good and of value. The semantic implications, in turn, seem to be that "value" and "good" are now at least four ways polysemous.

One may try to resist the quadripartition of being good and of value and their semantic correlates. I see two possible approaches to doing so. First, observe that I have characterized intentional, desiderative, biological, and artificial functional value respectively as follows:

> contribution to the realization of an intention
> contribution to the realization of a desire
> contribution to the realization of a biological function
> contribution to the realization of an artificial function.

In view of this, we might seek a superordinate kind of which intention, desire, biological function, and artificial function are sub-kinds. But, as I have already intimated, I know of none and so can offer no remedy of this form.

Accepting that intention, desire, biological function, and artificial function are not sub-kinds of a superordinate kind, a second idea is that intention and desire, on the one hand, and biological evolution and culture, on the other, all share the property of providing or endowing entities with ends or purposes. In this respect, one might call intention, desire, biological evolution, and culture "end-setters" or "purpose providers." Accordingly, entities such as the atom or shadow or seven, the fact that the Yankees' ace won't be pitching in the game, Sloan's heart and lungs, the watch and the toaster would all have ends or purposes. An entity's value might then be identified with its serving the purpose or realizing the end that it has. Accordingly, an entity's being good might be identified with its serving the purpose or realizing the end that it has to a significant degree.

Between the terms "end" and "purpose," I prefer "purpose." The term "end" is largely a philosophical term of art,[17] which derives from the Aristotelian tradition.[18] The legitimacy of its application here would depend on an independent account and justification of its meaning and use.[19] In contrast, "purpose" is an ordinary language term with well-established senses. Insofar as my proposed method is to pursue a metaphysical question by linguistic means, I aim to adhere

---

[17] I acknowledge that the term "end" has an ordinary use in contexts that draw a contrast with "means." But consider the infelicitous examples in footnotes 20 and 21.

[18] Arguably, for Aristotle, an end is the actualization of a potential for form that occurs through a natural biological process or through a deliberate artificial process. Cp. Allan Gotthelf, "The Place of the Good in Aristotle's Natural Teleology," *Proceedings of the Boston Area Colloquium in Ancient Philosophy* 4 (1988) 113–39.

[19] The term "end" is central to Finlay's "end-relational" analysis of "good." But he expressly stipulates his use of "end" as "a term of art for any proposition conceived as a potential outcome" (2014, 32). On Finlay's analysis, see footnote 63 in my chapter 5.

to ordinary language until I reach its explanatory limitations. At that point, there might be justification for introducing technical terminology. Meanwhile, I propose to employ the term "purpose" in considering this second strategy for preserving the unity of value and of being good.

Granted this, the term "purpose" is ambiguous. One sense of "purpose" is akin to "intention"; for example:

9.  Despite all that he has been through, Adam's purpose has not wavered.[20]

Here, "Adam's purpose" refers to an intention that Adam has and has had. We can substitute "purpose" with "intention" and preserve the meaning of (9):

Despite all that he has been through, Adam's intention has not wavered.

I will call this the "mental" sense of "purpose."

Contrast the mental sense of "purpose" with the sense that occurs in the following sentence:

10.  Over the last twenty years, the purpose of cell phones has changed.[21]

The sense of "purpose" here is clearly not the mental sense. If we try to force such a reading of "purpose" onto (10), we must animate these objects and precisely endow them with minds. On such a reading, cell phones would have once had aims that they no longer have. Instead, the natural reading of "purpose" in (10) is akin to "function," "use," or "role." Observe that we can substitute "purpose" for "function," "use," or "role" and preserve the meaning of (10):

Over the last twenty years, the function / use / role of cell phones has changed.

I will call this second sense of "purpose" the "modal" sense. I hasten to add that I do not think that "purpose," "function," "use," and "role" are all strictly synonymous. But I believe that they are semantically closely akin.

Consider now the sense of "purpose" in the phrase "serve a purpose," for example in

The heart serves a purpose.

---

[20] Cp. # "Despite all that he has been through, Adam's end has not wavered."
[21] Cp. # "Over the last twenty years, the end of cell phones has changed."

Here only the modal sense is acceptable; and "function" is a particularly felicitous gloss:

# The heart serves an intention.
The heart serves a function.
? The heart serves a role.[22]

Granted this, observe that in the contexts that I elaborated for sentences (1)–(4), the atom, shadow, seven, and the fact that the Yankees' ace will not be pitching in the game all serve purposes. To be clear, by "serve" a purpose, I understand "contribute to the realization of" a purpose. So all of these entities variously contribute to the realization of various purposes. Clearly the purposes that they have and serve are not biological functions. Nor are they characteristic functions. Atoms, shadows, sevens, and the fact the fact that the Yankees' ace will not be pitching in the game do not have characteristic functions. Insofar as we may felicitously say that they have and serve functions, the functions that they have and serve are ad hoc. But I think that especially in the case of the fact that the Yankees' ace will not be pitching in the game, it is more natural to speak of this entity as having and serving a purpose. Consequently, hereafter I will restrict my use of "purpose" to the modal sense and speak only of purposes, not functions, whether biological or artificial, whether characteristic or ad hoc.

The crucial point now follows that purpose providers may constitute a heterogeneous class, but that being good and value may nonetheless each be a single thing. Precisely, value may be purpose serving; and being good may be significant purpose serving. In short, this second strategy preserves the unity of being good and of value and correlatively the univocity of "value" and "good" by suggesting that purpose serving is a single thing, despite the fact that the class of purpose providers consists of fundamentally heterogeneous entities.

In light of this position, we can say that (descriptivist) interest theories definitely make one and possibly two mistakes. The possible mistake relates to biological purposes. If there are such things, then of course being good need not depend on any interest. But setting this possibility aside, the key error is that in appealing to such things as intentions and desires, interest theories include in their definition of what it is to be good something that is merely a source of what it is to be good, namely a purpose provider.

---

[22] The term "function" seems to denote a kind a purpose (in the modal sense of "purpose"), precisely a characteristic purpose. Consequently, we can speak of the purposes or equivalently the functions of artifacts as well as biological organs.

I cautiously endorse the second strategy that retains the unity of being good and of value. I do not take myself to be in a position here to offer a decisive defense of this strategy. But I will note two considerations in support of it. One is rather simple. There is a modal sense of "purpose"; and all of the following phrases in which it is employed are well formed and semantically acceptable:

ad hoc purpose
desire derived purpose
intention derived purpose
characteristic purpose
artificial purpose
biological purpose.

But in that case, it appears that the various modifiers, "biological," "artificial," "ad hoc," and "characteristic," contribute to denoting sub-kinds of purposes.

I say that this is a rather simple consideration. What seems to be needed to make a decisive case is a semantic analysis of "purpose" that, while clarifying what a purpose is, shows how such a thing may be ad hoc or characteristic, desire or intention derived, artificial or biological. As I said, I do not take myself to be in a position to advance such an analysis here. However, I can suggest the direction that I believe such an analysis is likely to take and which thereby gives me confidence in the semantic and metaphysical unity theses that I am here proposing.

I have given the name "modal" to the sense of "purpose" in question. This follows what I take to be a fact about the term and what it denotes. "Purpose" is a modal term. If $x$ has a purpose, then there is something that $x$ ought to or must do or there is some way that $x$ ought to or must be. Recall from chapter 1 that, at least according to the standard Krazterian theory, the meaning of modal auxiliary constructions varies in relation to two parameters: the kind of modality, for example deontic versus epistemic, and the strength of modality, for example weak as in "might" versus strong as in "must."[23] I am uncertain about the modal strength associated with purposes. I am unsure whether it is constant across purposes or whether it varies. That is why I have used the disjunction "ought to or must." But the distinctions between kinds of purposes—intention derived, desire derived, characteristic artificial and biological—correspond to familiar kinds of modality in the literature. So I am encouraged to believe that "purpose" is to be explained in modal terms; and therefore that "purpose" is univocal.[24]

---

[23] The best available survey of semantic theories of modality of which I am aware is Paul Portner, *Modality*, Oxford University Press, 2009.

[24] Insofar as "purpose" is a modal term, the meaning of "good" depends on the meaning of one or more modal auxiliary terms such as "ought" or "must."

In short, while I acknowledge that the preceding remarks are merely suggestive, once again I cautiously endorse the second strategy for retaining the unity of
being good and value and of the meanings of "good" and "value."

## 2.2. The Polysemy of Evaluative and Operational "Good"

In sections 2.3 and 2.4, I will corroborate the central theses of the preceding section: that value is purpose serving and that being good is purpose serving to a
significant degree. But in light of these theses, here is a convenient place to provide justification for a claim I introduced in section 5 of chapter 2.

Recall the claim that evaluative "good" and operational "good" are polysemes,
whereas quantitative "good" stands in a homonymous relation to the former two.
Given that value is purpose serving, there is a close semantic relation between
evaluative and operational "good." If something is functional or operational, it
serves a purpose or is disposed to serve a purpose. This encourages the view that
evaluative and operational "good" are polysemes.

Recall, in addition, that among the various semantic, syntactic, and phonological properties that I cited in comparing evaluative, quantitative, and operational "good," evaluative and operational "good" share all but two. Neither
evaluative "good" nor operational "good" is associated with the dimension-type
of non-evaluative quantity; both evaluative "good" and operational "good" have
antonyms: evaluative and operational "bad" respectively; both are predicative;
neither is sensitive to definiteness effects; both can modify mass and count
nouns; and in phrases of the form "good N," both normally stress both the adjective and the noun.

In contrast, as we've seen, quantitative "good" is associated with the
dimension-type of non-evaluative quantity. But functionality or purpose serving
are not required for non-evaluative quantity. In addition, quantitative "good" has
no antonym; it is sensitive to definiteness effects; it cannot modify a mass noun;
it is not predicative; in phrases of the form "good N," it normally stresses only the
noun; and in such phrases, it does not admit stress on only the adjective. On this
basis, but above all in terms of the dimension-type with which it is associated and
the fact that non-evaluative quantity does not require functionality, I suggest that
operational "good" stands in a homonymous relation to evaluative and operational "good."

The two respects in which evaluative and operational "good" differ from one another are that evaluative "good" is a gradable adjective, whereas operational "good"
is non-gradable; and in a phrase of the form "good N," evaluative "good" admits
stress on the adjective alone, whereas operational "good" does not. As far as I am

aware, these two respects in which evaluative and operational "good" differ are rather idiosyncratic to this pair. Assuming that evaluative and operational "good" are polysemes, this encourages the view that, more precisely, they are irregular polysemes.

Granted this explanation of the irregular polysemy of evaluative and operational "good," given that there are at least four fundamentally different kinds of value and ways of being evaluatively good, it is questionable whether there are correlatively at least four fundamentally different ways of being operationally good. In other words, it may be questioned whether operational "good" can be predicated of subjects or attributed to nominal expressions that denote entities with biological purposes and artificial functions, including both characteristic and ad hoc purposes. In fact, operational "good" is only applicable to characteristic artificial purposes, and indeed to a small subset of them. For example, the following sentences simply cannot be read in terms of operational "good":

> # Sloan's heart is good (working / operational / in effect).
> # That shadow is good (working / operational / in effect).
> # The fact that the Yankees' ace won't be pitching is good (working / operational / in effect).

I have no explanation for why operational "good" is restricted to characteristic artificial purposes and more precisely to a small subset of them. But this restriction is also noteworthy as distinguishing operational "good" from evaluative "good." Evaluative "good" can be predicated of and attributed to a wide range of subjects and nominal expressions.

Finally, given that one of the meanings of the adjective "purposive" is "purpose serving," in light of the preceding conclusions it would be natural hereafter to refer to the lexeme "good" that has two irregular polysemes, namely evaluative and operational "good," as "purposive 'good.'"

## 2.3. Purposive "for" Phrases

I return now to the main thread of the chapter: the relation between value, being evaluatively good, and purpose serving. Hereafter, I will drop the modifier "evaluative."

"Good" admits at least two kinds of "for" phrases. In chapter 3, I discussed one kind, exemplified by the following sentences:

11. Paolo is good for a beginner.
12. Isabella is good for a high school student.

As I explained, the nominal complement of the preposition "for" here specifies membership in a comparison class. Consequently, I will refer to such "for" phrases as "comparison class 'for' phrases." Sentence (11) claims that, compared to other beginners, the value that Paolo has is significant. Sentence (12) claims that, compared to other high school students, the value that Isabella has is significant. In both (11) and (12), I have intentionally left the kind of value unspecified. But in a certain context, (11) could mean that Paolo is good at Latin for a beginner; and in a certain context, (12) could mean that Isabella is good at accounting for a high school student.

"Good" admits comparison class "for" phrases because it is a relative gradable adjective. Granted this, I am here interested in a different kind of "for" phrase, exemplified by the following two sentences:

13.  This knife is good for carving a turkey.
14.  These tires are good for driving in snow.

The "for" phrases here indicate purposes that the subjects of these sentences serve. Compare the following incomplete expressions:

15a.  ??? The number π is irrational for . . .
15b.  ??? Pluto is a dwarf planet for . . .
15c.  ??? Magnesium is a type of mineral for . . .

Assume that "for" in (15a)–(15c) introduces phrases of the same kind as those that occur in (13) and (14). Examples (15a)–(15c) cannot be felicitously completed unless one assumes some fantastic metaphysical or cosmological views, precisely views that attribute purposes to the irrationality of π, Pluto's being a dwarf planet, and magnesium's being a type of mineral. Accordingly, I will refer to the kind of "for" phrases that occur in (13) and (14) as "purposive 'for' phrases."

Consider now the use of the "for" phrases in (13) in (14) as simple predicate expressions:

13p.  This knife is for carving a turkey.
14p.  These tires are for driving in snow.

I'll call these "for" phrases "predicate purposive 'for' phrases." The nominal complement of a predicate purposive "for" phrase indicates either the characteristic function of the subject of the predicate expression or an intention derived ad hoc purpose thereof. Sentences (13p) and (14p) are naturally read as describing the characteristic functions of their subjects.

By contrast, consider the following example. Gail may reserve a knife for cutting fruit, although that knife was designed for and so has the characteristic function of carving a turkey. In such a case, Gail may felicitously inform her sous-chef:

16.  This knife is for cutting fruit.

Observe that the felicity of (16) requires that "this knife" refer to a particular qua particular. In contrast, insofar as (13p) is used to state the characteristic function of the knife, "this knife" must refer either to the particular qua member of the kind or to the kind.

Because the nominal complement of a predicate purposive "for" phrase may indicate a characteristic function, such complements may denote biological functions:

Hemoglobin is for transporting oxygen from the lungs to tissues in the body.

It is curious—and I do not have an explanation for the fact—that predicate purposive "for" phrases exclude purposes derived from non-practical desires. Recall the example of Clay wanting the Red Sox to win. In this context, it is not possible to say:

# The fact that the Yankees' pitcher is sick is for the Red Sox winning.

In purposive "for" phrases, the nominal complement of "for" indicates a purpose that the subject of "good" significantly serves or is disposed to serve. Such purposes may derive from any type of purpose provider. For example, once again, in the context in which Clay desires that the Red Sox win, he may felicitously say:

17.  The fact that the Yankees' ace will not be pitching is good for the Red Sox winning.

Compare the following example, which denotes a biological function:

18.  Chloroplasts are good for conducting photosynthesis.

I acknowledge that (18) may initially seem semantically peculiar. But observe that this is due to the fact that it is difficult to determine a comparison class for chloroplasts. However, imagine a natural world in which plants have evolved various organelles, in addition to chloroplasts, whose function is to conduct photosynthesis. And assume that among these organelles, chloroplasts are particularly effective. In that case, (18) is felicitous.

Finally, in cases where the subject of a purposive "for" phrase has a characteristic function, the nominal complement "for" need not refer to that function. For example, the following two sentences are consistent:

> Coca-Cola is good for removing rust. But Coca-Cola is not for removing rust.[25]

In short, given the form of purposive "for" phrase constructions as

$x$ is good for $P$.

such phrases should be interpreted as follows:

$P$ indicates a purpose that $x$ significantly serves or is disposed to serve.

More precisely, purposive "for" phrases require that $x$ serve or be disposed to serve the purpose that $P$ indicates in an instrumental way. For example, consider the following sentences:

> 19a.  ? This painting is good for aesthetic purposes.
> 19b.  # She is good for moral purposes.

(19a) is rather odd, and (19b) is completely unacceptable. But, regarding (19a), imagine a situation in which there is debate over whether a painting should be displayed in an art gallery or at a political event. In such a context, someone might felicitously say:

> This painting is good for aesthetic purposes, but not for political purposes.

Regarding (19b), it is difficult to imagine a situation in which a person might be used for moral purposes. But imagine instead that we are speaking of a pamphlet whose content is devoted to moral conduct. In that case, it would be possible to felicitously say:

> This pamphlet is good for moral purposes.[26]

---

[25]  Compare: "Removing rust is a purpose of Coca-Cola, but it is not the purpose of Coca-Cola."

[26]  On the distinction between instrumental and non-instrumental uses of "good," cp. the discussion of service contributions in section 2.4, including footnote 37.

Infinitive phrases and gerund phrases are typical ways of representing purposes; for example:

The purpose of a watch is *to tell time.*
Chloroplasts have the purpose of *conducting photosynthesis.*

Purposive "for" phrases are syntactically incompatible with infinitive phrases:

\* This knife is good for to carve a turkey.

However, replacing the "for" phrase with an infinitive phrase is marginally acceptable, at least in cases where the infinitive phrase denotes an action:

? This knife is good to carve a turkey.
? These tires are good to drive in snow.
? Coca-Cola is good to remove rust.[27]

Consider now the following sentences:

20.  This medication is good for people with migraines.
21.  This soil is good for cacti and other succulents.

Sentences such as (20) and (21) ostensibly have a different syntactic form and meaning from sentences (13)–(14) and (17)–(18). In (20) and (21), the nominal complements of "for" are not gerund phrases, but ordinary common noun phrases. Semantically, these "good for" phrases are akin to verbal "benefit" or adjectival "beneficial for" predicate expressions. For example, we can substitute "good for" in (20) and (21) with "benefit" and "beneficial for" and yield felicitous sentences that preserve the truth-conditions of (20) and (21):

20b.  This medication benefits people with migraines.
21b.  This soil is beneficial for cacti and other succulents.

Precisely, (20) and (21) entail (20b) and (21b), respectively.

The subjects of "good" in sentences like (20) and (21) appear to be benefactors, and the nominal complements of "for" appear to be beneficiaries. Accordingly, we might call "for" phrases such as those in sentences (20) and (21) "beneficiary

---

[27] In all of these cases, the expression is improved by appending the preposition "with" to the end of the clause.

'for' phrases." In such cases, the nominal complements of "for," the beneficiaries, must either denote entities to which well-being can be attributed or at least denote entities that can be benefited in some way. As examples (20) and (21) demonstrate, such entities include living things. Indeed, well-being attribution seems to require an entity that has a life and perhaps more specifically a life consisting of sentience. However, the following examples indicate that beneficiaries are not limited to living things:

22. This sealer is good for the deck.
23. This varnish is good for oil paintings.

I suggest, however, that the differences between (13)–(14) and (17)–(19), on the one hand, and (20)–(23), on the other, are superficial. To see how and why, consider the following. For an entity $b$ to be benefited, the degree of value that $b$ has must increase. But given that value consists of purpose serving, the former point entails that $b$ must have and serve a purpose. Consequently, if $b$ is benefited, the degree to which it serves its purpose must increase. Accordingly, for $x$ to benefit $b$, $x$ must contribute to the realization of the purpose that $b$ serves. Finally, if $x$ is good for $b$, the contribution that $x$ makes to the realization of the purpose that $b$ serves is significant relative to the members of a comparison class.

So beneficiary "for" phrases are in fact mere variants of purposive "for" phrases. Consequently, it must be possible to substitute "good for" with "benefit" or "is beneficial" in sentences (13)–(14) and (17)–(18) and thereby produce felicitous sentences that preserve the truth-conditions of (13)–(14) and (17)–(18). Precisely, through such substitutions, (13)–(14) and (17)–(18) must entail the following:

13b. This knife is beneficial for carving a turkey.
14b. These tires are beneficial for driving in snow.
17b. The fact that the Yankees' ace will not be pitching is beneficial for the Red Sox winning.
18b. Chloroplasts are beneficial for conducting photosynthesis.

Conversely, what makes the "for" phrases in sentences such as (20)–(23) ostensibly different from those in sentences such as (13)–(14) and (17)–(18) is that a gerund phrase or something akin to it is assumed; for example:

20'. This medication is good for [alleviating the suffering of] people with migraines.

21'.  This soil is good for [the growth and flourishing of] cacti and other succulents.

22'.  This sealer is good for [preserving the condition of] the deck.

23'.  This varnish is good for [preserving the condition of] oil paintings.

In sum, according to the present account, purposive "for" phrase constructions, which have the form "$x$ is good for purpose $P$," require that the subject of "good" make or be disposed to make a significant contribution to the realization of $P$. And beneficiary "for" phrase constructions, which have the form "$x$ is good for beneficiary $b$," require that the subject of "good" and the nominal complement of "for" have purposes; and require that $x$ make or be disposed to make a significant contribution to the realization of the purpose that $b$ serves. Indeed, $x$'s purpose here must be to serve $b$'s purpose. Moreover, $x$ and $b$ may have their purposes in any of the ways described in section 2.1, namely by being a member of a biological or artificial functional kind or through their relation to an individual's intention or non-practical desire.

## 2.4.  Purpose Serving and the Basic Sentence

Section 2.1 argued that value is purpose serving. Consequently, for $x$ to be good, $x$ must serve a purpose to a significant degree. The preceding section in effect corroborated these metaphysical claims by successfully applying them to the interpretation of purposive "for" phrases. But—save for the suggestion that although there are at least four fundamentally distinct kinds of purposes, "value" and "good" are univocal—I have resisted further application of the metaphysical claims to semantic claims about "value" and "good." For example, I have cautiously avoided making the claim that "value" means "purpose serving" or that "to be good" means "to serve a purpose to a significant degree." The present section explains the reason for this cautious avoidance.

My discussion will precisely focus on the implications of the metaphysical claims for the meaning of the basic sentence "$x$ is good." My question then is how the metaphysical claims may be applied to a claim about the meaning of the basic sentence. The aim of this discussion is to expose some subtle points regarding the semantics of "good" and the basic sentence.

I begin with the following proposal:

B1. "$x$ is good" means "$x$ is serving a purpose to a significant degree."

In the following discussion, I note two problems with B1. One relates to the indefinite article in the nominal complement ("a purpose") of the verb "serve."[28] The other relates to the verbal aspect of the predicate expression "is serving a purpose." I'll discuss these problems in that order.

As it occurs in B1, "serve" is a binary predicate.[29] In other words, "serve" requires two syntactic arguments. The two arguments that "serve" requires are, in traditional grammatical terms, a subject and a direct object: $x$ serves $y$. In more contemporary syntactic terms, the subject argument here ($x$) is the external argument of this predicate, while the direct object ($y$) is the internal argument.[30]

Compare "serve" with "good." Ostensibly, "good" is a unary predicate, requiring only a subject. But "good" is a relative gradable adjective. According to the relational degree-based analysis of chapter 2, it requires a degree argument as well as a subject argument. In that case, "good" is also a binary predicate. The degree argument is the internal argument of the predicate "good." Consequently, while "serve" and "good" are both binary predicates, they require different kinds of internal arguments. Moreover, whereas "serve" requires that its internal argument be overtly realized, "good" does not require this.

Now, the indefinite article that introduces the phrase "a purpose," which is the direct object complement of the predicate "serve," is contentful. For example, contrast the following two sentences:

Pass me a cup.

Pass me the cup.

According to one prominent theory, the indefinite article is interpreted as a free variable.[31] Assuming so, if "$x$ is good" were strictly synonymous with "$x$ is serving a purpose to a significant degree," the predicate "good" would have to

---

[28] The expression "a purpose" may be interpreted as a so-called determiner phrase, headed by the determiner "a" and whose nominal complement is "purpose." I note this possibility, but will, for the sake of simplicity, here treat "a purpose" as a noun phrase. On determiner phrases, cp. section 1.2 of chapter 7.

[29] Note that I use "predicate" in this sort of context to denote a syntactic category. Contrast the use of "function" in section 3.4 of chapter 3 to denote a semantic type or category. I am regimenting this usage for the sake of clarity, precisely to distinguish syntactic and semantic categories.

[30] Recall the use of the terms "internal argument" and "external argument" in the discussion of the transitive verb "kiss" in section 3.4 of chapter 3.

[31] Cp. Hans Kamp, "A Theory of Truth and Discourse Representation," in *Formal Methods in the Study of Language*, J. Groenendijk et al., eds., Mathematical Centre, 1981, 277–322; Irene Heim, *The Semantics of Definite and Indefinite Noun Phrases*, University of Massachusetts Amherst, dissertation in linguistics, 1982.

contain content corresponding to the free variable expressed by the indefinite article in "a purpose."[32]

Absent a variable binder, a free variable is subject to existential closure. In other words, absent a variable binder, the meaning of, for example,

This button serves a purpose.

which may be formally represented as

$P(x) \wedge S(x,b)$

defaults to

$\exists x\, [P(x) \wedge S(x,b)].$

Consequently, the indefinite article engenders a scopal ambiguity. For example, compare the following sentences:

24. Toby saw a mark on the wall.
25. Toby did not see a mark on the wall.

On a narrow-scope reading, namely where the indefinite phrase scopes under the negation, (24) and (25) are contradictory. Formally, the contradictory reading can be represented as

$\exists x\, [M(x) \wedge S(x,t)]$
$\neg\exists x\, [M(x) \wedge S(x,t)].$

However, on a wide-scope reading, where the indefinite phrase scopes above the negation, the sentences are not contradictory:

26. There is a mark on the wall that Toby saw.
27. There is a mark on the wall that Toby did not see.

Formally, (26) and (27) can be represented as

$\exists x\, [M(x) \wedge S(x,t)]$
$\exists x\, [M(x) \wedge \neg S(x,t)].$

---

[32] Of course, "a significant degree" also contains an indefinite article. I ignore this fact for now, but return to it subsequently.

Likewise, $x$ serving purpose *P1* is compatible with $x$ is not serving a distinct purpose *P2*. Consequently, on a wide-scope reading, the following sentences are not contradictory:

> $x$ is serving a purpose.
> $x$ is not serving a purpose.

Compare:

> There is some purpose that $x$ is serving.
> There is some purpose that $x$ is not serving.

In contrast, the following pair is simply contradictory:

> $x$ is good.
> $x$ is not good.

Contrast this with the following pair, which admits both narrow- and wide-scope readings, and so in the latter case a non-contradictory reading:

> $x$ is good in a way.
> $x$ is not good in a way.

A simple fix to this problem with B1 is to replace the indefinite article in the phrase "a purpose" with the possessive "$x$'s":

> "$x$ is good" means "$x$ is serving $x$'s purpose to a significant degree."

Observe that the adverbial phrase "to a significant degree" also contains an indefinite article and so is subject to the same scopal ambiguity. That too can be remedied by rendering it as the adverb "significantly":

> B2. "$x$ is good" means "$x$ is significantly serving $x$'s purpose."

Compare the following metaphysical thesis derived from B2:

> For $x$ to be good is for $x$ to significantly serve $x$'s purpose.

Finally, note that by comparison with B1, the following construal of "$x$ is good" in terms of "value" requires no such emendations:

"*x* is good" means "*x* has significant value."

I turn now to a second problem with B1. This problem is also a problem for B2. Verbs have so-called aspects.[33] Verbal aspect is one of the ways that the temporality of the action, event, or state denoted by the verb is characterized. For instance, consider the following two pairs of sentences:

28. Ronan was cooking lamb.
29. Adam was speaking Spanish.

30. Ronan cooked lamb.
31. Adam spoke Spanish.

The verbs in (28)–(31) are in the past tense. So they denote activities in the past. But the verbs in (28) and (29) have different temporal aspects from those in (30) and (31). In (28) and (29), the activity is characterized as ongoing or in progress over the course of some past time. In (30) and (31), the activity is characterized as completed. Accordingly, the verbs in (28) and (29) are said to have "progressive" aspects, while the verbs in (30) and (31) are said to have "perfect" or "completed" aspects.

Verbal aspect is not limited to the distinction between progressive and perfect. Consider the following pairs of sentences:

32. Ronan is cooking lamb.
33. Adam is speaking Spanish.
34. Ronan cooks lamb.
35. Adam speaks Spanish.

Sentences (32)–(35) are in the present tense. With respect to aspect, the verbs in (32) and (33) are progressive: Ronan's activity is in progress or ongoing in the present; and Adam's activity is in progress or ongoing in the present. The aspect in (34) and (35) is called "habitual." At least, this is one of two possible ways that these sentences can be read. As such, these sentences may be glossed as

Ronan habitually cooks lamb.
Adam habitually speaks Spanish.

---

[33] For an overview, cp. Susan Rothstein, "Aspect," in *The Cambridge Handbook of Formal Semantics*, M. Aloni and P. Dekker, eds., Cambridge University Press, 2016, 342–68.

Sentence (35) can also be construed in a second way. This construal is in terms of a disposition or a potential, that is, a capacity, that Adam has. Accordingly, the construal is called "dispositional" or "potential." On this reading, "Adam speaks Spanish" is construed as

35d.   Adam is able to speak Spanish.

Observe that (35d) may be true, regardless of whether Adam habitually does speak Spanish.

It is noteworthy that a dispositional or potential reading does not seem available for (34). "Ronan cooks lamb" cannot reasonably be read to mean the same thing as

Ronan is able to cook lamb.

Precisely why (35) can be read both habitually and dispositionally, while (34) can only be read habitually, I leave unresolved.

Presently, let's return to B2, repeated here for convenience:

B2. "$x$ is good" means "$x$ is significantly serving $x$'s purpose."

In light of the preceding, it will be evident that the predicate expression "is serving $x$'s purpose" has a progressive aspect. Accordingly, contrast the following two sentences:

36.   $x$ is serving $x$'s purpose.
37.   $x$ serves $x$'s purpose.

Sentence (37) can be read with a habitual aspect or a dispositional aspect. In either case, (36) and (37) have different meanings. An entity may habitually serve its purpose without presently serving its purpose. Likewise, an entity may be disposed to or be capable of serving its purpose without presently serving its purpose.

Granted this, it may be questioned whether a predicate expression composed of an adjective, in this case "good," can have any aspect whatsoever. After all, I introduced aspect as a property of verbs. Indeed, some adjectives have aspects. But regardless of whether some adjectives have aspects, a single adjective cannot have both progressive and habitual or dispositional aspects simultaneously. Yet in some contexts, "$x$ is good" would more accurately be rendered as "$x$ is significantly *serving* $x$'s purpose," whereas in other contexts it would more accurately be rendered as "$x$ significantly *serves* $x$'s purpose." For example, assume

Joe and Adam are hiking. Adam falls and hurts his arm. Joe jerry-rigs a splint for Adam. They continue on the hike, and ten minutes on Joe asks: "How is the splint working?" Adam responds:

38.  It's good.

Compare the following two glosses of (38) in this context:

38p.  The splint is significantly serving its purpose.
38h.  The splint significantly serves its purpose.

In this context, (38p) is clearly preferable to (38h).

Contrast the following example. A patron at a hardware store is looking to buy a saw to cut metal piping. The clerk suggests a saw and says:

39.   This one is good.

Compare the following glosses of (39):

This saw significantly serves its purpose (of cutting metal piping).
This saw is able to significantly serve its purpose (of cutting metal piping).
# This saw is significantly serving its purpose (of cutting metal piping).

So "$x$ is good" should sometimes be glossed with a progressive aspect as "$x$ is significantly serving $x$'s purpose" and sometimes with a habitual or dispositional aspect as "$x$ significantly serves $x$'s purpose." But since these glosses have different meanings, "$x$ is good" cannot be strictly synonymous with the gloss in B2: "$x$ is significantly serving $x$'s purpose."

Granted this, we could replace B2 with the following disjunctive thesis:

B3. "$x$ is good" means "$x$ is significantly serving $x$'s purpose" or "$x$ significantly serves $x$'s purpose."

But the disjunction in B3 is unsatisfactory for a couple reasons. First, it entails that "$x$ is good" has two or even three meanings: one progressive, one habitual, one dispositional. That seems implausible. Second, an explanation is needed for why in glossing "$x$ is good" with the verbal predicate expression "serve $x$'s purpose," various aspects are required in various contexts. Arguably, "good" lacks an aspect. Consequently, aspectuality information that is conveyed in sentences of the form "$x$ is good" derives from something other than the term "good." This at least explains why "$x$ is good" would be compatible with various aspectual

readings. Granted that, it remains to specify the source of aspectuality information in "good" constructions. I offer a few preliminary considerations regarding
this topic here.

Basically, the aspectual distinctions that emerge in the attempt to gloss the
basic sentence using the verbal predicate expression "serve $x$'s purpose" owe to
the following two features related to the basic sentence: the nature of the subject of which "good" is predicated and the nature of the purpose that the subject
serves. For instance, consider again sentence (5):

5.  Sloan's heart is good.

Assume that the purpose associated with "good" here is the characteristic function of the heart, namely to circulate blood. More precisely, it is to circulate blood
for an extended period of time, say, for the typical lifespan of the vertebrate. This
fact would encourage a habitual or dispositional verbal gloss of (5) rather than a
progressive one. Granted this, in different contexts, the subject of (5) might be
understood as "the condition of Sloan's heart," that is, "the physical structure of
Sloan's heart" or instead "the operation of Sloan's heart." In the former case, a
dispositional gloss of (5) would be preferable to a habitual one. In the latter case,
a habitual gloss would be preferable.

Compare the following example. Assume that Beatrice is a professional dancer
and that someone says of her:

40.  Beatrice is good.

Assume that the type of value and so purpose that the predicate expression here
denotes relates to dancing. Now contrast the following two precisifications of
the context in which (40) is uttered. In one context, Beatrice is performing a
role on stage, and the speaker is an audience member watching her for the first
time. Plausibly then, the purpose that the predicate expression here denotes is
performance of the present role. In that case, a progressive verbal gloss of (40)
would be reasonable. In another context, two choreographers are considering
which member of a dance troupe to cast in a particular role; and the speaker is
one of the choreographers, who is familiar with Beatrice's abilities. In that case, a
dispositional gloss would be reasonable.[34]

---

[34] I note one further problem with the verbal gloss of "good." For the sake of simplicity, I will
present this problem in terms of the progressive predicate expression "is serving $x$'s purpose."
This expression admits adverbial "well" modification: "$x$ is serving $x$'s purpose well." "Good"
clearly does not admit adverbial "well" modification: * "$x$ is good well." * "$x$ is well good." To be
sure, "is significantly serving $x$'s purpose" also does not admit adverbial "well" modification: * "$x$

The two problems I have discussed with B1 are related to the fact that in this context "serve" is a verbal predicate expression, and precisely one that takes a direct object complement containing an indefinite article. Consequently, it might be questioned whether a gloss of the basic predicate expression using another adjective would be more successful. Given the limited success of "serve $x$'s purpose," an adjectival gloss with a similar meaning to this verbal predicate expression is clearly required. The following three possibilities occur to me:

serviceable
purposive
useful.

*The Concise Oxford Dictionary of Current English* glosses "serviceable" as "of use, useful or usable, willing and able to render or capable of rendering service." It glosses "purposive" as "having, serving, done with, a purpose." I will focus solely on "purposive" and "useful."

In some respects, "useful" seems to be a better gloss than "purposive." One is that "useful" is clearly gradable. The adjective "purposive" may be gradable, but it is a rare word; and I don't have clear semantic intuitions about its employment. For example, it is not clear to me whether the following sentences are acceptable:

? $x$ is very purposive.
? $x$ is more purposive than $y$.
? $x$ is the most purposive $F$ there is.

---

is significantly serving $x$'s purpose well." Precisely, here "well" and "significantly" appear to be in complementary distribution. Consequently, the fact that "is serving $x$'s purpose" but not "good" admits "well" modification may seem an idle point. But consider now a standard Davidsonian analysis of the sentence "$x$ is serving $x$'s purpose well." According to a Davidsonian analysis, both the subject ($x$) and the predicate ("is serving $x$'s purpose") are predicated of an event $e$. For example, consider first the simpler sentence "Joe is walking." On a Davidsonian analysis, this sentence is interpreted as follows: there is an event $e$, such that $e$ is an event of walking, of which Joe is the agent. Formally: $\exists e(W,j)(e)$. According to this analysis, adverbial modifiers are treated as predicates of the event. So consider "Joe is walking quickly." This is interpreted thus: there is an event $e$, such that $e$ is an event of walking, of which Joe is the agent, and $e$ is quick. Formally: $\exists e[(W,j)(e) \wedge Q(e)]$. Accordingly, the sentence "$x$ is serving $x$'s purpose well" would be interpreted thus: there is an event $e$, in which there is a purpose that $x$ has and that $x$ is serving, and of which $x$ is the agent, and $e$ is good. Formally: $\exists e[\exists P[Px \wedge S(P,x)](e) \wedge G(e)]$. But now given the analysis of "$x$ is good" as "$x$ is significantly serving $x$'s purpose," the final conjunct in the Davidsonian analysis corresponding to "$e$ is good" requires the analysis: "$e$ is significantly serving $x$'s purpose." Consequently, the following bizarre result follows: There is an event $e$, in which there is a purpose that $x$ has and that $x$ is serving, and of which $x$ is the agent, and there is an event $e'$, such that $e'$ is an event of purpose serving, $e$ is the agent of $e'$, and $e'$ occurs to a significant degree.

Contrast:

*x* is very useful.
*x* is more useful than *y*.
*x* is the most useful *F* there is.[35]

In addition to being regularly gradable, "useful" admits comparison class and purposive "for" phrases:

*x* is useful for an inexpensive model.
*x* is useful for an older model.

*x* is useful for driving on mountain roads.
*x* is useful for carving a turkey.

I have no semantic intuitions regarding whether "purposive" admits such phrases. A search for instances of the expression "purposive for" in the Brigham Young Corpus of Contemporary American English, which at the time of writing contains over 560 million words used between 1990 and 2017, returns only one instance.[36]

On the other hand, "useful" and "good" are not synonymous. "Useful" obviously derives from "use." There is some reason to think that "use" has both an active and a passive reading. For example, compare the following sentences:

Adam's use of the apparatus made his fingers numb. [ACTIVE]
Our use of the car is now confined to grocery shopping. [ACTIVE]

This knife has several uses.         [PASSIVE]
The chapel is still in use today.    [PASSIVE]

Assuming that "use" has both an active and a passive reading, "useful" derives from the passive reading of "use." That is to say, the adjective does not mean

---

[35] I note in passing that the participial phrase "purpose serving" as in "*x* is purpose serving" is not gradable: * "*x* is very purpose serving."

[36] corpus.byu.edu/coca. "Ruscha's books highlight the many layers of mediation through which they are constituted; editing and cropping appear at once arbitrary and yet all the more *purposive for* pointing to the conditions of the frame as the very matrix of vision." The example derives from Jaleh Mansoor, "Ed Ruscha's One-Way Street," *October Magazine* 111 (2005) 127–42. A Google search (May 1, 2018) for the expression "purposive for," where "for" introduces a purposive phrase, returns a number of additional examples. However, it is noteworthy that these are mainly confined to scholarship on Kant's Third Critique. For example, "Just as Kant's critical writings argue that agents must be able to assume that the natural world of efficient causes is *purposive for* morality's ultimate ends . . . " (Luke MacInnis, "Agency and Attitude: Kant's Purposive Conception of Human Rights," *Philosophy and Social Criticism* 42 [2016] 289–319, in abstract, with my italics). It is also noteworthy that the author of the single example in the BYU corpus characterizes herself as "a historian of modern and contemporary cultural production, specializing in twentieth-century European art, Marxism, Marxist feminism, and critical theory" (retrieved from ahva.ubc.ca/persons/jaleh-mansoor, on May 1, 2018).

"(someone's) considerable usage (of something)" but "(something's having) considerable usage."

Granted this, crucially, "useful" implies instrumentality, whereas "good" does not. This contrast is salient in the following three pairs of examples:

41g.  *x* is a good painting. (That is, *x* is an aesthetically good painting.)
41u.  *x* is a useful painting.

42g.  *x* is a good person. (That is, *x* is a morally good person.)
42u.  *x* is a useful person.

43g.  *x* is a good feeling. (That is, *x* feels good.)
43u.  *x* is a useful feeling.

In (41g), (42g), and (43g), the natural reading of "good" is non-instrumental. Consequently, the substitution of "good" for "useful" in (41u), (42u), and (43u) yields sentences with different meanings.

Compare the following three sentences that incorporate the same "useful *N*" phrases that occur in (41u), (42u), and (43u), but now in felicitous instrumental contexts:

44u.  Masaccio's *Holy Trinity* is a useful painting for illustrating early perspective technique.
45u.  Michael Nutter is a useful person to speak to if you are considering a career in city government.
46u.  Such pain is a useful feeling insofar as it indicates a buildup of lactic acid in the muscle and serves as a warning that you may be overexerting yourself.

In all of these cases, "useful" can be substituted with "good" while preserving the original meanings:

44g.  Masaccio's *Holy Trinity* is a good painting for illustrating early perspective technique.
45g.  Michael Nutter is a good person to speak to if you are considering a career in city government.
46g.  Such pain is a good feeling since it indicates a buildup of lactic acid in the muscle and serves as a warning that you may be overexerting yourself.

In short, "good" is compatible with, but in contrast to "useful" does not require, an instrumental reading.

In light of this consideration, the question arises how the distinction between something being instrumentally versus non-instrumentally good is related to the idea that for *x* to be good is for *x* to significantly serve *x*'s purpose. The answer here is akin to the one that I proposed in explaining the aspectual readings of the basic sentence. That is to say, it depends on the nature of the subject of "good" and the nature of the purpose that the subject serves. More precisely, it depends on the relation between these two things.

I have glossed "serve a purpose" as "contribute to the realization of a purpose." Accordingly, we may speak of various kinds of "service contributions." Some such contributions are instrumental to the realization of purposes, while some are non-instrumental. Among non-instrumental contributions are those that partially or wholly constitute realizations of purposes. For example, a natural way to read the expression "good painting" is as denoting a painting that significantly constitutively realizes some aesthetic purpose. Likewise, "good person" or "good deed" may be read as denoting a person who or deed that constitutively realizes a moral purpose.[37]

In sum, the basic sentence "*x* is good" can felicitously be glossed by the expression "*x* has significant value." But insofar as I have sought to clarify the nature of value and the meaning of "value," I have attempted to provide an alternate gloss in terms of purpose serving. The discussion has clarified some subtle difficulties involved in glossing the basic sentence in terms of the verbal predicate expression "serve a purpose" as well as in terms of semantically related adjectival predicate expressions. The problem of aspect in particular impedes the ability to gloss the basic sentence with the verbal predicate expression "serve *x*'s purpose." The disjunctive gloss of B3 appears to be as close as one can get. But we now have an explanation of the disjunction. With respect to the adjectival predicate expressions, there is no other English adjective that is synonymous with "good." That fact should not be surprising, let alone dispiriting. Natural language is extremely subtle as well as economical. Why would a natural language duplicate its basic terms? Finally, recognition of the precise limits of the various glosses has shed light on the semantics of "good" and the basic sentence.

---

[37] I acknowledge a resemblance between what I am characterizing as various kinds of service contributions and the traditional philosophical distinction between instrumental and final goods as well as Christine Korsgaard's more recent distinction between extrinsic and intrinsic goods ("Two Distinctions in Goodness," *Philosophical Review* 92 (1983) 169–95). I believe that the philosophical terms, especially intrinsic and final goods, need to be reconsidered in light of my interpretation of the ordinary language expressions. But I resist saying more than that here since an adequate treatment of the topic would require too large a departure from the train of the present discussion.

## 2.5.  Generic and Specific Value

I have resisted the view that "purpose" in the modal sense and so "value" and "good" are at least four ways polysemous. Granted this, in the present section I suggest that, for reasons that I have yet to discuss, "value" is in fact polysemous, precisely two ways polysemous. To begin, note that "value" is syntactically ambiguous: it may be a verb or a noun:

What is it to value something?
What is value?

Our concern here is of course with the noun "value." But the noun "value" itself is also ambiguous. There is both a mass noun "value" and a count noun "value."[38] The distinction between mass and count nouns will be central to chapter 6, and I postpone a more thorough discussion of it until then. Presently, it suffices to note the following two points that distinguish mass nouns from count nouns.

First, count nouns and most mass nouns are lexically singular in number. That is to say, they appear in the lexicon in the singular. But whereas count nouns can be pluralized, lexically singular mass nouns cannot. For example, "molecule" is a count noun and "helium" is a mass noun:

There are molecules in the chamber.
* There are heliums in the chamber.

Second, without modification by a so-called "determiner," count nouns in the singular cannot appear in argument positions, for example as the subject of a sentence, or as predicate expressions. Determiners are a syntactic category of contemporary syntactic theory, which I will explain more thoroughly in section 1.2 of chapter 7. Here, it suffices to note that the indefinite and definite articles are examples of determiners. In contrast, mass nouns can appear in argument

---

[38] As far as I am aware, this point is missed in philosophical discussions of value and its relation to goodness. For example, consider Gerald Gaus's remark: "Value language is grammatically complex, having a verb form (where someone *values* something), an adjectival form (where something is said to be *valuable*), and an abstract noun form (where something is said to be a *value*). Let us call these, respectively, *valuing, valuableness,* and *a value* (or *values*)" (*Value and Justification*, Cambridge University Press, 1990, 2). I also note here that, beyond the following comment, I will not investigate the semantic relation between the mass noun "value" and the adjective "valuable." The adjective appears to have two senses: "what is able to be valued" and "what ought to be valued" or, more weakly, "what there is reason to value." Evidently, explication of these senses of "valuable" requires explication of the verb "value." Consequently, the question is how the mass noun "value" is semantically related to the verb "value."

positions and as predicate expressions without determiners. For example, consider the following sentences:

47. * Molecule is in the chamber.
48. Helium is in the chamber.

In (47), the determiner-less singular count noun "molecule" is syntactically unacceptable as the subject of a clause. In contrast, in (48) the determiner-less mass noun "helium" is acceptable in that position.

Furthermore, as noted in section 2.2 of chapter 2, although mass nouns admit the definite article, they do not admit the indefinite article. Consider the following examples:

49. A molecule is in the chamber.
50. * A helium is in the chamber.

In (49), the singular count noun "molecule" admits the indefinite article, whereas in (50) the singular mass noun "helium" does not.[39]

Having clarified the distinction between mass and count nouns to this extent, observe that in the value thesis, repeated here for convenience, the noun "value" is a mass noun:

Value is the dimension type associated with evaluative "good."

Here "value" appears as the subject of the clause, an argument position, without a determiner.[40]

Likewise, in the following example, the mass noun "value" occurs as the complement of "has," another argument position, without a determiner:

This painting has value.

Contrast the following occurrences of "value" as a count noun:

51. Hope is a traditional Christian value.
52. Hope and love are traditional Christian values.

---

[39] Cp. "This is a molecule"; * "This is molecule"; * "This is a helium"; "This is helium."

[40] It is convenient to note here that dimensions and dimension-types are typically denoted by mass nouns. This is why in referring to the dimension-type encoded in quantitative "good," the term "magnitude" is preferable to "quantity." "Magnitude" here is a mass noun, whereas "quantity" is principally a count noun. (There is also a count noun "magnitude.")

In (51), the count noun "value" has a determiner, the indefinite article.[41] In (52), the count noun "value" is pluralized.

Throughout this chapter, my de facto concern has been with the mass noun "value." The mass noun "value" is two ways polysemous in the following respect. Linguists use the terms "hyperonymy" and "hyponymy" to denote semantic relations between words that themselves denote superordinate and subordinate kinds respectively. For example, "bird" is the hypernym of words such as "robin," "swallow," and "cardinal." Conversely, "robin," "swallow," and "cardinal" are hyponyms of "bird."[42] Granted this, there are a few polysemous words whose polysemes themselves stand in hyperonymous and hyponymous relations to one another. The word "moral" is an example. Consider the following sentences:

53.  That is a moral, not an aesthetic judgment.
54.  That judgment has moral, not aesthetic content.

In (53) and (54), "moral" denotes a type of value that is distinct from, but co-ordinate with, aesthetic value. The antonym of "moral" in this sense is "non-moral." I will call this the "generic" sense of "moral." The generic sense of "moral" comprises both what is morally good or right and what is morally bad or evil or wrong. Contrast the generic sense of "moral" with the sense of "moral" that occurs in the following sentences:

55.  Gail is a moral person.
56.  The situation is very difficult, but I believe you've made a moral deci-
     sion here.

In (55) and (56), "moral" is equivalent to "morally good." So this sense of "moral" is a hyponym of the generic sense of "moral." Accordingly, I will refer to this sense of "moral" as the "specific" sense. The antonym of "moral" in the specific sense is "immoral."

Analogously, there are generic and specific senses of the mass noun "value." The mass noun "value" comprises what is commonly called "positive," "neutral," and "negative" value. The very fact that the expressions "negative value" and "positive value" are felicitous confirms the existence of a generic sense of "value." The specific sense of the mass noun "value" denotes only positive value. In short, the specific sense of "value" is a hyponym of the generic sense. Conversely, the generic sense of "value" is a hypernym of the specific sense.

---

[41]  It is of course also modified by the adjectival expression "traditional Christian."
[42]  For example, cp. Saeed (2009) 69–70.

The following diagrams illustrate these two polysemes of the mass noun "value":

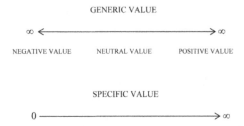

The distinction between the generic and specific senses of "value" bears on my analysis of "good" in the following way. According to the value thesis, "good" is associated with the dimension-type of value. But given that the mass noun "value" is polysemous between generic and specific senses, this claim is unclear. Accordingly, let's distinguish "generic" and "specific" versions of the value thesis:

GENERIC VALUE THESIS
Generic value is the dimension-type associated with evaluative "good."

SPECIFIC VALUE THESIS
Specific value is the dimension-type associated with evaluative "good."

The question, then, is which of these two precisifications of the value thesis is correct. By analogy with, for example, the dimension of height associated with "tall," we might expect the dimension-type of value to be generic rather than specific value. Entities that are short, of average stature, and tall all have height. So we would expect that entities that are bad, of neutral value, and good would all have the gradable property of value, which is to say, generic value. In that case, the generic value thesis is true.

There are, however, several problems with the generic value thesis. First, if the generic value thesis is true, then it appears to be at odds with the view that value is purpose serving. At least, it is questionable whether it is instead specific value that is purpose serving. Arguably, to *serve* a purpose is to have some degree of so-called positive value. Contrast thwarting the realization of a purpose. And consider contributions that neither significantly serve nor significantly thwart the realization of a purpose and so have neutral value. If purpose serving is so understood, then if the generic value thesis is true, generic value is not purpose serving, but something more general, which we might conveniently call "purpose contribution." By "purpose contribution," I here stipulatively mean to include thwarting the realization of a purpose as well as serving the realization of a purpose.

Unfortunately, there is a much more serious problem with the generic value thesis. While purpose serving and purpose thwarting might reasonably be viewed as kinds of purpose contribution, purpose contribution is not in fact a plausible candidate for the generic gradable property associated with both "good" and "bad." It does not follow that the greater the purpose contribution an entity makes, the better it is; or that the lesser the purpose contribution an entity makes, the worse it is. According to the intended sense of "purpose contri-bution," good and bad entities both make significant purpose contributions, but of polar opposite kinds. So again, while purpose serving and purpose thwarting might reasonably be viewed as kinds of purpose contribution, purpose contri-bution cannot be a dimension or dimension-type associated with both "good" and "bad."

A discussion by Bierwisch suggests a direction that the solution to this problem might take. Bierwisch argues that there is a subset of gradable adjectives, consisting of members of antonym pairs, each of which measures degrees on a scale based on a distinct dimension (or dimension-type).[43] In other words, the marked and the unmarked members of the antonym pair are each associated with a distinct dimension or dimension-type (rather than being associated with a single dimension or dimension-type and scales on that single dimension or dimension-type with inverse orientations). Bierwisch's signal example of such an antonym pair is "good"/"bad." In fact, Bierwisch refers to this subset of relative gradable adjectives as "evaluative adjectives." However, given my distinct use of "evaluative" here and throughout this study, I will instead call this class of an-tonym pairs "bidimensional."[44]

Adapting Bierwisch's view to the terms of my analysis, "good" and "bad" would not be associated with the same dimension-type. "Good" would be as-sociated with the dimension-type of specific value, that is, purpose serving. Consequently, the specific value thesis would be true. In turn, "bad" would be associated with a dimension-type to which I have yet to give a name. Call it "dis-value." In any case, the dimension-type with which "bad" is associated is pur-pose thwarting. Furthermore, although the term generic "value" cannot denote

---

[43] Bierwisch (1987), especially 199–219.
[44] Compare: "destructive"/"creative," "hateful"/"loving," "sad"/"happy," "unpleasant"/"pleasant." Observe that in none of these cases is there a generic *gradable* property that can explain the semantics of both members of the pair.

a dimension-type, it can and indeed does denote the concatenation of two dimension-types. This may be represented as follows:[45]

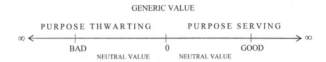

Note here that neutral value comprises certain degrees of both purpose serving and purpose thwarting, namely non-significant degrees.

Assume then that "good" and "bad" are associated with distinct, albeit semantically related dimension-types. And so assume that the specific value thesis is true. One consequence of this result is that I must emend or simply reject a claim regarding conditions for gradable antonymy that I introduced in section 2 of chapter 3. That claim was

> For an antonym pair of gradable adjectives *a* and *b*, the scales that are associated with *a* and *b* are based on the same gradable property.

The present proposal distinguishes a class of bidimensional antonym pairs, for which this claim does not hold. Consequently, precisely how conditions for gradable antonymy should be determined is unclear.

Beyond this problem, it also remains to consider whether my present commitments regarding the antonymy of "good" and "bad" are consistent with a range of other considerations. One especially problematic consideration is this. According to the present proposal, an entity that serves a purpose to any degree cannot be bad in the relevant respect, that is, with respect to that purpose. It could only have neutral value or be good. But this is questionable. For example, consider test taking. If Jett gets a D on a test and Dax gets an A on that test, then Jett gets a bad grade and Dax gets a good grade. According to my proposal, this entails that Jett's grade significantly thwarts the relevant purpose. But is that correct? What is the purpose that Jett's grade is thwarting? Could it be scoring in the upper quartile of test takers?

Even if something along these lines is the correct way to explain Jett's and Dax's bad and good grades, consider the following problem. Two entities may serve a purpose, but to different degrees. Consequently, one will be better than the other (in that respect). But now consider the following claims:

---

[45]   Cp. Bierwisch's diagram #403 at (1987) 212.

57. If *x* is better than *y*, then *y* is worse than *x*.

Conversely:

58. If *y* is worse than *x*, then *x* is better than *y*.

If (57) and (58) are true, then an account of the semantics of "good" and "bad" must be compatible with them and be capable of explaining them. But insofar as "good" and "bad" are not associated with scales with inverse orientations based on the same dimension-type, it is unclear how to explain (57) and (58). Precisely, how can the term "worse" apply to a scale based on the dimension-type associated with "good"? And how can the term "better" apply to a scale based on the dimension-type associated with "bad"?

The ostensible solution to this problem is to maintain that while "good" and "bad" are associated with distinct dimension-types, the scales with which their comparative forms "better" and "worse" are associated are in fact based on two dimension-types, precisely on the concatenation of the dimension-types associated with "good" and "bad." The antonymous comparatives will therefore share the same bidimensional structure, while, like other antonym pairs, having inverse scalar orientations. The main cost of this solution is that the semantics of each of the comparative forms, "better" and "worse," will not be derivable simply from the basic forms "good" and "bad."

Finally, to be clear, the general problem here is not with the dimension-type associated with "good." I can consistently maintain that "good" is associated with the dimension-type of specific value, where having specific value requires purpose serving. The problem is how to elaborate this view in terms of the semantics of "bad" and of the evident truth of (57) and of (58).

I will leave these problems of the antonymy of "good" and "bad" unresolved. Going forward, I will assume the specific value thesis, again that "good" is associated with the dimension-type of specific value.

## 3. Quality and Value

I have now completed my discussion of the first and main point regarding the explanatory adequacy of the value thesis. Recall that the basic concern here was that value is obscure. More precisely, in the value thesis, it is unclear what "value" denotes. The second and minor point regarding the explanatory adequacy of the value thesis concerns the relation between value and quality. In an effort to clarify this relation, I begin by clarifying the sense of "quality" at issue.

"Quality" occurs as a count noun and as a mass noun. The existence of a count noun "quality" is confirmed by the fact that it admits pluralization; for example:

59s.   One quality of the alloy is its hardness.

59p.   Increasing the platinum content will affect the qualities of the alloy, especially its hardness.

60s.   One quality a successful entrepreneur needs is creativity.

60p.   A successful entrepreneur needs two qualities: creativity and optimism.

As a count noun, "quality" is semantically akin to the count nouns "attribute" and "characteristic." We can felicitously substitute "qualities" for these terms in the examples just given:

59s'.   One attribute / characteristic of the alloy is its hardness.

59p'.   Increasing the platinum content will affect the attributes / characteristics of the alloy, especially its hardness.

60s'.   One attribute / characteristic a successful entrepreneur needs is creativity.

60p'.   A successful entrepreneur needs two attributes / characteristics: creativity and optimism.

In the following examples, "quality" is a mass noun:

61m.   This is a good quality shoe / vacuum cleaner / toaster.[46]

62m.   The quality of the painting / performance / service / institution is good.

63m.   He is a man of good quality.

64m.   The quality of their relationship / her life is good.

As so used, "good quality" or "quality that is good" is substitutable for "high quality" or "quality that is high":

61h.   This is a high-quality shoe / vacuum cleaner / toaster.

62h.   The quality of the painting / performance / service / institution is high.

63h.   He is a man of high quality.

64h.   The quality of their relationship / her life is high.

---

[46] Note that the count noun "shoe / vacuum cleaner / toaster," not "quality," is taking the indefinite article here.

That "quality" is a mass noun here may not be obvious. One reason for this non-obviousness is that the plural count noun "qualities" admits "good" modification and predication:

61c.   The shoe / vacuum cleaner / toaster has good qualities.
62c.   The qualities of the painting / performance / service / institution are good.
63c.   He is a man of good qualities.
64c.   The qualities of their relationship / her life are good.

But, as I noted in the preceding section, one property of mass nouns is that they are syntactically acceptable in argument or predicate position without determiners; for example:

65a.   Good quality is rare in the auto repair business.
65b.   He is a man of good quality.
65c.   The fabric is good quality.

In (65a)–(65c), "quality" is modified, but only by the adjective "good." I also note in passing that (65a) and (65b) have the same meaning if the adjective "good" is dropped:

65a'.   Quality is rare in the auto repair business.
65b'.   He is a man of quality.

Consequently, the mass noun "quality" is polysemous. In accordance with the treatments of "moral" and "value," I could refer to the polysemes as "generic 'quality'" and "specific (that is, positive) 'quality'" respectively. However, for the sake of simplicity, I will hereafter ignore the polyseme of specific "quality" and so limit my consideration to generic "quality." Instead, since my focus will be on the relation between the mass noun "quality" and the count noun "quality," I will refer to the former as "evaluative 'quality'" and to the latter as "non-evaluative 'quality.'"

What, if anything, is the relation between evaluative and non-evaluative quality? One possibility is that neither one is necessary for the other. In particular, evaluative quality does not require non-evaluative quality. But this idea should strike one immediately as implausible; and indeed I reject it. Consider a good-quality knife. A knife is of good quality in part on account of certain of its non-evaluative qualities, for example, the sharpness of its blade, the graspability of its handle, and the weight distribution between the handle and the blade. I suggest, then, that the evaluative quality of an entity $x$ is partially constituted by and therefore partially to be explained in terms of $x$'s non-evaluative qualities.

More precisely, it is a subset of the non-evaluative qualities of $x$ that partially constitute $x$'s evaluative quality. This is because some of the non-evaluative qualities of $x$ are simply irrelevant to its evaluative quality. For example, the fact that a knife was manufactured on a Thursday, packaged by a man of Lithuanian descent, or sent to its purchaser by a vehicle with Nebraska license plates is per se irrelevant to its evaluative quality. For convenience, I will call the subset of non-evaluative qualities of $x$ that contribute to $x$'s evaluative quality the "evaluatively relevant" non-evaluative qualities of $x$.

In some, perhaps most cases, the set of evaluatively relevant non-evaluative qualities of $x$ will consist of more than one member. That is, for some entities, a plurality of its non-evaluative qualities, rather than just one non-evaluative quality, contribute to its evaluative quality. For example, as just suggested, there are several attributes of a knife that contribute to its being a good- or bad-quality knife. The evaluative quality of an entity $x$ will then, in part, owe to the aggregate of its evaluatively relevant non-evaluative qualities.

I say that the evaluative quality of an entity $x$ owes, *in part*, to the aggregate of its evaluatively relevant non-evaluative qualities. The evaluative quality of an entity $x$ also owes to the purpose that $x$ has. As I have explained, generic value is purpose contribution; and specific value is purpose serving. In light of these considerations, I suggest that generic value and evaluative quality are related as follows:

The generic value of $x$ is the purpose contribution that $x$ makes.

The evaluative quality of $x$ is the purpose contribution that the aggregate of evaluatively relevant non-evaluative qualities of $x$ makes.

Later I will precisify the account of evaluative quality still further. But presently, note that since the purpose contribution that $x$ makes depends on the purpose contribution that the aggregate of evaluatively relevant non-evaluative qualities of $x$ makes, generic value depends on evaluative quality. Moreover, since the evaluatively relevant non-evaluative qualities of $x$ are partly constitutive of $x$, evaluative quality depends on generic value. In short, generic value and evaluative quality are interdependent.

Granted this, as the descriptions given above suggest, generic "value" and evaluative "quality" do not have the same meaning. Indeed, the non-synonymy of generic "value" and evaluative "quality" is easily demonstrated. In the following sentence, "value" cannot be substituted by "quality":

66v. The value of the appliance is due as much to its durability and
multifunctionality as its price.

66q. # The quality of the appliance is due as much to its durability and
multifunctionality as its price.

The reason that evaluative "quality" is unacceptable in (66q) owes to the fact
that evaluative "quality" requires characteristic purpose contribution. Previously
I claimed that the evaluative quality of $x$ is the purpose contribution that the
aggregate of evaluatively relevant non-evaluative qualities of $x$ makes. More
precisely:

The evaluative quality of $x$ is the contribution that the aggregate of evaluatively
relevant non-evaluative qualities of $x$ makes *to $x$'s characteristic purpose.*

In contrast, generic value does not require characteristic purpose contribution.
Accordingly, the appliance example is problematic with evaluative "quality" because the affordability of an appliance is extrinsic to its contribution to its characteristic purpose. In contrast, its durability and multifunctionality are (plausibly)
intrinsic to its contribution to its characteristic purpose. Consequently, (66q)
becomes acceptable if reference to the price of the appliance is dropped:

66d. The quality of the appliance is due to its durability and
multifunctionality.

Conversely, if we refer only to price, the resulting alteration to (66q) is
unacceptable:

66p. # The quality of the appliance is due to its price.

Contrast the more acceptable

66r. The quality of the appliance is related to its price.

The acceptability of (66r) owes to the substitution of the relation denoting expression "is due to" by the weaker relation denoting expression "in relation
to." There is at least a plausible relation between the cost of an appliance and its
quality. As it is said, good quality is rarely cheap.

Since the generic value of an entity $x$ has no purpose restriction, the generic value of an appliance may be a function of its affordability as well as those

properties relevant to the contribution it makes to its characteristic purpose. When purchasing appliances, customers take affordability as well as properties such as durability and multifunctionality into account.

The same considerations explain the following pair of sentences:

67v.   The value of the painting lies less in its handling of its chosen subject matter than in the influence that choice had on other nineteenth-century artists.

67q.   # The quality of the painting lies less in its handling of its chosen subject matter than in the influence that choice had on other nineteenth-century artists.

The characteristic purpose of a painting is aesthetic; and the handling of its chosen subject matter crucially contributes to its aesthetic purpose. In contrast, the influence of the chosen subject matter on other artists of the period is extrinsic to the contribution that the painting makes to its aesthetic purpose. Accordingly, if we drop reference to that influence, the sentence becomes acceptable:

67d.   The quality of the painting is due to its handling of its chosen subject matter.

In contrast, the value of a painting is not limited to its aesthetic value. For example, a painting can have historical value. And it is precisely historical value that is incorporated in (67v), the version of the sentence that uses the term "value."

In light of this distinction, compare the following sentences; and assume, for the sake of illustration, that the painting in question derives from the studio of Rembrandt and was produced collaboratively by Rembrandt and some of his apprentices:

The fact that Rembrandt assisted in the production of the painting enhances its value.

?? The fact that Rembrandt assisted in the production of the painting enhances its quality.

Strictly speaking, the *fact* that Rembrandt assisted in the production of the painting is extrinsic to the quality of the painting.[47] Contrast this with

---

[47] Compare: "The fact that George Washington once owned this chair enhances its value / # quality."

Rembrandt's contribution to the painting enhanced its quality.[48]

Consider now the following sentence in which evaluative "quality" is acceptable and generic "value" is unacceptable:

68q.  The fact that he happened to be present when the tragic event occurred in no way impugns the quality of his character.

68v.  # The fact that he happened to be present when the tragic event occurred in no way impugns the value of his character.

The unacceptability of (68v) seems to be due to the fact that "value" is not restricted to characteristic purpose. Indeed, absent an explicit specification of the kind of value in question, "value" here does not require characteristic purpose. Why "value" does not here require characteristic purpose, given the immediate linguistic context is, I confess, difficult to understand. Nonetheless, if we modify "value" by "moral," which specifies the characteristic purpose associated with human character, the acceptability of the sentence is ameliorated:

68m.  The fact that he happened to be present when the tragic event occurred in no way impugns the moral value of his character.

I will conclude this discussion of the relation between value and quality by noting one further point in support of the semantic distinction between generic "value" and evaluative "quality." Consider the following sentences:

69a.  ?? Paolo's height is tall.
69b.  ?? Sloan's age is young.
69c.  ?? The cabinet's weight is heavy.

In each of (69a)–(69c), a relative gradable adjective is, peculiarly, predicated of the dimension with which it is associated. The reason for the peculiarity of such sentences is that they mean that the dimension—here height, age, and weight—is predicated of itself. For example, the basic sentence "$x$ is tall" means "$x$ has significant height." Hence "Paolo's height is tall" means "Paolo's height has significant height."[49]

---

[48] The past tense here helps to convey that it was as a *result* of Rembrandt's assistance that the quality of the painting was (positively) affected.

[49] Note here that "height," "age," and "weight" also occur as count nouns; and in such cases the following are felicitous: "Six feet is a tall height for a woman"; "Twenty years old is a young age for a city council member"; "Thirty pounds is a heavy weight for a cat." Observe that in all of these cases, the nouns "height," "age," and "weight" are preceded by the indefinite article.

Consequently, felicitous predication must be of the entity that bears the dimension; for example:

Paolo is tall.
Sloan is young.
The cabinet is heavy.

In light of this, we would expect "good" predication of "value" to be unacceptable or at least awkward; and it is:

?? The painting's value is good.
?? The value of the painting is good.[50]

In contrast, "good" predication of evaluative "quality" is fine:

The painting's quality is good.
The quality of the painting is good.

Compare:

The painting is good.

The reason evaluative "quality" admits "good" predication seems to be due to the fact that an aggregate of certain qualities of the subject $x$, namely evaluatively relevant non-evaluative qualities of $x$, are part of the denotation of evaluative "quality." These qualities, both individually and in aggregate, admit "good" predication. To return to the knife example, we may say: the sharpness of the blade is good, the graspability of the handle is good, the weight distribution is good; and we may say that collectively these various features are good.

## 4. Multidimensionality

For the remainder of this study, unless otherwise noted, I will use the term "value" in the specific sense. As such, "$x$ has value" entails "$x$ is purposive." Accordingly, the value thesis, namely that value is the dimension-type associated with "good,"

---

[50] Such sentences are arguably less problematic than those originally cited such as "Paolo's height is tall" for the following reason: value of a given kind may have value of a different kind.

is to be understood in the terms of the specific value thesis, namely that specific value, which is purpose serving, is the dimension-type associated with "good."

Granted this, I return now to the thesis that "good" is multidimensional. In terms of the value thesis, the multidimensionality of "good" is explained by the fact that value is specifiable by kind. From the time that I introduced evaluative "good" in section 1 of chapter 2, I provided examples such as "This painting is good," which may be read in terms of aesthetic value, and "That person is good," which may be read in terms of moral value.

Given the thesis that value is purpose serving, the multidimensionality of "good" is explicable in terms of the fact that purpose serving is specifiable by kind. This specifiability is conceivable in at least two ways. One way is in terms of what I called kinds of service contributions. For example, there are instrumental and non-instrumental kinds of value and so ways of being good. But this way of specifying kinds of purpose serving does not correspond to the multidimensionality of "good." Distinctions between, say, aesthetic and moral value are themselves different in type from distinctions such as that between instrumental and non-instrumental value. Rather, the specifiability by kind of purpose serving that corresponds to the specifiability by kind of value that explains the multidimensionality of "good" is in terms of the specifiability of purpose.

I have suggested that there are at least four fundamentally different kinds of purposes: biological purposes; characteristic artificial purposes; and ad hoc purposes, some derived from intentions, others from non-practical desires. Each of these four basic kinds in turn subsumes countless, in some cases, in principle infinite sub-kinds of purposes. So the multidimensionality of "good" is explicable in terms of the specifiability of purpose and more precisely in terms of specifiability of at least four basic kinds of purpose. Granted this, it is questionable precisely how such specification occurs in tokenings of "good." In other words, in tokenings of "good," what linguistic operation explains such purpose and so dimensional specification? This is the subject of the following chapter.

# 5

# Dimensional Specification

## 1. Multidimensionality and Dimensional Specification

Multidimensionality is a property of a subset of relative gradable adjectives. It is the property of a relative gradable adjective being associated with a gradable property that is specifiable by kind. I have called gradable properties that are specifiable by kind "dimension-types." Evaluative "good" is a multidimensional gradable adjective. Value, the gradable property with which evaluative "good" is associated, is specifiable by kind and so is a dimension-type. Here and throughout this chapter, unless otherwise noted, I will be concerned with evaluative "good" and so will hereafter drop the modifier "evaluative."

Dimensional specification is the linguistic event in which tokening of a multidimensional adjective involves specification of the dimension-type associated with the adjective. The previous chapter concluded by posing the following question: In tokenings of "good," what linguistic operation explains dimensional specification? In other words, in various contexts of its use, what linguistic operation is responsible for "good" being associated with specific kinds of value?

In the secondary literature, there are several explanations of dimensional specification of "good"—albeit not in the precise terms in which I have articulated the phenomenon here. The various explanations are divisible into two types. According to one, multidimensional adjectives such as "good" are analyzed as having a complex syntactic structure that belies their superficial syntactic simplicity. The true, but non-apparent, syntactic structure is often referred to as the "logical form" or the "deep syntactic structure" of the expression, in this case of the adjective.[1] One of the constituents of the deep syntactic structure is a variable

---

[1] On the relation between the logical form and syntactic structure of a sentence, cp. Jason Stanley: "The logical form of a sentence is something like the 'real structure' of that sentence ... [According to this conception of logical form,] we may discover that the 'real' structure of a natural language sentence is in fact quite distinct from its surface grammatical form. Talk of logical form in this sense involves attributing hidden complexity to sentences of natural language, complexity which is ultimately revealed by empirical inquiry." ("Context and Logical Form," *Linguistics and Philosophy* 23 (2000) 391–434, at 392; this paper is also collected in Jason Stanley, *Language in Context*, Oxford University Press, 2007.) Note that Stanley here refers to Gilbert Harman, "Deep Structure as Logical Form," *Synthese* 21 (1970) 275–97; reprinted in *Semantics of Natural Language*, D. Davidson and G. Harman, eds., Reidel, 1972, 25–47.

or at least functions like a variable. Dimensional specification is then explained in terms of various values or content assignments that this variable constituent receives in various contexts in which "good" is used. Because the deep syntactic structure corresponding to the adjective contains a variable, tokens of the adjective syntactically require that the variable be valued or bound. Accordingly, I will refer to this type of explanation of dimensional specification as "determinism," short for "syntactic structural determinism."[2]

To gain some appreciation for a determinist explanation of dimensional specification, by way of analogy compare the inherent vagueness and relational analyses of gradable adjectives, introduced in section 3.4 of chapter 3. Recall that according to the inherent vagueness analysis, gradable adjectives are, in terms of both their semantic argument structure and their syntactic structure, like non-gradable adjectives. Semantically, both gradable and non-gradable adjectives are analyzed as unary semantic functions and precisely as functions from individuals to truth-values. Recall that in the standard semantic type theoretic notation, such functions are represented as $\langle e,t \rangle$. In contrast, according to the relational analysis, gradable adjectives are analyzed as binary functions that take a degree argument as well as an individual argument: $\langle d,\langle e,t \rangle \rangle$. So, the two analyses interpret the semantic type of gradable adjectives in different ways.

Assuming, if merely for the sake of illustration, a correspondence between semantic and syntactic structure,[3] the syntactic structures in terms of which gradable adjectives are interpreted will therefore differ in accordance with the two different semantic analyses. Precisely, according to the relational analysis, the deep syntactic structure corresponding to the basic sentence, for example "Thiebaud's 1969 *Candy Counter* is good," contains a constituent, conceived as a degree variable, corresponding to the semantic degree argument that the adjective requires. In contrast, according to the inherent vagueness analysis, the deep syntactic structures corresponding to these sentences contain no such variable constituent. Furthermore, in the case of the relational analysis, since basic sentences such as "Thiebaud's 1969 *Candy Counter* is good" are well-formed, yet lack any overt degree argument, the syntactic degree argument that the adjective is assumed to require is covert and so is a constituent of the deep, as opposed to superficial, syntactic structure corresponding to the predicate expression.

---

[2] I underscore that my use of the term "determinism" here is idiosyncratic. In the secondary literature, one rather finds terms such as "covert / hidden indexicalism." Also, I prefer to avoid the expression "logical form." Minimally, if logical form is identical to (deep) syntactic structure, then there is no need to employ two expressions for the same thing.

[3] I have in mind here what Alexander Williams calls "canonical correspondence," according to which "every syntactic argument of an expression is a functional semantic argument, and vice versa." (*Arguments in Syntax and Semantics*, Cambridge University Press, 2015, 89.)

In short, the contrast between the inherent vagueness and relational analyses of gradable adjectives provides an illustration of distinct interpretations of the deep syntactic structure corresponding to a natural language expression; and where one, but not the other, of these interpretations attributes a covert syntactic constituent, conceived as a variable, to that structure. Accordingly, what I am calling a "determinist" interpretation of dimensional specification consists in interpreting the deep, that is, true syntactic structure corresponding to a multidimensional gradable adjective as consisting of a covert syntactic constituent, conceived as a variable, a constituent that does not exist in the deep syntactic structure corresponding to a unidimensional gradable adjective. In the case of multidimensional gradable adjectives, the covert syntactic constituent is naturally understood as a dimension variable. Consequently, in various contexts of felicitous use, the dimension variable associated with the multidimensional gradable adjective receives and is required to receive various dimension-type specifying values.

According to the second type of explanation of dimensional specification, the deep syntactic structure corresponding to "good" or to any other multidimensional gradable adjective does not consist of any such variable constituent.[4] Consequently, some other kind of linguistic operation is responsible for dimensional specification. Crucially, whatever that other type of linguistic operation is, it is not mandated by and in this respect is free from the deep syntactic structure corresponding to the term in question. Contrast this with the determinist position according to which the variable constituent requires a value assignment. In

---

[4] At least, it does not consist of any covert variable constituent that explains dimensional specification. According to a relational analysis, it does consist of a covert degree variable. One might then wonder whether an advocate of the relational analysis might appeal to the degree variable associated with a gradable adjective to explain dimensional specification in determinist terms. On this view, context would provide not only a quantitative value for the degree variable as well as values relating to structural properties of the associated scale, such as un/boundedness and orientation, but also specification of the scale. For example, in one context, the scale associated with "good" might be specified as aesthetic goodness; and in another context, as moral goodness. Call this property of the scale associated with a multidimensional adjective its "specification." Then the degree variable associated with a multidimensional adjective will also have a scale specification variable associated with it or more precisely as a constituent of it. To be clear, this account involves scale specification, not dimensional specification. Nonetheless, presumably scale specification semantically entails dimensional specification. While I acknowledge the theoretical possibility of such a determinist account, I resist exploring it here. Such an account assumes and so depends on a defense of the relational analysis of gradable adjectives and more precisely on a defense of such a dimension specifying role for the degree variable. But I want to remain neutral between the relational and measure function analyses. For example, cp. Sassoon, who commits to a measure function analysis and suggests that the semantics of multidimensional gradable adjectives "includes a dimension parameter" (2013, 337). She then suggests that the syntactic structures corresponding to multidimensional gradable adjectival constructions possibly consist of a "dimension variable" that will be "implicitly saturated or bound" in a given context (338).

accordance with the terminology that I am appropriating from the free will literature, I will refer to this second type of explanation of dimensional specification as "compatibilism."[5] In short, compatibilist explanations of dimensional specification of "good" maintain that dimensional specification is syntactically compatible with, but not syntactically mandated by, the syntactic structure of "good."

The ensuing chapter is structured in two main parts followed by one brief section. Part one, which consists of sections 2.1 through 2.5, focuses on three determinist explanations of dimensional specification of "good." The authors of these accounts are Peter Geach, Zoltán Szabó, and Muffy Siegel respectively. Geach argues that "good" is a so-called logically attributive adjective, and as such "good" requires a nominal expression as its internal argument. This nominal expression, in effect, serves to specify the dimension-type with which "good" is associated. Szabó argues that "good" is an incomplete unary predicate, one component of which is a so-called role variable. This role variable, in effect, serves to specify the dimension-type with which "good" is associated. Siegel argues that "good" is polysemous and that each of its two polysemes has a distinct syntactic form. According to one of these, "good" is a type of so-called predicate modifier. A predicate modifier is an expression that syntactically requires a predicate and where the complex expression consisting of the predicate modifier and the predicate that it requires constitutes a predicate. Semantically, Siegel interprets this polyseme of "good" as a function from the intension of a unary function to the intension of a unary function. In this respect, Siegel's position is akin to Geach's. Both hold that the (nominal) predicate expression that "good" requires effectively serves to specify the dimension-type with which it is associated.

It should be noted that neither Geach nor Szabó recognizes or at least considers that "good" is a gradable adjective; and so neither considers an interpretation of "good" in terms of a degree argument. The composition date of Geach's paper, 1956, of course predates degree-based interpretations of gradable adjectives. Siegel does recognize that "good" is a gradable adjective, but, here too, the composition date of her work, 1976, concurs with Max Cresswell's introduction of a degree-based interpretive framework; and Siegel does not consider an interpretation of either polyseme of "good" in terms of a degree argument. Accordingly, in this chapter I will largely ignore discussion of a degree argument that might be associated with gradable adjectives. I underscore that this is a mere convenience for the sake of simplifying a complex discussion whose focus is elsewhere.

I criticize all three determinist treatments of "good" on various grounds. Granted this, the determinist accounts adduce several considerations that

---

[5] More commonly, what I am calling "determinism" is contrasted with so-called free pragmaticism. But I resist using the latter term since, as I will show, some compatibilist forms of dimensional specification involve semantic rather than pragmatic operations.

I believe any adequate explanation of dimensional specification of "good" must address. Among these considerations are the inferential properties of "good" in three types of inference schemas, which I call "*AN* splitting," "simple transfer inference," and "quantified transfer inference," respectively. I return to these inference schemas in part two of the chapter and consider how the constructive account that I ultimately defend can explain them.[6]

Part two of the chapter, which consists of sections 3.1 through 3.8, considers two types of compatibilist explanation of dimensional specification of "good." One is modulation by means of ad hoc conceptualization. The other is what I call "supplementation." Broadly speaking, compatibilist explanations of linguistic meaning are widespread in the linguistic and philosophical literature. But compatibilist explanations of dimensional specification of "good" in particular are almost non-existent.

To my knowledge, Ingrid Falkum is the only linguist or philosopher who appeals to modulation by means of ad hoc conceptualization to explain dimensional specification of "good." According to Falkum, the literal meaning of

---

[6] I note in passing here that one argument that some determinists—although not Geach, Szabó, or Siegel—have appealed to in support of their position is the so-called Binding Argument, which was originally presented by Stanley (2000). Cp. Adam Sennet, "The Binding Argument and Pragmatic Enrichment, or, Why Philosophers Care Even More Than Weathermen about 'Raining,'" *Philosophy Compass* 3 (2008) 135–57; Paul Elbourne, "The Argument from Binding," *Philosophical Perspectives* 22 (2008) 89–110; as well as discussions prior to Stanley's paper by Barbara Partee, "Binding Implicit Variables in Quantified Contexts," *Papers from the 25th Regional Meeting of the Chicago Linguistic Society*, C. Wiltshire, R. Grazyte, and B. Music, eds., Chicago Linguistic Society, 1989, 342–56; and Cleo Condoravdi and Jean Mark Gawron, "The Context-Dependency of Implicit Arguments," *Quantifiers, Deduction, and Context*, M. Kanazawa, C. Piñón, and H. de Swart, eds., CSLI, 1996, 1–32. In his paper, Stanley is principally concerned with covert syntactic constituents associated with verbal predicate expressions, in particular "rain." (For the focus on "rain," cp. John Perry, "Indexicals, Contexts, and Unarticulated Constituents," in A. Aliseda-Llera et al., eds., *Computing Natural Language*, CSLI Publications, 1998, 1–11.) Stanley does not discuss the adjective "good," and—so far as I am aware—no proponent of determinism has applied the Binding Argument to the interpretation of "good." However, the Binding Argument arguably could be applied to "good." For example, consider sentences such as "In whatever genre she writes, Janet is good"; "At whatever position the rookie plays, he is good." Beyond this footnote, however, I have chosen not to discuss the Binding Argument further. I find the Binding Argument unpersuasive on both semantic and more fundamentally syntactic grounds. For semantic criticisms of the Binding Argument, cp. Kent Bach, "Quantification, Qualification, and Context: A Reply to Stanley and Szabó," *Mind and Language* 15 (2000) 262–83; François Recanati, "Unarticulated Constituents," *Linguistics and Philosophy* 25 (2002) 299–345 (but note also the response to Recanati's paper in Luisa Martí, "Unarticulated Constituents Revisited," *Linguistics and Philosophy* 29 (2006) 135–66); Allison Hall, "Free Enrichment or Hidden Indexicals," *Mind and Language* 23 (2008) 426–56, especially at 428–33; Lenny Clapp, "Three Challenges for Indexicalism," *Mind and Language* 27 (2012) 435–65. For syntactic criticisms, cp. John Collins, "Syntax, More or Less," *Mind* 116 (2007) 805–50; Francesco Pupa and Erika Troseth, "Syntax and Interpretation," *Mind and Language* 26 (2011) 185–209; John Collins, "The Nature of Linguistic Variables," in *Oxford Handbooks Online*, 2014. Cp. also the general discussions in Rajesh Bhatt and Roumyana Pancheva, "Implicit Arguments," in *Blackwell Companion to Syntax*, M. Everaert and H. van Riemsdijk, eds., Blackwell, 2006, 558–88; and Williams (2015) 94–118. Regarding the syntactic problems, consider a sentence such as "Whenever Leonard visits Philadelphia, it rains." The expression "Whenever Leonard visits Philadelphia" is an adjunct free relative. Cp. Henk van Riemsdijk, "Free Relatives," in Everaert and van Riemsdijk (2006) 338–82.

"good" is modulated, that is, adjusted, and precisely narrowed relative to the very general lexical meaning of "good." Such narrowing, which in effect amounts to dimensional specification, is explained in terms of so-called ad hoc conceptualization. Ad hoc conceptualization consists of ad hoc mental tokening of a concept, called an "ad hoc concept." The content of the ad hoc concept, which in this case is symbolized as GOOD*, is narrower than that of the concept GOOD corresponding to the lexical meaning of "good." (Note that I follow standard practice in using capitals to denote mental content or concepts.) The narrower concept GOOD* provides what I call the "semantic grounding," that is, the modulated, precisely narrowed meaning of the token of "good."[7] I criticize Falkum's account as incoherent. Moreover, I suggest that she conflates ad hoc conceptualization with conceptual combination. For example, the so-called ad hoc concept GOOD* is simply a complex of concepts such as AESTHETICALLY GOOD or GOOD AT SPELLING.

Supplementation is my own and so is a novel explanation of dimensional specification. I propose that supplementation is realized in two principal ways: by garden variety modification and by a pragmatic phenomenon that I dub "reciprocal modification." Garden variety modification of "good" that effects dimensional specification consists of an adverb or a prepositional phrase modifying "good"; for example:

This is *morally* good.
That is good *for growing roses.*

Observe that in the latter case, the prepositional phrase functions adverbially. So both kinds of garden variety modification of "good" in fact involve adverbial modification.

In contrast, reciprocal modification consists of a nominal expression semantically modifying the adjective that syntactically modifies it. Examples of expressions in which reciprocal modification of "good" effects dimensional specification are

He is a good *father.*
This is good *bread.*

Precisely, the nominal expression $N$ that "good" syntactically modifies semantically modifies the adjective "good" by freely pragmatically enriching the adjectival phrase with an implicit adverbial modifier whose content

---

[7] Note that Falkum too does not recognize or consider "good" as a gradable adjective.

derives from the content of *N*. The implicit adverbial modifier + "good" phrase has the sense of "good in the typical or at least contextually salient way that an *N* is good." For example, in the sentence "He is a good father," "He is good" means "He is good in the typical or at least contextually salient way that a father is good"; and in the sentence "This is good bread," "This is good" means "This is good in the typical or at least contextually salient way that bread is good." I suggest that reciprocal modification is a widespread phenomenon. In other words, the occurrence of reciprocal modification in the dimensional specification of "good" is just one way in which reciprocal modification is realized. At the same time, reciprocal modification has not been recognized as such.

Supplementation is further complicated by the fact that the so-called supplement, namely the adverbial expression that modifies "good" or the nominal expression that "good" modifies, may be elided. I characterize such ellipsis as "semantic ellipsis" and contrast it with both syntactic and implicative ellipsis. I underscore that semantic ellipsis is to be distinguished from, although it may occur in conjunction with, pragmatic enrichment of the adjective phrase by an implicit adverbial modifier in cases of reciprocal modification.

After clarifying the semantic and syntactic implications of supplementation and how it can explain the inferential properties of "good" in *AN* splitting, simple, and quantified transfer inference, I also consider pro-form replacement tests to corroborate supplementation as an explanation of dimensional specification of "good."

Finally, the short section 4 that concludes the chapter suggests that an operation akin to supplementation explains how the comparison class and standard of comparison associated with a relative gradable adjective is determined in a context of use.

## 2.1. Three Determinist Explanations of Dimensional Specification

I begin with three determinist explanations of dimensional specification, those of Geach, Szabó, and Siegel, in that order.

## 2.2. Geach on "Good" as a Logically Attributive Adjective

In 1956, when Geach published his short, seminal article "Good and Evil," non-cognitivist and non-descriptivist views of ethical and generally evaluative thought and language were dominant in mainstream anglophone philosophy. According to non-cognitivism, evaluative concepts do not contribute to propositional contents and therefore cannot be contents of cognitive attitudes such as belief and knowledge. According to non-descriptivism, evaluative terms do not contribute to the truth-conditions of utterances and therefore cannot be contents of assertions. Some striking expressions of these views from the thirties by Wittgenstein, Carnap, and Russell follow:

> My whole tendency and the tendency of all men who ever tried to write or talk Ethics or Religion was to run against the boundaries of language. This running against the walls of our cage is perfectly, absolutely hopeless. Ethics so far as it springs from the desire to say something about the ultimate meaning of life, the absolute good, the absolute valuable, can be no science. What it says does not add to our knowledge.[8]

> In the domain of metaphysics, including the philosophy of value and normative theory, logical analysis yields the negative result that the alleged statements in this domain are entirely meaningless.[9]

> Questions as to "values" lie wholly outside the domain of knowledge. That is to say when we say that this or that has "value," we are giving expression to our own emotions, not to a fact which would still be true if our feelings were different.[10]

In his article, Geach is particularly concerned to criticize the version of non-descriptivism endorsed in Richard Hare's 1952 *The Language of Morals* and called "prescriptivism." According to Hare, "good" has a commendatory, rather than a descriptive, meaning. As such, sentences of the form "*x* is good" are not used to make assertions, but to commend *x* to their audiences. Against Hare, Geach argues that "good" has a descriptive meaning.

Central to his defense of this semantic thesis, Geach draws what he calls a "logical" distinction between two kinds of adjectives, adjectives that he accordingly calls "logically attributive" and "logically predicative." This terminology loosely relates to the traditional grammatical distinction between attributive and predicative adjectives, that is, to adjectives occurring in attributive and predicative positions. The traditional grammatical distinction is then a syntactic one.

---

[8] Ludwig Wittgenstein, "I: A Lecture on Ethics," *Philosophical Review* 74 (1965) 1–12, at 12. The lecture from which this quotation derives was originally delivered in late 1929 or early 1930.
[9] Rudolf Carnap, "Überwindung der Metaphysik durch logische Analyse der Sprache," *Erkenntnis* 2 (1932) 219–41; translated in A. J. Ayer, ed., *Logical Positivism*, Free Press, 1959, 60–81, at 60–61.
[10] Bertrand Russell, *Science and Religion*, Oxford University Press, 1935, 230–31.

When an adjective modifies a nominal expression, the adjective is attributive. For example, "gray" is attributive in the following two sentences:

That is a gray mouse.
The gray mouse is sleeping.

I underscore that "gray" is attributive because it modifies a nominal expression, and regardless of whether the entire phrase "a / the gray mouse" is in the subject or predicate position within the sentence. In contrast, when an adjective constitutes the predicate expression in a sentence, the adjective is predicative. For example, "gray" is predicative in the following sentence:

The mouse is gray.

Geach's argument for the distinction between logically attributive and logically predicative adjectives turns on certain inferences that these two types of adjectives license or prohibit.[11] Geach focuses on the following inference schema, which he does not name, but which I will call "*AN* splitting." Assume that *A* stands for an adjective and that *N* stands for a common nominal expression:

*x is A N.*

_____

*x is A.*
*x is N.*[12]

I'll call the first inference the "adjectival inference" and the second inference the "nominal inference." Geach's account turns on the adjectival inference. His claim is that only certain adjectives license the adjectival inference. Such adjectives are the ones that he calls "logically predicative." Other adjectives do not license the adjectival inference; and these adjectives are the ones that he calls "logically attributive."

For example, consider the adjective "gray" in the following *AN* splitting argument:

Casey is a gray mouse.

_____

Casey is gray.
Casey is a mouse.

---

[11] Throughout this discussion, I speak of "inferences" rather than "entailments." One could recast the discussion in terms of entailments with minor adjustments.

[12] Note that throughout this chapter I often use the same fonts for symbols in the main text as I use in the examples set off from the main text. This is done to avoid confusion.

Both inferences are valid. So the adjective "gray" admits *AN* splitting and is therefore logically predicative. In other words, regardless of whether "gray" occurs in predicate position, as in the adjectival inference, or in attributive position, as in the premise, "gray" is a logically predicative adjective.[13]

Contrast "gray" with "large" in the following *AN* splitting argument:

Casey is a large mouse.

---

Casey is large.
Casey is a mouse.

Geach maintains that the adjectival inference here is invalid: although Casey is a large mouse, he is not large. That is, Casey is not a large animal or a large thing. Consequently, "large" is a logically attributive adjective.

The central thesis of Geach's paper is that "good" is a logically attributive adjective. For instance, consider the following argument:

Bernie is a good lawyer.

---

Bernie is good.
Bernie is a lawyer.

Again, Geach maintains that the adjectival inference here is invalid: although Bernie is a good lawyer, he need not be good. That is, Bernie may be a bad man or a bad person.[14]

I pause here to remark on the sense in which the logically attributive and logically predicative adjective distinction is a logical distinction. Geach himself does not clarify this matter. One possibility is that Geach employs the term "logical(ly)" here because he is concerned with the inferential properties of the adjectives. But observe then that licensing of or prohibition on *AN* splitting is not a matter of logical inference. That is, the inferential properties in question are not properties of logical terms such as conjunction or negation. Rather, the inferential properties are properties of adjectives.

Instead, Geach's use of "logical(ly)" might be explained in terms of the deep, as opposed to superficial, syntactic properties of the adjectives in question. Superficially, a logically attributive adjective such as "good" may appear in predicate position without overtly modifying a nominal expression. However, so Geach thinks, a covert nominal expression must be understood; and this explains

---

[13] Although "gray mouse" admits *AN* splitting, "gray" and other color terms do not always license *AN* splitting. I discuss this topic in section 3.6.4.
[14] Again, I find the adjectival inference questionable. I return to this topic in section 3.6.4.

the adjective's distinctive inferential properties. I propose to understand Geach's use of "logical(ly)" in this way—whether or not it accords with his original intention. In short, Geach is concerned with what others have referred to as the "logical forms" corresponding to the two classes of adjectives and what I prefer to refer to as the "deep syntactic structures" corresponding to the adjectives of these classes.

A logically predicative adjective corresponds to a unary predicate. A logically attributive adjective corresponds to a binary predicate, whose internal argument is itself a predicate, and more precisely a predicate corresponding to an explicit or implicit nominal expression (such as "mouse" or "lawyer" in the arguments above). So understood, the internal argument of the binary predicate corresponding to "good" might be understood as a dimension variable. For instance, in the Bernie argument, the nominal expression "lawyer" in the premise "Bernie is a good lawyer" specifies the dimension-type associated with "good" as lawyer value; whereas in the adjectival inference, the implicit nominal expression "man" or "person" specifies the dimension-type associated with "good" as moral value.

I will return to Geach's position and to *AN* splitting in the ensuing discussion. Presently, I turn to Szabó's interpretation of "good" as an incomplete unary predicate.

## 2.3.  Szabó on "Good" as an Incomplete Unary Predicate

Szabó's interpretation of "good" occurs in his 2001 paper "Adjectives in Context." The principal concern of Szabó's paper is not the semantics or syntax of "good." Rather, consideration of the semantics and syntax of "good" plays a central role within a broader discussion whose focus is the relation between context and the semantic principle of compositionality. Precisely, Szabó is concerned with the question whether the role that context may play in determining the content of a complex expression jeopardizes the principle of compositionality. In examining this question, Szabó is specifically concerned with context-sensitive predicate expressions and more precisely with context-sensitive adjectives. He focuses on "good" for two reasons. One is historical: through the twentieth century, "good" has played a central role in theories of adjectival semantics. The other and more important reason is that Szabó takes "good" to be a paradigm case of the kind of context-sensitive adjective that interests him, namely an adjective that he interprets as an incomplete unary predicate, one aspect or part of which is a variable of some kind.

According to the version of the compositionality principle that concerns Szabó, the literal meaning, which is to say, the truth-conditional content of a complex expression, say, an atomic declarative sentence, depends on the literal meanings of its constituents, the syntactic structure of those constituents, and nothing else.[15] Observe that what Szabó calls "the Context Thesis" is consistent with his commitment to the principle of compositionality, so understood. According to the Context Thesis:

> The content of a complex expression may depend on context, but only insofar as the contents of its constituents do.[16]

For example, consider the following complex expression:

1. I was born in Pretoria.

Sentence (1) contains an indexical expression, the first-person pronoun "I." Consequently, the content of an utterance of (1) depends on context insofar as the content of its indexical constituent "I" does. For example, if Gail asserts (1), the proposition, that is, the truth-conditional content, that she expresses is: Gail was born in Pretoria; and what she asserts is true. If Joe asserts (1), the proposition that he expresses is: Joe was born in Pretoria; and what he asserts is false. The contents, that is, literal meanings of "I" in the two contexts of the utterance are Gail and Joe respectively. So again, the content or literal meaning of a complex expression may depend on context, but only insofar as the contents of its constituents, such as the constituent "I," do.

That context contributes to the content of constituents like indexicals is not in dispute. Indeed, in the case of indexicals, this is true by definition. Indexicals are expressions whose lexical meanings encode semantic rules that specify the contribution of context to the determination of content. The question is whether context can contribute to the literal meaning of a complex expression in a way that is not mandated by the constituents of the complex expression. We might conveniently distinguish the former as "determinist" contextual contributions and the latter as "compatibilist" contextual contributions.

In considering the possibility of compatibilist contextual contributions, we should also be mindful of the distinction between truth-conditional and non-truth-conditional compatibilist contextual contributions. Recall the distinction, introduced in section 3.3 of chapter 3, between what is said or asserted and what is implicated. Again, that implicature occurs is not in dispute. For example, when, as I walk out of the kitchen, Janet says to me: "There are dishes in the sink," the truth-conditional content of her utterance is that there are dishes in the sink;

---

[15] Szabó (2001) 119.
[16] Szabó (2001) 122.

but what Janet implicates by her assertion is that I ought to do the dishes. Again, when a spectator at a tennis match mocks a lousy shot by saying: "That was brilliant," the truth-conditional content of this utterance is that the shot was brilliant; but the ironic remark implicates that the shot was lousy.

That context can compatibilistically contribute to the non-literal, that is, non-truth-conditional content of utterances is not in dispute. The contentious issue is whether context can compatibilistically contribute to fixing the truth-conditional content, that is, literal meaning of an utterance. Indeed, I have already discussed a case in section 3.3 of chapter 3. Recall that according to Rett's theory, in contexts such as the basic sentence, the degree associated with a relative gradable adjective undergoes a semantic adjustment. That is, in "Paolo is tall," the meaning of the predicate expression shifts from denoting some degree of height ("Paolo has some degree of height") to a significant degree of height ("Paolo has a significant degree of height"). Moreover, and crucially, although Rett appeals to aspects of Grice's theory of implicature to explain this adjustment in meaning, she maintains that the adjustment is truth-conditional. As discussed, evidence supporting the truth-conditionality of the semantic adjustment derives from the fact that such content is preserved when embedded under truth-functional operators such as negation and the material conditional; for example: "Paolo is tall"; "Paolo is not tall"; "If Paolo is tall, then he ought to try out for the basketball team." In short, Rett's theory exemplifies a compatibilist contextual contribution to truth-conditional content.[17]

It is this, then, that is at stake in Szabó's defense of the principle of compositionality: denial that context can compatibilistically contribute to the literal meaning, that is truth-conditional content, of a complex expression. Or rather, granted Rett's position, the question is whether Szabó's defense of the principle of compositionality, as he understands this principle, succeeds in the sorts of cases that concern him.

Szabó advances his position in response to an argument by Charles Travis that challenges the compositionality principle.[18] In arguing against the compositionality principle and for free contextual contributions to truth-conditional content, Travis is concerned with the meanings of predicate expressions. In support of his position, Travis focuses on the adjective "green" as it occurs in the sentence "The leaf is green":

---

[17] To be clear—although here it is the meaning of a constituent, namely the degree associated with the relative gradable adjective "tall," that is adjusted, the adjustment is a function of the uninformative meaning of the whole expression ("Paolo has some degree of height"). Consequently, such semantic adjustment does not conform to the Context Thesis.

[18] Charles Travis, "On Constraints of Generality," *Proceedings of the Aristotelian Society* n.s. 44 (1994) 165–88.

The words "is green," while speaking of being green, may make any of indefi-
nitely many distinct contributions to what is said [that is, to the literal meaning]
in words of which they are part . . . The same holds of any English predicate
[expression].[19]

In support of this thesis, Travis invites consideration of the following kind of
situation. Assume that Isabella is using leaves for decoration and paints green
a maple leaf whose natural color is red. In a decorating context, where Isabella
is sorting leaves by painted color, she may, in reference to the maple leaf, truly
say: "The leaf is green." But in describing leaves to identify their species, it could
be false, despite the paint, for her to say: "The leaf is green."[20]
Observe now that the adjective "green" does not appear to be context sensitive
in any familiar way. It is not an indexical of the standard kind such as "I," "here,"
or "now." To be sure, "green" is polysemous. In addition to the color sense, "green"
has the sense of "young" or "inexperienced." But the Travis case obviously does
not turn on this polysemy of "green." The only sense at issue is the color sense. We
may also assume that, in the example, the painted color of the leaf is a paradigmatic shade of green.[21] As such, the contradictory readings cannot be explained
by the fact that "green" is vague; that is, that there are borderline cases of, say,
blue-green or yellow-green, where, depending on additional contextual features,
"green" may or may not be truly predicated of one and the same blue-green or
yellow-green object. Consequently, Szabó admits, unless some aspect of "green"
is responsible for its application in one context to the painted surface of the leaf
and in another context to the natural surface, the sentence "The leaf is green"
presents "a genuine counterexample to the principle of compositionality."[22]
In pursuing an alternative explanation of the context sensitivity of "green,"
Szabó turns to "good." He argues that "good" illustrates a general thesis about the
context sensitivity of adjectives that resolves the problem of the painted leaf example and counters Travis's challenge to the principle of compositionality. Szabó
argues that "good" should be interpreted as an "incomplete" unary predicate.
Here, we need to pause over this peculiar syntactic category.
Qua unary predicate, "good" requires only a subject to constitute a proposition. But, Szabó maintains, the predicate is "incomplete" in that it contains
a variable constituent. Because the predicate contains a variable constituent, it
determines an extension "only if additional information [in this case, a value for

---

[19]  Travis (1994) 172, cited by Szabó (2001) 124.
[20]  I am quoting Travis (1994, 171–72) here almost verbatim, cited by Szabó (2001) 123.
[21]  Note that Szabó also refutes the idea that the phrase "the leaf" is referentially indeterminate,
denoting the leaf with or without the paint. "There is no context in which one can hold up a painted
leaf and say truthfully 'The leaf is unpainted' " (2001, 123–24).
[22]  Szabó (2001) 126.

the variable] is provided."[23] The idea here seems to be that certain predicates, while being unary, are nonetheless syntactically complex, and precisely that they consist of two components or perhaps better two aspects: one whose content is constant, another whose content is variable. It seems questionable to me whether this idea is coherent. It would seem preferable to interpret "good" as a binary predicate whose internal argument is a variable of some kind. On the other hand, the interpretation of "good" as a binary predicate entails that "good" has a certain syntactic complexity that belies its superficial simplicity. Perhaps Szabó's incomplete unary predicate interpretation of "good" (and other adjectives) should be understood by loose analogy with ordinary indexicals, part of whose meaning is context invariant. For example, the content of tokens of "now" is always a time; the content of tokens of "here" is always a place. So the content of tokens of "good" might always be value (in the sense of purpose serving), but different kinds of value in different contexts. In defense of Szabó's proposal, he does suggest that the context sensitivity of "good" and other adjectives of its kind is of a hitherto unrecognized variety.

In any case, whether Szabó's notion of an incomplete unary predicate is ultimately coherent, I believe that we can profitably proceed through the remainder of his account. Accordingly, assume that we represent an ordinary unary predicate as

$$F(x).$$

We might then represent an incomplete unary predicate as

$$(\mathcal{I}(v))(x).$$

Here $\mathcal{I}$ stands for the component or aspect of the predicate whose content is contextually invariant; and $v$ stands for that component or aspect of the predicate whose content is variable. In a given utterance, context determines a value for $v$.[24] Subsequently, I will explain how Szabó employs such an interpretation of "green" to defend the principle of compositionality in response to Travis's green leaf example. But presently, I will continue to focus on Szabó's treatment of "good."

Szabó maintains that the variable constituent of the incomplete unary predicate that corresponds to "good" "stands for a certain role in which something can

---

[23] Szabó (2001) 133.

[24] I underscore that in the preceding formal representations, I have used distinct fonts to distinguish distinct formal syntactic categories. I employ such typographical means throughout the chapter when providing formal representations.

be good."[25] Accordingly, Szabó characterizes this constituent as a "role variable." As such, sentences of the form "*x* is good" entail "*x* is good in some role." The term "role" that Szabó uses here might suggest functionality or purpose serving. As such, Szabó's position would in this respect be akin to the account that I advanced in chapter 4. However, Szabó insists that, as he is using it, the term "role" is merely a place-holder:

> "Role" is used here as a more or less technical term. An actor can be good in a given role. Stretching the meaning of "role" a little, one can say that a good dancer or pianist is good in that role. Perhaps one can say that a good pencil is good in a role, but it certainly makes no sense to say that a good nap, a good sunset, or a good painting is good in some role. The variable *R* [Szabó represents the deep syntactic structure corresponding to "good" as $(G(R))(x)$][26] stands for some contextual information that specifies the incomplete [unary] predicate [corresponding to] "good."[27]

Granted that Szabó is, in this regard, non-committal about his use of "role," in terms of explaining dimensional specification, Szabó's role variable may be viewed as equivalent to a dimension variable, that is, to a variable constituent that is a part or aspect of the predicate corresponding to "good" and whose valuation or saturation specifies the dimension-type associated with "good" in a context of use.

Given this, let's concretize Szabó's account with a couple of examples. First, consider a context in which one is trying to find an object in a living room to prop up a television set. One locates a thick book and says:

This book is good.

One does not mean here that the object is, for instance, a good book to read. In this context, the book's being good is not even a function of its being a book. Rather, the book is good for propping up the television. In seeking an object to prop up the television, one might even consider various books and, upon locating a useful one, say:

This is a good book.

---

[25] Szabó (2001) 134. With respect to this aspect of his interpretation, Szabó acknowledges (at n. 27) a debt to Judith J. Thomson, "On Some Ways in Which a Thing Can Be Good," *Social and Political Policy* 9 (1992) 96–117.

[26] On Szabó's formalization, see my footnote 35.

[27] Szabó (2001) n. 31.

In this example, context is—as one would in any case presume—extra-sentential. However, Szabó states that the context that supplies the completing information for the incomplete predicate may also be intra-sentential. For example, consider the following sentence:

Bernie is a good lawyer.

In this case, the noun "lawyer" may provide the completing information. That is, the sentence may express the content

Bernie is a good-as-a-lawyer lawyer.

Indeed, Szabó states that: " 'good' within [the phrase] 'good $N$' normally has the content of 'good as an $N$.' "[28]

In arguing for his incomplete unary predicate interpretation, Szabó, like Geach, appeals to a type of inference schema. This, he calls "transfer inference." More precisely, Szabó distinguishes two types of transfer inference. For convenience, I will call these "simple" and "quantified" (short for "universally quantified") transfer inference. The following represents the form of simple transfer inference:

$x$ is $A$ $N$.
$x$ is $M$.
_____
$x$ is $A$ $M$.

Here again $A$ stands for an adjective and $N$ stands for a common nominal expression. $M$ stands for a distinct common nominal expression. I'll call adjectives that license transfer inference "transferable."[29] Adjectives that are transferable with respect to simple transfer inferences are akin to Geach's logically predicative adjectives. For example, consider "American" in the following example:

[28] Szabó (2001) 135. "I suggest that the content of certain expressions within the utterance may be part of the context that contributes to determining the content of other expressions within the *same* utterance. The content of 'good' in an utterance of 'Sue is a good dancer' may depend, in part, on the content of 'dancer' " (135).

[29] Szabó calls them "transparent." This term is employed by Cornelia Hamman, "Adjectivsemantik/ Adjectival Semantics," in *Semantik/Semantics: Ein internationals Handbuch der zeitgenössischen Forschung*, A. von Stechow and D. Wunderlich, eds., de Gruyter, 1991, 657–73, at 666. Cp. Edward Keenan and Leonard M. Faltz, *Logical Types for Natural Language*, UCLA Occasional Papers in Linguistics, no. 3, 1978, which seems to be the ultimate source of the expression.

Bernie is an American lawyer.
Bernie is a surfer.

---

Bernie is an American surfer.

Compare the use of "American" in the following case of *AN* splitting:

Bernie is an American lawyer.

---

Bernie is American.
Bernie is a lawyer.[30]

Now consider simple transfer inference, substituting "American" for "good":

Bernie is a good lawyer.
Bernie is a surfer.

---

Bernie is a good surfer.

The inference is invalid. So "good" is non-transferable in simple transfer inferences.

Szabó discusses Geach's interpretation of "good" and distinguishes it from his own. Szabó maintains that according to Geach's interpretation, "good" should be interpreted as a type of predicate modifier. However, Szabó interprets the semantics of expressions interpreted as predicate modifiers here in an unexpected way, namely merely extensionally rather than intensionally. To appreciate this point, it will be helpful to introduce a distinction between what I will call "extensional predicate modifiers" and "intensional predicate modifiers."

Recall that I am using the expression "predicate" to denote a syntactic category (and, by contrast, reserving the expression "function" to characterize semantic types). Accordingly, a predicate modifier is an expression that syntactically requires a predicate as its argument. Unless otherwise stated, by "predicate" I intend "unary predicate." Let us here understand modification as a syntactic construction consisting of two constituent expressions, a modifier and its modificand (the expression that the modifier modifies), in which the complex expression, that is, the expression consisting of the modifier and its modificand,

---

[30] I discuss problems with the inferential properties of territorial and nationality denoting adjectives in section 3.6.4.

belongs to the same syntactic category as the modificand itself. For example, consider the italicized phrases in the following two sentences:

Janet likes *chocolate*.
Janet likes *dark chocolate*.

In the first sentence, the simple expression "chocolate," which is unmodified, itself constitutes a noun phrase.[31] In the second sentence, the complex expression, which consists of the adjective "dark" modifying the noun "chocolate," also constitutes a noun phrase. So while, in the second sentence, the adjective "dark" modifies the noun "chocolate," the phrase "dark chocolate" is of the same syntactic category as the phrase "chocolate" itself, again a noun phrase. Accordingly, in the case of a predicate modifier, the syntactic category that the complex expression consisting of the predicate modifier and its modificand belongs to is the syntactic category of predicate, the same syntactic category as the predicate itself.[32]

Granted this, in principle, the semantic relation between a given modifier and its modificand may be interpreted in various ways. What I am calling an "extensional" predicate modifier is a function from the extension of a unary function to the extension of a unary function: $\langle et, et \rangle$. Note that as such, an extensional predicate modifier admits substitution of coextensional unary functions *salva veritate*. An "intensional" predicate modifier is a function from the intension of a unary function to the intension of a unary function: $\langle \langle s, \langle et \rangle \rangle, \langle s, \langle et \rangle \rangle \rangle$.[33] As such, an intensional predicate modifier does not admit substitution of coextensional unary functions *salva veritate*. Whether there are in fact any natural language expressions that should be interpreted as extensional predicate modifiers is a reasonable question. Nonetheless, Szabó's treatment of Geach compels us to recognize this as a theoretical option.

Let's focus first on Szabó's construal of Geach's interpretation of "good" as an extensional predicate modifier. Once again, consider the following natural language argument:

Bernie is a good lawyer.
Bernie is a surfer.

_____

Bernie is a good surfer.

---

[31] This point will be elaborated in section 1.2 of chapter 7.

[32] Note that the term "predicate modifier" is potentially misleading in that in contemporary syntactic theory, expressions that function as modifiers are not generally taken to *require* modificands. For example, the adjective "dark" does not require a nominal expression. For instance, "The liquid was dark" is syntactically well-formed and arguably consists of no covert nominal expression that "dark" is modifying. I return to the contemporary syntactic conception of modification in section 3.7.

[33] Note that the symbol *s* is used to represent the semantic type of a possible world.

The interpretation of "good" as an extensional predicate modifier can explain the non-transferability of "good" in this example of simple transfer inference:

$(G(L))(b)$
$S(b)$
———
$(G(S))(b)$.

Here G stands for the extensional predicate modifier corresponding to "good," and $L$ and $S$ stand for ordinary unary predicates corresponding to "lawyer" and "surfer" respectively. Evidently, the conclusion is invalid. "Lawyer" and "surfer" are not coextensive.

Note that insofar as "good" is a predicate modifier, be it extensional or intensional, its true syntactic structure must be represented in something like the following way:

$(G(F))(x)$.

Since a predicate modifier requires a predicate, the deep syntactic structure corresponding to "good" consists of a predicate variable.

On the other hand, Szabó argues that Geach's extensional predicate modifier interpretation "falls prey" to a second type of transfer inference, what I am calling "quantified" transfer inference.[34] For example, assume a world in which every lawyer is a surfer and every surfer is a lawyer. In other words, assume a world in which "lawyer" and "surfer" are coextensive. Now consider the following argument:

Bernie is a good lawyer.
All lawyers are surfers and all surfers are lawyers.
———
Bernie is a good surfer.

---

[34] This argument appears to be adapted from Richard K. Larson, "Events and Modification in Nominals," *SALT* 8 (1998) 145–68, at 147–48. But Larson employs it in discussing Siegel's interpretation of "good" as an intensional predicate modifier: "Suppose *dancer* and *singer* are coextensive, so that if one applies to Olga the other does too. Then, even so, the inference fails from *Olga is a beautiful dancer* to *Olga is a beautiful singer* and vice versa. This is captured by the intensional operator in function-argument combination."

Formally, we may represent this argument as follows:

$$(G(L))(b)$$
$$\forall x: L(x) \equiv S(x)$$

$$(G(S))(b).$$

Insofar as "good" is interpreted as an extensional predicate modifier, given the universally quantified premise, the predicate $L$ can be substituted for the predicate $S$ *salva veritate*. Contrary to the natural language argument, then, the conclusion of the formal language argument is valid. So, Szabó concludes, the interpretation of "good" as an extensional predicate modifier must be mistaken.

In contrast, consider a formalization of the second type of transfer inference according to Szabó's incomplete unary predicate interpretation. In the following, G stands for the constant content of an incomplete unary predicate; and l and s stand for role values, that is, values assigned to the role variable that is a constituent of the incomplete unary predicate corresponding to "good." Note also that since "good" is interpreted as a predicate, that is, a unary predicate, albeit an incomplete one, a sentence such as "Bernie is a good lawyer" must be formalized as

$$(G(l))(b) \wedge L(b).$$

That is to say, "Bernie is good in the role of a lawyer and Bernie is a lawyer." Accordingly, this instance of quantified transfer inference would be formalized as follows:

$$(G(l))(b) \wedge L(b)$$
$$\forall x: L(x) \equiv S(x)$$

$$(G(s))(b) \wedge S(b).$$

In this case, the conclusion of the formal argument, like that of the natural language argument, is invalid. Precisely, the fact that "lawyer" and "surfer" are coextensive does not license the inference from "$x$ is good in the lawyer role" to "$x$ is good in the surfer role."[35]

---

[35] As noted above, Szabó represents the incomplete predicate as follows: $(G(R))(x)$. Here G stands for the incomplete unary predicate, and R stands for the role variable. Compare this formalization with the following formalization that Szabó offers for Geach's predicate modifier interpretation: $(G(F))(x)$. In this latter case, F is a predicate variable. Comparing the two formalizations, one immediate problem is that the symbol G cannot mean the same thing in each formula. In the first formula, G stands for an incomplete predicate; in the second G stands for a predicate modifier. This problem is easily remedied; we simply need a different symbol for one or the other term in the

Szabó's interpretation of "good" as an incomplete unary predicate is, therefore, preferable to an interpretation of "good" as an extensional predicate modifier, insofar as the former can explain the non-transferability of "good" in quantified as well as simple transfer inferences. In other words, by postulating a role variable in the deep syntactic structure corresponding to "good," Szabó can explain why "good" constructions yield invalidity in both types of transfer inference.

With this result in hand, here is a convenient point to briefly return to Travis's green leaf example and to consider how Szabó's incomplete unary predicate interpretation answers Travis's challenge to the principle of compositionality. Szabó proposes that there are various types of incomplete unary predicates. Whereas the deep syntactic structure corresponding to "good" consists of a role variable, the deep syntactic structure corresponding to "green" and other color adjectives consists of a so-called part variable, that is, a variable corresponding to the part of the object (for example, the leaf), denoted by the external argument of the predicate, that has the color. Accordingly, we might represent the deep syntactic structure corresponding to a color adjective as

$$(C(p))(x).$$

Here $C$ stands for the invariant color content of the color adjective, and $p$ stands for the part variable, again the part of the object denoted by the subject of which the color adjective is predicated. Consequently, in a context where leaves are being sorted by painted color for decoration, the part variable receives as its value the painted surface of the leaf. And in a context where leaves are being sorted to identify their species, the value assignment of the part variable is the natural surface of the leaf. Since these variables are constituents of the (incomplete unary) predicate, truth-conditional contextual contributions are mandated rather than optional. Consequently, the principle of compositionality is, in this sort of case, preserved.

Granted this, for our purposes the crucial point to derive from the discussion of Szabó's interpretation of "good" is the one that we derived from Geach's interpretation of "good": the deep syntactic structure corresponding to "good" consists of a variable constituent that is interpretable as a dimension variable. This variable explains dimensional specification of "good" in determinist terms.

---

formulae. I ignore this minor problem. A more serious problem with Szabó's formalization of his incomplete predicate interpretation lies in the meaning of $G$: $G$ cannot stand for the incomplete predicate corresponding to "good," for if the role variable is indeed a constituent of the incomplete predicate, then a vicious regress follows. $G$ would then be equivalent to $G(R)$. So Szabó's formula should be equivalent to $((G(R))(R))(x)$, and so on. If the role variable is a constituent of the formal syntactic category corresponding to "good," Szabó cannot represent "good" as $G$ and commit himself to the view that $R$ is a constituent of $G$. Rather, he could maintain that $G$ stands for the non-variable constituent of "good," while $R$ stands for the variable constituent.

## 2.4. Siegel on "Good" as a Doublet

The last determinist explanation of dimensional specification of "good" that I will consider here is Muffy Siegel's. Siegel's account occurs in the context of a general theory of adjectives. According to her theory, there are three basic types of adjectives: exclusively intersective, exclusively non-intersective, and so-called doublets which have intersective and non-intersective readings. Although the semantics and syntax of "good" are not Siegel's principal interest, she does regard "good" as a key example of a doublet.

Intersective adjectives are (ordinary)[36] unary predicates. Examples include "carnivorous," "infinite," "speckled," and "drunk."[37] For instance, the phrase "carnivorous plant" is true of the intersection of the set of individuals that are carnivorous and the set of individuals that are plants. In Geach's terminology, intersective adjectives are logically predicative. For example:

Nepenthes is a carnivorous plant.

---

Nepenthes is carnivorous.
Nepenthes is a plant.

Semantically, non-intersective adjectives are functions from the intensions of common nominal expressions to the intensions of common nominal expressions. In the terminology that I employed above, they are a type of intensional predicate modifier. If, contra Szabó, we take Geach to interpret terms such as "good" as intensional, rather than extensional, predicate modifiers, then non-intersective adjectives correspond to Geach's logically attributive adjectives.[38]

Observe that insofar as "good" is a non-intersective adjective, it is non-transferable in both simple and quantified transfer inferences. In particular, recall the following example of quantified transfer inference:

Bernie is a good lawyer.
All lawyers are surfers and vice versa.

---

Bernie is a good surfer.

---

[36] Hereafter, the reader should assume that all talk of predicates refers to complete predicates, unless explicitly noted.
[37] Cp. Siegel (1980) 179, Appendix II.
[38] Unfortunately, Siegel does not mention Geach in her book.

Assume that $G$ stands for the intensional predicate modifier corresponding to "good." We can formalize this argument as follows:

$$(G(L))(b)$$
$$\forall x: L(x) \equiv S(x)$$

$$(G(S))(b).$$

Because $G$ is an intensional predicate modifier, the fact that "lawyer" and "surfer" are coextensive does not license substitution of $L$ for $S$ as an argument of the predicate modifier. Consequently, the conclusion of the formal argument, like that of the natural language argument, is invalid.

Nothing in Geach's discussion excludes such an interpretation or, conversely, encourages an interpretation of "good" as an extensional predicate modifier. In fact, Szabó entertains "an intensionalized version of Geach's proposal."[39] He acknowledges that on this view, "good" is not transferable in either kind of transfer inference.[40] Nonetheless, Szabó rejects the interpretation of "good" as an intensional predicate modifier. The reason that he offers for the rejection is the following:[41]

> By assigning $[(G(L))(b)]$ as [the] logical form [that is, deep syntactic structure] to ["Bernie is a good lawyer,"] we implicitly commit ourselves to an explanation why the inference [in a case of quantified transfer inference] fails. The *reason* why [Bernie] may be a good [lawyer] and a [surfer] without being a good [surfer] even if all [lawyers are surfers] and *vice versa* is that there is another possible world where someone ([he], or someone else) is a [lawyer], but not a [surfer]. This does not sound very convincing. How could the possibility that someone is a [lawyer], but not a [surfer] have anything to do with the question whether [Bernie] has to be a good [surfer], given that [he] is a good [lawyer] and a [surfer].[42]

---

[39]  Szabó (2001) 130–31.

[40]  Even if "lawyer" and "surfer" are coextensive, "the intensions of the complex predicates $[(G(L))$ $(x)$ and $(G(S))(x)]$ are different functions, and therefore the expressions $[(G(L))(x)$ and $(G(S))(x)]$ have different intensions too. But then there is no reason why the sentences ['Bernie is a good lawyer'] and ['Bernie is a good surfer'] should have the same truth-value in the actual world" (2001, 131; note that I have made minor changes to the formulae and examples here to make them accord with my formulae and examples above).

[41]  Szabó's reason essentially repeats one stated by Larson (1998) 149–50.

[42]  Szabó (2001) 131; note that here too I have made minor changes to the formulae and examples to make them accord with my formulae and examples above.

I find this ground for rejecting the intensional predicate modifier interpretation of "good" misguided. The appeal to intensionality and thereby to possible worlds is intended to capture our intuitions about the meanings of expressions. We make such appeals because extensional accounts of meaning are not fine-grained enough. The semantic intuitions also correlate with metaphysical intuitions and commitments. We assume that being a lawyer and being a surfer are properties of individuals. So, even if everyone who practiced law surfed and vice versa, being a lawyer and being a surfer would remain distinct properties of individuals. Insofar as we understand the meanings of common terms to correspond to properties, we can say that the intensionalized version of Geach's proposal does in fact provide an explanation for why "good" is non-transferable. In this respect, the interpretation of "good" as an intensional predicate modifier is just as satisfactory as Szabó's interpretation of "good" as an incomplete unary predicate.

With respect to Siegel's view, once again, non-intersective adjectives are intensional predicate modifiers. But, as I also said, Siegel distinguishes three basic types of adjectives: purely intersective, purely non-intersective, and doublets. In contrast to the intensionalized Geachean proposal, Siegel in fact maintains that "good" is not a purely non-intersective adjective. Instead, she claims that "good" and in fact most adjectives are doublets.[43] Again, doublets are adjectives that have intersective and non-intersective readings. In other words, doublets are adjectives that occur as unary predicates and as intensional predicate modifiers. Accordingly, doublets would best be understood as adjectives that are polysemous, and more precisely as adjectives that lexically encode two polysemes: one corresponding to a unary predicate, the other corresponding to an intensional predicate modifier.[44]

Siegel initially uses the following sort of example to illustrate the thesis that "good" is a doublet:

2.   Beatrice is a beautiful dancer.

As Siegel notes, sentence (2) is ambiguous between the following two readings:

2m.   Beatrice is beautiful and Beatrice is a dancer.
2i.   Beatrice dances beautifully.

Sentence (2m) corresponds to the interpretation of "beautiful" in (2) as a unary predicate; (2i) corresponds to the interpretation of "beautiful" in (2) as an intensional predicate modifier. I underscore that the difference between the two readings is not merely that "beautiful" can occur either as a unary predicate or

---

[43]  Examples of purely non-intersective adjectives are "alleged," "former," "blithering," "mere." Cp. Siegel (1980) 180, Appendix III.
[44]  I note that Siegel herself does not characterize doublets as polysemous.

as an intensional predicate modifier. In other words, the difference between the two readings is not merely syntactic; it is semantic. Compare Siegel's following remark: "It is the purpose of this thesis to show that the dual semantic roles of members of the adjective category are actually predictable from the dual syntactic roles that define the part of speech 'adjective.'"[45]

The semantic differences between the two syntactic structures are particularly clear in the following examples of "dirty," "present," and "sorry":[46]

| | |
|---|---|
| Bernie's son is dirty. | (unclean) |
| Bernie's son is a dirty liar. | (terrible, immoral) |
| The minister's son is present. | (physically) |
| The minister's son is our present caretaker. | (temporally) |
| The councilman is sorry. | (remorseful) |
| The councilman is a sorry public official. | (bad example of) |

I will not here question whether there are adjectival doublets. Rather, I will focus on whether "good" is a doublet. What grounds then does Siegel offer for thinking that "good" occurs as both a unary predicate and as an intensional predicate modifier? The main reason that Siegel offers for taking "good" to occur as an intensional predicate modifier is that "good" is, in my terminology, non-transferable. In corroborating this claim, she focuses on an argument form that is more or less equivalent to simple transfer inference. For an adjective $A$ and two distinct common nominal expressions $N$ and $M$, if the following set of four sentences is consistent, then $A$ has a non-intersective reading:

$x$ is $N$.
$x$ is $M$.
$x$ is $A$ $M$.
$x$ is not $A$ $N$.

For example:

Bernie is a lawyer.
Bernie is a surfer.
Bernie is a good lawyer.
Bernie is not a good surfer.[47]

---

[45] Siegel (1980) 1.
[46] These are adapted from Siegel (1980) 95–97.
[47] Siegel (1980) 4. I have simplified Siegel's presentation of the argument form.

The problem here is that this argument form, like that of simple transfer inference, does not entail the interpretation of *A* as an intensional predicate modifier. It is compatible with the interpretation of *A* as an extensional predicate modifier (as well as an incomplete unary predicate).

Granted this limitation of Siegel's argument, I want to focus on her grounds for taking "good" to also have an intersective, that is, a unary predicate, reading. Here, she offers syntactic as well as semantic considerations. There are basically two syntactic considerations. Before introducing these, let me briefly remark on one syntactic consideration that, as Siegel herself suggests, does not support the view that "good" occurs as a unary predicate. This is the fact that "good" can constitute the predicate expression in what I have called the basic sentence; for example:

This is good.

The problem with a mere appeal to this kind of example is that a defender of the view that "good" always occurs as an intensional predicate modifier can claim that English includes "a dummy common noun . . . [which] may be syntactically deleted by [the following rule]":

be an *A* Δ    →    be *A*.

Here *A* stands for a non-intersective adjective and Δ for a dummy common noun.[48] As Siegel writes:

The dummy [common noun] Δ remains part of the semantic interpretation. Its own interpretations range over common nouns, but it is interpreted uniquely for any given utterance. Most often, the Δ is interpreted according to linguistic context. [For example,] "The lutist is good" on its non-intersective reading is more likely interpreted as "The lutist is a good lutist" than as "The lutist is a good plumber." However, the second interpretation would be possible, given the right pragmatic context.[49]

In response, a defender of the view that "good" occurs as a unary predicate could insist that the syntactic deletion rule is ad hoc and question-begging. I note this

---

[48] Siegel (1980) 54. I have simplified Siegel's presentation. Siegel also suggests that this dummy common noun may be explicitly represented, at least in this case of count nouns, by the noun "one(s)"; for example: "the good one"; "the beautiful ones."

[49] Siegel (1980) 54–55. Siegel explicitly refers to Δ as an "indexical" (e.g. on p. 29). Cp. her remark on the sentence "The woman is a tall Δ." Here, "the Δ would be interpreted indexically, so that in a sentence like 'She is tall', with underlying structure 'She is a tall Δ', the Δ could be interpreted as 'woman' or 'ship' or anything else that the speaker happened to be talking about" (63–64).

point, but will not dwell on it here since Siegel offers more suggestive considerations on behalf of the view that "good" occurs as a unary predicate. She cites two syntactic constructions in which adjectives are prohibited from modifying nominal expressions. One type is "there" insertion. As Siegel writes: "roughly, 'there' insertion must take a sentence with an indefinite subject [symbolized by $i$ below], followed by [a form of the verb 'be'] or certain other verbs, insert 'there', and move the subject":[50]

$i$ be F   →   There be $i$ F.

For example, consider the following pairs of sentences:

A bat is suspended from the ceiling.   →
There is a bat suspended from the ceiling.

A chinchilla is a good pet.   →
* There is a chinchilla a good pet.

Some members of the board are willing to speak to the press.   →
There are some members of the board willing to speak to the press.

Some members of the board are experienced lawyers.   →
* There are some members of the board experienced lawyers.[51]

The key point for our purposes is that "there" insertion constructions do not permit an adjective that follows the moved subject $i$ to modify a nominal expression. In fact, these constructions do not allow nominal expressions sans adjectives following the moved subject $i$; for example:

Some chinchillas are pets.   →
* There are chinchillas pets.

A member of the board is a lawyer.   →
* There is a member of the board a lawyer.[52]

Consequently, if there are "there" insertion constructions with "good," these must be cases of "good" without an implicit dummy common noun, let alone an explicit common noun. Siegel does not cite any examples. Indeed,

---

[50] Siegel (1980) 81.
[51] Some of these examples are derived or adapted from Siegel (1980) 80–84.
[52] I acknowledge that "a lawyer" may be interpreted, instead, as a determiner phrase. On the notion of a determiner phrase, cp. section 1.2 of chapter 7.

I cannot think of any felicitous examples in which "good" occurs bare. For instance, consider the use of "good" meaning "well-behaved" in the following sentence:

Some children were good.

Now consider "there" insertion:

# There were some children good.

I have affixed the pound symbol here because I find this sentence semantically unacceptable. It may well be syntactically unacceptable too. Granted this, I do think that there are some "there" insertion constructions that are acceptable with "good" modified by prepositional phrases; for example:

Some of the rookies were good on both sides of the plate.     →
There were some rookies good on both sides of the plate.

Some relievers were good on no day's rest.     →
There were some relievers good on no day's rest.

I will return to discuss these examples later. Presently, I turn to the second syntactic construction that prohibits adjectives from modifying nominal expressions. These constructions consist of small clauses composed of a nominal expression and an adjectival predicate expression following verbs like "saw," "found," "caught";[53] for example:

I saw / found / caught the swimmers nude.
I saw / found / caught him shouting.
I saw / found / caught my employees drunk.

In these cases, the adjective cannot modify a nominal expression; for example:

* I saw / found / caught the swimmers nude pleasure-seekers.
* I saw / found / caught him a shouting protestor.
* I saw / found / caught my employees drunk revelers.[54]

---

[53] Recall from section 5 of chapter 2 that a small clause consists of a subject and a predicate, but the predicate expression is untensed.

[54] Note that when "find" occurs with an (explicit or implicit) infinitive complement (for example, "I find her to be duplicitous"), it admits an adjective plus nominal object of the infinitive ("I find her to be a duplicitous colleague"). But this is a distinct use of "find." Cp. Siegel (1980) 87.

In this case, Siegel offers the following example of "good":

I've seen those children good, but not very often.

I don't find this to be a felicitous sentence. But I offer the following alternative:

Anna was rushed to the emergency room complaining of heart palpitations. By the time I arrived, the doctors had given her a mild sedative and run some standard tests, all fortunately negative. I found her good, quite relaxed and comfortable. She didn't have an explanation for the incident, but she also seemed relatively unperturbed by it.

Although examples are scarce, the evidence from the two syntactic constructions—"there" insertion and small clauses consisting of a noun + adjectival predicate expression following verbs such as "see," "find," and "catch"—supports the view that there are instances of "good" that involve no modification of a nominal expression, indeed that are syntactically prohibited from such modification.

Granted this, the next question is whether in such cases, that is, when it occurs as a unary predicate, "good" has a different meaning from "good" when it occurs as an intensional predicate modifier. Siegel makes two specific remarks about the meaning of "good" as a unary predicate. In the first remark, she is commenting on the meaning of "good" in the following two sentences:

3. That lutist is good.
4. That is a good lutist.

I underscore that Siegel maintains that "good" can occur as a unary predicate and as an intensional predicate modifier in both contexts, that is, both in syntactically predicate position (3) and in syntactically prenominal, that is, attributive position (4). Granted this, she claims that in predicate position, "good" is "vague," whereas in prenominal position it is merely "ambiguous."[55] What she means by this is the following. In prenominal position, "good" has two possible meanings. If it occurs as a unary predicate, it has what she calls a "general meaning"—more on this shortly. If it occurs as an intensional predicate modifier, its meaning is relative to the common noun that it modifies. So in (4), "good" as an intensional predicate modifier means "good as a lutist." In contrast, when "good" occurs in predicate position, as in (3), its meaning is

---

[55] Cp. "adjectives [that are doublets] are ambiguous in prenominal position, but vague in the predicate" (1980, 66).

"vague" in the following sense. As a unary predicate, again "good" has a general meaning. But as an intensional predicate modifier, the deleted dummy common noun can take a wide range of values. In particular, in the case of (3), the deleted dummy common noun is not restricted to "lutist." It is in this sense that the meaning of "good" as an intensional predicate modifier in this construction is "vague."

Here now is Siegel's first comment on the "general" meaning of "good" as a unary predicate:

> [Both (3) and (4)] could be taken to be commenting on either the lutist's playing ("good as a lutist") [hence, an intensional predicate modifier occurrence] or her morals or general qualities ("generally or absolutely good") [hence a unary predicate occurrence].[56]

In this passage, Siegel vacillates between "good" meaning "morally good" and "good" meaning "generally or absolutely good."

In a second passage, she is commenting on the ambiguity of "good" in (4):

> "A good lutist" can only be good as a lutist [according to the intensional predicate modifier reading] or good in general [according to the unary predicate reading].[57]

One further remark Siegel makes about the "general" meaning of a doublet used as a unary predicate in prenominal position is worth noting:

> Prenominally [doublets] can only be read as applying either to the following [common noun, for example "lutist"], or to something so general that, in fact, they don't apply to anything.[58]

Siegel therefore seems to hold that the meaning of "good" as a unary predicate is something like "good in general" or "absolutely good." Yet she clearly vacillates between that position and the view that when "good" as a unary predicate is attributed to a person it means "morally good." Recall also her example, cited previously:

> I've seen those children good, but not very often.

---

[56] Siegel (1980) 53.
[57] Siegel (1980) 65.
[58] Siegel (1980) 74.

Regardless of the fact that I find this sentence semantically awkward, in this case "good" can be glossed as "well-behaved."[59] But note also that "well-behaved," when used of a child, does not have the same meaning as "morally good." For instance, to predicate "good" in the sense of "well-behaved" of an adult is patronizing and strange. Recall also the example that I offered of patient Anna, which I repeat here:

> Anna was rushed to the emergency room complaining of heart palpitations. By the time I arrived, the doctors had given her a mild sedative and run some standard tests, all fortunately negative. I found her good, quite relaxed and comfortable. She didn't have an explanation for the incident, but she also seemed relatively unperturbed by it.

In this case, "good" means something like "content" or "in a good state of mind." So here behavior, moral or otherwise, is not part of or associated with the meaning of "good."

At any rate, neither morally good nor well-behaved is a maximally general sense of "good." But, setting aside this vacillation on Siegel's part, it remains unclear what "good" in a general or absolute sense does mean. I take this obscurity to be a serious defect in Siegel's account of "good" as a unary predicate. Indeed, it calls into question her view that as a unary predicate "good" has a distinctive meaning. I will return to this point subsequently.

## 2.5. Additional Considerations and Problems with the Determinist Explanations

Recall my conclusion that the interpretation of "good" both as an intensional predicate modifier and as an incomplete unary predicate can explain the non-transferability of "good" in simple and quantified transfer inferences. Granted this—and setting aside what I have suggested is a misguided criticism of the interpretation of "good" as an intensional predicate modifier—Szabó appeals to two additional considerations to support his interpretation of "good" as an incomplete unary predicate.

According to both Geach's and Siegel's views, the argument that "good," interpreted as an intensional predicate modifier, requires must be supplied by a common nominal expression. Both Geach and Siegel grant that this nominal

---

[59] Confirmation that Siegel is committed to this comes from her gloss of "bad" in an analogous context: "I don't think I've ever seen that child bad" (1980, 87). She explicitly glosses "bad" here as "naughty" and refers to it as a "non-relative quality."

expression needn't be explicit. However, they maintain that it must be recoverable from context. In contrast, Szabó maintains that the predicate-completing content that the incomplete unary predicate requires need not derive from a nominal expression at all. He offers the following example to support this claim. Assume that students in a chemistry class are trying to produce a substance that can be used in a later experiment. "The teacher points to a certain blue liquid and says to the students: 'This is good.'" Szabó denies that in order to interpret the teacher's statement the students must be able to distinguish some nominal expression $N$ such that the blue liquid is a good $N$. All they know is that the blue liquid is good for the purposes of the experiment. A defender of Geach or Siegel might object here that "the [$N$] in question is something like 'stuff that can be used in a later experiment.'" But Szabó responds: "Why should we believe that standards of goodness are provided by the content of this complex [nominal expression], rather than simply by the context in which the teacher's utterance was made?"[60]

Szabó's second additional consideration in favor of his incomplete unary predicate interpretation is that in a case where "good" modifies a nominal expression, it should be possible for something other than the modified nominal to supply a value for the role variable. In other words, in a case where "good" modifies a nominal expression, it should be possible for something other than the modified nominal to provide a value that specifies the dimension-type associated with "good." In support of this claim, Szabó suggests the following sort of example. Assume that there is a musical theater troupe, half of whose performers are singers and the other half dancers. The troupe's treasurer discovers that money has been stolen from the company's safe. He reports the theft to the troupe's manager. It is clear that some of the dancers are responsible for the theft. The manager suggests that they speak to some of the dancers, whom they know to be morally upstanding, to see if these dancers might have some information on the identity of the thieves. In suggesting this, the manager has in mind Beatrice as an especially morally upstanding dancer; and he says:

Beatrice is one of the good dancers.

In this case, the role variable receives a moral role value rather than a dancing role value.

In short, the two additional considerations that Szabó appeals to in support of his interpretation are that "good" does not require a nominal expression to provide a value for the covert role variable; and that in the phrase "good $N$," the nominal expression $N$ needn't provide the value for the role variable.

---

[60]   Szabó (2001) 133.

On these points, I agree with Szabó. I do not regard his blue liquid example as particularly successful. But I think that other examples could be cited in support of his claim. Consider the following one. The two cords used to raise and lower some Venetian blinds have become tortuously entangled and Gail is having trouble untangling them. Adam suggests that she ask David for help and says:

5.   David is good with his hands.

In this case, the predicate expression is familiar and intelligible; and no nominal expression readily comes to mind that could well substitute for the prepositional phrase "with his hands."

Granted this particular example and Szabó's general point, Geach's and Siegel's views that "good" requires a nominal expression to provide an argument for the intensional predicate modifier are wrong. This defect in their positions could be remedied simply by altering their view to the following one: "good" corresponds to an intensional predicate modifier, but the predicate argument it requires needn't be supplied by a nominal expression. Call this the "non-restrictive" intensional predicate modifier interpretation of "good."

The non-restrictive predicate modifier interpretation, however, faces the following problem. Consider again example (13). As it occurs here, the prepositional phrase "with his hands" is not interpretable as a predicate. Rather, in ordinary syntactic terms, it is an adverbial expression. For example, compare

David untangled the cords with his hands.

In particular, from "David is good with his hands," we cannot infer

# David is with his hands.[61]

As such, Szabó's incomplete unary predicate interpretation is preferable to a non-restrictive intensional predicate modifier interpretation. Granted this, Szabó's account also needs to provide an explanation of the prepositional phrase in (13). Recall that Szabó's position commits him to the following interpretation of sentence (10) "Beatrice is a good dancer":

$(\mathcal{G}(\mathfrak{d}))(b) \wedge D(b)$.

---

[61] The sentence "The untangling was with his hands" seems awkward. The only acceptable use of "with his hands" as a predicate expression that I can think of is in the following expression describing a manual laborer or craftsman: "His work is with his hands."

That is, "Beatrice is good-in-the-dancing-role and Beatrice is a dancer." But Szabó cannot interpret (13) analogously as

$$(\mathcal{G}(\hat{h}))(d) \wedge H(d).$$

That is, "David is good with his hands and David is with his hands."

Modification of "good" by an adverb brings out this problem particularly well. For example, consider the following sentence:

Joseph is morally good.

The adverb "morally" cannot constitute a predicate expression:

\* $x$ is morally.

Finally, consider purposive "for" prepositional phrase modification of "good," which presents a different problem for Szabó's interpretation:

6.   Coca-Cola is good for removing rust.

In this case, the phrase "for removing rust" can occur as a predicate expression, what in section 2.3 of chapter 4 I called a "predicate purposive 'for' phrase":

This is for removing rust.

However, as I noted in chapter 4, although Coca-Cola is good for removing rust, it does not follow that Coca-Cola is for removing rust. In other words, removing rust is not the characteristic function of Coca-Cola. So the following formalization of (6) is inaccurate:

$$(\mathcal{G}(r))(c) \wedge R(c).$$

I note one final problem with Szabó's account, which is unrelated to the preceding considerations. Consider once again the following example of simple transfer inference:

Bernie is a good lawyer.
Bernie is a surfer.
_____

Bernie is a good surfer.

I formalized this, according to Szabó's incomplete unary predicate interpretation, as

$(G(l))(b) \land L(b)$
$S(b)$
_____

$(G(s))(b) \land S(b)$.

The conclusion of the formal argument, like that of the natural language argument, is invalid. But observe that nothing in Szabó's account prohibits the following formalization of the argument:

$(G(l))(b) \land L(b)$
$S(b)$
_____

$(G(l))(b) \land S(b)$.

Note in particular the first conjunct of the conclusion: $(G(l))(b)$. Here, contrary to the natural language argument, the conclusion is valid. In other words, the argument so formalized can be rendered in natural language as

Bernie is good-in-the-lawyer-role and Bernie is a lawyer.
Bernie is a surfer.
_____

Bernie is good-in-the-lawyer-role and Bernie is a surfer.

But there is in fact no natural way to read the original argument as such. It is incumbent on the interpreter to explain why this is so.[62]

One possibility is that the nominal expression that "good" modifies provides the value of the covert role variable. But note that Szabó cannot simply rely on this position, since he expressly maintains that in a phrase of the form "good N," the nominal expression need not provide the value of the role variable. Rather, what he needs to claim here is that, all other things being equal, the nominal expression that "good" modifies provides the value of the role variable.

Although I find that Geach's, Szabó's, and Siegel's determinist explanations of dimensional specification of "good" are ultimately unsuccessful, I acknowledge that a number of the considerations that they adduce on behalf of their

---

[62] Clearly, the same problem afflicts quantified transfer inference.

interpretations must be addressed by any adequate explanation of dimensional specification of "good." These considerations include the inferential properties of "good" in *AN* splitting inference, simple transfer inference, and quantified transfer inference; and Szabó's two additional considerations: that "good" needn't modify an explicit or implicit common nominal expression; and that in a case where "good" modifies a nominal expression, it is possible for something other than the modified nominal expression to specify the dimension-type associated with "good." I will return to these considerations when I advance my own explanation of dimensional specification of "good."[63]

---

[63] I note here that the analysis of "good" that forms part of the interpretation of normative language in Stephen Finlay's *Confusion of Tongues* is also interpretable as a determinist explanation of dimensional specification. I will briefly comment on Finlay's position here. To a first approximation, Finlay interprets "good" as a binary propositional operator $G$. Qua binary propositional operator, $G$ relates one proposition $p$ to another proposition $e$. The symbol $e$ here stands for an "end-proposition." (Recall, from footnote 19 of chapter 4, that for Finlay an end is a potential outcome, which is to say a possible state of affairs, which is to say, a proposition.) The relation between $p$ and $e$ that "good" denotes is that of probability increasing. So, if we represent what Finlay calls the "logical form," which is to say, the deep syntactic structure, corresponding to "good" as $G(e,p)$, this formula can be read as stating that $p$ increases the probability of $e$. (Finlay himself uses the following representation: $G_e(p)$ [2014, 34].) Broader worldly conditions are necessarily relevant to one proposition increasing the probability of another proposition. Accordingly, Finlay analyzes $p$ increasing the probability of $e$ as relative to a background $b$, where a background is a partial description of a world-state. (I acknowledge that I am simplifying Finlay's account here.) Given that the increasing probability relation between $p$ and $e$ requires a background, the deep syntactic structure corresponding to "good" can more precisely be represented as $G_b(e,p)$. (Finlay himself uses the following representation: $G_{e,b}(p)$ [2014, 45].) Consequently, the truth of an expression of the form "$p$ is good for $e$, given $b$" in a given context entails that the probability of $e$, given the conjunction of $b$ and $p$, is greater than the probability of $e$, given the conjunction of $b$ and $\neg p$. My account differs from Finlay's in a number of respects. One difference relates to my view that "good" is a relative gradable adjective. Insofar as the predicate expression in the basic sentence denotes a significant degree of the relevant gradable property, in this case value, given $b$, $p$ could not be good for $e$ unless the probability of $e$, given the conjunction of $b$ and $p$, were significantly greater than the probability of $e$, given the conjunction of $b$ and $\neg p$; where significance consists in relativization to a standard of comparison based on a comparison class. Absent such relativization, it could only follow that, given $b$, $p$ was better for $e$ than $\neg p$. (I note that Finlay does in fact briefly consider the view that "good" is a gradable adjective [2014, 41–42].) Assuming that my view is correct, I think that, in this respect, Finlay's account needs a relatively minor adjustment. A more important difference—perhaps the most important difference—between our views lies in the fact that Finlay conceives of ends and so of end-propositions merely as potential outcomes. On my view of value, the denotation of "good" consists of purpose serving. So, to the extent that "good" requires an end-proposition $e$, $e$ would have to be essentially associated with a purpose that the subject of which "good" was predicated significantly served. Related to this criticism is Finlay's paradigmatic expression of "good" constructions, once again: $p$ is good for $e$, given $b$. I draw special attention to the preposition "for" that introduces the end-proposition. The preposition "for" is contentful. So what is its content in this construction? On the basis of my discussion in section 2.3 of chapter 4, it appears to have a purposive meaning and indeed to head a purposive "for" phrase. If so, then Finlay is committed to end-propositions denoting purposes. In addition, it appears that, according to his own terms, Finlay has not provided an analysis of "good," but rather of "good for" as a binary propositional operator. (This also assumes that the gerund phrase complement of "for" has propositional content. I think that this is at least questionable,

## 3.1. Two Compatibilist Explanations
## of Dimensional Specification

I turn from determinist to compatibilist explanations of dimensional specification of "good." Precisely, I will discuss two compatibilist explanations: modulation, more precisely modulation by means of ad hoc conceptualization, and supplementation. There are various compatibilist approaches to linguistic meaning and considerations that might be recruited in support of modulation and supplementation.[64] My discussion of modulation will largely consider its treatment within the framework of relevance theory.[65] In addition to the fact that relevance theory is the most prominent compatibilist approach to linguistic meaning, so far as I am aware the only explanation of dimensional specification of "good" that has been advanced in terms of modulation, namely Ingrid Falkum's, has been within a relevance theoretic framework.

As I mentioned in section 1 of this chapter, supplementation is realized in two ways: by means of adverbial modification of "good" and by means of what I dub "reciprocal modification" of "good" by a nominal expression. No explanation of dimensional specification of "good" has been advanced in terms of supplementation. However, my account of supplementation in terms of adverbial modification of "good" is

but I will not pursue that point here.) Another difference between our views also relates to the preceding point. Given that "purpose" is a modal term, "good" must be analyzed in terms of modality. Consequently, "good" and, say, "ought" cannot, as Finlay holds, be semantically coordinate terms. A final difference between our accounts lies in our analyses of the deep syntactic structure corresponding to "good." Clearly, my view that, degree argument aside, "good" is a unary predicate differs from Finlay's view that "good" is a binary propositional operator with a background condition. I suspect that our respective conceptions of what so-called logical form is and therefore of the sorts of evidence that bear on the determination of the logical form of an expression differ in important ways.

[64] As noted above, what I am calling syntactic "determinism" is commonly contrasted with free pragmaticism. On the latter, cp. François Recanati, "Pragmatics and Semantics," in *Handbook of Pragmatics*, L.R. Horn and G. Ward, eds., Blackwell, 2004, 442–62; Recanati, "Pragmatic Enrichment," in *Routledge Companion to Philosophy of Language*, G. Russell and D. G. Fara, eds., Routledge, 2012, 67–78; Yan Huang, *Pragmatics*, Oxford University Press, 2014², 297–334. Cp. also François Recanati, *Literal Meaning*, Cambridge University Press, 2004; Recanati, *Truth-Conditional Pragmatics*, Oxford University Press, 2010; Robyn Carston, "Explicit Communication and 'Free' Pragmatic Enrichment," in *Explicit Communication: Robyn Carston's Pragmatics*, B. Soría and E. Romero, eds., Palgrave Macmillan, 2010, 217–85; Delia Belleri, *Semantic Under-determinacy and Communication*, Palgrave Macmillan, 2014; Kristin Börgjesson, *The Semantics-Pragmatics Controversy*, de Gruyter, 2014; Ilse Deparaetere and Raphael Salkie, eds., *Semantics and Pragmatics: Drawing a Line*, Springer, 2017.

[65] For overviews, cp. Deirdre Wilson and Dan Sperber, "Relevance Theory," in Horn and Ward (2004) 607–32; Robyn Carston, "Relevance Theory," in Russell and Fara (2012) 163–76; Billy Clark, *Relevance Theory*, Cambridge University Press, 2013. The principal primary texts are Dan Sperber and Deirdre Wilson, *Relevance: Communication and Cognition*, Blackwell, 1995²; Sperber and Wilson, *Meaning and Relevance*, Cambridge University Press, 2012; Robyn Carston, *Thoughts and Utterances: The Pragmatics of Explicit Communication*, Blackwell, 2002.

informed by various sources, especially the works of Kent Bach,[66] Stephen Neale,[67] and John Collins.[68] And my account of supplementation in terms of reciprocal modification is in part inspired and informed by a paper of Dwight Bolinger's on the distinction between predicate and attributive adjectives.[69]

I begin with modulation.

## 3.2. Modulation

Modulation is a form of polysemy. Assume that word $W$ has a lexical meaning $M$, and where the lexical meaning of $W$ is not a function from context to content such as that of an indexical or deictic expression (for example, "this" or "that"). Assume that a token of $W$, that is, an occurrence of $W$ in a context, has a meaning $M^*$, where $M^*$ derives, but differs, from $M$. Modulation, then, consists in a tokening of $W$ with the meaning $M^*$. I will refer to $M^*$ as the "modulated meaning" of $W$. Modulation is a compatibilist position insofar as it holds that the semantic adjustment to the meaning of $W$ in a context of use is not syntactically mandated.

There are two principal types of modulation: narrowing and broadening. Narrowing occurs when the extension of $M^*$ is a subset of the extension of $M$. Broadening occurs when the extension of $M$ is a subset of the extension of $M^*$.[70] In a paper on lexical pragmatics, Deirdre Wilson and Robyn Carston, two prominent relevance theorists, suggest several examples of narrowing, three of which

---

[66] Kent Bach, "Conversational Implicature," *Mind and Language* 9 (1994) 124–62; Bach, "Semantic Slack: What Is Said and More," in *Foundations of Speech Act Theory*, S. Tsohatzidis, ed., Routledge, 1994, 267–91; Bach, "Context ex machina," in Z. Szabó, ed., *Semantics and Pragmatics*, Oxford University Press, 2005, 15–44; Bach, "Context Dependence," in *The Bloomsbury Companion to the Philosophy of Language*, M. García-Carpintero and M. Kölbel, eds., Bloomsbury, 2014, 153–84.

[67] Stephen Neale, "This, That, and the Other," in *Beyond Descriptions*, A. Bezuidenhout and M. Reimer, eds., Oxford University Press, 2004, 68–182; Neale, "On Location," in *Situating Semantics*, M. O'Rourke and C. Washington, eds., MIT Press, 2007, 251–393.

[68] John Collins, "The Syntax of Personal Taste," *Philosophical Perspectives* 27 (2013) 51–103; Collins, "On the Linguistic Status of Context Sensitivity," in *A Companion to the Philosophy of Language*, B. Hale, C. Wright, and A. Miller, eds., John Wiley & Sons, 2017, 151–73. Cp. also Brendan Gillon, "English Relational Words, Context Sensitivity, and Implicit Arguments," unpublished MS; Wolfram Hinzen, "Nothing Is Hidden: Contextualism and the Grammar of Meaning," *Mind and Language* 30 (2015) 259–91; Wolfram Hinzen and Michelle Sheehan, *The Philosophy of Universal Grammar*, Oxford University Press, 2013.

[69] "Adjectives in English: Attribution and Predication," *Lingua* 18 (1967) 1–34.

[70] Nicholas Allott and Mark Textor, "Lexical Pragmatics and the Nature of *Ad Hoc* Concepts," *International Review of Pragmatics* 4 (2012) 185–208, at 193–94, propose a third type of modulation in which $M^*$ and $M$ have the same extension, but differ in meaning. I will discuss yet a fourth type in section 1.3 of chapter 7.

I cite here.[71] For reasons that I will provide shortly, I distinguish the first example from the following two. Assume that the following is uttered by a speaker to his friends, as they are preparing to go out for the evening:

7.   I'm not drinking tonight.

"Drink" is a common example in the literature. It is assumed that the lexical meaning of "drink" is something like: take liquid into the mouth and swallow. However, in the context described, the natural construal of "drink" in (7) is something like: take alcoholic liquid into the mouth and swallow. However, I think that the example is infelicitous; and I am introducing it here for instructive purposes. There is a lexeme "drink" that encodes two polysemes, one of which has the meaning: "take alcoholic liquid into the mouth and swallow."[72] In the context described, "drink" in (7) is employed in this sense. Consequently, no modulation occurs here.

Contrast the following example, which I discussed in section 5 of chapter 2, and which I renumber here:

8.   In order to buy a house in Brookline, you need money.[73]

I assume that the use of "money" in (8) is a genuine case of narrowing. The extension of "money" includes any quantity of money. But in (8), "money" denotes a significant amount of money. I note in passing that although "money" is a noun, precisely a mass noun, the case of its modulation in (8) appears akin to the modulation of the degree associated with a relative gradable adjective in the basic sentence.[74]

The third example that Wilson and Carston cite is

9.   Churchill was a man.

I assume that the use of the count noun "man" in (9) is another genuine example of narrowing. The extension of "man" includes every man. But in (9), "man"

---

[71] Deirdre Wilson and Robyn Carston, "A Unitary Approach to Lexical Pragmatics: Relevance, Inference, and Ad Hoc Concepts," in *Pragmatics*, N. Burton-Roberts, ed., Palgrave-Macmillan, 2007, 230–59, 232. Cp. Allison Hall, "Lexical Pragmatics, Explicature, and Ad Hoc Concepts," in Depraetere and Salkie (2017) 85–114.

[72] *Concise Oxford English Dictionary*, Oxford University Press, 2011[12], s.v.

[73] I have adjusted Carston and Wilson's example, but in trivial ways.

[74] I note this kinship, but am not suggesting that (8) should be explained in the same way.

denotes only those men who have, to an outstanding degree, certain traits that have traditionally been regarded as masculine, for example, leadership and courage.

Here are three examples of broadening:

10a.    That bottle is empty. (said of a bottle containing a little bit of liquid.)
10b.    France is hexagonal.
10c.    The ATM swallowed my card.[75]

On natural readings of each of these sentences, the extensions of "empty," "hexagonal," and "swallow" are broader than the extensions of the lexical meanings of these words. For example, in (10a) the extension of "empty" includes containers that have some quantity of a relevant content, for example, liquid. I note these examples, but will have no more to say about broadening.

To the extent that modulation plausibly explains dimensional specification of "good," the kind of modulation involved must be narrowing. "Good" is associated with the dimension-type of value. Value is purpose serving. And in most contexts of use, "good" is associated with specific purposes that are served and thereby specific kinds of value.

The one linguist of whom I am aware who has proposed a modulation explanation of dimensional specification of "good" is Ingrid Falkum. Falkum's discussion occurs in her dissertation *The Semantics and Pragmatics of Polysemy: A Relevance-Theoretic Account*.[76] As the title indicates, Falkum's treatment is formulated within a relevance theoretic framework. In fact, Falkum worked directly with both Carston and Wilson.[77] I will present the gist of Falkum's view, which is encapsulated in a single passage, shortly. To do so, I need to introduce some further background information, specifically two points: the technical term "ad hoc concept" and the general inferentialist model of linguistic communication. I'll introduce these points in that order.

The idea of ad hoc concepts and ad hoc conceptualization ultimately derives from the psychological research of Lawrence Barsalou.[78] Barsalou suggests that we often construct concepts on the fly for ad hoc purposes. The term that he has used to refer to such concepts is "ad hoc category." Here, "category" correlates with "concept." Barsalou's original description follows:

---

[75] Example (10a) is from Wilson and Carston (2007) 234. Example (10b) was originally discussed by J. L. Austin, *How to Do Things with Words*, Harvard University Press, 1962², 143. I draw example (10c) from Recanati (2012) 72.
[76] University College London, dissertation in linguistics, 2011.
[77] Carston directed Falkum's dissertation.
[78] "Ad Hoc Categories," *Memory and Cognition* 20 (1983) 211–27.

The study of natural categories has been limited mostly to common categories such as "birds," "furniture," and "fruit." However, the use of highly specialized and unusual sets of items pervades everyday living. Some examples are "things to take on a camping trip," "possible costumes to wear to a Halloween party," and "places to look for antique desks." Since categories like these often appear to be created spontaneously for use in specialized contexts, I refer to them as ad hoc categories.

For example, assume Ronan and Katie are going on a camping trip. Ronan might ask Katie: "What are you taking?" In this context, plausibly the ad hoc concept THINGS TO TAKE ON A CAMPING TRIP is a constituent of Ronan's thought. Likewise, insofar as Katie understands Ronan's question as intended, the ad hoc concept THINGS TO TAKE ON A CAMPING TRIP is a constituent of her thought.

Ad hoc concepts provide what might be called the "semantic grounding" of the modulated meaning $M^*$ of a word $W$. To illustrate this, let us return to example (9) of narrowing above: "Churchill was a man." Assume that the lexical meaning of "man" is identical to the content of a lexical concept MAN. So, insofar as the modulated meaning $M^*$ of "man" in (9) departs from the lexical meaning $M$ of "man," the modulated meaning differs from the content of the lexical concept MAN. But insofar as "man," with meaning $M^*$, is intelligibly used by a speaker and understood by an audience, it must correspond to a concept that is distinct from, although evidently related to, the concept MAN. This distinct, but related, concept is standardly represented by appending an asterisk to the lexical concept. So, in this case, the ad hoc concept would be represented as: $MAN^*$. Accordingly, in the tokening of "man" in (9), the speaker's thought must consist of an ad hoc concept $MAN^*$; and as I am suggesting, this ad hoc concept provides the semantic grounding of the modulated meaning $M^*$ of "man" as tokened in this context.

So much, then, for why ad hoc conceptualization is invoked to explain modulation and specifically narrowing. A second piece of background information that informs Falkum's account is a so-called inferentialist model of linguistic communication. Assuming that the speaker employs a word with a modulated meaning, what reason does the audience have for understanding the speaker's use of the word according to the modulated meaning? Likewise, what reason does that speaker have to expect her audience to understand her use of the word according to the modulated meaning? Broadly speaking, compatibilists respond to such questions by appealing to a general inferentialist model of linguistic communication, which they contrast with the so-called classical code model of linguistic communication.

According to the classical code model of linguistic communication, when we communicate in language, something like the following occurs. A speaker has a thought T, which the speaker wants to communicate to an audience. The speaker makes a linguistic utterance $U$ whose meaning encodes T. The audience decodes $U$, and the result is that the audience now possesses the thought T that the speaker aimed to communicate.

In some cases, the classical code model may be applicable. But compatibilists reject the classical code model as a general explanation of linguistic communication. In most instances, it is too cumbersome for a speaker to make an utterance whose contents wholly encode the speaker's thought. Instead, when a speaker wants to communicate something, she utters only so much linguistic content as is relevant, within the context of utterance, to make it likely for the audience to infer what she intends to communicate. In many cases, the context in which the utterance occurs provides enough information to make it possible for a speaker to convey her thought without wholly encoding that thought in the linguistic utterance.

As relevance theorists sometimes characterize it, in saying something, the speaker offers the hearer evidence of the thought that she intends to convey; and, on the basis of this evidence, the audience infers the thought that the speaker intends to convey. On this view, effective communication consists of a balance between how much background and contextual information a speaker and a hearer can mutually rely on, and how much linguistic content the speaker needs to make explicit. The goal is to conjointly optimize intelligibility and facility in the conveyance of information. Always having to make explicit every intended detail jeopardizes facility in the conveyance of information; while at the other extreme, leaving too much information implicit or unsaid places too high a demand on the audience to interpret the utterance and as such risks unintelligibility.[79]

With this background information in mind, I come now to the passage in Falkum's dissertation where she provides her account of dimensional specification of "good" in terms of modulation via ad hoc conceptualization. Note that I have added some content in square brackets to clarify Falkum's remarks:

> Adjectives such as "good" can be seen as encoding highly general concepts, which have to be narrowed into more specific *ad hoc* concepts on each

---

[79] Note that determinists must, of course, admit an inferentialist model of communication at least insofar as speaker and audience rely on context to supply values for linguistic variables as well as to resolve ambiguous terms and syntactic structures. But determinists insist that, at least as far as fixing the truth-conditional content of (assertoric) utterances is concerned, the inferentialist model provides no further explanation of linguistic communication.

occasion of use (e.g., GOOD* KNIFE, GOOD** BOOK, GOOD*** MOTHER, GOOD**** STUDENT, etc.).[80] Depending on the context, "good" may express different *ad hoc* concepts in describing one and the same thing (e.g., a "good job" could be one that is well paid [GOOD* JOB], offers interesting tasks [GOOD** JOB], has an inclusive social environment [GOOD*** JOB], offers special benefits to the employees [GOOD**** JOB], gives a certain social status [GOOD***** JOB], and so on, each of which might involve a distinct *ad hoc* concept) . . . The pragmatic inferential process will take as input information stored in the encyclopedic entry of other lexical concepts in the utterance in the derivation of the *ad hoc* concept. In the case of "good," encyclopedic information stored about the concept encoded in the head noun [for example, "knife" in the case of "good knife" and so the concept KNIFE] is of particular importance. However, this information is not restricted to a particular, linguistically-specified purpose (e.g., knives are for cutting), but might include any information relevant to the interpretation of the speaker-intended meaning of the adjective, as shown by the following examples: "To become a member of Billy's exclusive gang you had to have a good knife"; "This is a good knife for people with wrist arthritis." Here it appears that information such as "knives can be used for stabbing people," "knives can be designed in different ways," etc. plays an important role in the derivation of the *ad hoc* concepts communicated by "good."[81]

In light of this passage, Falkum's account can be understood as follows. Falkum claims that use of terms such as "good" requires narrowing because the meanings of such terms are "highly general." It would be more reasonable for her to say here that insofar as a speaker desires to communicate more specific information and to do so with facility, then, insofar as she relies on terms such as "good," these terms may need to be narrowed.

Granted this, in the case of "good," Falkum notes that the ad hoc concept semantically grounding the modulated meaning is typically made salient to the audience by means of "encyclopedic information" relating to the nominal expression that "good" modifies. By "encyclopedic information" here, we may understand the following:

The encyclopedic [information] comprises a wide array of different kinds of knowledge, including commonplace assumptions scientific

---

information, culture-specific beliefs and personal, idiosyncratic observations and experiences.[82]

For example, in a tokening of "good knife," the noun "knife," which heads this phrase,[83] makes salient a body of information pertaining to knives. Given "good" modification of this noun, other things being equal, the characteristic purpose of a knife will be most salient in this context. However, as Falkum rightly notes, such encyclopedic information is by no means restricted to the characteristic purpose of knives.[84] The broader context of the phrase or utterance can make all manner of encyclopedic information relevant for the audience's "interpretation of the speaker-intended meaning," which is to say, relevant to the audience's ability to access the ad hoc concept GOOD* associated with the speaker's tokening of the adjective "good."

So much then for Falkum's account of dimensional specification of "good" in terms of modulation, precisely, narrowing via ad hoc conceptualization. I turn now to a criticism of Falkum's position. I assume that modulation and specifically narrowing occurs. But I doubt that it involves ad hoc conceptualization as this notion has been understood. And, to my main point, I doubt that modulation by means of ad hoc conceptualization is a tenable explanation of dimensional specification of "good." To see why, consider an example adapted from Falkum: "good knife," used in a context where we are concerned with knives suitable for slicing vegetables. Falkum's account suggests that in using the phrase "good knife" in such a context, the speaker has in mind the ad hoc concept GOOD*, which derives from the lexical concept GOOD. But now consider the following question: How does one think of GOOD*? That is, how does the speaker or, if you prefer, the speaker's mind engender such a concept here? In considering this question, consider the following conceptual gloss of GOOD* as GOOD FOR SLICING VEGETABLES. This latter concept appears to involve conceptual combination, that is, combination of the stable lexical concept GOOD with other stable lexical concepts such as SLICE and VEGETABLE. But then, why not admit that the content of the speaker's thought simply involves conceptual combination rather than ad hoc conceptualization as defined?

---

[82]   Carston (2002) 321.

[83]   The so-called head of a phrase is the word whose syntactic category endows the phrase with its syntactic category. For example, "good knife" is a noun phrase headed by the noun "knife"; "extremely sharp" is an adjective phrase headed by the adjective "sharp." The syntactic term "head" is discussed further in section 1.2 of chapter 7.

[84]   The reason that Falkum makes this point here owes to the broader context in which she is advancing her position. This is precisely as part of a critical response to James Pustejovsky's generative theory of polysemy and specifically his account of the polysemy of "good." On this, cp. James Pustejovsky, *The Generative Lexicon*, MIT Press, 1995.

Indeed, we can press this point further. There can be no such concept as GOOD*. Again, GOOD* here has the content GOOD FOR SLICING VEGETABLES. But then GOOD* just is the complex concept GOOD FOR SLICING VEGETABLES. My fundamental criticism, then, is that I see no way for a person to think of GOOD* otherwise than by thinking of GOOD FOR SLICING VEGETABLES. In short, the representations of lexical concepts with asterisks suggest that ad hoc concepts are being thought of, but in fact they aren't. In light of this criticism, it is telling to recall the ad hoc categories that Barsalou introduced in his original paper: THINGS TO TAKE ON A CAMPING TRIP, POSSIBLE COSTUMES TO WEAR TO A HALLOWEEN PARTY, PLACES TO LOOK FOR ANTIQUE DESKS. Clearly, these are all conceptual complexes.

In short, modulation, specifically narrowing by means of ad hoc conceptualization, cannot explain dimensional specification of "good." Granted this, it remains possible that some other compatibilist linguistic operation might explain dimensional specification of "good" in terms of narrowing.[85] Observe, however, that the one other sort of case that we have seen, namely Rett's uninformativity-based quantity implicature theory in section 3.3 of chapter 3, is unlikely to be applicable to the present case. When someone says, "$x$ is good," it cannot simply be as a result of uninformativity that "good" is modulated. More precisely, no explanation is here available for why informativeness via narrowing would yield the appropriate dimensional specification. Whereas modulation of a degree is always from non-significance to significance, modulation of general value is, from context to context, to countless distinct species of value.

Rather than pursue other possible leads in this general theoretical domain, I propose to turn to a second type of compatibilist explanation of dimensional specification of "good": supplementation.

## 3.3. Introduction to Supplementation

With respect to explaining dimensional specification of "good," I here stipulatively employ the word "supplementation" to denote three basic types of constructions consisting of "good":

- modification of "good" by a dimension-type specifying pre-adjectival adverbial expression; for example, "morally good"

---

[85] Noteworthy here is Nicholas Allott and Mark Textor, "Lexical Modulation without Concepts," *Dialectica* 71 (2017) 399–424; unfortunately their discussion of narrowing is limited (421–22).

- modification of "good" by a dimension-type specifying post-adjectival adverbial expression; for example, "good for slicing vegetables"
- "good" modification of a dimension-type specifying nominal expression; for example, "good wine."

Note that my use of "adverbial" here is intended to include modification of "good" both by phrases consisting of adverbs and by non-adverbial phrases, in particular prepositional phrases such as "for slicing vegetables," functioning adverbially.[86]

Syntactically, the three basic types of supplementation share the fact that "good" and another expression are adjoined. I will refer to the dimension-type specifying expression with which "good" is adjoined as the "supplement." So, in the three examples given, the supplements are "morally," "for slicing vegetables," and "wine" respectively. Moreover, among the three primary types of supplementation, "good" and its supplement are adjoined in one of two ways: either the supplement modifies "good," as in the first two types, or "good" modifies the supplement, as in the third type. I will refer to the former way in which "good" and its supplement are adjoined as "adverbial" supplementation; and I will refer to the latter way in "good" and its supplement are adjoined as "nominal" supplementation.

In addition to the three basic types of supplementation, supplementation may occur through the combination of two or three of the basic types. Consider the following examples:

11a.   That is an aesthetically good lamp.
11b.   This is a good watch for scuba diving.
11c.   That is an economically good bulb for outdoor lighting.

In (11a), supplementation is realized through combination of a pre-adjectival adverbial expression modifying "good" and "good" modifying a nominal expression. In (11b), supplementation is realized through "good" modifying a nominal expression and a post-adjectival prepositional phrase modifying "good." In (11c), supplementation is realized through a pre-adjectival adverbial expression modifying "good," "good" modifying a nominal expression, and a post-adjectival prepositional phrase modifying "good."

---

[86] In the linguistics literature, these are referred to as "adverbials." Cp. Claudia Maienborn and Martin Schäfer, "Adverbs and Adverbials," in *Semantics: An International Handbook of Natural Language Meaning*, vol. 3, Claudia Maienborn, Klaus von Heusinger, and Paul Portner, eds., de Gruyter, 2011, 1390–1420; Denis Delfitto, "Adverb Classes and Adverb Placement," in Everaert and van Riemsdijk (2007) 83–120; Monika Rathert, "Adverbials," in *Oxford Handbook of Tense and Aspect*, R. I. Binnick, ed., Oxford University Press, 2012, 237–68.

Semantically, the three basic types of supplementation constructions share the fact that the expression with which "good" is adjoined, that is, the supplement, specifies the dimension-type associated with "good." I suggest that in the cases of pre-adjectival adverbial modification of "good" and post-adjectival prepositional phrase modification of "good," the supplement specifies the dimension-type associated with "good" directly. In contrast, in the case of nominal supplementation, the nominal expression that "good" modifies specifies the dimension-type associated with "good" indirectly and precisely by means of a phenomenon that I will dub "reciprocal modification." I will clarify these claims regarding the direct and indirect dimensional specification of the supplements subsequently.

Presently, note the following semantic claim pertaining to supplementation as an explanation of dimensional specification of "good." When, in a tokening of "good," dimensional specification occurs,[87] the token of "good" semantically contributes nothing to dimensional specification. To appreciate this claim, compare, by analogy, a rather different type of expression, the following noun phrase:

toasted bagel.

Here "toasted" modifies "bagel," with the result that the expression "toasted bagel" denotes a specific kind of bagel. But the meaning of "bagel" is unaltered; it is the lexical meaning of "bagel."

Viewed as such, dimensional specification of "good" in terms of supplementation should seem completely unremarkable. Indeed, I maintain that it is and that this is a virtue of the account. Granted this, there are two complicating features of supplementation. One relates to elliptical forms of supplementation, which involve what I call "semantic ellipsis." The other relates to nominal supplementation and what I have described as the indirect way that the nominal supplement contributes to specifying the dimension-type associated with "good." These features of supplementation will be focal points of my ensuing account.

## 3.4. Semantic Ellipsis

Supplementation may be explicit or implicit. In cases of explicit supplementation, the supplement is explicitly expressed. The examples in section 3.3 were all

---

[87] I say "when, in a tokening of 'good,'" dimensional specification occurs, because, although I take it that dimensional specification occurs in almost all tokenings of "good," I do not assume that dimensional specification must occur when "good" is tokened. I discuss the possibility of so-called unsupplemented and so dimensionally unspecified tokens of "good" in section 3.5.

examples of explicit supplementation. The following are examples of explicit adverbial supplementation, constructed on the basis of the basic sentence, and with the supplement italicized:

> *x* is good *with a paintbrush.*
> *x* is good *at accounting.*
> *x* is *aesthetically* good.
> *x* is good *for roasting potatoes.*

The following are examples of explicit nominal supplementation, again constructed on the basis of the basic sentence, and with the supplement italicized:

> *x* is a good *doctor.*
> *x* is good *furniture.*
> *x* is a good *way to tell time.*
> *x* is a good *example of a cover letter.*

I will return to explicit supplementation below. The remainder of this section will focus on implicit supplementation.

Implicit supplementation may also be either adverbial or nominal. What distinguishes implicit supplementation from explicit supplementation is that in the case of implicit supplementation, the supplement is not explicitly expressed, but nonetheless conveyed in the tokening of "good." For example, in a given context, what is explicitly stated may be

> This is good.

But what may be conveyed is

> This is good [for roasting potatoes].

or

> This is [a] good [example of a cover letter].

Here, the contents in square brackets are implicit.

Note that explicit and implicit supplementation are not mutually exclusive. For example, assume two children are looking for pebbles to use in playing marbles. Upon finding a suitable pebble, one child may say to the other:

This is a good pebble [for playing marbles].[88]

Here, we have a combination of explicit nominal supplementation and implicit adverbial supplementation. Conversely, the following is an example of implicit nominal supplementation and explicit adverbial supplementation. Two children are looking for stones to skip on a lake. Upon finding a suitable stone, one child says to the other:

This is [a] good [stone] for skipping.

For convenience, in this section I will focus on purely implicit supplementation. Implicit supplementation is a kind of ellipsis, precisely what I will call "semantic ellipsis." In his paper "This, That, and the Other," Stephen Neale distinguishes three kinds of ellipsis.[89] I will refer to these here as "implicative," "syntactic," and "semantic."[90] Implicative ellipsis involves implicature. It consists in saying one thing S, which implicates another thing I, where the intention in saying S is to convey I. Neale illustrates implicative ellipsis using the following example from Grice.[91] Asked for his opinion of a student Smith's philosophical ability, a professor replies:

Smith has wonderful handwriting and is always punctual.

Here, the professor's reply implicates that Smith's philosophical ability is poor. The professor does not explicitly say that Smith's philosophical ability is poor, and in this respect elides that content. I will say no more about implicative ellipsis here.

Syntactic ellipsis occurs when a statement S elides syntactic constituents that are recoverable in virtue of the broader syntactic structure of S, but whose elision would otherwise be syntactically unacceptable. Consider the following example:

12.   Joe works as a pediatric endocrinologist, and Gail as a social worker.

---

[88] The example is inspired by Szabó (2001) 132–33. Note that the prepositional phrase "for playing marbles" modifies "good" rather than "pebble." If it were modifying "pebble," then, contrary to fact, the sentence would entail "This is a pebble for playing marbles."

[89] Neale (2004) at 97–105.

[90] My implicative ellipsis corresponds to Neale's conversational ellipsis; my syntactic ellipsis corresponds to Neale's sentence ellipsis; and my semantic ellipsis corresponds to Neale's utterance ellipsis.

[91] Neale (2004) 98; after Paul Grice, "The Causal Theory of Perception," *Proceedings of the Aristotelian Society*, supp. vol. 35 (1961) 121–52.

In the second clause of (12), the verb is elided. The ellipsis can be represented by strikethrough as follows:

Joe works as a pediatric endocrinologist, and Gail ~~works~~ as a social worker.

A syntactically well-formed clause requires a verb. But the elided verb in the second clause can be recovered from the parallel structure of the first clause. Compare the following example:

13.   Ernest's first marriage lasted ten years; his second, three.

Here, multiple constituents have been elided in the second clause of (13): the noun that heads the phrase "his second," the verb, and the noun that heads the phrase "three":

Ernest's first marriage lasted ten years; his second marriage lasted three years.

Again, a clause requires a verb. Moreover, the elided verb "last" is a binary predicate. It requires an external argument corresponding to nominal expression that denotes a state or event and an internal argument whose meaning corresponds to a duration. Again, the ellipses are licit because they are recoverable from the preceding clause with parallel structure.

I note that there are strict constraints on syntactic ellipsis. For example, compare the following unacceptable examples (where the second member of each pair provides a representation of the intended elided elements):

Dax drank the orange juice, * and Jett grapefruit.
Dax drank the orange juice, * and Jett ~~drank the~~ grapefruit ~~juice~~.

Ronan bought Toby a shirt, * and Katie pajamas.
Ronan bought Toby a shirt, * and Katie ~~bought Toby~~ pajamas.[92]

By "semantic ellipsis" I mean the following. Assume a grammatically well-formed expression type, for example a word type, $W$. Assume a complex expression type $C$ of which $W$ is a proper part. Assume that the lexical meanings of $W$ and $C$ differ. Let us refer to the proper part of $C$ that when added to $W$ yields $C$ as $S$, short for "semantic supplement." So, $C$ is wholly constituted by $W$ and a semantic supplement $S$. Semantic ellipsis occurs when a tokening of $W$ that consists in the ellipsis of $S$ has the literal meaning of $C$. As such, we can represent the truth-conditional content that is conveyed as

---

[92] The sentence is of course felicitous if understood as "Ronan bought Toby a shirt, and ~~Ronan bought~~ Katie pajamas."

*W* [*S*].

Here I use square brackets, rather than strikethrough, to indicate semantic, in contrast to syntactic, ellipsis of *S*. I underscore that in this case the meaning of *W* is not modulated. The meaning of the token of *W* is the lexical meaning of *W*. However, the meaning of the token of *W* is *C* because the tokening of *W* consists in the semantic ellipsis of *S*. Implicit supplementation is precisely semantic ellipsis of the supplement.

Neale draws an example from Quine to illustrate semantic ellipsis occurring in the use of a definite description.[93] Consider the following sentence:

14.   The yellow house is on fire.

Here we are to imagine an utterance of (14) in a context that makes it clear that by "The yellow house" what is to be understood is "The yellow house in the third block of Lee Street, Tulsa." Consequently, we can represent the token of (14) as

The yellow house [in the third block of Lee Street, Tulsa] is on fire.

As Neale emphasizes, the definite description "the yellow house" is not syntactically elliptical. It is a "perfectly well-formed description." Consequently, the explicit expression constituting (14) is a syntactically well-formed sentence. Rather, the use of the definite description "The yellow house" in (14) in the given context is semantically elliptical. Consequently, what makes semantic ellipsis a compatibilist position is that the supplementary content *S* of *W*, as tokened, is not syntactically mandated.

Compare the following examples of semantic ellipsis, adapted from Bach:[94]

15.   Ronan and Katie are married.
16.   Joe turned off the light and walked out of his office.
17.   Adam has two children.

In many contexts, required interpretations of these sentences would be

15s.   Ronan and Katie are married [to each other].
16s.   Joe turned off the light and [subsequently] walked out of his office.
17s.   Adam has [exactly] two children.

---

[93] Neale (2004) 98, drawing on Willard Van Orman Quine, *Mathematical Logic*, Harvard University Press, 1940, 146.
[94] Bach (2000) 262–63.

Consider also the following exchange:

> Ronan: Would you like some breakfast?
> 18. Adam: I've already eaten.[95]

In ordinary contexts, the required interpretation of Adam's response is

> 18s. Adam: [No,] I've already eaten [breakfast today].

In examples (15s)–(18s), the bracketed expressions represent contents that are semantically elided in (15)–(18). In other words, in the appropriate contexts, the bracketed expressions are intended by the speaker, and rational norms of communication require that the audience infer them.

To be sure, one can easily imagine contexts where other intentions and inferences are preferable and indeed required. Here is such an example for (28). Ronan, Katie, and Adam are siblings. Joe is their father, and he is speaking to an old family friend, Ann. Ann asks Joe how his children are doing, and Joe replies: "Ronan and Katie are married." In this context, Joe's statement entails that Ronan and Katie are not married to each other.

Granted this, in contrast to our definition of modulation, our definition of semantic ellipsis suggests—and here I state expressly—that the elided supplement $S$ of $W$ contributes to truth-conditional content. In any case where an elided supplement did not contribute to truth-conditions, implicature or implicative ellipsis rather than semantic ellipsis would occur.

Hereafter, unless otherwise stated, I will refer to semantic ellipsis simply as "ellipsis." Given the definition of ellipsis, I'll now provide an illustration of ellipsis, and so of implicit supplementation, to explain dimensional specification of "good." Assume that Gail and Joe are at a kitchenware store and that they are testing knives for slicing vegetables. Gail says to Joe:

> 19. It's good.

Assume here that the pronoun "it" refers to the knife that Gail and Joe are testing. Recall that according to the modulation explanation, the meaning of this token of "good" in (19) undergoes semantic narrowing, precisely with respect to dimensional specification. Instead of denoting mere significant value, "good" denotes significant vegetable-slicing value. Now, according to the supplementation

---

[95] This example is adapted from François Recanati, "The Pragmatics of What Is Said," *Mind and Language* 4 (1989) 296–329, at 303.

explanation, the meaning of "good" in (19) is unchanged. "Good" is associated with unspecified value; but the token of "good" in (19) involves ellipsis. The elided supplement is "for slicing vegetables":

19s.  It's good [for slicing vegetables].

This elided supplement specifies the type of value with which "good" is associated.

Furthermore, we can confirm that the elided supplement, as represented in (19s), is part of the truth-conditional content of the utterance of (19) in this context, on the basis of the following considerations. First, assume that Gail says (19). Within this context, it would not be consistent with rational norms of communication for Gail to mean something other than (19s). Second, observe that the predicate expression in (19), as uttered in this context, can be embedded under truth-conditional operators such as negation and the material conditional, while preserving the content of the predicate expression (19s). For instance, Joe may reply to Gail's utterance of (19):

19c.  If you think it's good, then we should buy it.

Here, the meaning conveyed by the antecedent of (19c) must be

If you think it's good [for slicing vegetables].

Alternatively, Joe may be having trouble using the knife on a turnip and reply to Gail's utterance of (19):

19n.  No, it's not good.

Again, here the meaning conveyed by (19n) must be

No, it's not good [for slicing vegetables].

## 3.5.  Four Syntactic and Semantic Implications of Supplementation

Here I underscore or clarify two syntactic and two semantic implications of the account of supplementation that I am proposing to explain dimensional specification of "good" in a context of use. These implications pertain to the syntactic relation between "good" and its supplement, the formal syntactic category in terms of which "good" is interpreted, the semantic contribution of the supplement in relation to the thesis that value is purpose serving, and the lexical meaning of the basic sentence without a supplement.

Insofar as supplementation of "good" is a compatibilist explanation of dimensional specification, supplements are not syntactically required. In syntactic terms, the relation between "good" and its supplement is "adjunctive" rather than "complementary." This is just to say that the supplement is not syntactically required by "good," in which case it would be a syntactic complement. Rather, the supplement is merely syntactically admissible; consequently, it is a syntactic adjunct.[96] More precisely, adverbial modification of "good" is adjunctive. And "good" modification of a nominal expression is adjunctive.[97]

Ignoring, for convenience, any additional degree argument associated with "good," this entails that "good" is an ordinary unary predicate. And that entails that the following views are false: Geach's view that "good" is a logically attributive adjective (whether this be interpreted as an extensional or intensional predicate modifier whose predicate argument derives from a nominal expression), Szabó's view that "good" is an incomplete unary predicate, and Siegel's view that "good" occurs as an intensional predicate modifier. On the other hand, the view that "good" is a unary predicate conforms to Siegel's view of "good" in one of its two forms.

The claim that "good" is a unary predicate may be difficult to accept. But consider the following sentence:

20. If an entity is good, then it has value.

I defended the truth of sentence (20) in section 1 of chapter 4, in the context of introducing what I called "the value thesis." If the basic sentence "an entity is good" in the antecedent of the conditional did not express a proposition, then (20) could not be true.

Assume then that "good" is a unary predicate.[98] In section 4 of chapter 4, I proposed that dimensional specification of "good" precisely consists in the specification of purpose.[99] Accordingly, I propose that the semantic contribution of the supplement to dimensional specification is precisely the following:

---

[96] On the adjunct-complement distinction, cp. Williams (2015) 51–74.

[97] This point is elaborated in section 3.7.

[98] If instead we assume, according to the relational analysis, that "good" is a binary predicate, the key point in the present context remains that one of the arguments of the binary predicate is not a dimension argument.

[99] When convenient and for the sake of simplicity, I will hereafter elide reference to significance of degree.

The supplement specifies, that is, contributes to the specification of, the purpose that is being served.

Granted this, what is the lexical meaning of the basic sentence "$x$ is good"? Assume that *pos* is not a covert constituent of the predicate expression. In that case, lexically, the predicate expression denotes a degree of unspecified value. Given the semantic adjustment to the degree that occurs in the basic sentence, in that context the predicate expression denotes a significant degree of unspecified value.[100]

While "good" almost always occurs with a supplement, explicit or implicit, given its interpretation as a unary predicate or, at any rate, as a predicate that does not have a dimension argument, one may wonder what truth-value an unsupplemented sentence of the form "$x$ is good"—call it an "unsupplemented basic sentence"—may have. Assume a universe without purposes and so without value. Said of an entity in such a universe, an instance of an unsupplemented basic sentence—whose literal meaning is "$x$ has significant [unspecified] value" or "$x$ is significantly purposive [in an unspecified way]"—will be false.[101] Conversely, said of such a universe, the following sentence will be true:

Nothing is good.

Consider now a universe that contains values and so purposes, for example ours. Prima facie, it may seem that there are entities in this universe of which the unsupplemented basic sentence is true. For example, consider, by analogy, the following implication: if $x$ is red or has some other specific color, then $x$ is colored. Accordingly, if $x$ is good in such-and-such a way, then $x$ is good simpliciter. There is, however, a problem with the latter inference, which relates not to the distinction between specific and general value, but rather to the gradability of "good" and the sense of significance of degree in the basic sentence. The problem is this: there is no universal scale of value. To clarify this problem, assume, for the sake of simplicity, a universe with exactly two kinds of purpose and so with two ways in which entities might serve purposes to a significant degree. Absent a third kind of purpose according to which the other two kind are coordinated, one kind of value would have no more or less value than the other. Of course, if there exists in our universe some superordinate kind of value and so a kind of value whose value coordinates the values of all other subordinate kinds of value,

---

[100] Compare Siegel's view that as a unary predicate, "good" has a very general meaning.

[101] I note that the term "unspecified" here is not to be confused with the term "specific" in the phrase "specific value," which denotes so-called positive value. Unspecified value is value of an indeterminate kind. In the case of unsupplemented "good," this will be specific (versus generic) value of an unspecified kind.

then the unsupplemented basic sentence might be true or false of some $x$ in our universe. However, I don't see any reason to believe that there is a superordinate kind of value.

There may be a second reason that, said of a universe with multiple uncoordinated types of value, an instance of the unsupplemented basic sentence would lack a truth-value. Absent determination of a comparison class, there can be no sense to the comparative notion that significance consists in. If $x$ has a significant degree of some gradable property, that degree is significant relative to the degrees to which members of a comparison class have that property. Comparison class determination precisely delimits a set of entities. Absent such determination, the comparison class will consist of all entities in the universe. But arguably the notion of *all* entities in the universe is incoherent.

In short, there are few contexts where instances of the unsupplemented basic sentence have a truth-value.

### 3.6.1. Supplementation and Inferences

I turn now to consider how supplementation may explain transfer inferences and *AN* splitting. In the course of this discussion, I will also address the two additional considerations that Szabó cites in favor of his position over Geach's.

### 3.6.2. Supplementation and Transfer Inferences

Consider the following instance of simple transfer inference:

Joe is a good doctor.
Joe is a father.

---

Joe is a good father.

In the first premise, "doctor" explicitly supplements "good" and so specifies the dimension-type of value associated with "good" as value relating to being a doctor. Likewise, in the conclusion, "father" explicitly supplements "good" and so specifies the dimension-type of value associated with "good" as value relating to being a father.

Granted this, insofar as we aim to formally represent supplementation, we need a clearer understanding of the way that nominal supplementation effects dimensional specification. In considering this topic, I suggest that we look at how adverbial supplementation effects dimensional specification.

I assume that, syntactically, dimensional specification involves adverbial modification of "good." As we've seen, explicit adverbial supplementation has two forms: a pre-adjectival adverb modifying "good," for example, "economically / prudentially / morally / aesthetically good"; and a post-adjectival prepositional phrase functioning adverbially modifying "good" such as "good in such-and-such a way / a respect." I presume that these two forms of adverbial supplementation perform the same semantic function. For example, compare the following pairs of sentences:

> x is aesthetically good.
> x is good with respect to aesthetic considerations.

> x is morally good.
> x is good in a moral way.

The members of each pair are semantically equivalent or at least nearly so.

Observe also that, with ordinary stress, the normally pre-adjectival adverb is syntactically awkward if it occurs post-adjectivally:

> * x is good aesthetically.
> * x is good morally.[102]

Likewise, with ordinary intonation, the prepositional phrase that functions adverbially and ordinarily occurs post-adjectivally is unacceptable pre-adjectivally:

> * x is with respect to aesthetic considerations good.
> * x is in a moral way good.[103]

The reasons for the syntactic infelicities in the two types of cases are related, but different. The natural site of an adverbial modifier of "good" is pre-adjectival. However, when an adverbial modifier is "heavy," that is, when it is a lengthy syntactic constituent, it is "extraposed" rightward and so occurs post-adjectivally.

Syntactically, adverbial modifiers of adjectives are a type of predicate modifier. Semantically, I take adverbial modifiers—more precisely, the sorts of adverbial modifiers of "good" that effect dimensional specification— regardless of their overt position, to be functions from the intensions of

---

[102] With a heavy stress, such constructions, which focalize the adverb, are acceptable. For example: "When I said that the painting was good, I meant that it was good *aesthetically*; I didn't mean that it was good *morally*."

[103] With suitable pauses, which can be represented by commas, both sentences are more acceptable: "x is, with respect to aesthetic considerations, good"; "x is, in a moral way, good."

predicate expressions to the intensions of predicate expressions. Accordingly, for example, "morally good" and "good in a moral respect" would both be represented as

$$(\mathbf{M}(G))(x).$$

And "aesthetically good" and "good with respect to aesthetic considerations" would both be represented as

$$(\mathbf{A}(G))(x).$$

Given these commitments regarding adverbial modification of "good" and so adverbial supplementation, I am committed to the view that nominal supplementation effects dimensional specification by adverbial means. But, of course, no overt adverbial modifier appears in sentences such as "Beatrice is a good dancer" and "Joe is a good doctor." Rather, I suggest that the truth-conditional content of such sentences is enriched and enriched precisely with adverbial content. Informally, such content may be represented in some such ways:

21a.  Beatrice is a good (as a dancer) dancer.
21b.  Beatrice is a (dancer-wise) good dancer.

22a.  Joe is a (doctor-wise) good doctor.
22b.  Joe is a good (with respect to being a doctor) doctor.

I have placed the enriched contents in parentheses to indicate that they derive from supplementation and as such are not syntactically mandated. I hasten to add that some of these sentences are semantically, if not syntactically infelicitous. I merely offer them for heuristic purposes. What is common to all four sentences is that they involve semantic redundancy. Precisely, on natural readings of these sentences, the adverbial contents in parentheses are redundant. In other words, on a natural reading, "Joe is good" in the sentence "Joe is a good doctor" means "Joe is good with respect to doctoring" or "Joe is good in the role of doctor." In short, while, syntactically, nominal supplements are indeed nominal and not adverbial, semantically, they suggest adverbial contents. Moreover, in these occurrences, it would be semantically infelicitous to overtly express the adverbial contents that they suggest because such expressions would be redundant. For example, consider:

# Joe is a good doctor and good as a doctor.

Granted this, to formally represent the contents of such sentences and their operation within inference schemas, we need make these redundancies explicit. Recall then our natural language argument:

Joe is a good doctor.
Joe is a father.
_____

Joe is a good father.

I suggest that we formalize the first premise as follows:

$(\mathbf{D}(G))(j) \wedge D(j).$

In the first conjunct, $\mathbf{D}$ stands for an intensional predicate modifier. Its meaning is something like "doctor-wise." Its argument is the unary predicate $G$ corresponding to "good." The value of $\mathbf{D}(G)$ is a unary predicate whose meaning is something like "good at doctoring" or "good as a doctor." Likewise, we can represent the conclusion as

$(\mathbf{F}(G))(j) \wedge F(j).$

Accordingly, the formal conclusion is invalid. And so, we have a formal representation of the simple transfer inference argument that corresponds to the invalidity of the natural language argument.

Generalizing, a sentence of the following form, where *Nom* stands for a nominal expression,[104]

*x* is a good *Nom.*

should be formalized as

$(\mathbf{N}(G))(x) \wedge N(x).$

Here, $\mathbf{N}$ stands for an intensional predicate modifier variable and $N$ stands for a unary predicate variable, where the meaning of $N$ corresponds to the meaning of the nominal expression *Nom* and the meaning of $\mathbf{N}$ suitably derives from the meaning of $N$.

---

[104] I note in passing that if the nominal expression *Nom* is a mass noun, the indefinite article should be dropped, viz.: *x* is good *Nom*; for example "*x* is good wine."

Granted this, let me now pause over the second conjunct: $N(x)$. For convenience, I'll call this the "nominal conjunct." For most nominal expressions modified by "good," the nominal conjunct is entailed. For example, consider the following sentences:

23a.   x is a good painting.
23b.   x is a good person.
23c.   x is good wine.
23d.   x is good chocolate.

Sentences (23a)–(23d) entail, respectively,

23a'.   x is a painting.
23b'.   x is a person.
23c'.   x is wine.
23d'.   x is chocolate.

Granted this, there are some nominal expressions that do not entail the nominal conjunct. Some agentive nominals with "-er" suffixes are among them.[105] For instance, consider:

Beatrice is a good dancer.

———————————

Beatrice is a dancer.

The premise seems to require merely that if Beatrice dances, she typically dances well. In contrast, the conclusion seems to require that Beatrice typically dances. Contrast:

Joe is a good father.

———————————

Joe is a father.

The crucial difference between "dancer" and "father" is that being a father is a permanent or relatively stable property of individuals. In contrast, being a dancer need not be so. I note then that some agentive nominals modified by "good," including some with "-er" suffixes, do not entail the nominal conjunct. But since

---

[105] I underscore that these inferences are valid for "good." I am not generalizing beyond "good."

the inferential property here turns on the semantics of these agentive nominals, rather than on "good," I will say no more about such cases.[106]

In light of the preceding, we can be brief in our treatment of quantified transfer inference. Consider the following example:

Joe is a good doctor.
All doctors are fathers and vice versa.

———————————————————

Joe is a good father.

I formalize this argument as

$(\mathbf{D}(G))(j) \wedge D(j)$
$\forall x: D(x) \equiv F(x)$

———————

$(\mathbf{F}(G))(j) \wedge F(j).$

The conclusion of the formal argument is clearly invalid; and so it accords with the invalidity of the natural language argument.

Finally, let's briefly return to adverbial supplementation of "good," both by a pre-adjectival adverb and by a post-adjectival prepositional phrase functioning adverbially.

Assume that $V$ stands for an adverb. Then we can formalize the following,

$x$ is $V$ good.

as

$(\mathbf{V}(G))(x).$

Here, $\mathbf{V}$ is an intensional predicate modifier whose meaning corresponds to that of $V$. Assume now that $P$ stands for a prepositional phrase:

$x$ is good $P$.

———

[106] Cp. Malka Rappaport and Beth Levin, "-er Nominals: Implications for the Theory of Argument Structure," in *Syntax and Semantics*, vol. 26, T. Stowell and E. Wehrli, eds., Academic Press, 1992, 127–53. (A kindred problem relating to generic statements was first discussed in the 1662 *La Logique ou l'art de penser* and has, accordingly, been referred to as the "Port Royal Puzzle." Consider the following sentences: "The French are good soldiers" and "The Dutch are good sailors." From these sentences, the following cannot be inferred: "The French are soldiers" and "The Dutch are sailors." Cp. Antoine Arnauld and Pierre Nicole, *Logic or the Art of Thinking*, J. V. Buroker, ed., Cambridge University Press, 1996, 116; Sarah-Jane Leslie, "Generics: Cognition and Acquisition," *Philosophical Review* 117 (2008) 1–47, at 16–18; Bernhard Nickel, "Dutchmen Are Good Sailors: Genericity and Gradability," in Alda Mari et al., eds., *Genericity*, Oxford University Press, 2013, 390–405.)

We can formalize this as

$$(\mathbf{P}(G))(x).$$

Here, $\mathbf{P}$ is an intensional predicate modifier whose meaning corresponds to that of $P$.

I underscore that, in contrast to our formalization of nominal supplementation, the formalization of adverbial supplementation involves no analogous "adverbial" conjunct. For example, as I noted above, from

Cola-Cola is good for removing rust.

it does not follow that

Cola-Cola is for removing rust.[107]

In light of the preceding, I can now clarify my claims from section 3.3 that an adverbial supplement—be it a pre-adjectival adverb or a post-adjectival prepositional phrase functioning adverbially—*directly* specifies the dimension-type associated with good, whereas a nominal supplement specifies the dimension-type associated with good *indirectly*. I have suggested that dimensional specification semantically requires adverbial modification of "good." Adverbial supplements constitute such modifiers. In contrast, a nominal supplement specifies the dimension-type associated with good by suggesting an adverbial modifier of "good." And so nominal supplementation effects dimensional specification indirectly. I will elaborate on this phenomenon, which I call "reciprocal modification," in section 3.7.

### 3.6.3. Szabó's Two Additional Considerations

I turn now to the two additional considerations that Szabó cites in support of his interpretation of "good" as an incomplete unary predicate. Again, these are that "good" does not require a nominal expression to provide a value for its covert role variable, and that a noun phrase "good $N$" does not entail "good in the $N$

---

[107] I should note here that my treatment of adverbial supplementation considerably oversimplifies. Prepositional phrases in particular can be of various kinds and can be of various degrees of complexity. In addition, I am considerably oversimplifying the relation between adverbial supplements consisting of adverbs and adverbial supplements consisting of prepositional phrases functioning adverbially. A more adequate treatment of adverbial supplementation would address such points and such distinctions. Nonetheless, so far as I can see, the absence of refinements does not compromise the basic points being advanced.

role." Regarding the first point, recall Szabó's example: "This liquid is good for the purpose of the experiment." Here we have a case of adverbial supplementation, precisely a "for" prepositional phrase and more precisely still a purposive "for" phrase. Likewise, recall my example:

5. David is good with his hands.

Here "with his hands" is a prepositional phrase functioning adverbially. Consequently, without accepting Szabó's interpretation of "good" as an incomplete unary predicate, my supplementation account admits Szabó's first point. More strongly, given my claim that nominal supplementation effects dimensional specification indirectly by suggesting an adverbial modifier of "good," I am claiming that, strictly speaking, the nominal expression that "good" modifies is never sufficient for dimensional specification.

With respect to Szabó's second point, recall the following sort of example:

24. Beatrice is a good dancer.

Assume that (24) is uttered in a context where certain members of the troupe have been stealing money from the company's safe, and so where (24) means

24m. Beatrice is a dancer who is morally good.

I accept this example. Nothing in the preceding account of supplementation entails that when "good" modifies a nominal expression, the nominal expression must contribute to dimensional specification. Recall that I characterized nominal supplementation as "'good' modification of a dimension-type specifying nominal expression." So, it is not the case that every nominal expression that "good" modifies contributes to dimensional specification. Granted this, in explaining the reading of (24) as (24m), I take it that (24) involves semantic ellipsis of the adverb "morally," viz.:

Beatrice is a [morally] good dancer.

Evidently, the implicit adverbial modifier is not suggested by "dancer." Rather, the elided adverb "morally" is supplied by the broader context in which (24) occurs. Furthermore, it should also be noted that in order to achieve the reading of (24) as (24m) in the given context, the stress pattern of the sentence must be non-ordinary. Precisely, "good" in (24) must have a heavy stress accent:

Beatrice is a góod dancer.

Without the heavy stress on "good," (24) cannot be felicitously read as (24m).

According to our formalism, we would render (24), read as (24m), as

$$(\mathbf{M}(G))(b) \wedge D(b).$$

Contrast this with the following sentence—read with ordinary stress patterns—involving a combination of adverbial and nominal supplements:

25.   Joseph is a morally good doctor.

The natural reading of this sentence is not

Joseph is morally good and Joseph is a good doctor.

but rather

Joseph is morally good in the context of his role as a doctor.

### 3.6.4.  Supplementation and *AN* Splitting

I turn now to the relation between supplementation and *AN* splitting. Recall that *AN* splitting consists of adjectival and nominal inferences of the following form:

*x* is *A N.*
_____

*x* is *A.*
*x* is *N.*

Adjectives that do not license the adjectival inference are, in Geach's terminology, logically attributive. For example, consider the following example of *AN* splitting:

Garth is a good surgeon.
_____

Garth is good.
Garth is a surgeon.

Geach's thought here is that the adjectival inference

26a.   Garth is good.

is illicit precisely because it is naturally read as

26r.   Garth is morally good.

or

26r′.   Garth is a good person.

I am not convinced. I grant that if we understand "Garth" to refer to a person, then, absent any further context, that is, absent the premise "Garth is a good surgeon," the natural reading of (26a) may be (26r) or (26r′). However, there is a further context, namely the context of the argument; and from the premise "Garth is a good surgeon," I think that a reasonable inference is in fact

26s.   Garth is a good surgeon.

Accordingly, I think that the argument is reasonably formalizable as

$(\mathbf{S}(G))(g) \wedge S(g)$

---

$(\mathbf{S}(G))(g)$
$S(g)$.

Likewise, consider the following example of *AN* splitting:

Casey is a large mouse.

---

Casey is large.
Casey is a mouse.

Here too, I think, the claim that the adjectival inference is invalid is dubious. In other words, there is a reasonable reading of this argument as

$(\mathbf{L}(M))(c) \wedge M(c)$

---

$(\mathbf{L}(M))(c)$
$M(c)$.

On the other hand, if we understand "Casey" to refer to a mouse, then, absent any further context, that is, absent the premise "Casey is a large mouse," "Casey is large" might reasonably be a false claim.

In short, I suggest that *AN* splitting is not a well-conceived inference schema to diagnose a distinction among adjective classes. At least, *AN* splitting is not a well-understood inference schema. In reflecting further on *AN* splitting, I suggest that we return to nominal supplementation and precisely to the phenomenon that I dub "reciprocal modification."

## 3.7. Nominal Supplementation and Reciprocal Modification

According to the strict sense in which the term "modification" is used in contemporary syntactic theory, modification is a syntactic construction in which "a head is accompanied by an [expression] not typically required by it."[108] Recall that the syntactic term "head" here denotes the word in a phrase that endows that phrase with its syntactic categorical identity. For example, the head of a noun phrase is a noun; the head of an adjective phrase is an adjective. I will elaborate on the notion of a head in section 1.2 of chapter 7. Presently, our concern is limited to noun phrases and so to phrases headed by nouns. According to the contemporary syntactic theoretic definition of modification, then, modification of a noun phrase consists of a noun accompanied by an expression, in our case an adjective, not typically required by it. Indeed, I am not aware of any noun that requires an adjective.

Granted this, in the following sentence,

27. Janet likes dark chocolate.

the adjective "dark" modifies the noun "chocolate."[109] Accordingly, in the case of nominal supplementation, the adjective "good" modifies a dimension-specifying nominal expression. For example, in

28. Joe is a good doctor.

"good" modifies the count noun "doctor."

---

[108] P. H. Matthews, *Oxford Concise Dictionary of Linguistics*, Oxford University Press, 2007, s.v. modification (1).

[109] This example is adapted from Matthews (2007) s.v. modification (1).

In sentence (27), the phrase "dark chocolate" is a noun phrase, not an adjective phrase. Accordingly, "dark chocolate" is headed by the noun "chocolate," which is modified by the adjective "dark." "Dark chocolate" is precisely not an adjective phrase headed by the adjective "dark" and modified by the noun "chocolate." Likewise, in (28) the phrase "good doctor" is a noun phrase headed by "doctor," not an adjective phrase headed by "good."

Granted this, since I am interpreting "good," like "doctor," as a unary predicate, I have formalized (28) as

$$(\mathbf{D}(G))(j) \wedge D(j).$$

Contrast a case of adverbial supplementation such as

29.  Garth is morally good.

In (29), the adverb "morally" modifies the adjective "good." The semantic effect of this syntactic fact—after all, modification is a syntactic construction—is uncontroversial: "good" is dimensionally specified in terms of morality. That is, (29) states that Garth is good in a moral way.

Relative to (29), the case of (28) is strange. Once again, in (28) "good" modifies "doctor," not the other way around. So why should it follow that, on a natural reading, "$x$ is a good doctor" entails "$x$ is a good as a doctor"? What appears to be occurring here is that as a result of the syntactic modification of "doctor" by "good," the nominal expression "doctor" in turn has a semantic effect on the adjective that modifies it. I dub this phenomenon "reciprocal modification." Precisely:

Reciprocal modification consists of a nominal expression semantically modifying the adjective that syntactically modifies it.

In such a case, what I am calling "semantic modification" amounts to enrichment of the adjective phrase with content relating to the nominal expression. Above, I argued that such enrichment is adverbial and implicit. More precisely then:

Reciprocal modification consists of a nominal expression semantically modifying the adjective that syntactically modifies it, and where the semantic modification consists of the enrichment of the explicitly articulated expression by an implicit adverbial expression that modifies the adjective and whose meaning derives from the meaning of the nominal expression.

Reciprocal modification seems to occur for at least two reasons: one syntactico-semantic, the other semantico-pragmatic. The syntactico-semantic reason is that the adjective modifies the nominal expression. This syntactic relation suggests a semantic association between the adjective and the noun. For example, compare (28), repeated here, with the following variant that introduces a conjunction between the adjective and the nominal expression:

28.   Joe is a good doctor.
28c.  Joe is good and a doctor.

It is difficult to read (28c) as (28)—and that is puzzling; for if "good" is a unary predicate, then (28c) is, at least informally, akin to (28). It is, in effect, precisely such a consideration that should tempt an interpreter to analyze "good" as a predicate modifier or as an incomplete unary predicate. However, I have provided grounds for rejecting such analyses. Instead, I suggest that precisely because in (28) "good" modifies "doctor," this syntactic fact has a semantic effect. It suggests, precisely, that Joe is good in the way that a doctor is.

Compare the relation between (28) and (28c) with the relation between the following two sentences:

30.   This is a red wagon.
30c.  This is red and a wagon.

In this case, it is not difficult to read (30c) as (30). And that in turn should be puzzling for one who adopts the sort of account that I am proposing. In contrast, the semantic kinship between (30) and (30c) precisely encourages interpreters such as Geach to maintain that "red" is a member of a different class of adjective than "good." So I, in turn, need to explain the relation between (30c) and (30).

Here I note the second reason why reciprocal modification seems to occur. Again, this reason is semantico-pragmatic. Consider the following question. For an entity $x$, what is the typical way for $x$ to be good? This question does not admit a positive answer. There is no typical way for entities to be good. Insofar as there is a typical way for a subset of entities to be good, it is in virtue of their belonging to purposive kinds. So if $x$ is a member of a purposive kind $P$, then the typical way for $x$ to be good is for $x$ to significantly serve the characteristic purpose of a $P$. For example, there is a typical way for a doctor to be good, namely, by serving a medical therapeutic purpose.

In (28c), "good" is predicated of "Joe," and not attributed to "doctor." The natural reading of (28c) is that "Joe" denotes a man or at least a person. It is questionable whether there is a typical way for a man or a person to be good. Perhaps there is; and if so, that way is moral. But then (28c) would naturally be read as

Joe is morally good and a doctor.

Now consider (30) and (30c). There is a typical way for entities to be colored, for example, to be colored red. That typical way is for the exterior surface, or at least a contextually salient part of the exterior surface of the entity to be red. This explains why it is natural to read (30c) as (30): the typical way for an entity to be red happens to be the same as the typical way for a wagon to be red. But now contrast this with the following:

31.  This is a red grapefruit.
31c.  This is red and a grapefruit.

As it happens, there is a typical way for a grapefruit to be red; but this typical way differs from the typical way in which an object is red. The typical way for a grapefruit to be red is for the interior flesh of the grapefruit to be red. This explains why (31) cannot naturally be read as (31c). The same holds for the following:

32.  This is a red pen.
32c.  This is red and a pen.

The divergence between (32) and (32c) might be less striking than that between (31) and (31c). But there is a typical way for a pen to be red that consists of the pen having red ink, rather than having the surface of its exterior be red.[110]

Observe now that on account of examples such as (31) and (32), color terms are not always "transferable." For example, consider the following case of simple transfer inference:

This is a red grapefruit.
This is a spherical object.
_____
This is a red spherical object.

---

[110] I note in passing that recognition of such facts will serve to explain the green leaf example over which Travis and Szabó contend.

The inference is invalid. Again, the invalidity owes precisely to the fact that the typical way for a grapefruit to be red differs from the typical way for a spherical object to be red.

We can formalize the argument as follows:

$$(\mathbf{G}(R))(t) \wedge G(t)$$
$$S(t)$$

$$\overline{\qquad\qquad\qquad}$$

$$(\mathbf{T}(R))(t) \wedge S(t).^{111}$$

Here $\mathbf{G}$ and $\mathbf{T}$ stand for intensional predicate modifiers whose meanings correspond to the way in which color is attributed to a grapefruit and to the typical way in which color is attributed to a spherical object respectively.

Likewise, compare:

This is a red pen.
This is a cylindrical object.

$$\overline{\qquad\qquad\qquad}$$

This is a red cylindrical object.

Again, the inference is shaky, if not simply invalid.

Contrast the following argument:

This is a red ball.
This is a spherical object.

$$\overline{\qquad\qquad\qquad}$$

This is a red spherical object.

The inference is valid. That is because the typical way that color is attributed to a ball is also the typical way that color is attributed to a spherical object. Accordingly, we can formalize this argument as

$$(\mathbf{T}(R))(t) \wedge B(t)$$
$$S(t)$$

$$\overline{\qquad\qquad\qquad}$$

$$(\mathbf{T}(R))(t) \wedge S(t).$$

---

[111] For the sake of simplicity, I am treating "spherical object" as a simple predicate whose meaning is the same as "sphere." Likewise, in the example of "cylindrical object" and "cylinder" below.

Territorial and nationality terms provide another helpful illustration of the general phenomenon. Consider the adjective "American" in the basic sentence:

x is American.

Is there is typical way for an entity to be American? I suggest that there is not. If x ranges over people, presumably the typical way for a person to be American is for that person to be a citizen of (the United States of) America. But what if x ranges over manufactured products? In that case, the typical way for a manufactured product to be American is for that product to have been manufactured in America. But now, what if x ranges over colonies? Territorial terms applied to colonies typically refer to the mother country that is the source of the colony. We might be inclined to think that the typical way for a colony to be American is for a colony to be from America. But assume now that we are speaking of the early eighteenth century and specifically of Virginia as an American colony. Since Virginia was a British colony, in this case being an American colony requires being located in, rather than from America.

In light of such remarks, consider the following simple transfer inference involving the term "Syrian." Note that at the time of writing, Syria is a war-wracked country:

These packages are Syrian aid relief.
These packages are coffee.

---

These packages are Syrian coffee.

The inference is invalid or shaky at best. The typical way for coffee to have a territorial attribute is for coffee to have been grown in the territory in question; compare "Columbian coffee," "Ethiopian coffee." But the typical way for aid relief to have a territorial attribute is for the aid relief to be for individuals in that territory.

These considerations help to explain the phenomenon of reciprocal modification, both in the particular case of nominal supplementation of "good" and, as the range of examples has shown, more generally. If we return to the peculiar sentences adapted from Ziff in section of 2.1 of chapter 4, the present considerations also shed light on them:

This atom is good.
This shadow is good.
This seven is good.

There is no typical way for an entity to be good; and more precisely in these cases, there is no typical way for an atom, shadow, or seven to be good. Precisely, none of these entities is a member of a functional kind.

The preceding considerations also shed light on $AN$ splitting by helping to explain why attributive and predicative adjectives have different readings. In an example such as "Garth is a good surgeon," the fact that "good" modifies "surgeon" strongly encourages a reading of the sentence as "Garth is (surgeon-wise) good and a surgeon." But in the sentence "Garth is good," with the knowledge that "Garth" refers to a person and absent any further context, if the sentence is truth-evaluable at all, it is naturally read as suggesting that Garth is good in the typical way that a person is good; and that typical way is (arguably) moral. Likewise, in the sentence "Casey is a large mouse," the fact that "large" modifies "mouse" strongly encourages a reading of the sentence as "Casey is (mouse-wise) large and a mouse." But in the sentence "Casey is large," with the knowledge that "Casey" refers to a mouse and absent any further context, if the sentence is truth-evaluable at all, it is naturally read as suggesting that Casey is large in the typical way that an animal or perhaps ordinary macroscopic object is large. Compared to ordinary macroscopic objects, Casey is not large.

In sum, ignoring the question of an internal degree argument, "good" is a unary predicate. Consequently, in constructions of the form "$x$ is (a) good $N$," the readings of the complex predicate expression "good $N$" are intersective.[112] That is, such sentences are true if $x$ is a member of the intersection of the sets of which "good" and $N$ are true. However, because "good" modifies $N$, ceteris paribus, "good" is enriched by $N$ operating as a nominal supplement. Consequently, in these constructions, $N$ plays two semantic roles: it provides a property of the subject; and it suggests an adverbial modifier that specifies a property, of that subject, denoted by "good." In the latter case, $x$ is good in the typical or at least contextually salient way that an $N$ is.

## 3.8. Dimensional Specification, Ambiguity, and Pro-form Replacement

As an explanation of dimensional specification, supplementation differs from both Falkum's theory of modulation by means of ad hoc conceptualization and Szabó's incomplete unary predicate theory, in the following way. Supplementation entails that when dimensional specification occurs, tokens of

---

[112] That is, with the exception of certain agentive nominals.

"good" have the same meaning as that of the lexical word, that is, the lexeme "good."[113] In contrast, Falkum's and Szabó's theories maintain that when dimensional specification occurs, the meaning of a token of "good" differs from the meaning of the lexical word "good." Consequently, according to Falkum's and Szabó's theories, in this respect, various tokens of "good" may be and in fact often are ambiguous.

Although it has rarely, if ever, been put in quite the preceding terms, "good" has been viewed as an ambiguous term. Aristotle, who uses the Greek word *agathon*, translated as "good," is the most illustrious case. For instance, in a passage of the *Topics* he writes:

> Look also at the classes of predicates signified by the term and see if they are the same in all cases. For if they are not the same, then clearly the term is homonymous. For example, "good" in the case of food is what is productive of health, whereas when applied to the soul it is to be of a certain quality, for example, temperate or courageous or just; and likewise also, as applied to a man. Sometimes it signifies what happens at a certain time, as what happens at the right time; for what happens at the right time is called "good." Often it signifies what is of a certain quantity, for example, as applied to the proper amount; for the proper amount too is called "good." So then "good" is homonymous.[114]

Aristotle's understanding of "homonymous" (*homōnymon*) is not equivalent to the one that I defined in section 5 of chapter 2. But it is close enough so that according to the view that he is here stating,[115] Aristotelian homonymy entails ambiguity.

David Wiggins maintains that the following sentence illustrates the ambiguity of "good":

33.  She has good legs.

---

[113] More precisely, of one of the polysemes, namely evaluative "good," of the lexical word purposive "good." Note also that I am here ignoring the degree associated with the lexical meaning of evaluative "good" and its tokens.

[114] *Topics*, 107a3–9. Cp. *Eudemian Ethics*, 1217b26–34, *Nicomachean Ethics*, 1096a23–29.

[115] "Things are said to be homonymous when they share the same name, but the account of their being according to the name differs. For example, a man and a painting of a man can both be said to be animals; but they have only the name 'animal' in common, for the account of their beings according to the name differs" (*Categories*, 1a1–4). On Aristotle's conception of homonymy, cp. Christopher Shields, *Order in Multiplicity*, Oxford University Press, 1999, especially 194–215; Julia K. Ward, *Aristotle on Homonymy: Dialectic and Science*, Cambridge University Press, 2007.

Wiggins claims that in (33) "good" can be read in at least the following two ways:[116]

33b.   She has beautiful legs.

33h.   She has healthy legs.

We can adapt Wiggins's claim and say that according to the reading in (33b), "good" itself is associated with the dimension of aesthetic value; while according to the reading in (33h), "good" itself is associated with the dimension of physical health value.

As we have seen, Falkum argues that tokens of "good" exhibit polysemy, which is generated as a result of modulation, specifically narrowing by means of ad hoc conceptualization. For example, she claims that in the phrase "good knife," "good" may mean "good for cutting," "good for stabbing," and so on.[117] Again, we can adapt Falkum's claim and say that on one reading "good" itself is associated with the dimension of knife cutting value, and on another reading with the dimension of knife stabbing value, and so on.

Kennedy has also suggested that dimensional specification is a form of polysemy.[118] Kennedy does not discuss the semantics of "good"; but on his view of the polysemy of dimensional specification, tokens of "good" in, for example, "good painting" and "good person" are polysemes because the meanings of these tokens are themselves associated with various dimensions of value.

Insofar as the question at hand is whether tokens of "good" are ambiguous, we can test the claim by appealing to the sort of pro-form replacement tests that we introduced in section 4 of chapter 2 to corroborate the thesis that evaluative, quantitative, and operational "good" have distinct meanings. For example, assume that Adam is a good singer and Inga is a good dancer; and that Ronan, speaking of their respective abilities, says:

34.   Adam is good and so is Inga.

In (34), "so" replaces "good" and therefore must have exactly the same meaning as "good." But Adam and Inga are not good in the same way; for, intuitively, what (34) conveys is

34i.   Adam is good at singing and Inga is good at dancing.[119]

---

[116] "On Sentence-Sense, Word-Sense, and Difference of Word-Sense: Towards a Philosophical Theory of Dictionaries," in *Semantics: An Interdisciplinary Reader in Philosophy, Linguistics, and Psychology*, D. Steinberg and L. Jakobovits, eds., Cambridge University Press, 1971, 14–34, at 30–34.

[117] Falkum (2011) 46.

[118] Kennedy (2007) 6. Kennedy refers to multidimensionality as "indeterminacy."

[119] Cp. examples such as "The produce is good, and so are the prices"; "The film was good, and so was the popcorn"; "The graduate program is good, and so is the location."

Falkum's and Szabó's theories will have difficulty explaining how (34) can be read as (34i), for according to these views "good" in (34) literally means "good at singing." But if that is so, then—contrary to (34i)—"so" in (34) must mean "good at singing."

Contrast how supplementation handles (34). According to supplementation, in (34) "good" is associated with the dimension-type of unspecified value. Likewise, "so." And this is consistent with (34i). For in (34), what specifies the dimension-type that "good" and the pro-form "so" are associated with are implicit adverbial supplements, namely the "at" prepositional phrases in (34i).

Observe that according to this manner in which supplementation explains a sentence such as (34), the very fact that the supplements are implicit also explains why they are not semantically captured by pro-form replacement. This is confirmed by altering (34) to make the supplement of "good" explicit:

35. Adam is good at singing and so is Inga.

In (35), "so" must be read as replacing the entire phrase "good at singing" and not merely the adjective "good"; viz.:

Adam is good at singing and Inga is good at singing.

Even the following explicit supplement will not yield the intuitive reading of (35):

36. Adam is good at what he does and so is Inga.

Strictly, (36) must be read to mean:

Adam is good at what he does and Inga is good at what he (Adam) does.

Considerations of pro-form replacement therefore lend support to the theory of supplementation and present a further challenge to Falkum's and Szabó's theories.[120]

## 4. Standard and Comparison Class Determination

Having completed my explanation of dimensional specification in terms of supplementation, I will conclude this chapter by considering the way that the standard of comparison and comparison class associated with tokens of "good" and relative gradable adjectives generally are determined in contexts of use. I will

[120] In light of the preceding, it follows that in one important respect "good" is not a context-sensitive word.

refer to these phenomena as "standard (of comparison) determination" and "comparison class determination." I use the term "determination" here rather than "specification" because, as far as I can tell, "good" and other relative gradable adjectives are not associated with standard of comparison or comparison class content analogously to the dimension or dimension-type with which they are associated. In other words, there is no *specification* of the standard of comparison or of the comparison class in the way that there is specification of the dimension-type. Little hangs on the particular terms that I am using here, "specification" versus "determination"; but the use of distinct terms for the distinct phenomena is substantive.

Granted this, I suggest that an operation akin to supplementation explains standard of comparison determination and comparison class determination associated with "good" and so with relative gradable adjectives generally. (Hereafter, for convenience, I will simply speak of "good.") That is, in the context in which "good" is tokened, it is supplemented, explicitly or implicitly, with content that determines the standard and the comparison class. I say that this operation is "akin" to supplementation. I have defined supplementation precisely in terms of dimensional specification. For the most part, different kinds of supplements—that is, different kinds of expressions—are involved in the determination of standards of comparison and comparison classes; although, as we will see, there is some overlap between dimensional specifying supplements and standard and comparison class determining supplements.

Before I turn to these, I should be clearer about the relation between standard determination and comparison class determination. First, two aspects of standard of comparison determination should be distinguished: the particular quantity of the gradable property borne by the subject and the significance of that quantity. For instance, consider the adjective "tall" in the basic sentence:

37.   $x$ is tall.

Observe that a tokening of (37)—that is, precisely that open sentence employing the individual variable $x$—is equivalent to

$x$ has significant height.

But what quantity a significant degree of height consists in is wholly undetermined.

Granted this, the quantity that constitutes significance of degree is, I have tentatively assumed, based on a statistical algorithm consisting of median values and an absolute median derivation. Crucially, determination of the inputs to this algorithm requires determination of a comparison class. Once a comparison class is determined, the quantity constituting the standard of comparison that is the significant degree is fixed.[121]

So, determination of the quantity constituting the significant degree depends on determination of the comparison class. Consider then the kinds of supplementary expressions that serve to determine the comparison class. I have identified and commented on one kind at several points earlier in the study, namely "for" comparison class phrases such as those italicized in the following sentences:

> Paolo is tall *for a sixteen-year-old boy*.
> Paolo is good at chess *for a high school student*.

As I have said, the nominal complement of the preposition "for" denotes a property—for example, being a sixteen-year-old boy or being a high school student—that determines membership in the comparison class.

Generalizing, comparison class determination requires the context in which a relative gradable adjective is tokened to make salient, if not explicit, a property that determines membership in such a class. Such a property must be supplied by an explicit or implicit nominal expression. For convenience, let's call a nominal expression that serves this purpose a "comparison class determiner." A "for" comparison class phrase is a kind of adverbial supplement, whose complement is, again, a nominal expression, which here serves as a comparison class determiner. Compare the following nominal supplementary expressions, which derive from simple predicate expressions:

> Paolo is a tall *sixteen-year-old boy*.
> Paolo is a tall *high school student*.

As in dimensional specification, these nominal supplementary expressions contribute to comparison class determination through a phenomenon akin to reciprocal modification.

---

[121] It should be emphasized here that the speaker of a sentence such as (37) need not and invariably will not know the algorithm that determines the quantity that determines the standard of comparison, let alone the quantities of the relevant degrees of each individual in the comparison class. Accordingly, the account that I am proposing here is semantically externalist with respect to such information. For example, Ronan may say of Paolo: "Paolo is taller than the average sixteen-year-old boy." And while Ronan may have access to height statistics and so may utter this sentence in a relatively informed state of mind; he might just as well utter it in a relatively uninformed state of mind. Indeed, we express basic sentences all the time, on the basis of limited information. Cp. footnote 82 in chapter 3.

But context may also supply comparison class determiners in the following more indirect manner. Consider:

Paolo is tall.

So long as we are aware that "Paolo" is a personal name, the natural reading of the comparison class is

Paolo is a tall person.

or

Paolo is tall for a person.

In other words, being a person determines membership in the comparison class. Consequently, the comparison class determiner here derives from an inference to the most salient kind to which the subject, here Paolo, belongs.

Finally, observe that in the case of "good," nominal supplements often play a dual role as both dimension-type specifiers and comparison class determiners. For example:

Adam is a good teacher.

Here the nominal supplement "teacher" both specifies the dimension-type of value, namely as teaching value, and determines a comparison class, namely teachers.

# 6

# Adjectival Nominalization

## 1. Summary of the Interpretation of "Good"

I have completed my interpretation of the meaning and use of "good." My central results have been the following. "Good" is fundamentally three ways ambiguous between evaluative, quantitative, and operational senses. Evaluative and operational "good" are irregular polysemes encoded in one lexeme, call it "purposive 'good.' " Quantitative "good" is a distinct lexeme, whose meaning stands in the relation of homonymy to the former two. So purposive "good" and quantitative "good" are homonyms.

Evaluative "good" is the sense of "good" that, de facto, has been of principal interest to philosophers and that has been the focus of chapters 3, 4, and 5. Evaluative "good" is the unmarked member of an antonym pair of relative gradable adjectives, the marked member being evaluative "bad." Evaluative "good" is a multidimensional gradable adjective. It is associated with the dimension-type of value. The lexical meaning of evaluative "good" is associated with a non-significant degree on an open scale of unspecified value.

In tokenings of the basic sentence "$x$ is good," the degree associated with evaluative "good" is modulated to a significant degree, if not through the operation of a covert positive degree morpheme *pos*, then arguably through an uninformativity based quantity implicature. In the latter case, although the modulation is explicable in terms of implicature, which is standardly conceived as a pragmatic operation, the effect is truth-conditional and so the sense of significance is a constituent of the literal meaning of tokens of the basic predicate expression and so of the basic sentence.

Significance of degree is, arguably, a statistical quantity, precisely a quantity that exceeds the upper bound of a range of numeric values based on a contextually determined comparison class, and where the range is determined by the median value of the degrees to which individuals constituting the comparison class have the gradable property in question plus or minus, say, three-quarters of the median absolute derivation based on the degrees to which the individuals in the comparison class have the gradable property in question.

Regarding the nature of the dimension-type associated with evaluative "good," value is purpose serving. Consequently, for an entity $x$ to be good is for $x$ to serve a purpose to a significant degree. "Purpose," as here employed, is a univocal modal term, whose denotation comprises at least four basic kinds: biological and characteristic artificial purposes and ad hoc purposes derived from either intentions or desires.

Evaluative "good" admits purposive "for" phrases, of which beneficiary "for" phrases are a syntactic variant. Such phrasal adjuncts corroborate the identification of value with purpose serving. On the other hand, owing to the semantic properties of the indefinite article and verbal aspect, the basic sentence "$x$ is good" is not synonymous with "$x$ is serving a purpose to a significant degree." Indeed, aside from "$x$ has significant value," there is no gloss of the basic sentence, with either a verbal or adjectival predicate expression, that is strictly synonymous with "$x$ is good." Natural language abhors redundancy.

The term "value" that denotes the dimension-type with which evaluative "good" is associated is a mass noun. This mass noun is polysemous between generic and specific senses; where the former comprises so-called negative, neutral, and positive value; and the latter denotes only positive value. Accordingly, specific value is a hyponym of generic value. The terms "negative" and "positive" are merely heuristic here. They can and should be understood in terms of "thwarting" and "serving" a purpose respectively. Accordingly, generic value can be understood as purpose contribution, which includes both thwarting and serving a purpose. Arguably, evaluative "good" is precisely associated with the dimension-type of specific value. Assuming so, I hereafter use "value" in this context in the sense of "specific 'value.'"

Tokenings of evaluative "good" almost always involve specification of the dimension-type associated with evaluative "good." Such dimensional specification is tantamount to specification of a kind of value and in turn a kind of purpose that the entity of which evaluative "good" is predicated serves. The linguistic operation that explains dimensional specification is neither mandatory saturation of a covert dimension variable that is a constituent of the deep syntactic structure, that is, the so-called logical form, corresponding to evaluative "good," nor free pragmatic modulation, precisely narrowing of evaluative "good" by means of ad hoc conceptualization. Rather, dimensional specification results from compatibilist supplementation of evaluative "good" with an explicit or implicit adverbial or nominal expression. Implicit supplementation is semantic ellipsis.

In cases of nominal supplementation, the nominal expression semantically modifies evaluative "good," which syntactically modifies it. Such reciprocal modification, as I call it, involves the nominal supplement $N$ suggesting an implicit adverbial modifier of "good." Semantically, the implicit adverbial modifier functions as an intensional predicate modifier. Ceteris paribus, the meaning of the adverbial modifier plus "good" phrase is "good in the typical or at least contextually salient way that an $N$ is good." This explains the distinctive inferential properties of "good" in schemas such as *AN* splitting and simple and quantified transfer inference.

Szabó begins his analysis of "good" with the following historical reflection:

> It is a curious fact that contemporary views on the semantics of adjectives evolved from a debate that started in moral philosophy. In their effort to articulate theories about what goodness consists in, philosophers turned to questions about the semantics of "good." "Good" is an adjective with some peculiar characteristics, so any analysis of its content had to say something about the interpretation of adjectives in general as well as about the semantic features that distinguish "good" from less problematic adjectives, like "round" or "tall."[1]

The semantics of "good" is more complicated than that of "round" because "good" is a gradable adjective and "round" is a non-gradable adjective. The semantics of "good" is more complicated than that of "tall" because "good" is a multidimensional gradable adjective and "tall" is a unidimensional gradable adjective. More to the point—Szabó's pithy remark on the role that "good" has played in contemporary semantics serves as a fitting conclusion to our interpretation of this adjective.

## 2.1. Three Preliminary Remarks on "Goodness"

I turn now from the adjective "good" to the noun "goodness." I will begin with three preliminary remarks on "goodness." The first of these is a morphological one concerning the bound morpheme "-ness" and the reasons for its concatenation with "good." The second and third are semantic points. The second point concerns the fundamental univocity of "goodness" in contrast to the fundamental three way ambiguity of "good." The third point concerns the gradability of "goodness" and precisely the degree associated with the lexeme "goodness."

## 2.2. "-ness"

"Goodness" is composed of two morphemes: the free morpheme "good" and the bound morpheme "-ness."[2] "Goodness" is precisely an adjectival nominalization,

---

[1] Szabó (2001) 216.

[2] On the suffix "-ness" from a diachronic perspective, cp. Seichi Suzuki, "On the Origin and Development of the Action Noun Forming Suffix *-nis* in Old English," *Indogermanische Forschungen* 95 (1990) 184–207. Note Elizabeth M. Riddle, "A Historical Perspective on the Productivity of the Suffixes *-ness* and *-ity*," in *Historical Semantics: Historical Word Formation*, J. Fisiak, ed., de Gruyter

that is, a nominal expression, precisely, a noun, morphologically derived from an adjective, hence adjectival; "-ness" is a deadjectival nominalizing affix, more precisely suffix.

The suffixation of "-ness" to "good" results in a distinct lexeme. Affixes that yield distinct lexemes are called "derivational." In contrast, affixes that alter the case or number of a noun or the tense or mood of verb, rather than yielding a new lexeme, are called "inflectional." For example, the pluralizing suffix "-s," which changes "dog" into "dogs," does not yield a distinct lexeme, but inflects the lexeme "dog." Likewise, the past tense suffix "-ed," which changes "walk" into "walked," is an inflectional suffix rather than a derivational one.

Let us briefly discuss "-ness" suffixation of "good" in contrast to concatenation of "good" with other nominalizing suffixes. For example, consider the following non-existent words:

*goodhood, *goodment, *goodship, *goodity, *gooddom, *goodth.[3]

In contrast, we do have the following:

brotherhood, entertainment, kinship, purity, wisdom, truth.

Why don't words such as "goodment," "goodity," and "gooddom" exist? In some respects, the answer to this question is simple. In others, it is complex and almost impossible to answer without undertaking a large and detailed historical study.

The simple respects are the following. The nominalizing suffix "-hood" is denominal. That is, it concatenates with a noun and yields a distinct nominal lexeme. Likewise, "-ment" is a deverbal nominalizing affix; it concatenates with a verb and yields a noun. This explains why "goodhood" and "goodment" do not occur: "good" is neither a noun nor a verb. The same point largely explains the non-existence of "goodship." For the most part, "-ship" is a denominal nominalizing suffix.[4]

"Goodity" presents perhaps the most informative case. By far, "-ity" and "-ness" are the most productive deadjectival nominalizing suffixes in English. By "productive" here is meant that the typical way that English forms a noun from an adjective is by "-ness" or "-ity" suffixation. Granted this, the reason that "goodity" does not exist is at least partly explicable as follows.[5] English belongs to the Germanic

---

Mouton, 1985, 435–62. I do not, however, find Riddle's argument regarding the semantic distinction between "-ness" and "-ity" clear or compelling.

[3] The prefixed asterisks here indicate that there is no such word.

[4] In fact "goodship" is attested. At least, there are a few occurrences of "gōdscipe" in Old English and a few of "gōdshipe" (also "gōdschupe") in Middle English.

[5] To be precise, the OED lists one occurrence of "goodity." Cp. "hardship."

language family. However, particularly in the eleventh century, in the wake of the Norman Conquest of England, and following, English acquired a large number of French words, which are themselves of Latin derivation.[6] Subsequently, particularly through the growth and influence of specialized studies such as theology, philosophy, and the empirical sciences, English acquired a large number of additional Greek and Latinate words. "Good" is a word of Germanic origin. Likewise, "-ness" is a nominalizing suffix of Germanic origin. So, "goodness" derives from Old English, that is, Anglo-Saxon. In contrast, "-ity" is a French and therefore Latinate nominalizing suffix. For example, consider the Latin noun *veritas*, meaning "truth," which derives from the Latin adjective *verus* plus the Latin nominalizing suffix *-itas*. So, "goodity" would be a case of a Latinate suffix concatenated with a Germanic root. This is not impossible by any means. However, since "goodness" already existed, this would at least discourage creation of "goodity." More precisely, "-ity" and "-ness" tend to have the same or very similar meanings; and, crucially, as I noted in section 1 and at the end of section 2.4 in chapter 4, natural language is semantically economical. If it is to admit a new word into the lexicon, that word should contribute something semantically that is not already extant. So, "goodity" would be in semantic competition with "goodness."

This last point supports an explanation of why there is only one word with the sense of "goodness." Consequently, if "goodity," "goodth," or "gooddom" did exist, their meanings would likely be slightly or perhaps not so slightly different from "goodness."

The morphemes "-th" and "-dom" are in fact Germanic deadjectival nominalizing suffixes. One reason to think that "goodth" doesn't exist is that it appears phonetically and so morphologically weird. In other words, the thought is that perhaps English lacks words with the consonant string "dth." But that is not true. Consider "width" from "wide"; compare "strength" from "strong." Likewise, "gooddom" is not attested, but I don't see an obvious compelling reason why it isn't. As noted above, we have "wisdom" from "wise."[7]

In sum, the existence of "goodness" is explicable on the grounds that "good" is a Germanic root and "-ness" is the most productive Germanic deadjectival nominalizing suffix. But granted this, it remains somewhat unclear why other possible words such as "goodity," "goodth," and "gooddom," each with a slightly different meaning from "goodness" and from one another, don't exist.

---

[6] Cp. Albert C. Baugh and Thomas Cable, *A History of the English Language*, Routledge, 2002[6], 104–21.

[7] The suffix "-dom" is both deadjectival and denominal. Cp. Carola Trips, *English Suffixes and Diachronic Morphology: The Development of –hood, -dom, and –ship in the History of English*, Max Niemeyer Verlag, 2009.

## 2.3. The Fundamental Univocity of "Goodness"

The governing question of this study is "What is goodness?" I am undertaking to answer this question by clarifying the meaning of "goodness." The meaning of "goodness" obviously depends on the meaning of "good." The governing question presupposes that "goodness" is univocal. Insofar as the meaning of "goodness" depends on the meaning of "good," the presupposition of the governing question may be false. Since "good" is fundamentally three ways ambiguous, "goodness" is presumably three ways ambiguous as well. In other words, presumably there is an evaluative "goodness," a quantitative "goodness," and an operational "goodness."

In fact, this does not appear to be the case. There is only one "goodness," and that is evaluative "goodness." In other words, "-ness" only concatenates with one word and more precisely with one sense of the one word "good." Confirmation of this claim comes from consideration of the impossibility of reading "goodness" quantitatively or operationally. For example, consider the following sentences:

> Our company understands that your appliance is malfunctioning; # and given the goodness of your warranty, we can reimburse you for the cost of the repairs.

> Since the power went out at least three days ago, # we can't be assured of the goodness of the milk.

> # Given the goodness of the distance from here to City Hall, I would suggest that you take a taxi instead of walking.

> The board has decided to renew our grant, # in view of the goodness of the number of last year's subscribers.

In short, "goodness" is formed from evaluative "good" concatenated with the deadjectival nominalizing suffix "-ness." Why operational and quantitative "goodness" do not exist is unclear to me. In any case, the question I want to answer now is this: What does evaluative "goodness" mean? Since evaluative "goodness" is the only sense of "goodness" there is, I will hereafter drop the modifier "evaluative."

## 2.4. "Goodness" and Significance

Since "goodness" derives from a gradable adjective, it is not merely an adjectival nominalization, but a gradable adjectival nominalization.[8] Accordingly,

---

[8] To be clear, even though "goodness" is gradable, I am using the expression "gradable adjectival nominalization" to mean "a nominal expression derived from a gradable adjective," and not "a gradable nominal expression derived from an adjective."

"goodness" inherits gradability of some kind from the gradable adjective from which it derives. Since "goodness" is a noun, it does not admit the same set of degree expressions that the adjective "good" admits. However, it does admit degree expressions; for example:

1. There was more goodness in that one action than in all of his other actions combined.
2. There is a lot of goodness in him.
3. A little goodness can go a long way.

Since the lexical meaning of "good" is associated with a non-significant degree of value, which, in tokenings of the basic sentence, is modulated to a significant degree, it is questionable whether the lexical meaning of "goodness" is also associated with a non-significant degree of value. As far as I can tell, none of the preceding examples encourages that view. The truth of sentence (1) does not merely entail that his one action had more value than all of his other actions combined, but that his one action was good. In that case, his one action had significant value. With respect to examples (2)–(3), whether one speaks of "a lot of" goodness or "a little" goodness or even of "little" goodness, the implication is a significant degree of value. For example,

There is little goodness in him.

entails

There is little of significant value in him.

Certainly, all of the following examples imply a significant degree of value:

4. The museum is noted for the goodness of its Flemish and Spanish collections.
5. The goodness of the engineering is evident in the original models.
6. The goodness of the soil could not compensate for the inadequate sunlight.

This claim is corroborated by the fact that (4)–(6) entail the following:

4s.  The museum's Flemish and Spanish collections are good.
5s.  The engineering of the original models is good.
6s.  The soil is good.

Recall now from section 2 of chapter 3 that interrogative "how" constructions with unmarked relative gradable adjectives have a non-significant sense; for example:

How tall is Paolo?
How wide is the entryway?
How good was the movie?

In light of this, consider the following sentences:

7.  The committee wants to evaluate how good the proposal is.
8.  The board is assessing how good the curriculum is.
9.  An independent firm is reviewing how good the audit is.

The felicity of these sentences suggests that the following construction would support the claim that lexical "goodness" is associated with a non-significant degree of value:

To evaluate / assess / review the goodness of x.

But none of the following examples is acceptable:

7n.  # The committee wants to evaluate the goodness of the proposal.
8n.  # The board is assessing the goodness of the curriculum.
9n.  # An independent firm is reviewing the goodness of the audit.[9]

Contrast the following acceptable sentences:

7s.  The committee wants to evaluate the proposal.
8s.  The board is assessing the curriculum.
9s.  An independent firm is reviewing the audit.

And compare the following sentences, which are also felicitous:

7q.  The committee wants to evaluate the quality of the proposal.
8q.  The board is assessing the quality of the curriculum.
9q.  An independent firm is reviewing the quality of the audit.

---

[9] The following sentence does seem acceptable or at least marginally so: "Her parents want to assess the goodness of his character." However, here too "goodness" requires significant (moral) value.

The preceding considerations encourage the thesis that, in contrast to lexical "good," lexical "goodness" is not associated with a non-significant degree of value, which, in tokenings, contextual factors, be they intra- or extra-clausal, are responsible for modulating to a significant degree.[10] Rather, lexical "goodness" itself is associated with a significant degree of value.

## 2.5. Overview of the Rest of the Chapter

Having offered these three preliminary points regarding the morphology and semantics of "goodness," the remainder of the chapter consists of two parts. The first part, sections 3.1 through 3.4, is motivated by the fact that "goodness" is a gradable mass noun. Consequently, these sections examine the semantics of mass nouns. Section 3.1 begins with an account of the distinction between mass and count nouns. Section 3.2 proposes a pair of properties, which I call "semantic cumulativity" and "semantic divisibility," to explain the semantic distinction between mass and count nouns. Section 3.3 explains the so-called lattice theory of the denotation of mass nouns. And section 3.4 clarifies how gradable mass nouns are distinct from non-gradable mass nouns.

Part two, sections 4.1 through 4.2, applies the preceding results, indeed various linguistic results from all of the preceding chapters, to explain the metaphysics of goodness. The gist of section 4.1 is that the metaphysical elements constitutive of the denotation of "goodness" are instances of goodness. An instance of goodness itself consists of a quantitative trope $q1$ of value of a certain kind $K$ in relation to an abstract, higher-order quantitative trope $q2$ of value of kind $K$ (where $q2$ is a standard of comparison based on a comparison class), such that $q1$ exceeds $q2$. If the kind of value in question is biological, then $q1$ is a mind-independent entity; and otherwise, $q1$ is a mind-dependent entity. But in either case, the relation between $q1$ and $q2$ is mind- or at least language-dependent. Consequently and more precisely, goodness in each of its at least four basic kinds, which correspond to four basic kinds of purposes, consists of comparison of $q1$ with $q2$.

Section 4.2, which is a brief conclusion to the discussion of the metaphysical implications of the linguistic results, revisits the discussion in section 3.4 of chapter 3 regarding the claims that scales are abstract representations of measurement and ultimately, albeit not necessarily occurrently, derived from psychological acts of comparative judgment. The central point of this section is that the relation between quantitative tropes $q1$ and $q2$ is, fundamentally, an artifact of the mind and more precisely of a mental act of quantitative comparison.

---

[10] Cp. Moltmann's distinction between what she calls "positive" and "absolute" adjectival and verbal nominalizations (2013, 80–82).

Accordingly, the scales associated with gradable adjectives and adjectival nominalizations encode such comparison.

## 3.1. Mass Nouns and Count Nouns

I introduced the distinction between mass nouns and count nouns in section 2.2 of chapter 2, when I argued that quantitative "good" modifies count, but not mass, nouns. I returned to the mass-count noun distinction in section 2.5 of chapter 4, when I clarified that the term "value" that denotes the dimension-type associated with "good" is a mass noun. There, I offered a cursory account of the mass-count noun distinction. "Goodness" is also a mass noun. In fact, almost all adjectival nominalizations formed with "-ness" are mass nouns.[11] Here, I present a more thorough account of the distinction between mass and count nouns. This distinction is intended to be instructive in its own right. But it will serve as background to the account of the semantics of mass nouns and in particular of "goodness" that follows.

The term "mass noun" or rather "mass word" originates with the Danish linguist Otto Jespersen. In his 1913 *A Modern English Grammar*, Jespersen distinguishes mass words from so-called "countables":

> The categories of singular and plural naturally apply to all such things (this word taken in the widest sense possible) as can be counted; such "countables" are either material things like *houses, horses* . . . or immaterial things of various orders, like *days, miles . . . events . . . errors . . . ideas . . . plans . . .* But beside these we have a great many words which represent "uncountables," that is, [words] which do not call up the idea of any definite thing, having a certain shape or precise limits. These words are here called mass-words; they may be either material, in which case they denote some stuff or substance in itself independent of form, such as *silver . . . water, butter . . . air . . .* or else immaterial, such as *leisure, music . . . commonsense, knowledge,* and especially many "nexus-substantives" [that is, nominalizations] from verbs, like *admiration, satisfaction . . .* and from adjectives, like *restlessness . . . clearness, safety, constancy.*[12]

Observe here that Jespersen makes a morphological claim—that certain nouns admit both singular and plural forms—in view of semantic or metaphysical

---

[11]   An exception is the word "likeness," which can occur as a count noun, for example: "He created three likenesses of the president in clay, one of which he is planning to cast in bronze."

[12]   *A Modern English Grammar*, part II, *Syntax*, vol. 1), George Allen & Unwin, 1913, §5.211. Cp. Jespersen, *The Philosophy of Grammar*, George Allen & Unwin, 1924, 198, as well as Jespersen's criticisms of his predecessors, Sweet and Cross at 200ff.

properties, namely that the entities denoted can be counted. And conversely, certain nouns do not admit both singular and plural forms insofar as the entities denoted "do not call up the idea of any definite thing, having a certain shape or precise limits."

Observe further that Jespersen's distinction between mass nouns and what have since been called "count nouns"[13] cuts across the distinction between so-called "concrete" and "abstract" nouns, or, as Jespersen characterizes them, material and immaterial nouns, that is, nouns that (in some sense) denote concrete or material versus abstract or immaterial entities.[14] Hereafter, I will employ the terminology of "concrete" and "abstract" nouns, and I will return to the distinction at various points in the chapter.[15]

Presently, I will enumerate three properties that serve to distinguish count nouns and mass nouns.[16] Consider again the grammatical property that Jespersen cites:

A count noun admits both singular and plural morphology. A mass noun does not.

[13] Although Jespersen uses the term "countables," he does not use the term "count noun" or "count word." As Peter Lasersohn notes: "[The term 'count noun'] is considerably more recent than 'mass noun'; the earliest occurrence [known to Lasersohn] is in the anonymous (1952) *Structural Notes and Corpus*; the term was popularized by [Henry Gleason, *An Introduction to Descriptive Linguistics*, Holt, 1955]. However, earlier authors did employ comparable terms such as . . . 'bounded nouns' [Leonard Bloomfield, *Language*, Holt Reinhart and Wilson, 1933], or 'individual nouns' [Benjamin Whorf, 'The Relation of Habitual Thought and Behavior to Language,' in *Language, Culture, and Personality*, L. Spier, ed., Sapir Memorial Fund, 1941, 75–93]." (Peter Lasersohn, "Mass Nouns and Plurals," in *Semantics*, K. von Heusinger, C. Maienborn, and P. Portner, eds., 2001, de Gruyter, 1131–53, at 1133.)

[14] I note in passing the following remark on the entry of the distinction between abstract and concrete nouns into the English grammatical tradition. In contrast to the distinction between proper and common nouns, which first occurs in Alexander Gill's *Logonomia Anglica* (1619/1621, 36), "the dichotomy concrete vs. abstract nouns appears relatively late. It is first found in Cooper's (1685) grammar [*Grammatica Linguae Anglicanae*] (pp.97–100) and is taken over by all following authors (Lane: 'Corporeal' vs. 'incorporeal', p.20)." (Ute Dons, *Descriptive Adequacy of Early Modern English Grammars*, de Gruyter, 2012, 31.)

[15] Note that Quine imported the term "mass noun" from linguistics into philosophy (*Word and Object*, MIT Press, 1960, 90–98). Since then, it has become common both among linguists and philosophers to employ the mass-count noun distinction in these terms. A critical review of the literature from Quine to 1989 can be found in F. J. Pelletier and L. K. Schubert, "Mass Expressions," in *Handbook of Philosophical Logic*, vol. 4, D. Gabbay and F. Guenther, eds., Reidel, 1989, 327–407, at 349–73. For more recent work with bibliography, cp. Kathrin Koslicki, "Nouns, Mass and Count," in *Encyclopedia of Philosophy*, D. M. Bouchert, ed., Macmillan, 2005; Henry Laycock, *Words without Objects*, Oxford University Press, 2006; Laycock, "Mass Nouns, Count Nouns and Non-count Nouns: Philosophical Aspects," in *Encyclopedia of Language and Linguistics*, K. Brown, ed., 2006, 534–38; Brendan S. Gillon, "Mass Terms," *Philosophy Compass* 7 (2012) 712–30; David Nichols, "The Logic of Mass Expressions," *Stanford Encyclopedia of Philosophy*, 2013.

[16] My discussion of these three properties consists in a distillation and in some cases elaboration of the discussion by Gennaro Chierchia, "Plurality of Mass Nouns and the Notion of a 'Semantic Parameter,'" in *Events and Grammar*, S. Rothstein, ed., Kluwer, 1998, 53–103, at 55–57. Cp. Brendan Gillon, "Towards a Common Semantics for English Count and Mass Nouns," *Linguistics and Philosophy* 15 (1992) 597–639, at 599–613, which is especially lucid. See also Gillon (2012) 716–17.

For example, "shoe" is a singular count noun and "footwear" is a singular mass noun. Observe that in the following sentences the noun phrases headed by "shoe" and "footwear" agree with the third-person singular form of the verb "be":[17]

> A shoe is lying on the beach.
> Footwear is lying on the beach.

But whereas "shoe" can be pluralized (as long as the indefinite article is dropped), "footwear" cannot:

> Shoes are lying on the beach.
> * Footwears are lying on the beach.

Note that there is a subclass of mass nouns, called "mass plurals," which are lexically plural. Examples include "clothes," "lees," "winnings," and "dregs."[18] The claim that such nouns are lexically plural means that they occur in the lexicon in plural form and that they cannot be singularized, for example:

> * He washed a clothe in his duffle bag.
> * She poured a dreg out of the container.

Although mass plurals constitute a small number of mass nouns, they encourage the following precisification of our first property distinguishing count nouns and mass nouns:

> A count noun admits both plural and singular morphology. The singularity or plurality of a mass noun is lexically fixed and unalterable.

A second property that distinguishes count nouns and mass nouns is numeral licensing:

> Count nouns admit numerals. Mass nouns do not.

For example, consider the count noun "drop" in the singular and plural:

> There is one drop of blood on the stairwell.
> There are three drops of blood on the stairwell.

---

[17] Recall from footnote 83 of chapter 5 that the so-called head of a phrase is the word whose syntactic category endows the phrase with it syntactic category.

[18] This is noted by Jespersen, 1913, §5.28. On the subject of mass plurals, see Almerindo E. Ojeda, "The Paradox of Mass Plurals," in *Polymorphous Linguistics: Jim McCawley's Legacy*, MIT Press, 2005, 389–410.

While we would not expect a lexically singular mass noun to admit a numeral denoting a number greater than one on the grounds that lexically singular mass nouns resist pluralization, it is noteworthy that lexically singular mass nouns do not even admit the numeral "one." For example, consider the lexically singular mass noun "blood":

* There are three bloods on the stairwell.
* There is one blood on the stairwell.[19]

Likewise, while we would not expect a lexically plural mass noun to admit the numeral "one" on the grounds that lexically singular mass nouns resist pluralization, it is noteworthy that lexically plural mass nouns do not admit numerals that denote numbers greater than one. For example, consider the lexically plural mass noun "clothes":

* There are two clothes on the floor.

Compare:

* There is one clothe on the floor.
* There is one clothes on the floor.

In considering the unacceptability of numerals with mass nouns, it should be observed that mass nouns, whether abstract or concrete, admit so-called classifying or classifier phrases, one subset of which includes terms such as "kind," "type," and "sort." These classifiers are count nouns and so do admit numerals; for example:

There are three kinds of irony.
There are two types of jade.
There are five sorts of blood.[20]

---

[19] Laycock has claimed that mass nouns are not singular (or plural), but rather non-count. However this confuses a grammatical with a semantic property. For argument's sake, assume with Laycock that, for example, "water" does not denote any individual object or unified or single thing. Regardless, "water" is grammatically singular. Compare: "Water *is* common." "Water *has* seeped through the floorboards." * "Water *are* common." * "Water *have* seeped through the floorboards."

[20] Compare the third property Chierchia (1998, 55–56) that discusses in distinguishing mass and count nouns: numeral + mass noun phrases require either a classifier phrase or a measure phrase; for example: "two heaps of clothes," "three drops of blood," "two pounds of sugar," "one gallon of milk." I discuss such constructions in section 3.4.

Moreover, there are cases where a mass noun admits numerals, but where the mass noun denotes a kind or kinds. For example, a forensic pathologist might say:

> There are two bloods on this article of clothing.

Note also that through a process that has been called "conversion,"[21] most count nouns can be converted into mass nouns:

> There are two rabbits in the hutch.     [COUNT]
> There is rabbit in the stew.     [MASS]

Jeffrey Pelletier invites us to conceive of count-to-mass noun conversion through the thought experiment of a so-called universal grinder:

> Consider a machine, the "universal grinder." This machine is rather like a meat grinder in that one introduces something into one end, the grinder chops and grinds it up into a homogeneous mass and spews it onto the floor from its other end. The difference between the universal grinder and a meat grinder is that the universal grinder's machinery allows it to chop up any object no matter how large, no matter how small, no matter how soft, no matter how hard.[22]

Contrast the universal grinder with the so-called universal sorter, which converts mass nouns into count nouns by sorting and packaging the entities denoted by mass nouns:[23]

> There is water on the floor.     [MASS]
> There are two waters in the cooler.     [COUNT]

There is some question just how universal conversion in either direction is. For example, imagine a room in which a boy has been mutilated and his mutilated body parts are strewn all over the floor:

> ??? There was boy all over the floor.[24]

---

[21] Cp. Nichols (2013) n. 1.

[22] F. Jeffrey Pelletier, "Non-singular Reference: Some Preliminaries," *Philosophia* 5 (1975) 451–65, at 456.

[23] This term is introduced in H. C. Bunt, *The Formal Semantics of Mass Terms*, University of Amsterdam, dissertation, 1981.

[24] Lisa Cheng, Jenny Doetjes, and Rint Sybesma, "How Universal Is the Universal Grinder?" *Linguistics in the Netherlands*, 2008, 50–62.

Likewise, some mass nouns, in particular abstract mass nouns, resist conversion into count nouns:

* There are three honesties.
* There are several wisdoms.
* There are a few goodnesses.

Contrast:

There are three forms of honesty.
There are several types of wisdom.
There are a few kinds of goodness.

The third property that distinguishes mass and count nouns is the following:

Only count nouns admit so-called individuating quantifier expressions.

The following individuating quantifier expressions occur only with count nouns in the singular: "every," "each," "a":

Every horse has been vaccinated.
Each proposal was discussed.
An idea has been proposed.

* Every water has been tasted.
* Each advice was considered.
* A wisdom is worth pursuing.

The following individuating quantifier expressions occur only with count nouns in the plural: "several," "few," "a few," "many," "both":

Several horses escaped.
Several ideas are worth pursuing.
A few horses escaped.
A few ideas are worth pursuing.
Many proposals were discussed.

* Several water is / are worth tasting.
* Several wisdom should be pursued.
* A few water is / are worth tasting.
* A few wisdom is / are worth pursuing.
* Many advice was / were considered.

Here, it is also worth noting that the quantity expressions "little" and "much" can only modify mass nouns:

much / little water / wisdom
* much computer / idea.[25]

In sum, I have identified three grammatical properties that distinguish mass nouns from count nouns:

- A count noun admits both plural and singular morphology. The singularity or plurality of a mass noun is lexically fixed and unalterable.
- Only count nouns admit numerals.
- Only count nouns admit individuating quantifier expressions.[26]

It may seem as if these three properties derive from a common principle. Indeed, the following three sections are devoted clarifying the nature of this common principle.

## 3.2. Material and Semantic Cumulativity and Divisibility

I turn now to the semantics of mass nouns. One way of trying to explain the grammatical distinctions between mass nouns and count noun appeals to natural or metaphysical distinctions between the entities that the two classes of nouns denote. Recall that this is how Jespersen seems to have conceived of the distinction. He suggests that mass nouns "do not call up the idea of any definite thing, having a certain shape or precise limits." For convenience, I will call this kind of explanation "metaphysical."

According to one version of the metaphysical explanation—to speak in somewhat vague terms—count nouns denote entities that are individuals, whereas mass nouns denote entities that are stuffs. For example, compare the count noun "bottle" with the mass noun "water." The entities of which the count noun

---

[25] Some linguists have referred to "much" and "little" as determiners. This seems dubious to me. For example, "much" and "little" admit the degree modifier "very," whereas determiners are not gradable. When they occur with nouns, "much" and "little" may therefore be better classified as adjectives. In any case, the licensing of "much" and "little" is diagnostic of mass nouns.

[26] In addition, Chierchia (1998, 56) notes that the following expressions occur only with plural count nouns and mass nouns: "a lot of," "all," "plenty of," "more," "most." Contrast the following expressions which are "unrestricted," that is, admissible with plural and singular count nouns and mass nouns: "the," "some," "any," "no."

"bottle" are true are individuals, precisely individual bottles. Perhaps it is this that explains why "bottle" admits the indefinite article, other individuating quantifier expressions, as well as numerals and pluralization:

    a bottle
    each bottle
    several bottles
    two / three bottles.

In contrast, the entities of which the mass noun "water" are true are stuffs, in this case (typically) liquids. Qua stuff, water has no determinate form or shape. Consequently, the entities of which "water" is true are not individuals; and this explains why the term does not admit the indefinite article (assuming that the indefinite article semantically requires individuality); individuating quantifier expressions; numerals or pluralization:

    * a water
    * every water
    * several water
    * two / three water.

Such expressions are only acceptable if "water" is converted to a count noun whose meaning is akin to "a bottle / portion of water" or "a kind of water."

An objection to this way of advancing the metaphysical explanation of the distinction between mass nouns and count nouns is that the entities of which—to continue with our example—"bottle" is true also come in different forms or shapes. There may be a stereotypical bottle form, but there is no definitive shape that a bottle must take. Moreover, to the extent that the explanation succeeds at all, it does so only with respect to concrete or material count nouns, that is, with respect to count nouns that denote concrete or material entities. If we take into consideration abstract count nouns, for example "intention" or "misconception," the entities of which these terms are true seem no more or less formally determinate than the entities of which concrete mass nouns such as "water" and "wine" and abstract mass nouns such as "anger" or "fear" are true.

A somewhat different set of considerations that has been offered in an effort to explain the mass-count noun distinction along metaphysical lines concerns properties that have been called "divisibility" and "cumulativity." Consider that for a given entity of which "bottle" is true, it is not the case that physical division or partitioning of that entity yields two entities, of each of which "bottle" is true. Nor is it the case that physical aggregation, concatenation, or conjunction of two entities, of each of which "bottle" is true, yields a single entity of which "bottle" is true. In contrast, at least down to its molecular constituents, physical division or partitioning of an entity of which "water" is true yields two entities, namely two bodies or portions, of which "water" is true. And physical conjunction or aggregation of two entities, of each of which "water" is true, yields a single entity of which "water" is true. Arguably then, physical or material divisibility and cumulativity are properties of the sorts of entities that mass nouns denote, again stuffs, and not properties of the sorts of entities that count nouns denote, again individuals.

Since this appeal is precisely to physical or material cumulativity and divisibility, even if these properties did hold for the entities that concrete mass nouns denote, they do not hold for the entities that abstract mass nouns denote. Nor is it evident what non-material analogues of these properties would be that might be applied to the denotations of abstract mass nouns. For example, what sense is there to be made of the partitioning of an entity of which "anger" or "fear" is true. Likewise, what sense is there to be made of the aggregation of two entities, of each of which "anger" or "fear" is true?

A related criticism appeals to count nouns that apparently satisfy the properties of material cumulativity and divisibility. Examples include both concrete and abstract count nouns such as "fence," "wall," and "bouquet," as well as "sequence" and "line segment." The example of "line segment" is arguably the most compelling. One can divide an entity of which "line segment" is true and thereby render two entities, of each of which "line segment" is true. Likewise, one can aggregate or conjoin two line segments endpoint to endpoint along a single vector and thereby produce a single entity of which "line segment" is true. Such examples encourage the conclusion that material cumulativity and divisibility and, in a case such as "line segment," the non-material analogues of material cumulativity and divisibility are not at the root of the mass-count noun distinction.

A more general criticism advanced against metaphysical explanations of the mass-count noun distinction appeals to the fact that a number of pairs of terms, one member of which is a plural count noun, the other a (singular) mass noun, are near synonyms. For example, consider the following pairs:

| MASS | PLURAL COUNT |
| --- | --- |
| advice | suggestions |
| ammunition | bullets |
| clothing | garments |
| company | guests |
| footwear | shoes |
| infantry | foot soldiers |
| luggage | suitcases |
| pottery | pots. |

In view of these examples, Brendan Gillon concludes:

> Though the[se] pairs of words are not perfect synonyms, it seems far-fetched to say that part of what distinguishes the pairs is that the denotation of the first [member of each pair does not consist of individuals], while the denotation of the second [does consist of individuals].[27]

One further criticism advanced against metaphysical explanations of the mass-count noun distinction relates to so-called object mass nouns in contrast to so-called substance mass nouns. Note that both of these terms—which have recently been introduced by David Barner and Jesse Snedeker—are limited to concrete mass nouns. The term "substance mass noun" applies to those mass nouns such as "water," "wine," "gold," and "air" whose denotations consist of entities traditionally taken to be stuffs. In contrast, the denotations of so-called object mass nouns include objects, in other words, individuals. Examples of object mass nouns are "footwear," "furniture," "silverware," "clothing," and "cutlery." As mass nouns, these terms do not admit individuating quantifier expressions, numerals, or pluralization; for example:

* a furniture
* three footwear(s)
* each / every clothing
* several / many silverware(s)
* footwears / cutleries.

But, again, the denotations of these terms include entities that are individuals. For example, the denotations of "footwear," "furniture," and "clothing" include individual shoes, individual pieces of furniture, and individual articles of clothing, respectively.

Perhaps all of the preceding criticisms of metaphysical explanations of the distinction between mass nouns and count nouns are not equally or entirely compelling. Nonetheless, some of them, in particular the last one concerning object mass nouns, seem to me to tell against metaphysical explanations.

The alternative approach to explaining the difference between mass and count nouns focuses on features of the semantics of these classes of terms that are distinct from the natural or metaphysical properties of the entities that they denote. This approach in fact goes back at least to Quine. In introducing the topic of mass nouns from linguistics into philosophy in *Word and Object*, Quine suggests that

---

[27] Gillon (2012).

"the contrast [between the two classes of nouns] lies in the terms and not the [entities that] they name." Following Quine's statement, for convenience I will refer to this way of attempting to explain the distinction between mass nouns and count nouns as "linguistic."

What exactly it means to say that the contrast between mass nouns and count nouns is "linguistic" rather than "metaphysical" and that it lies "in the terms" and not in the entities that they name is questionable. We can clarify the view by reconsidering the properties of cumulativity and divisibility. Above, we treated cumulativity and divisibility in material or physical terms. For example, we spoke of partitioning entities such as a portion of water and a line segment. And again, we spoke of aggregating portions of water and concatenating line segments, for instance, by pouring two separate portions of water into a single container to yield a single portion or by conjoining line segments endpoint to endpoint.

Properties called "cumulativity" and "divisibility" (among other names) have also been invoked in linguistic explanations of the distinction between mass nouns and count nouns. But according to a linguistic approach, these properties are understood differently. For the sake of clarity, I will hereafter distinguish "material" cumulativity and divisibility from what I will call "semantic" cumulativity and divisibility.

I'll begin with a semi-formal description of semantic cumulativity. For a mass noun $M$,[28] semantic cumulativity is the property whereby

If $x \neq y$ and $M$ is true of $x$ and $M$ is true of $y$, then $M$ is true of the sum of $x$ and $y$.

For example:

If liquid $a$ and liquid $b$ are distinct entities, and "water" is true of liquid $a$ and "water" is true of liquid $b$, then "water" is true of the sum of liquid $a$ and liquid $b$.

The crucial term here is "sum." In this context "sum" does not denote any sort of physical or material conjunction, concatenation, agglomeration, or aggregation such as, once again, the pouring of separate portions of water into a single container, or more generally the physical bringing of two distant entities into proximity. Nor, in the case of the abstract entity line segment does it denote the quasi-material conjoining of two line segments endpoint to endpoint along a single vector.

---

[28] Note that here and throughout this chapter, to facilitate intelligibility, I tend to use Gill Sans MT font to represent select variables both in the text constituting ordinary paragraphs and in the indented texts where I introduce examples, principles, and claims that I want to highlight.

Summation, as it is here invoked, is an abstract operation. In mereology, this operation is called "mereological summation"; in algebra it is called "join." I will use the term "join."

Join is a binary operation on any two entities $x$ and $y$, be they abstract or concrete, which yields an entity $z$ constituted of $x$ and $y$. The join operation is often symbolized as ∨ or as ⊕. I will use the symbol ⊕. Join has the following three properties:

IDEMPOTENCY:        $x \oplus x = x$.

That is to say, the join of any entity $x$ with itself yields the original entity $x$. For example, if we join Janet Lorenz and Janet Lorenz, the yield is simply Janet Lorenz.

COMMUTATIVITY:        $x \oplus y = y \oplus x$.

That is to say, the entity that join yields is identical regardless of the order in which the two constituent entities $x$ and $y$ are joined. For example, if we join Janet Lorenz and David Wolfsdorf, the result is the same complex entity as if we join David Wolfsdorf and Janet Lorenz.

ASSOCIATIVITY:        $x \oplus (y \oplus z) = (x \oplus y) \oplus z$.

That is to say, for any three constituent entities $x, y, z$, the entity that join yields is identical regardless of whether one joins the first entity $(x)$ to the join of the second and third $(y \oplus z)$ or whether one joins the join of the first and second entities $(x \oplus y)$ to the third $(z)$.[29]

Intuitively, the operation of join can be thought of as a constitution operation. We take two entities and by joining them yield an entity, which in all cases, save for when we join something and itself, is distinct from and more complex than either of the original two entities. However, again, join should not be thought of as involving the physical manipulation or agglomeration of two entities. For example, the application of join to two physically separate bodies of water yields, as Quine himself puts it, a "scattered object," that is, an entity consisting of those two bodies of water, regardless of how those two bodies of water may be physically related to one another. I suggest that the term "scattered" should here be taken as heuristic. It serves, again, to underscore that the operation does not involve physical or material manipulation of concrete entities. In any case, insofar as the operation is applicable to abstract entities, physical manipulation is impossible. For this reason as well, the term "object" is also misleading. Since join

---

[29] Since the associativity property is basically an extension of the commutativity property, I will skip an example.

is an abstract operation, the entity it yields is abstract—and this is so regardless of whether the entities joined are concrete. For example, we can join the water in Lake Michigan and the water in Lake Eerie with the result that we have two bodies or quantities of water. But we can also join Isabella's desire to become an environmental scientist with the number seven and thereby yield the bizarre complex entity consisting of a particular woman's particular motivation and a number.

In light of these remarks, compare the concatenation of two line segments endpoint to endpoint along a single vector with the join of two line segments. In the latter case, the result is not a single line segment whose length is equal to the sum of the lengths of the original two line segments. Instead, the result is an abstract entity consisting of two line segments. Observe that both cases—quasi-material concatenation in the original case and join in the present case—involve an abstract operation. However, the former operation includes structural specifications regarding the way that the two entities are to be concatenated, once again contiguity endpoint to endpoint along a single vector. Join involves no such specifications. Consequently, in the case of semantic cumulativity, the term "line segment" is false of the join (or sum) of two line segments. Analogous points could be made with respect to examples such as "wall" and "fence."

Since join operates on any two entities of which $M$ is true—recall our earlier example: liquid $a$ and liquid $b$, of both of which "water" is true—insofar as the denotation of a mass noun consists of at least two entities, it will then trivially follow that the denotations of all mass nouns consist of entities, which are the result of joins, that is, sums, that have the following property of semantic divisibility:

For a join $j$ of which $M$ is true, there are two proper and non-identical mereological parts $a$ and $b$ of $j$, of each of which $M$ is true.

For example, for a join of liquid $a$ and liquid $b$ of which "water" is true, there are two proper and non-identical parts, namely liquid $a$ and liquid $b$ of that join, of each of which "water" is true.

In light of these points, consider the falsity of the following count noun analogues of semantic cumulativity and divisibility. Consider first the count noun analogue of semantic cumulativity. For a singular count noun $C$:

If $x \neq y$ and $C$ is true of $x$ and $C$ is true of $y$, then $C$ is true of the join (that is, mereological sum) of $x$ and $y$.

For example, assume "cat" is true of Abby and "cat" is true of Benny. It is not the case that "cat" is true of the join of Abby and Benny. In other words, it is false that "cat" is true of the join of Abby and Benny. Instead, what is true of the join of Abby and Benny is the plural count noun "cats."

In light of this, the falsity of semantic divisibility for count nouns trivially follows:

> For a join j of which C is true, there are two proper and non-identical parts a and b of j, of each of which C is true.

The only sort of cases where this principle might seem true are those that conform to material cumulativity and divisibility such as "fence" and "line segment." But as we have shown, in order to yield an entity that is a fence or a line segment from two fences or line segments, structural specifications beyond what the join operation consists in are required.

I conclude then that mass nouns are distinguishable from count nouns in that semantic cumulativity and divisibility are properties of mass nouns but not count nouns.

## 3.3. The Lattice Theory of Mass Nouns and Plural Count Nouns

As I explained, count noun analogues of semantic cumulativity and divisibility are false. If the count noun "cat" is true of Abby and the count noun "cat" is true of Benny, what is true of the join of Abby and Benny is not the singular "cat," but the plural "cats." Conversely, for a join $j$ of which a plural count noun $CC$ is true, there are two proper and non-identical parts $a$ and $b$ of $j$, of each of which $C$ is true. For example, if "cats" is true of some join $j$, say, the join of Abby and Benny, then there are proper and non-identical parts of $j$ of each of which "cat" is true, namely Abby, on the one hand, and Benny, on the other hand.

Granted this last point, observe that it does not follow from there being proper and non-identical parts of a join $j$ of each of which "cat" is true that those two proper and non-identical parts wholly constitute $j$. The reason for this is simply that the denotation of a plural count noun $CC$ is not limited to sums consisting merely of two entities of each of which $C$ is true. Rather, for instance, "cats" is true of all pluralities of cats. This includes pluralities whose cardinality is two, but also pluralities whose cardinality is greater than two. So, for example, "cats" is true of the plurality consisting of Abby, Benny, Casey, and Denny, of each of which "cat" is true. And in that case, there is a join $j$ of the join Abby $\oplus$ Benny and the join Casey $\oplus$ Denny, where Abby $\oplus$ Benny, on the one hand, and Casey $\oplus$ Denny, on the other hand, are proper and non-identical parts of $j$, but of which the plural "cats," rather than the singular "cat," is true. In short, "cats" is true of Abby $\oplus$ Benny; and "cats" is true of Casey $\oplus$ Denny.

Assume now a join consisting of three cats: Abby, Benny, and Casey. The plural count noun "cats" is true of this join. But it is also true of the following diverse constituent parts of that join: Abby $\oplus$ Benny; Abby $\oplus$ Casey; and Benny $\oplus$ Casey.

Unsurprisingly, one upshot of this is that the denotations of plural count nouns differ from the denotations of singular count nouns. But, interestingly and crucially, the denotations of plural count nouns are akin to those of mass nouns. The denotations of both classes of nouns share a structure that, in mathematical terms, is called a "join semilattice." This structure is most easily apprehended visually:

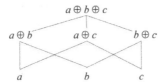

This diagram in effect represents a set consisting of all possible joins derived from three entities: $a, b, c$. There are seven possible joins.[30]

Let us call the entities at the base of the join semilattice, in our example $a,b,c$, the "elements" of the join semilattice. For a mass noun $M$, the entities that constitute the elements of the join semilattice that represents the denotation of $M$ are the metaphysical elements of which $M$ is true. For example, in the case of "water" these elements will be water molecules, the most fundamental entities of which "water" is true. In the case of an abstract mass noun like "kindness" these elements will be individual instances of kindness.

I said that the denotations of plural count nouns are also representable as join semilattices. The one difference between plural count nouns and mass nouns is that the elements constituting the join semilattices that represent the denotations of plural count nouns $CC$ are sets of two entities, of each entity of which the singular count noun $C$ is true. For example, the most basic entities of which "cats" is true are sets of two cats, for example, the set of Abby and Benny; and the singular count noun "cat" is true of each of "Abby" and of "Benny." So, more precisely, the following join semilattice represents the denotation of a plural count noun:

---

[30] I enumerate these here for the sake of clarity: 1. $a$ (recall that $a \oplus a = a$), 2. $b$, 3. $c$, 4. $a \oplus b$, 5. $a \oplus c$, 6. $b \oplus c$, 7. $a \oplus b \oplus c$.

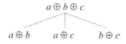

One additional point regarding a subset of mass nouns, which are called "non-atomic" or "non-elemental," is worth noting here. Consider the mass noun "time" or "space." It is possible, as a truth of physics, that time and space are infinitely divisible. If so, then there are no metaphysical atoms of time or of space. And if that is true, then there are no elements at the base of the join semilattice that represents the denotation of "time" or "space." I note this point because it is interesting in its own right. On the other hand, it does not bear on our term "goodness," since the denotation of "goodness" is atomic or elemental. At its base are instances of "goodness."

Finally, if the preceding account of the denotation of mass nouns is correct, then it should be possible to use a lexically singular mass noun of the form "*F*-ness" to denote a plurality of things, of each of which "*F*-ness" is true. And indeed it is. Here is an example:

10.   I encountered kindness throughout my trip to Italy.

Compare this sentence with the following plural and singular count noun versions:

11p.   I encountered cats throughout my trip to Italy.
11s.   I encountered a cat throughout my trip to Italy.

Observe that for (11s) to be true, I must have encountered one and the same cat in many different places as I traveled through Italy. In contrast, it is natural and reasonable to understand the truths of (10) and (11p) to entail that I encountered distinct instances of kindness and distinct cats throughout my trip.

## 3.4. Counting, Measuring, and Gradable Adjectival Mass Nominalizations

I have explained that the denotations of mass nouns, singular count nouns, and plural count nouns have different structures. The denotations of mass nouns and the denotations of plural count nouns have join semilattice and so mereological structures; the denotations of singular count nouns do not. The mereological structures that plural count nouns denote are atomic, and the atoms of these structures are pluralities of cardinality two. In contrast, the mereological structures that mass nouns denote may or may not be atomic; and when they are atomic, they are not pluralities of cardinality two.

Whether or not the denotation of a mass noun is atomic is language independent. In contrast, all of the other properties of the denotations of the various classes of nouns just described are language dependent. Following an established terminological distinction in the philosophy of language, we may refer to the language-independent properties of the denotation of a common noun as "externalist," and the language-dependent properties as "internalist." For example, it is an internalist property of the denotations of mass nouns that they have a mereological structure; and it is an externalist property whether a given mass noun's denotation is atomic.

Since it is a necessary condition on singular count nouns that they denote individuals, this must be an internalist property of singular count nouns. In other words, singular count nouns must semantically encode individuality. If this is correct, then we ought to distinguish semantically encoded individuality from natural or metaphysical individuality. For example, object mass nouns such as "furniture," "jewelry," and "cutlery" do not semantically encode individuality, but the denotations of object mass nouns include natural or metaphysical individuals, an externalist property of these nouns.

The fact that singular count nouns semantically encode individuality explains why singular count nouns do not have the properties of semantic cumulativity and divisibility. Moreover, the fact that singular count nouns semantically encode individuality seems to be the ultimate explanation for why singular count nouns admit the indefinite article, individuating quantifier expressions, numerals, and pluralization. Another way to understand these claims is that in semantically encoding individuality, singular count nouns, of themselves, provide a unit of quantification. Such a unit enables the noun to admit the indefinite article, individuating quantifier expressions, numerals, and pluralization.

Units are the basis for counting. So a count noun's internalist provision of a unit enables the quantificational operation of counting. Counting consists of setting entities in one-to-one relations with the natural numbers. Entities can only be set in such relations if they are taken to be members of a kind, whether natural or non-natural. For example, one may count units that are members of the kind cat or units that are members of the kind item that Isabella bought at Macy's on Christmas Eve. The count noun $C$ therefore provides units of that kind, or in Isabella's case heads a noun phrase that provides such units, for example, "item that Isabella bought at Macy's on Christmas Eve."

Since plural count nouns are compositionally derived from singular count nouns, for example "dogs" from "dog," their denotations consist of units of a kind, again the kind specified by the singular count noun. But insofar as plural count nouns are plural, their denotations consist of pluralities of units, rather than of individuals.

The cardinality of these pluralities is specified only to the extent that it must be at least as great as two.

Mass nouns do not semantically encode individuality. Consequently, whether the denotation of a mass noun is atomic, that is, whether it consists of units, is an externalist property of these nouns. This appears to be the fundamental explanation for why mass nouns do not admit the indefinite article, individuating quantifier expressions, numerals, or pluralization. Once again, the case of object mass nouns brings out particularly clearly the division between internalist and externalist properties of these expressions. For example, the denotation of "furniture" includes individuals. Consequently, furniture can be counted. For example, it is felicitous to respond to the question

How much furniture does the room contain?

by saying:

Three pieces.

But qua mass noun, "furniture" does not admit numerals. And, since the individuating quantifier expression "many" requires a plural count noun, it is unacceptable to ask:

* How many furniture / furnitures does the room contain?

Since mass nouns do not semantically encode individuality and yet their denotations may consist of individuals, counting here requires the use of a count noun. Again, in the example above the answer to the question was

Three pieces [of furniture].

The count noun here heads what is called a "partitive" or "pseudo-partitive" construction.[31] The form of such constructions is

n C of (det) M.

Here n stands for a numeral or the like (such as the indefinite article); C stands for a count noun; det in parentheses stands for an optional determiner; and M stands for a mass noun. In section 1.2 of chapter 7, I will clarify the term

---

[31] For example, cp. Roger Schwarzschild, "The Role of Dimensions in the Syntax of Noun Phrases," *Syntax* 9 (2006) 67–110, at 81.

"determiner," which denotes a category of contemporary syntactic theory. Presently, it suffices to note that determiners include at least the following sub-kinds: generalized quantifiers (for example, "all," "some"); articles ("the," "a"), demonstratives ("this," "that");[32] and possessives ("my," "your," "their").[33] For example, the following phrases consist of a determiner and a noun:

> some sandwiches
> a pretzel
> this orange
> your napkin.

Granted this, partitives consist of a determiner that facilitates reference to a particular entity; for example:

> three slices of *that* pizza
> two glasses of *their* wine.

Pseudo-partitives lack such a determiner and so such reference; for example:

> three slices of pizza
> two glass of wine.

Count nouns such as "article," "piece," "body," or "portion," which Susan Rothstein calls "individuating classifiers,"[34] typically provide the value of $C$ in such constructions; for example:

> three articles of clothing
> six pieces of furniture
> two bodies of water
> one portion of rice.

Compare individuating classifiers such as "instance" and "occurrence":

> three instances of irony
> two occurrences of arson.

---

[32] Note that these are to be distinguished from the homophonous demonstrative pronouns "this" and "that." For example, contrast "Janet likes this / that" and "Janet likes this / that soup."

[33] Numerals such as "eight" and "three" are often included; but their inclusion is contested, and I will not assume that numerals are determiners.

[34] *Semantics for Counting and Measuring*, Cambridge University Press, 2017, 49–81. Cp. also Rothstein, "Counting, Measuring, and the Mass Count Distinction," *Journal of Semantics* 27 (2010) 343–97.

For convenience, I will call such phrases of the form *n C* "individuating phrases." When they head pseudo-partitive constructions, individuating phrases appear to be measure phrases. For example, compare

| | |
|---|---|
| two articles of clothing | [INDIVIDUATING PHRASE] |
| two yards of cloth | [MEASURE PHRASE] |
| three planks of wood | [INDIVIDUATING PHRASE] |
| three pounds of sawdust | [MEASURE PHRASE]. |

However, as Rothstein argues, counting and measuring are two distinct quantificational operations; and the two phrase types, individuating and measure, differ semantically:

> Individuating classifiers cannot be assimilated to measure classifiers since . . . they have a very different semantic function. Individuating classifiers like "bottle of," "glass of" (as well as other non-container classifiers like "piece of") pick out the relevant individual entities which are to be counted, while measure classifiers like "kilo," "liter," and "glass" (on its measure reading), specify the unit in terms of which a dimensional scale is calibrated.[35]

Rothstein illustrates this distinction using the phrase "two glasses of water," which she argues to be ambiguous between an individuating phrase and a measure phrase. For example, compare the following sentences:

12i.   Put two glasses of water on the table.

12m.  Put two glasses of water in the soup.

Sentence (12i) is equivalent to

Put two glasses containing water on the table.

In contrast, although it is possible to read (12m) as, oddly, requiring that two glasses containing water be placed in the soup, the natural reading of (12m) is

Put two glassfuls of water in the soup.

Rothstein proposes several semantic diagnostics for distinguishing individuating phrases and measure phrases or individuating and measure readings of an ambiguous phrase such as "two glasses of water." I note three

---

[35] Rothstein (2017) 106. Rothstein also argues that they differ syntactically (55–60); and I agree with her syntactic analysis. However, I will ignore this aspect of her discussion here.

of these here. First, the bound morpheme "-ful" cannot be added to contexts favoring an individuating reading; for example:

Add one glass(ful) of wine to the soup.
Bring one glass(#ful) of wine for our guest.

We need three bucket(ful)s of cement to build that wall.
Three bucket(#ful)s of mud were standing in a row against the wall.

Second, plural individuating classifiers provide natural antecedents for individuating pronouns:

There are two glasses of wine on this tray. They are blue.
There are two glasses of wine in this soup. # They are blue.[36]

Third, whereas plural individuating phrases require plural agreement, measure phrases may admit singular agreement, especially in existential and copular constructions:

There are two glasses of wine on this tray.
# There is two glasses of wine on this tray.

Two spoonfuls of sugar were added to the sauce.
Two spoonfuls of sugar was added to the sauce.

In sum, the distinction between individuating and measure phrases is a genuine semantic (and syntactic) distinction, which correlates with the distinct quantificational operations of counting and measuring respectively.[37] As we will now see, these distinctions are in turn applicable to the distinction between gradable and non-gradable mass nouns.

While all mass nouns have denotations representable as join semilattices and so as mereological structures, mass nouns derived from gradable adjectives, such as "goodness," have additional semantic structure due to gradability that they inherit from the gradable adjective that they morphologically incorporate. This semantic complexity, the combination of mereological and gradable structure, correlates with the distinction between individuating and measure phrases and the correlative distinction between counting and measuring respectively. Recent discussions by Stefan Hinterwimmer, on the one hand, and

---

[36] Contrast: "There are two glasses of wine in this soup. It adds flavor."
[37] Rothstein (2017) 55.

Itamar Francez and Andrew Koontz-Garboden, on the other, indicate two linguistic constructions that, in different ways, expose this semantic complexity of gradable mass nouns.[38]

Hinterwimmer discusses mass nouns preceded by the "vague quantifier" expressions "a lot of" and "(a) little." I will focus here on the phrase "a lot of." The phrase "a lot of $M$"—where, as above, $M$ stands for a mass noun—is semantically akin to "a large quantity of $M$."[39] The quantity that "a lot of $M$" denotes can be read in terms of the mereological structure that the mass noun denotes; for example:

13.   I drank a lot of wine.

14.   I bought a lot of jewelry.

Sentences (13) and (14) assert that the speaker drank or bought large quantity of wine or of jewelry. Here, "large quantity" requires many externalistically determined units of wine and of jewelry; for example, many glasses or bottles of wine and many pieces or items of jewelry. Contrast the following pair of sentences:

15i.   I encountered a lot of beauty during my trip to Sicily.

15d.   There is a lot of beauty in that painting.

Both (15i) and (15d) require a large quantity of beauty. But the natures of the quantities differ. In (15i), the speaker encountered many instances of beauty. In (15d), a painting has a single instance of the gradable property of beauty to a high degree. Accordingly, in (15i) "a lot of $M$" is read, as it is in (13) and (14), in mereological terms. In contrast, in (15i) "a lot of $M$" is read in terms of the degree structure, rather than the mereological structure, associated with "beauty."

---

[38]   Stefan Hinterwimmer, "A Comparison of Abstract and Concrete Mass Nouns in Terms of Their Interaction with Quantificational Determiners," forthcoming; Itamar Francez and Andrew Koontz-Garboden, *Semantics and Morphosyntactic Variation*, Oxford University Press, 2017, especially at 103–40. Note that Francez and Koontz-Garboden's discussion is indebted to Lucia M. Tovena, "Between Mass and Count," in *Proceedings of WCCFL*, K. Mergerdoomian and L. A. Bar-el, eds., Cascadilla Press, 2001, 565–78; and Rebekah Baglini, *Stative Predication and Semantic Ontology*, University of Chicago, dissertation in linguistics, 2015.

[39]   I note in passing—and because Hinterwimmer does not seem to recognize this—that the terms "little" and "a little" do not have the same meaning. For example, compare: "She received little sympathy from her boss"; "She received a little sympathy from her boss." The truth of the first sentence does not require that she received sympathy from her boss. The truth of the second sentence requires that she received sympathy from her boss. "A little" is akin to "a small amount / quantity of." So the antonym of "a lot of" is "a little." "A little" also heads a pseudo-partitive construction. "A little" licenses the preposition "of" in partitive, but not pseudo-partititve constructions; for example: "He has a little money hidden under his mattress." * "He has a little of money hidden under his mattress." "He has a little of his money hidden under his mattress." * "I'd like to use a little of sugar." "I'd like to use a little sugar." "I'd like to use a little of your sugar."

In light of this distinction, recall sentences (1)–(3) introduced in section 2.3 and repeated here for convenience:

1. There was more goodness in that one action than in all of his other actions combined.
2. There is a lot of goodness in him.
3. A little goodness can go a long way.

In these sentences, "more," "a lot of," and "a little" are naturally read in gradable terms and therefore function here as degree expressions. Contrast the following sentence:

16. Much goodness goes unrecognized.

In (16), "much" is naturally read in mereological terms. For instance, (16) entails:

Many instances of goodness go unrecognized.

On the other hand, "much" in (16) is not an individuating quantifier expression, since mass nouns do not admit individuating quantifier expressions:

* many goodness.

Rather, "much goodness" denotes a large amount of externalistically determined instances, where instances of goodness are countable.

I turn now to a second linguistic construction that manifests the semantic complexity of gradable mass nouns. In a section of their recent book *Semantics and Morphosyntactic Variation*, Francez and Koontz-Garboden discuss exclamatives, more precisely *wh*-exclamatives. Exclamatives are sentences used to "express an affective response to what is taken to be a fact" and to "convey the speaker's surprise that some . . . situation is remarkable." Exclamatives have various forms. Consider the following four:

Wow, Katie bakes delicious desserts!   [SENTENCE EXCLAMATIVE]
Boy, does Katie bake delicious desserts!   [INVERSION EXCLAMATIVE]
My, the delicious desserts Katie bakes![40]   [NOMINAL EXCLAMATIVE]
My, what delicious desserts Katie bakes!   [*WH*-EXCLAMATIVE][41]

---

[40] The initial exclamative word in these sentences—"Wow," "Boy," "My"—is clearly optional and included in the examples for illustrative purposes.

[41] One is surprised by what one takes to be atypical. So surprise is a response to perceived atypicality. Consequently, a *wh*-exclamative cannot felicitously be followed by the statement that the nominal complement of the *wh*-term is of average quality. For example:

"What water the Aegean has! # The quality of the Aegean's water is average." "What fruit the farmers' market is selling! # The quality of the fruit the farmers' market is selling is average."

One distinguishing feature of *wh*-exclamatives is that they have both expressive and descriptive content. Moreover, a "key property of *wh*-exclamatives is that their descriptive and expressive contents always involve a gradable [property]." Francez and Koontz-Garboden contrast *wh*-exclamatives with plural count noun and non-gradable mass noun complements, on the one hand, and *wh*-exclamatives with gradable mass noun complements, on the other. These distinct variants of *wh*-exclamatives "involve" gradable properties in distinct ways.

To begin, consider the following *wh*-exclamative whose nominal complement is the plural count noun "boys":

17.  What boys Gail has!

Observe that, in a typical context,[42] sentence (17) cannot felicitously be glossed as

17h.  How many boys Gail has!
17l.  Wow, Gail has a lot of boys!

To be clear, (17h) and (17l) are both well-formed and intelligible sentences. However, in a typical context, they fail as glosses of (17). Likewise, consider the following examples of *wh*-exclamatives whose nominal complements are the plural count nouns "ideas" and the non-gradable mass nouns "silverware" and "fruit":

18.   What ideas he has!
18h.  How many ideas he has!
18l.  Wow, he has a lot of ideas!

19.   What silverware they used at dinner!
19h.  How much silverware they used at dinner!
19l.  Wow, they used a lot of silverware at dinner!

20.   What fruit they are selling at the farmers' market!
20h.  How much fruit they are selling at the farmers' market!
20l.  Wow, they are selling a lot of fruit at the farmers' market!

Again, all of these sentences are well-formed and intelligible. However, in typical contexts, neither (18h) nor (18l) accurately glosses (18), neither (19h) nor (19l) accurately glosses (19), and neither (20h) nor (20l) accurately glosses (20).

---

[42] This qualification is explained in footnote 43.

In contrast, in typical contexts, such glosses are acceptable with gradable mass nouns. For example, consider "goodness," "kindness," and "beauty":

21.   What goodness / kindness Janet displayed!
21h.  How much goodness / kindness Janet displayed!
21l.  Wow, Janet displayed a lot of goodness / kindness!

22.   What beauty this painting has!
22h.  How much beauty this painting has!
22l.  Wow, this painting has a lot of beauty!

Once again, as Francez and Koontz-Garboden state, *wh*-exclamatives always "involve" gradable properties. But since the lexical meanings of the plural count nouns "boys" and "ideas" and the non-gradable mass nouns "fruit" and "silverware" are not lexically associated with gradable properties, the gradable properties that the *wh*-exclamatives (17)–(20) involve must, in these cases, be more loosely related to the contents of these nouns. Precisely, the nouns are related to contextually salient gradable properties. In the case of sentence (17), the contextually salient gradable property related to "boys" may be personal fineness or goodness. For example, (17) may be glossed as

What fine / good boys Gail has!

In the case of sentence (18), the contextually salient gradable property related to "ideas" may be creativity or impressiveness. For example, (18) may be glossed as

What creative / impressive ideas he has!

In the case of sentence (19), the contextually salient gradable property related to "silverware" may be beauty or expensiveness. For example, (19) may be glossed as

What beautiful / expensive silverware they used at dinner!

And in the case of sentence (20), the contextually salient gradable property related to "fruit" may be tastiness or again beauty. For example, (20) may be glossed as

What tasty / beautiful fruit they are selling at the farmers' market![43]

---

[43] Granted the preceding points, since quantity or magnitude itself is a gradable property, it should in fact be possible, in select contexts, for a *wh*-exclamative whose nominal complement $N(s)$ is not lexically associated with a gradable property to mean "What a lot of $N(s)$ . . . !" For example, assume that Helen has an extraordinarily large collection of shoes. Upon seeing this, Ron might reasonably respond: "What shoes Helen has!" In this context Ron's exclamation means: "What a lot of shoes Helen has!"

In contrast, since gradable mass nouns are lexically associated with gradable properties, the *wh*-exclamatives derive the requisite gradable property directly from their gradable nominal complements.

In sum, gradable mass nouns have a semantic complexity that non-gradable mass nouns and plural count nouns lack. We have considered two constructions that exhibit this semantic complexity: the vague quantifier expression "a lot of *M*" and *wh*-exclamatives. With gradable mass nouns, the vague quantifier expression "a lot of *M*" admits two readings: an individuating phrase reading and a degree or measure phrase reading. In contrast, with plural count nouns and non-gradable mass nouns, the vague quantifier expression admits only an individuating reading. Consequently, *wh*-exclamatives require a gradable property and precisely a degree reading of this gradable property. The gradable mass nominal complement of the *wh*-expression provides this gradable property directly. In contrast, in the case of plural count nouns and non-gradable mass nouns, the broader context of the expression provides the gradable property, and so that property is more loosely related to the nominal complement.

## 4.1. Metaphysical Implications

Having clarified the semantics of gradable mass nouns, I turn now to consider the metaphysical implications of the linguistic results.[44] Once again, my lead question is "What is goodness?" and my proposal has been to answer this metaphysical question by means of answering the semantic question "What does 'goodness' mean?" So what does "goodness" mean?

Assume that the meaning, which is to say the denotation, of a common noun *N* is, at the actual world and at each possible world, the set of all entities of which *N* is true. Since the actual world is a possible world, we can rephrase this assumption to suggest that the meaning of *N* is, at each possible world, the set of all entities of which *N* is true.

The denotation of a mass noun *M* has a lattice structure. Consequently, the entities of which *M* is true include both individuals and joins or mereological sums, which is to say pluralities, of those individuals. The individuals of which mass nominalizations with "-ness" suffixes are true are precisely instances. Accordingly, the meaning of *M* is, at each possible world, the set of all instances

---

[44] Note that I have yet to remark on how tokenings of gradable mass nouns in contexts affect their denotations. Precisely, I did not remark on how the standard of comparison and comparison class associated with significance of degree affects the denotation of gradable mass nouns. And I did not remark on how the multidimensionality of multidimensional gradable mass nouns—of which "goodness" is an example—affects the denotation of multidimensional gradable mass nouns. The role of context on gradable and multidimensional gradable mass nouns requires a crucial adjustment, or rather a crucial supplement, to the preceding results. I will add and explain that supplement in the course of the present section.

and pluralities of those instances of which *M* is true. Accordingly, in the case of "goodness" we may say that

> The meaning of "goodness" is, at each possible world, the set of all instances and pluralities of those instances of which "goodness" is true.

This entails that

> The meaning of "goodness" is, at each possible world, the set of all instances and pluralities of those instances of goodness.

While I take this to be true, at least to a first approximation, if we had no more to say about goodness, this result would be unsatisfying. But we certainly have more to say about goodness.

"Goodness" is a gradable mass noun. Moreover, "goodness" is associated with a significant degree of the dimension-type with which it is associated. This dimension-type is value. Accordingly, we may, at least to a second approximation, say that

> The meaning of "goodness" is, at each possible world, the set of all instances and pluralities of those instances of significant value.

Insofar as value is purpose serving or, as I will gloss it here, purposiveness and insofar as the expression "significant purposiveness" is sensible, we may also say that

> The meaning of "goodness" is, at each possible world, the set of all instances and pluralities of instances of significant purposiveness.

At this point, it would be helpful to clarify what an instance of goodness or significant value or significant purposiveness is. But before I do that, I need to pause over two points. One concerns a crucial implication of the fact that "goodness" is associated with a significant degree. The other is a peculiar feature of questions of the form "What is *N*?" where, as above, *N* stands for a common noun. I'll discuss these points in that order.

The phrase "a significant degree of some gradable property" is meaningful. But given what significance of degree consists in—namely exceeding the upper bound of a range based on certain values of a comparison class—absent a comparison class determination, there are no instances of significant value or purposiveness and so no instances of goodness. In other words, absent a comparison class determination, "goodness" or "significant value" or "significant purposiveness" is true of nothing. This entails that the denotation of "goodness" must be more complex than the preceding proposals have suggested.

Observe further that because "goodness" is a multidimensional gradable mass noun, determination of a comparison class does not in fact suffice to make "goodness" or "significant value" or "significant purposiveness" true of anything.[45] To appreciate why consider the following example using the adjective "good":

23. Paolo is good for a beginner.

Here, the "for" phrase determines a comparison class. Even so, (23) is not truth-evaluable. Given the array of kinds of value in the actual world, absent a dimensional specification, the natural response to an utterance of (23) would be: Good in what way?

To resolve these problems, we must incorporate into our account of the denotation of "goodness" a function from contexts to instances and pluralities of those instances. Consider then the following proposal:

The meaning of "goodness" is, at each possible world, a function from a context C to a set of instances and pluralities of those instances of goodness$_C$ (equivalently, of significant value$_C$ or of significant purposiveness$_C$).

The subscript "C" here serves to indicate factors of context C that determine the particular kind of goodness and so the particular instances of goodness of that particular kind. Precisely, the contextual factors that the present account requires are a dimension-type specifier and a comparison class determiner.[46] Accordingly, I will call context C a "context of (dimension-type) specification and (comparison class) determination." Consequently, I will lightly emend the preceding proposal as follows:

The meaning of "goodness" is, at each possible world, a function from a context of specification and determination C to a set of instances and pluralities of those instances of goodness$_C$ (equivalently, of significant value$_C$ or of significant purposiveness$_C$).

---

[45] I assume here that we are concerned with the actual world.

[46] Since we are here dealing with a noun "goodness," rather than the adjective "good," a distinct account of dimensional specification is needed. For example, adjectival modification of "goodness" can effect dimensional specification: "moral goodness," "aesthetic goodness." But certain prepositional phrases may also be acceptable: "goodness as a dancer," "goodness in / at dancing." I acknowledge, then, the need for a theory of how dimensional specification is effected in the case of multidimensional gradable mass nouns, but I will not attempt one here.

I come now to a point about the peculiarity of the question "What is $N$?" Consider the following two questions:

24p.  What are kumquats?
24s.  What is a kumquat?

Although (24p) contains the plural "kumquats" and (24s) contains the singular "kumquat," the force of the questions appears to be equivalent. In particular, (24p), containing the plural, is equivalent to asking what *a* kumquat is. This is a curious characteristic of "What is $N$?" questions, where $N$ stands for a plural count noun. The plural count noun in this interrogative definitional or identificational construction functions equivalently to a singular (indefinite) count noun.

Likewise, although mass nouns include pluralities as well as individuals or instances within their denotations, questions of the form "What is $M$?" where $M$ is a mass noun are equivalent to questions that ask what *an* individual or instance of $M$ is. For example, consider the following question:

25.  What is water?

The correct answer to (25) will state what constitutes an instance or particular body of water qua water. Likewise, the following question,

26.  What is goodness?

will state what constitutes an instance of goodness. In short, a satisfactory answer to (26) will state what an instance of goodness is, even though the denotation of "goodness" includes pluralities of instances as well as individual instances.

Granted this, let us now clarify what an instance of goodness is. In an effort to do so, it will be helpful first to consider a more concrete example. So, I will first focus on "tallness" rather than "goodness"; and I will consider what an instance of tallness is. I underscore that my employment of "tallness" here is intended to provide theoretical scaffolding.

An instance of tallness is an instance of significant height. We characterized significance in relational terms, namely as a degree of some gradable property, for example height, in relation to some contextually determined degree that is the standard of comparison based on a contextually determined comparison class, such that the former degree exceeds the latter degree. As such, an instance of tallness consists of

a quantity $q1$ of height in relation to a quantity $q2$ of height, such that $q1$ exceeds $q2$.

*q1* is the quantity of height of the entity that is said to be tall or to have tallness. I will initially call *q1* the "subject quantity." *q2* is the quantity of height of the standard of comparison based on the contextually determined comparison class. I will initially call *q2* the "comparison quantity." And again, the relation between *q1* and *q2* is such that *q1* exceeds *q2*.

Let's concretize these claims on the basis of the following example:

27.   Paolo is tall for a twelve-year-old boy.

On the basis of (27), Paolo's tallness is

the quantity *q1* of height that Paolo has, in relation to the quantity *q2* of height that is the standard of comparison based on twelve-year-old boys, such that *q1* exceeds *q2*.

I'll now clarify three aspects of this description: the subject quantity, the comparison quantity, and the comparative relation between the former and the latter.

The subject quantity *q1* is the degree or quantity of height that Paolo has. Observe that *q1* is a trope. A trope is a particular feature or a particular attribute of a particular. I'll call the particular that possesses, has, or bears the trope the "trope bearer." In this case, Paolo is the trope bearer. The trope *q1* here borne by Paolo is quantitative in nature. So, more precisely, the trope *q1* that Paolo bears is a quantitative trope.[47] Accordingly, I will now interchangeably use the phrases "subject quantity" and "subject trope."

To clarify the claim that *q1*, which Paolo here bears, is a quantitative trope, I will contrast quantitative tropes with qualitative tropes. Consider two particular line segments *s1* and *s2*, which are both exactly the same uniform color red and which both measure exactly one inch in length.[48] The redness of *s1* is a trope, and the redness of *s2* is a trope. In other words, the redness of *s1* is a particular feature or attribute of the particular line segment *s1*. Call it *r1*. And the redness of *s2* is a trope. In other words, the redness of *s2* is a particular feature or attribute of the particular line *s2*. Call it *r2*. More precisely, *r1* and *r2* are each qualitative tropes. That is, they are tropes that are qualitative in nature. Furthermore, as stipulated, *r1* and *r2* are qualitatively identical. However, they are not strictly identical. By "strict identity," I understand: having all the same features. So *r1* and

---

[47] My understanding of quantitative tropes is informed by Moltmann's discussion in (2013), especially at 61–69. More broadly, the following account of the metaphysics of the entities denoted by gradable mass nouns is informed by her discussion, especially at 1–94. Cp. also Moltmann (2009), in which Moltmann first argues for an account of degrees as tropes.

[48] Since the line segments have color, they must have width and so cannot be line segments in a strict sense. But the artificiality of the example in this respect serves my instructive purpose.

*r2* are not strictly identical because *r1* and *r2* themselves have distinct features. For example, *r1* and *r2* have distinct locative features. *r1* is located where *s1* is located; and *r2* is located where *s2* is located.

Contrast the qualitative tropes of redness, *r1* and *r2*, of *s1* and *s2* with the following tropes of *s1* and *s2*. *s1* is one inch long, and *s2* is one inch long. The length of *s1*, call it *l1*, is a trope of *s1*; likewise, the length of *s2*, call it *l2*, is a trope of *s2*. More precisely, *l1* and *l2* are quantitative tropes of *s1* and *s2* respectively. That is, they are tropes that are quantitative in nature. Furthermore, as stipulated, *l1* and *l2* are quantitatively identical. However, they are not strictly identical. They are not strictly identical because *l1* and *l2* themselves have distinct features. For example, they have distinct locative features. *l1* is located where *s1* is located; and *l2* is located where *s2* is located.

In sum, *r1* is a qualitative trope, that is, a particular qualitative feature, of *s1*. *l1* is a quantitative trope, that is, a particular quantitative feature of *s1*. *r2* is a qualitative trope, that is, a particular qualitative feature, of *s2*. And *l2* is a quantitative trope, that is, a particular quantitative feature of *s2*.

I return now to Paolo's tallness based on (27). Recall the subject quantity *q1*, which, in this example, is the degree or quantity of height that Paolo has. Our discussion of line segments *s1* and *s2* was in the service of clarifying the claim that *q1* is a quantitative trope. Assume that Ronan is exactly the same height as Paolo. Still, the quantitative trope *q1* is not strictly identical to the quantitative trope that is the height Ronan has. *q1* is not strictly identical to the quantitative trope that is the height Ronan has because the two quantitative tropes have distinct features, for example, distinct locative features.

Observe now that the quantitative trope *q1* is the referent of the phrase "Paolo's height." In contrast, it is not the referent of the phrase "Paolo's tallness." Paolo's tallness is distinct from Paolo's height in that the former consists of Paolo's height in relation to another quantity. In our example, Paolo's height, *q1*, is related to *q2*, the quantity that is the standard of comparison based, in this example, on the comparison class consisting of twelve-year-old boys. Given this, we turn to the nature of the comparison quantity *q2*.

Metaphysically, the comparison quantity *q2*, which is the standard of comparison, is of course a quantity. Indeed, I suggest that it is a quantitative trope. But, at least relative to *q1*, *q2* is a peculiar quantitative trope. *q2* is the value of a function. Following Solt's proposal, the function in question is a statistical one. Consequently, we may say that the value constituting *q2* is a statistical one. The statistical value that constitutes *q2* is precisely the upper bound of a range *R*, where *R* is based on the median value of the degrees of the gradable property, here height, borne by members of the comparison class, here twelve-year-old boys (at the time of utterance or inscription), plus or minus, say three-quarters of the median absolute derivation based, again, on the degrees of the gradable property borne by individuals constituting the comparison class (at the time of utterance or inscription).

I underscore that while $q2$ is the value of a function, metaphysically $q2$ is not a mere number. To clarify the metaphysical distinction between $q2$ and a mere number, consider the following two sentences:

28m. Paolo is six feet tall.

28b. Six is greater than five.

In (28m), the numeral "six" precedes the noun "feet," which denotes a standard of measurement. The phrase "six feet" constitutes a measure phrase. The measure phrase in turn precedes the adjective "tall," which specifies the function of the measure phrase, namely to measure vertical extension. Contrast "Paolo is six feet wide" or "Paolo is six feet deep." In (28b), the numeral "six" is the sole constituent of the phrase that constitutes the subject of (28b). Assume here, if merely for the sake of illustration, that "six" is a singular term that refers to the number six.[49] The phrases "six feet tall" and "six" have different meanings. For example, substituting the one for the other in (28m) and (28b) does not preserve the sense of these sentences:

28m'. Paolo is six.

28b'. Six feet tall is greater than five.[50]

Returning now to Paolo's tallness on the basis of (27) and precisely to the comparison quantity $q2$ that is a constituent of Paolo's tallness—$q2$ is not a mere number, but more precisely a quantity of height and more precisely still the quantity of height derived from a particular statistical function, in this case a particular statistical function based on the quantities of height borne by the twelve-year-old boys that constitute the comparison class. Granted this, I suggest that $q2$ is a quantitative trope because it is borne by a particular. The particular in question is a set. Precisely, the set consists of the quantities of height of each of the members of the comparison class. Insofar as a set is an abstract particular, the quantitative trope $q2$ borne by this abstract particular may itself be characterized as an abstract quantitative trope. Nonetheless, it is a quantitative trope.

---

[49] This is a controversial claim. For example, cp. Thomas Hofweber, "Number Determiners, Numbers, and Arithmetic," *Philosophical Review* 114 (2005) 179–225.

[50] In both (28m') and (28b'), pragmatic factors encourage novels readings. (28m') is naturally read as semantically elliptical for: "Paolo is six [years old]," since years of age is the typical reading when an integer between one and one hundred is predicated of a person. (28b') is naturally read as semantically elliptical for: "Six feet tall is greater than five [feet tall]."

To appreciate how sets can bear quantitative tropes, consider the following more concrete example, adapted from a discussion by Moltmann.[51] Assume that Ronan is laying the table for a dinner party:

29.   Ronan laid out eight knives and eight forks.

The phrases "eight knives" and "eight forks" as used in (29) each refers to a distinct set, of knives and of forks respectively. Call the set of knifes K and the set of forks F. Call the cardinality of K $c1$, and the cardinality of F $c2$. $c1$ and $c2$ are quantitatively identical. But they are not strictly identical, since $c1$ is the cardinality of K, whereas $c1$ is the cardinality of F. So $c1$ and $c2$ are quantitative tropes of K and F respectively.

In the case of Paolo's tallness based on (27), more precisely the comparison quantity $q2$ constitutive thereof, this quantity is based on the set of quantities of height of twelve-year-old boys. The quantities of height of each of the twelve-year-old boys are themselves quantitative tropes. So, the comparison quantity $q2$ is a higher-order quantitative trope, precisely, once again, derived from a particular statistical function. Observe that the statistical function, although complex relative to the measure of the height of an individual, is nonetheless a measure of an entity, in this case of a set.

So much then for the metaphysics of the comparison quantity $q2$, which I will now also refer to as the "comparison trope." I turn finally to the comparative relation between the subject trope $q1$ and the comparison trope $q2$. I will be brief here and return to this relation below. Paolo's tallness consists of the subject trope, Paolo's height, $q1$, *in relation to* the comparison trope, the standard of comparison, $q2$, such that $q1$ is greater than $q2$. Accordingly, the comparative relation consists of a quantitative relation between $q1$ and $q2$ such that $q1 > q2$. In sum, on the basis of (27), Paolo's tallness consists of a quantitative trope $q1$, which is Paolo's height, in relation to an abstract, higher-order quantitative trope $q2$, which is the standard of comparison, such that $q1$ is greater than $q2$. Moltmann, adapting an idea from Kit Fine, has suggested that we regard such an entity as a so-called qua trope.[52] A qua trope is a trope qua something. In this case, the qua trope is the quantitative trope of the subject, the subject trope, qua exceeding the quantitative trope that constitutes the standard of comparison, the comparison trope. I will return to this idea subsequently.

[51] Moltmann (2013) 61–69.
[52] Moltmann (2013) 81. Cp. Kit Fine, "Acts, Events, and Things," in *Language and Ontology*, W. Leinfellner and E. K. J. Schank, eds., Holder-Pichler-Tempsky, 1982, 97–105.

Presently, having clarified the metaphysics of an instance of tallness to this extent, I'll now apply the results to an instance of goodness. Since an instance of goodness is an instance of significant value, it should follow that an instance of significant value is

a quantity $q1$ of value in relation to a quantity $q2$ of value (where $q2$ is a standard of comparison based on a comparison class), such that $q1$ exceeds $q2$.

Let's exemplify and concretize this description. For example, let's say we are analyzing the following sentence:

Wayne Thiebaud's 1969 *Candy Counter* is a good painting.

Assume that the comparison class is a collection of paintings of candy counters. Assume, as naturally, that the value in question is aesthetic. Thiebaud's painting's goodness here is

the quantity $q1$ corresponding to the degree of aesthetic value that Thiebaud's 1969 *Candy Counter* has, in relation to a quantity $q2$ of aesthetic value, where $q2$ is a standard of comparison based on a comparison class of candy counter paintings, such that $q1$ exceeds $q2$.

Note that $q1$ is a quantitative trope of aesthetic value, and $q2$ is an abstract higher-order quantitative trope of aesthetic value.

We may also describe the goodness of Thiebaud's painting in terms of purposiveness as follows:

the quantity $q1$ corresponding to the degree to which Thiebaud's 1969 *Candy Counter* serves a given aesthetic purpose, in relation to the quantity $q2$, the standard of comparison, which on the basis of the statistical function quantifies the degree to which the members of the comparison class serve the given aesthetic purpose, such that $q1$ exceeds $q2$.

Let us return now to our instance of tallness, Paolo's tallness vis-à-vis twelve-year-old boys. The quantitative trope that is Paolo's height is a mind-independent entity. But, as we've explained, Paolo's tallness consists of the relation of Paolo's height to an abstract, higher-order quantitative trope, which constitutes the standard of comparison. More precisely, and crucially, it consists of the *relating* of Paolo's height to the standard of comparison. Such relating of the subject trope to the comparison trope is semantically encoded in gradable nominalizations such as "tallness" and "goodness." But this encoded content must ultimately—albeit not occurrently—derive from a psychological perspective and precisely a judgment in which one thing is compared to members of a kind. In other words, comparative judgment, which involves perspective taking, is the psychological basis of the comparative relation encoded in gradable nominalizations such as "tallness" and "goodness." This point is crucial because I see no reason to think that there is a mind-independent relation between the subject trope and the comparison trope. In other words, while, for example, Paolo's height is a mind-independent entity, Paolo's height *in relation to* a standard of comparison is not a mind-independent entity. It consist in perspective taking and precisely comparative judgment. In the case of gradable mass nouns such as "tallness" and "goodness," such perspective taking and precisely comparative judgment is semantically encoded in the language.

The upshot of this point is that an instance of tallness is, metaphysically speaking, a hybrid of mind-independent and mind- or language-dependent features. In short, although height and degrees or quantities of height are objective features of the world, instances of tallness are not wholly objective features of the world. Rather, they are ways that we conceive and talk of degrees of height in relation to other degrees of height, in particular degrees based on comparison classes.

Finally, observe that in contrast to instances of F-ness (where "F-ness" stands for a gradable adjectival nominalization with a "-ness" suffix) that partly consist of mind-independent features (such as tallness and so height), an instance of goodness will only consist of mind-independent features if the kind of value in question is biological, in other words, if a biological purpose is being served to a significant degree. All other kinds of value and so purposes, namely characteristic artificial, and ad hoc intentional and desiderative, are mind-dependent. So in these three kinds of cases, instances of goodness will be wholly mind-dependent.

## 4.2. Scales and Comparison

In section 3.4 of chapter 3, I remarked that the scales associated with gradable adjectives are abstract representations of measurement. They are abstract representations insofar as they are ultimately, albeit not necessarily occurrently, derived from psychological acts of comparative judgment. Since the degrees associated with gradable adjectives are constituents of scales, these degrees must likewise be abstract representations of measurement and again ultimately, albeit not occurrently, derived from psychological acts of comparative judgment. I underscore that scales and degrees ultimately, but not necessarily occurrently, derive from comparative judgments insofar as gradable adjectival constructions, which are meaningful linguistic expressions, linguistically encode abstract representations of measurement.

Given this, I noted that the term "degree" is ambiguous between what I called "metaphysical" and "semantic" senses. Insofar as the degrees that are constituents of scales are abstract entities in the sense just stated, they are not features of mind-independent entities. On the other hand, there is a sense of "degree," namely the metaphysical sense, according to which mind-independent entities do have degrees, that is, quantities or amounts, of gradable properties (insofar as the gradable properties themselves are mind-independent entities). For example, Paolo has a mind-independent degree, quantity, or amount of height. And so Paolo has a degree, in the metaphysical sense, of height. The relation between semantic degrees and metaphysical degrees is, I suggest, that semantic degrees denote metaphysical degrees.

Granted this, there is a disanalogy between semantic and metaphysical degrees, on the one hand, and semantic scales and their metaphysical denotata, on the other. Precisely, there are no, so to speak, metaphysical scales that semantic scales might denote. The case of open (semantic) scales associated with relative gradable adjectives corroborates this claim particularly well. What could an open scale, that is, a scale that is infinitely extended in one direction, denote in the mind-independent world?!

Insofar as gradable adjectival nominalizations such as "tallness" and "goodness" are associated with degrees, precisely degrees with a significant value, they must also be associated with scales and, in their case, precisely open scales. So here too, while the semantic degrees with which the nominalizations are associated denote metaphysical degrees, precisely quantitative tropes,[53] the scales with which they are associated do not denote mind-independent entities. Rather, the scales associated with gradable adjectival nominalizations denote relations of comparison, precisely the relations in which a subject trope is compared to a comparison trope.

In short, terms such as "tallness" and "goodness" and the phrases that they head, such as "Paolo's tallness" or "the goodness of Thiebaud's 1969 *Candy Counter*," have complex denotations, partly world-involving and partly mind- or language-involving. And the scales, in these examples open scales, that are associated with their meanings precisely denote relations of comparison, which

---

[53] I acknowledge that the comparison trope itself is, as I have said, an abstract entity, but abstract in a different way.

ultimately, if not occurrently, derive from mental acts of comparison and so of perspective taking, precisely comparison of one entity with respect to one of its quantitative features with the quantitative features of other entities of the same class. In a word, the "qua" in "qua (quantitative) trope" corresponds to this comparison relation.

# 7

# Bare Noun Phrases

## 1.1. Bare Noun Phrases and the Ambiguity of "Goodness"

I have answered my lead question, "What is goodness?" by means of answering the question "What does 'goodness' mean?" Beyond numerous explicit points of irresolution in the preceding chapters, a great deal more remains to be said about "good" and about "goodness." In this final chapter, I will advance the inquiry one step further. I will introduce a problem that has been much discussed in the linguistics literature, but which in the philosophical literature has almost entirely been overlooked: the ambiguity of bare noun phrases.[1] The problem of bare noun phrases does not jeopardize the preceding results. Rather, it concerns their application to certain tokenings of "goodness" and mass nouns and plural count nouns generally. Insofar as bare noun phrases are ambiguous, tokens of "goodness" may be. Accordingly, the present chapter concerns one feature of the use of "goodness."

By way of orientation and contrast, it may be helpful to briefly summarize the respects in which, according to the foregoing analysis, "goodness" is univocal and in which it is not. I have claimed that there are at least four fundamentally distinct kinds of goodness: biological, characteristic artificial, and ad hoc intentional and desiderative. Moreover, within these four fundamental kinds, there are countless, in most cases in principle infinite sub-kinds. Nonetheless, I have

---

[1] The linguistics literature here is vast. A brief, recent overview is Bert Le Bruyn, Henriëtte de Swart, and Joost Zwarts, "Bare Nominals," in the *Oxford Research Encyclopedia of Linguistics*, 2017, online. Some other valuable overviews include Gregory Carlson, "No Lack of Determination," in *The Second Glot International State of the Article Book*, L. Cheng and R. Sybesma, eds., Mouton de Gruyter, 2003, 149–78; Denis Delfitto, "Bare Plurals," in Everaert and van Riemsdijk (2006) 214–59; Artemis Alexiadou, Liliane Haegeman, and Melita Stavrou, *Noun Phrase in the Generative Perspective*, Mouton de Gruyter, 2007, 159–226; and Veneeta Dayal, "Bare Noun Phrases," in von Heusinger, Maienborn, and Portner (2011) 1088–109. I cite a number of additional linguistic contributions subsequently. With respect to works that have appeared in philosophical journals, the following three come to mind: Frederike Moltmann, "Properties and Kinds of Tropes: New Linguistic Facts and Old Philosophical Insights," *Mind* 113 (2004) 1–43; Leslie (2008); Gennaro Chierchia, "Mass Nouns, Vagueness and Semantic Variation," *Synthese* 174 (2010) 99–149—although among these Moltmann's and Leslie's papers merely touch on the issue.

suggested that "goodness" is univocal, both insofar as there is only evaluative, not operational or quantitative, goodness; and insofar as "purpose" in the modal sense and so "value" in the specific sense are univocal. In other words, the lexeme "goodness" is univocal.

I have also discussed the fact that tokens of "good" almost always involve dimensional specification. The theory of supplementation presented in chapter 5 to explain dimensional specification of "good" is, in certain respects, applicable to "goodness." Consequently, when dimensional specification of the noun occurs, for example when "goodness" is explicitly or implicitly modified by an adjective such as in "aesthetic goodness" and "moral goodness," the meaning of "goodness" is unaffected. With one possible qualification, the same point applies to comparison class determination. For example, whether in a tokening of "goodness" the comparison class is a class of paintings or a class of actions, the meaning of "goodness" is unaffected. The one possible qualification is that since the lexical meaning of "goodness" is associated with a significant degree, in contexts of use that degree is, externalistically, quantitatively precisified in virtue of the determination of the comparison class. In other words, the quantity that constitutes significance of degree varies according to the standard of comparison, which is determined by the contextually determined comparison class. If the degree associated with "goodness" is, precisely, lexically encoded in the noun, then the meanings of tokens of "goodness" will vary in this, admittedly limited respect.[2]

The possible ambiguity of "goodness" that I will be considering here is, in any case, of an entirely different kind. Once again, it concerns the ambiguity of bare noun phrases. In the ensuing discussion, I will introduce the problem of the ambiguity of bare noun phrases. In doing so, I will address the question whether the literal meanings of the nouns that head these phrases have meanings that differ from the lexical meanings of the nouns. In cases where they do, I will clarify those meanings and the contexts in which they occur.

Finally, let me underscore that my objective here is to introduce the problem of the ambiguity of bare noun phrases, including the outlines of the principal types of solution to the problem that have been offered. I am not in a position to offer what I regard as a cogent or comprehensive explanation of the phenomena.

---

[2] The point being made here may be easier to grasp by considering the term "tallness." Compare "Paolo's tallness for a twelve-year-old boy" and "Paolo's tallness for a player on his school's basketball team." The standards of comparison vary in the two cases as a function of the two different comparison classes. Consequently, the quantity that constitutes significance of degree with which "tallness" is associated varies. So if the degree to which the subject, here Paolo, is tall is encoded in the meaning of "tallness," then this aspect of the meaning of "tallness" will vary across contexts.

## 1.2.  Introduction to Bare Noun Phrases

I begin by clarifying what a bare noun phrase is. Recall that grammar is standardly divided into two fields: morphology and syntax. Morphology is the study of the internal structure of words. For instance, the description of "goodness" as composed of one of the adjectives "good"—namely purposive "good" in its evaluative sense—and the suffix "-ness" is a morphological one. Syntax is the study of the structural relations between words. Each word belongs to a syntactic category, traditionally called a "part of speech," for example: noun, verb, preposition. Given the description of syntax as the study of the structural relations between words, consideration of words as members of syntactic categories is tantamount to consideration of the interrelations of syntactic categories. For example, a syntactic property of nouns that distinguishes them from verbs is that only nouns admit modification by adjectives; for example:

Ronan owns *numerous* houses.
\* Ronan *numerous* owns houses.

In turn, a syntactic property of verbs that distinguishes them from nouns is that only verbs admit modification by adverbs; for example:

Ronan rapidly expanded his business.
\* Ronan expanded his rapidly business.

A phrase is a functional syntactic unit whose syntactic category derives from the syntactic category of the word that serves as its so-called head. For example, a verb phrase is a phrase whose head is a verb; an adjective phrase is a phrase whose head is an adjective; and a prepositional phrase is a phrase whose head is a preposition. Consider the italicized phrases in the following sentences:

1.  Joe *walks to work.*
2.  The building is *closed on Sundays.*
3.  The net is *in the pool.*

In sentence (1), "walks to work" is a verb phrase because it is headed by the verb "walks." In (2), "closed on Sundays" is an adjective phrase because it is headed by the adjective "closed." And in (3), "in the pool" is a prepositional phrase because it is headed by the preposition "in."[3]

---

[3] According to the syntactic principle of endocentricity, every expression with syntactic parts has a head. According to the syntactic principle of single headedness, expressions have only one head. Cp. Williams (2015) 48–49.

In sentences (1)–(3), the head of the phrase is the first word in the phrase. However, the head of a phrase need not be the first word in the phrase. Consider the italicized phrases in the following three sentences:

1a. Joe *quickly walks to work*.
2a. The building is *sometimes closed on Sundays*.
3a. The net is *partially in the pool*.

In sentences (1a)–(3a), the adverbs "quickly," "sometimes," and "partially" are the first words in the respective phrases. However, the phrases remain verbal, adjectival, and prepositional respectively. The syntactic category of a phrase owes to the syntactic properties of the phrase, that is, to how the phrase relates or may relate to other syntactic constituents of a clause or sentence; and, again, this in turn owes to the syntactic properties of the word that heads the phrase. For example, the phrase "salty pretzels" is a noun phrase headed by the (plural count) noun "pretzels." It is not an adjective phrase headed by the adjective "salty." This is because "salty pretzels" can serve as an argument—be it the subject or the direct object—of a transitive verb, which is a syntactic property of noun phrases; for example:

4a. Saul eats salty pretzels.
4b. Salty pretzels have sold out.

Contrast sentences (4a) and (4b) with the following syntactically ill formed constructions:

* Saul eats salty.
* Salty has sold out.

Note also that although a noun phrase is a phrase headed by a noun, it need not consist of anything more than a noun. For example, in the following sentences, "pretzels" is a noun phrase consisting solely of the noun "pretzels":

Dax and Jett are eating pretzels.
Pretzels are in the snacks aisle.

Nouns admit so-called determiners as well as adjectives. Whereas noun, adjective, and verb are traditional grammatical categories, determiner is a recently theorized one.[4] Membership in the category of determiner is some-what contested. As I mentioned in section 3.4 of chapter 6, the following are standardly accepted as kinds of determiners: generalized quantifiers, articles, demonstratives, and possessives. So the following are examples of determiner phrases or determined noun phrases:

some pretzels
the pretzels
these pretzels
her pretzels.[5]

Determiners are said to function so as to limit "the potential referent of a noun phrase."[6] If this is a necessary condition of a determiner, it is not a suffi-cient one; for it fails to distinguish determiners from adjectives. One distinc-tion between adjectives and determiners is that adjectives—like nouns, verbs, and adverbs—are so-called "open" word classes. This means that the language, here English, readily admits new members belonging to these classes. In con-trast, determiner is a closed word class.[7] So English does not readily admit new determiners.

A second difference between adjectives and determiners is that most adjectives are gradable. In contrast, determiners do not admit degree expressions, for example:

* more the book
* this-er book.

Third, if a noun phrase admits both a determiner and an adjective, the deter-miner must precede the adjective; for example:

the black dog
* black the dog.

---

[4] The term "determiner" apparently first occurs in Bloomfield (1933) 203–6. Note that some linguists use the term "determinative" to denote the lexical category and "determiner phrase" to denote the syntactic category. Cp. Rodney Huddleston and Geoffrey K Pullman, *The Cambridge Grammar of the English Language*, Cambridge University Press, 2002, 54.

[5] If the determiners in these phrases head the phrases, then the phrases are determiner phrases. If instead the noun "pretzels" heads the phrases, then they are determined noun phrases. I note, but will not take a stand on, this substantive question of syntactic theory.

[6] Matthews (2007) s.v.

[7] For instance, prepositions are also closed class words.

In light of these considerations, I can now define a bare noun phrase as a noun phrase that satisfies the following two conditions:

- The noun phrase lacks a determiner; in other words, the noun phrase is determiner-less.
- The occurrence of the determiner-less noun phrase is syntactically acceptable in a clause or sentence.

To appreciate the idea of a determiner-less noun phrase being syntactically acceptable in a clause or sentence, consider the following two sentences:

5a.  * Black dog lay asleep on the lawn.
5b.  * She saw black dog asleep on the lawn.

The determiner-less noun phrase "black dog" is not syntactically acceptable in either (5a) or (5b). Consequently, "black dog" is not a bare noun phrase in either of these sentences. In fact, it is not syntactically acceptable in any sentence.[8] For syntactic acceptability, some determiner is required, for example the definite or indefinite article:

A black dog lay asleep on the lawn.
She saw the black dog asleep on the lawn.

Only certain types of nouns can constitute bare noun phrases. Moreover, among the types of nouns that can constitute bare noun phrases, only some of these types engender the distinctive ambiguity problem that I am in the process of introducing.

The following are types of nouns that can constitute bare noun phrases: proper nouns, pronouns, mass nouns, and plural count nouns. Examples of bare proper noun phrases and bare pronoun phrases are the subjects and direct objects in the following sentences:

David loves Janet.
He loves her.

In fact, proper nouns and pronouns in English generally do not admit determiners, and so the noun phrases that they constitute must be bare; for example:

---

[8] This claim assumes that "dog" is a count noun. If "dog" is taken as a mass noun, then "dog" and so "black dog" can constitute a bare noun phrase. I return to this point momentarily.

\* The David loves Janet.

\* David loves a Janet.[9]

\* The he loves her.

\* He loves a her.[10]

But the distinctive ambiguity problem of bare noun phrases does not arise for pronouns, and, with few exceptions, it does not arise for proper nouns.

In English, the sorts of nouns that can constitute bare noun phrases with various readings are, for the most part, limited to plural count nouns and mass nouns. Recall the ill-formed sentences (5a) and (5b). I have said that the noun phrase "black dog" is not syntactically acceptable in any sentence without a determiner. More precisely, insofar as "dog" is a singular count noun, without a determiner the noun phrase "black dog" is not syntactically acceptable in any sentence. The reason for this can be expressed as a generality:

> In English, singular count nouns generally cannot constitute bare noun phrases.

In fact, it has been claimed that bare singular count noun phrases are "totally impossible" in English.[11] I believe that this claim is an overstatement. Below, I will consider some possible examples of singular count nouns that can constitute bare noun phrases. Even so, the general point holds.[12]

"Dog" is usually a count noun. However, it can be converted to a mass noun; and in such cases, it can constitute a bare noun phrase; for example:

> The Chinese eat dog.
>
> Dog is considered a delicacy in China.

---

[9] This sentence is acceptable if the intended meaning is that David loves a person named "Janet." However, then "Janet" is no longer functioning as a proper noun, but as a count noun. This is evident from the fact that it admits pluralization and numerals: "There are three Janets in our class."

[10] A sentence such as "He is a she" is not an exception, since "she" here is not functioning as a pronoun, but as a count noun. This is evident from the fact that it admits pluralization: "They are all shes."

[11] Gennaro Chierchia, "Reference to Kinds across Languages," *Natural Language Semantics* 6 (1998) 339–405, at 341.

[12] There has been some discussion of bare singular count nouns in English. Cp. Laurel Smith Stvan, *The Semantics and Pragmatics of Bare Singular Noun Phrases*, Northwestern University dissertation in linguistics, 1998; Stvan, "The Functional Range of Bare Singular Count Nouns in English," in *Nominal Determination: Typology, Context, Constraints, and Historical Emergence*, E. Stark, E. Leiss, and W. Abraham, eds., John Benjamins, 2007, 171–87; Henriëtte de Swart and Joost Zwarts, "Less Form—More Meaning: Why Bare Singular Nouns Are Special," *Lingua* 119 (2009) 280–95.

As I mentioned in the previous chapter, almost all adjectival nominalizations formed with the suffix "-ness" are mass nouns. Accordingly, "goodness" can constitute a bare noun phrase; for example:

> Goodness is rare.
> Goodness is a measure of value.

In addition, note the following important point:

> A noun phrase may be bare even if the noun that heads the phrase is modified.

For example, consider the following two sentences:

> 6a.  Moral goodness is rare.
> 6b.  Aesthetic goodness is relatively widespread.

In (6a) and (6b), the noun phrases "moral goodness" and "aesthetic goodness" are bare. Even so, in both sentences "goodness" is modified, by the adjectives "moral" and "aesthetic" respectively.

## 1.3. The Ambiguity of Bare Noun Phrases

Gregory Carlson first systematically examined the topic of the ambiguity of bare noun phrases in his 1977 dissertation *Reference to Kinds in English*.[13] The focus of Carlson's study was bare plural count noun phrases.[14] Following Carlson, I will introduce the ambiguity of bare noun phrases on the basis of bare plural count noun phrases. I will then apply the account to bare mass noun phrases, including bare noun phrases headed by "goodness."

As Carlson writes, bare plural count noun phrases "have a notorious reputation for defying consistent semantic analysis. This is due to the fact that [their] meanings ... seem to change with context."[15] For example, consider the following

---

[13]  Carlson (1980). Cp. also Carlson, "A Unified Analysis of the English Bare Plural," *Linguistics and Philosophy* 1 (1977) 413–57. Earlier remarks occur, for example, in Noam Chomsky, *Aspects of the Theory of Syntax*, MIT Press, 1965; James Gough, "The Syntax-Based Semantics of the English Determiner Ø, A, The," *Papers in Linguistics* 1 (1969) 41–48.

[14]  Following Noam Chomsky, "Questions of Form and Interpretation," *Linguistic Analysis* 1 (1975) 75–109, Carlson refers to this class of phrases as "bare plurals"; and this is the way that this class of terms is often referred to in the literature, despite the fact that it is now recognized as including bare (singular) mass noun phrases.

[15]  Carlson (1980) 1.

four sentences, which employ the bare plural count noun phrase "dogs" as their subject:

D1. Dogs are mammals.
D2. Dogs bark.
D3. Dogs barked at the passing cyclist.
D4. Dogs are common.

Carlson suggests, and others have consistently followed him in suggesting, that (D1) seems equivalent to the following universally quantified sentences:

All dogs are mammals.
Every dog is a mammal.

(D2) seems equivalent to the following generically quantified sentences:

Generally dogs bark.
The typical dog barks.

(D3) seems equivalent to the following existentially quantified sentence:

Some dogs barked at the passing cyclist.

(D4) does not seem equivalent to a universally, existentially, or generically quantified sentence. In other words, the following sentences do not provide accurate renditions of (D4):

# All dogs are common.
?? Generally dogs are common.
There are dogs that are common. / Some dogs are common.[16]

Instead, arguably, (D4) is equivalent to the following sentences:

Dogs, as a kind, are common.
The kind dog is common.

---

[16] In addition to failing to capture the meaning of (D4), I have noted that these sentences are semantically dubious in their own right. "There are dogs that are common" and "Some dogs are common" are acceptable only if they are read as equivalent to "There are kinds of dogs that are common" and "Some kinds of dogs are common" respectively.

Assuming so and following Carlson, in (D4) "dogs" is said to have a "kind-denoting" reading. Granted this, the problem that Carlson presents is how to explain the various—again universal, existential, generic, and kind-denoting—readings of the one bare plural count noun phrase that occurs in (D1)–(D4).

While Carlson's original study focuses on bare plural count noun phrases, as he himself observes and as subsequent scholars have discussed, the same array of readings can be generated using bare mass noun phrases. Here, I offer two sets of examples: one using the concrete mass noun "water," the other using the abstract mass noun "goodness":

W1.   Water is composed of hydrogen and oxygen.
W2.   Water is a liquid.
W3.   Water covered the floor of Ronan's basement.
W4.   Water is widespread.

(W1)–(W4) can be glossed in terms of universally quantified, generically quantified, existentially quantified, and kind-denoting readings respectively as follows:

W1g.   All water is composed of hydrogen and oxygen.
W2g.   Water is generally a liquid.
W3g.   Some water covered the floor of Ronan's basement.
W4g.   The (chemical) kind water is widespread.

Note that, semantically, "goodness" is so general that it is difficult to generate all four readings without some modification. But recall that bare noun phrases may consist of nouns that are modified by adjectives. So consider "moral goodness" in the following sentences:

G1.   Moral goodness consists of serving a moral purpose.
G2.   Moral goodness promotes collective well-being.
G3.   Moral goodness sustained Ernest and Teresa's relationship, despite the extremely trying circumstances in which they found themselves.
G4.   Moral goodness is rare.

(G1)–(G4) can be glossed in terms of universally quantified, generically quantified, existentially quantified, and kind-denoting readings respectively as follows:

G1g. All moral goodness consists of serving a moral purpose.[17]

G2g. Moral goodness generally promotes collective well-being.

G3g. Ernest's and Teresa's moral goodness sustained their relationship, despite the extremely trying circumstances in which they found themselves.

G4g. The (psychological or behavioral) kind moral goodness is rare.

One response to the variety of readings to which the bare plural count noun phrases and bare concrete and abstract mass noun phrases are subject would be that the nouns that head these phrases lexically encode four distinct meanings: one universal, one existential, one generic, and one kind-denoting. In other words, the nouns are four ways polysemous. Prima facie, that seems implausible; and no one who has offered an explanation of the ambiguity of bare noun phrases endorses this position. Instead, what theorists have proposed is that, in various contexts, either the lexical meaning of the noun that heads the phrase is modulated or the meaning of some other constituent of the phrase of which the noun is a constituent is modulated or in some way altered.

Broadly speaking, there are two principal approaches to explaining the ambiguity of bare noun phrases. One descends from Carlson. The other has developed in opposition Carlson and Carlsonian theories. Following common usage, and for reasons that will become clear shortly, I will refer to Carlsonian theories as "kind-denoting" and to the alternative group as "ambiguity" theories. For reasons that will also become evident below, the ambiguity theory has alternatively been called "quantificational" and "indefinite."[18]

I will begin, in section 2, with a brief account of Carlson's original kind-denoting theory. This will enable me, in section 3.1, to explain the ambiguity theory. I will then, in section 3.2, identify six problems of the ambiguity theory: four relating to conditions of scopal ambiguity, one relating to the application of the theory to mass nouns, and one relating to the application of the theory to singular so-called date-denoting nouns. Consequently, in section 4, I will return to a Carlsonian kind-denoting theory, precisely Gennaro Chierchia's neo-Carlsonian account.

---

[17] Cp. "Every instance of moral goodness consists of serving a moral purpose."

[18] I should note here a third theory, according to which bare noun phrases are generalized quantifier phrases, which has been advanced by Carmen Dobrovie-Sorin and Claire Beyssade, *Redefining Indefinites*, Spring, 2012, especially at 31–93. Their discussion includes criticisms of both kind-denoting and ambiguity theories.

## 2. Carlson's Kind-Denoting Theory

A fundamental point that any account of bare noun phrases must acknowledge is that, syntactically, common nouns—and therefore mass and count nouns, whether singular or plural—are standardly interpreted as predicates. Accordingly, with respect to their semantic type, common nouns are, in principle, true of many entities, whereas proper nouns are, in principle, true only of one entity.[19] More precisely, insofar as they are unary functions, common nouns are functions from individuals or entities to truth-values. Indeed, this is how I treated the denotation of "goodness" and mass nouns generally as well as singular and plural count nouns in chapter 6. Such functions are then equivalent to sets, namely sets of entities of which the common noun is true, and whether those sets are mereologically structured, as in the case of mass and plural count nouns, or not, as in the case of singular count nouns.

Granted this, bare noun phrases occur in argument positions, for example as subjects, as in all of preceding examples: (D1)–(D4), (W1)–(W4), and (G1)–(G4). Subjects are not predicates. Consequently, some explanation is required of the semantic type of the noun that heads the bare noun phrase in such a position. If it is a function, then how can it occur in the subject position? If it is not a function, then what is it? And also in that case, what of the standard syntactic interpretation of common nouns as predicates?

According to Carlson's original kind-denoting theory, the nouns that head bare noun phrases in argument positions are a sort of proper noun; in other words, they are a sort of name. This at least explains why they occur in argument positions. But granting this, an explanation is then needed for why they also occur in non-argument positions, precisely in predicate positions. I note this point and will return to it in section 4.

Presently, assuming that at least in argument positions the nouns that head bare noun phrases have the semantic type of a sort of proper noun, what is it that they name? Rather than naming familiar sorts of individuals or entities such as individual persons, ordinary objects, and places, Carlson's view is that they name so-called kinds. For example, "dogs" names the animal kind dog; "water" names the chemical kind water; and "moral goodness" names the evaluative or purposive kind moral goodness.[20] Contrast kinds as individuals with what may be considered ordinary individuals such as a particular dog (Lassie), a particular mass of water (Lake Erie), and a particular instance of moral goodness (the

---

[19] This semantic claim is often made by saying that common nouns have plural reference, whereas proper nouns have singular reference. Cp. Andrew Radford, *Syntactic Theory and the Structure of English*, Cambridge University Press, 1997, 60.
[20] Carlson briefly treats "mass terms" as well as "abstract terms" at (1980) 293–300.

moral goodness of Sidney Kimmel's charitable donation to the Philadelphia Symphony Orchestra).

In contrast to such ordinary individuals, Carlson identifies two "major" distinguishing features of kinds as individuals. Ordinary individuals "may, in a certain pedestrian sense, occupy only one place at a time." In contrast, kinds "may function in such a way as to be in many places at a given time." For example, consider the animal kind ground squirrel: "quite clearly the presence of ground squirrels in New York City does not preclude the possibility of the presence of ground squirrels in Albany at that very same moment."[21] For convenience, I will call this feature of ordinary individuals "spatiotemporal continuity" and of kinds "spatiotemporal discontinuity."

According to Carlson, a second feature that distinguishes kinds from ordinary individuals is that "kinds . . . serve as whatever it is that ties together [the ordinary individuals that are members of or that instantiate a kind]."[22] For example, a ground squirrel in Central Park in New York City and a ground squirrel in Washington Park in Albany are "tied together" in that both are instances of a kind, the kind ground squirrel. Although suggestive, the term "tie together" is clearly theoretically inadequate. Nonetheless, I will conveniently refer to this feature of kinds—namely the fact that they are in some sense responsible for unifying a set of individuals—as "set unification."

Carlson's attribution to kinds of spatiotemporal discontinuity and set unification suggests that he is committed to a view of kinds as properties, in some philosophical sense of the term "property." But, as Carlson himself acknowledges, the metaphysical implications of his theory are underdeveloped.

Presently, assume that the nouns that head bare plural count noun phrases unambiguously name kinds so conceived. On this view, from among (D1)–(D4), only (D4) would provide the expected reading. What then explains the universal, generic, and existential readings in (D1)–(D3)? Carlson claims that "what gives rise to the different readings in those sentences is the manner in which the context of the sentence interacts with the bare [noun phrase]."[23] More precisely, the key contextual feature of the sentence engendering the various readings of the bare noun phrases is the predicate expression.

Carlson introduces what has since become a familiar distinction between two types of predicate expressions.[24] This distinction turns on the sorts of subjects

---

[21] Carlson (1980) 69.
[22] Carlson (1980) 69.
[23] Carlson (1980) 3.
[24] This distinction is inspired by Gary Milsark, *Existential Sentences in English*, MIT, dissertation in linguistics, 1974. Cp. Carlson (1980) 71: "A similar set of facts holds among the adjectives of English, as noted by Milark (1974) (who serves as a primary source of the line of thinking pursued in this section)."

that, semantically, the predicate expressions select. Loosely speaking, one sort of predicate expression semantically selects temporal stages of individuals.[25] For example, consider the following sentences:

7a.   Toby is smiling.
7b.   Toby is sitting.

Contrast the predicate expressions in (7a) and (7b) with those in the following two sentences:

8a.   Toby is male.
8b.   Toby is human.

The predicate expressions "smiling" and "sitting" in (7a) and (7b) apply to temporal stages of an individual, in this case to temporal stages of the individual Toby. In contrast, the predicate expressions "male" and "human" in (8a) and (8b) apply to the subject permanently or at least with relative permanence. Accordingly, "smiling," "sitting," and predicate expressions of their class are characterized as "stage-level," while "male," "human," and predicate expressions of their class are characterized as "individual-level."[26]

In sentences whose subjects are bare plural count noun phrases, and therefore according to Carlson's theory whose subjects are kind-denoting terms, different classes of predicate expressions may apply in one of three ways. They may apply to individuals that instantiate the kind; they may apply to stages of those individuals that instantiate the kind; or they may apply to the kind itself. For example, individual-level predicate expressions give rise to universal or generic readings, as in sentences (D1) and (D2); while stage-level predicate expressions give rise to existential readings, as in sentence (D3). It is claimed that predicate expressions such as "common," "widespread," and "rare" are members of a third class, so-called "kind-level" predicate expressions. These predicate expressions apply to kinds themselves, as in sentence (D4).

In sum, I underscore that according to Carlson's original kind-denoting theory, the bare noun phrases all name kinds; and the various readings that are generated owe to various ways that distinct types of predicate expressions apply to the kind-denoting terms. Finally, I repeat the notice above that insofar as, lexically, plural count nouns and mass nouns are interpreted as predicates,

---

[25] Carlson (1980, 68) appropriates the term "stage" from Quine (1960) 52–54.
[26] Carlson is explicit that "the sole criterion for separating the classes of predicate [expressions] cannot simply be a temporal one." However, he does not "attempt to give any criteria for distinguishing the two classes" (1980, 73).

when tokens of these nouns head bare noun phrases in argument positions, their syntactic category shifts and so their semantic type shifts from that of (unary) functions to kind-denoting expressions and therefore to individuals, albeit individuals of a non-ordinary sort. Such tokens of plural count nouns and mass nouns, including "goodness," are therefore ambiguous, at least in this respect. Again, I will consider the linguistic mechanism that has been posited to explain this shift below. However, according to Carlson, bare noun phrases in argument positions are consistently and so unambiguously kind-denoting terms. Presently, I turn to a general account of the ambiguity theory that arose in response to Carlson's kind-denoting theory.

### 3.1. The Ambiguity Theory

According to the ambiguity theory, bare plural count noun phrases are ambiguous in argument positions, precisely two ways so.[27] (I conveniently ignore other ways that, according to the ambiguity theory, plural count noun phrases may be ambiguous between their occurrences in argument and non-argument positions.) One sense of bare plural count noun phrases in argument positions is as kind-denoting terms. Bare plural count noun phrases have this sense when they are the arguments of kind-level predicate expressions such as in (D4). In this respect, the ambiguity theory and the kind-denoting theory are in agreement.

But the ambiguity theory maintains that in other contexts, albeit still in argument positions, such as those exemplified by (D1)–(D3), bare noun phrases have a different meaning. Moreover, strictly speaking, the phrases are not actually bare, only ostensibly so. In contexts such as (D1)–(D3), the noun phrases are actually constituents of determiner phrases. Determiner phrases consist of a determiner, which heads the phrase and so endows the phrase with its syntactic identity, followed by a nominal complement.[28] In cases such as (D1)–(D3), the

---

[27] For example, cp. Angelika Krazter, "Die Analyse des bloßen Plural bei Gregory Carlson," *Linguistische Berichte* 70 (1980) 47–50; Brendan Gillon, "Bare Plurals as Plural Indefinite Noun Phrases," in *Knowledge Representation and Defeasible Reasoning*, H. E. Kyburg et al., eds., Kluwer, 1990, 119–66; Karina Wilkinson, *Studies in the Semantics of Generic Noun Phrases*, University of Massachusetts, Amherst, dissertation in linguistics, 1991; Molly Diesing, *Indefinites*, MIT Press, 1992; Cleo Condoravdi, *Descriptions in Context*, Yale University, dissertation in linguistics, 1994; Manfred Krifka, "Common Nouns: A Contrastive Analysis of Chinese and English," in *The Generic Book*, G. Carlson and F. J. Pelletier, eds., University of Chicago Press, 1995, 398–411; Angelika Kratzer, "Stage-Level and Individual-Level Predicates," in Carlson and Pelletier (1995) 125–74; Peter Lasersohn, "Bare Plurals and Donkey Anaphora," *Natural Language Semantics* 5 (1997) 79–86; Manfred Krifka, "Bare NPs: Kind-Referring, Indefinites, Both, or Neither?" *SALT 13* (2003) 180–203.

[28] My characterization of the phrases as determiner phrases is in fact an expository convenience. I could just as well have characterized them as determined noun phrases.

nominal complement of the determiner, namely the plural count noun "dogs," is explicit. In contrast, the determiner is covert. Such determiner phrases therefore may be represented as

(Det) N.

Here N stands for the nominal expression, in our example "dogs"; and Det in parentheses is intended to indicate that the determiner is a covert constituent.[29]

More precisely, the ambiguity theory maintains that the covert determiner that heads the determiner phrase is an indefinite article. Various considerations are adduced to support this claim. First, observe that a singular indefinite phrase may, more or less accurately, gloss sentences such as (D1)–(D3):

D1s.   A dog is a mammal.
D21s.  A dog barks.[30]
D3s.   A dog barked at the passing cyclist.

Moreover, consistently with the ambiguity theory, (D4) cannot felicitously be rendered by a singular indefinite phrase:

D4s.   # A dog is common.

Next, observe that whereas the definite article admits both singular and plural nominal complements, the indefinite article only admits a singular nominal complement; for example:

the dog
the dogs

a dog
* a dogs.

So English does not license the indefinite article with a plural noun phrase.[31] More precisely, so the ambiguity theory maintains, English does not license an overt indefinite article with a plural noun phrase. Insofar as an indefinite article

---

[29] Note that here and occasionally elsewhere in this chapter, as in chapter 6, to facilitate intelligibility, I tend to use Gill Sans MT font to represent select variables both in the text constituting ordinary paragraphs and in the indented texts where I introduce examples, principles, and claims that I want to highlight.

[30] I acknowledge that this sentence admits a second reading, according to which the action of occurrent barking is attributed to a single dog.

[31] This point is forcefully made in Gillon (1990).

heads the determiner phrase, it is required to be covert. Accordingly, let the symbol α stand for a covert indefinite article that takes a plural count noun in argument position. Consequently, sentences (D1)–(D3) can be represented as

D1c.  α dogs are mammals.
D2c.  α dogs bark.
D3c.  α dogs barked at the passing cyclist.

To be clear, since the plural indefinite article α is covert, it is not pronounced or written. Consequently, sentences (D1c)–(D3c) are to be read, respectively, as I originally introduced them; once again:

D1.  Dogs are mammals.
D2.  Dogs bark.
D3.  Dogs barked at the passing cyclist.

Recall and compare the theory of *pos*, introduced in section 3.2 of chapter 3, which is motivated to explain the compositionality problem for basic sentences such as

10.  Thiebaud's 1969 *Candy Counter* is good.
11.  Paolo is tall.

Advocates of *pos* claim that this covert positive degree morpheme is a constituent of the predicate expressions in such sentences. Accordingly, sentences (10) and (11) can be represented as

10c.  Thiebaud's 1969 *Candy Counter* is *pos* good.
11c.  Paolo is *pos* tall.

However, again, since *pos* is covert, it is unpronounced and unwritten.

In the case of the ambiguity theory of bare noun phrases, one might well object that the fact that the indefinite article is not explicitly licensed with plural noun phrases calls into question the very claim that sentences such as (D1)–(D3) consist of a covert indefinite article.[32] The following consideration is crucially supposed to support the ambiguity theory's commitment in this regard.

---

[32] Cp. Gillon (1990): "There is a plural form of the indefinite article but . . . it is phonetically null. This claim accrues plausibility from the fact that, of all the determiners which go together with count nouns to form acceptable [determined] noun phrases, only the indefinite article has no overt phonetic form" (120).

Defenders of the ambiguity theory largely follow Hans Kamp's or Irene Heim's theories of the indefinite article. As in section 2.4 of chapter 4, I will here adopt Heim's account. Recall that Heim analyzes the indefinite article as a free variable, which is to say, an unbound variable.[33] Consequently, so-called "unselective" quantificational operators in the sentence or in the broader context in which the noun phrase occurs can bind the variable. An unselective quantifier is a quantifier that binds any free variables in its scope.[34] The universal, generic, and existential readings of sentences such as (D1)–(D3), then, result from the fact that these quantificational operators may be of correlative kinds, namely universal, generic, or existential. As an illustration of this idea, consider sentences consisting of the singular indefinite phrase "a dog" as their subject and with explicit universal and generic quantificational operators (here italicized):

A dog is *always* a mammal.

$\forall x \, (Dx \rightarrow Mx)$

A dog *generally* barks.

$Gen \, x \, (Dx \rightarrow Bx).$[35]

Analogously, the ambiguity theory claims, in the cases of (D1), "Dogs are mammals," and (D2), "Dogs bark," universal and generic quantifiers bind the covert plural indefinite article that heads the determiner phrase "α dogs" that is the subject of these sentences.

Granted this, observe now that the existential reading in (D3), "Dogs barked at the passing cyclist," is explained as follows. In the absence of any quantificational operator to bind it, a free variable is subject to existential closure. This occurs in (D3) and so yields the existentially quantified reading:

Some dogs barked at the passing cyclist.

$\exists x \, (Dx \wedge Bx).$

Recall the semantic type theoretic notation introduced in section 3.4 of chapter 3 according to which $e$ stands for an individual and $t$ stands for a truthvalue. The semantic type of the indefinite article is a function from a unary function to a function from a unary function to a truth-value. Consequently, the indefinite article is represented as $\langle\langle e,t\rangle,\langle\langle e,t\rangle,t\rangle\rangle$ or more simply as $\langle\langle et\rangle,\langle et,t\rangle\rangle$. In other words, the indefinite article requires a nominal complement (for

---

[33]  See especially Heim (1982) 131–67.
[34]  Cp. Wilkinson (1991) 10–16.
[35]  Here, as standardly, *Gen* stands for the generic quantifier.

example, "dog" or "dogs"), whose semantic type is a unary function, and the resulting indefinite phrase requires a predicate expression (for example, "barked at the passing cyclist"), again interpreted as a unary function, to yield a proposition. Consequently, insofar as the nouns or nominal expressions constituting the noun phrases are complements of a covert indefinite article, these nominal expressions retain their lexical semantic type as unary functions. It is only in contexts such as (D4) that the nouns heading the noun phrases are truly bare, that is, that they occur with no determiner, and as such undergo a semantic type shift from the type of unary functions $\langle e,t \rangle$ to the type of individuals $\langle e \rangle$.[36] For example, observe that the intuitive meaning of a sentence such as (D4), "Dogs are common," could not result from a universal or generic or existential quantifier binding a covert indefinite article heading the phrase "a dogs":

# Dogs are always common.
# Dogs are generally common.
# Dogs are sometimes common.

In sum, the ambiguity theory maintains that in argument positions such as the subject position of a sentence, bare noun phrases are two ways ambiguous. When they receive kind-denoting readings, the nouns that head bare noun phrases are indeed bare and kind-denoting and so have the semantic type of individuals. Once again, in such cases the ambiguity theory and Carlson's kind-denoting theory are in agreement. But in all other cases, the ambiguity theory holds that the nouns retain their lexical meanings as unary functions from individuals to truth-values, and syntactically they occur as complements of a covert indefinite article.

## 3.2. Problems with the Ambiguity Theory

The ambiguity theory's commitment to the view that in most instances, the allegedly bare noun phrases are in fact complements of a covert plural indefinite article faces several problems. In this section, I describe six. The first four concern scopal ambiguity and have been discussed in the secondary literature since Carlson.[37] The fifth problem concerns the application of the ambiguity theory to

---

[36] I acknowledge that in the case of plural count nouns, the individuals of which these nouns are true must be pluralities. On the topic of semantic type shifting, the seminal contribution is Barbara Partee, "Noun Phrase Interpretation and Type Shifting Principles," in *Studies in Discourse Representation and the Theory of Generalized Quantifiers*, J. Groenendijk, D. de Jongh, and M. Stokhof, eds., Foris, 1987, 115–43. For an overview, cp. Helen de Hoop, "Type Shifting," in Maienborn, von Heusinger, and Portner (2011) 2259–71.

[37] For example, cp. Wilkinson (1991) 4–6.

mass nouns. The sixth problem relates to the ambiguity of what I will call "date-denoting" count noun phrases.

One of the most widely cited criticisms of the ambiguity theory concerns the scopal properties of indefinite or quantificational phrases versus bare plural count noun phrases. Recall that I discussed this topic in section 2.4 of chapter 4. For example, consider the following sentence:

12.  Everyone read some books about Philadelphia.[38]

Sentence (12) is two ways ambiguous. One reading, where "everyone" takes scope over "some books," is compatible with different readers reading different books about Philadelphia. The other reading, where "some books" takes scope over "everyone," requires that the readers read the same books. Contrast the following sentence:

12n.  Everyone read books about Philadelphia.

In (12n), "books" only admits narrow scope. In other words, it cannot take scope over "everyone."

Likewise, recall the following example from chapter 4, here renumbered:

13.  Toby did not see a mark on the wall.

Sentence (13) is also two ways ambiguous. The indefinite phrase "a mark" can take wide scope, that is, scope above the negation. In that case, (13) is equivalent to

13w.  There is some mark on the wall that Toby did not see.

Alternatively, "a mark" can take narrow scope, below the negation; in which case (13) is equivalent to

13n.  Toby did not see any marks on the wall.

In contrast, in the following sentence, the bare plural count noun phrase "marks" only take narrow scope:

13b.  Toby did not see marks on the wall.

---

[38] For example, cp. Ariel Cohen and Nomi Erteschik-Shir, "Are Bare Plurals Indefinites?" in *Empirical Studies in Formal Syntax and Semantics* vol. 2, F. Corbin, C. Dobrovie-Sorin, and J. Marandin, eds., Thesus, 1999, 99–119, at 102.

Sentence (13b) can only be read as equivalent to (13n). It cannot be read as

> There are some marks on the wall that Toby did not see.

Consider next the following sentences:

14a.  Inga is looking for a policeman.
14b.  Inga is looking for some policemen.[39]

The verb "looking for" introduces an opaque context. The phrases "a policeman" in (14a) and "some policemen" in (14b) may be read *de dicto* or *de re*. According to the former readings, there is no particular policeman or there are no particular policemen that Inga is looking for. According to the latter readings, there is a particular policeman or there are particular policemen that Inga is looking for. In contrast, the bare plural count noun phrase does not admit a *de re* reading. That is, the following sentence,

> Inga is looking for policemen

cannot be read to mean that there are particular policemen that Inga is looking for.

A third problem concerns anaphoric constructions. An anaphor must have the same denotation as its antecedent. For example, consider the following sentence, to which I have added subscripted indices i to represent coreference:

15.  Joe loves Gail$_i$ and thinks of her$_i$ all the time.

The pronoun "her" must have the same denotation as its antecedent "Gail"; and here in sentence (15) it does. With this fact in mind, consider the following sentence:

16.  Katie polished apples and Toby ate them.

One circumstance that would make (16) true is if Toby ate the very apples that Katie polished. Accordingly, (16) is read as

16s.  Katie polished apples$_i$ and Toby ate them$_i$.

---

[39]  Cp. Delfitto (2006) 226.

However, the truth of (16) does not require (16s). Instead, (16) would be true if Toby ate a distinct set of apples from the set that Katie polished, an event represented by the following sentence:

16d.   Katie polished apples$_i$ and Toby ate them$_j$.

Contrast this with the following sentences:

16a.   Katie polished an apple and Toby ate it.
16b.   Katie polished some apples and Toby ate them.

For (16a) and (16b) to be true, Toby must have eaten the very apple or apples that Katie polished.

A fourth difficulty concerning scope relates to noun phrase deletion in coordinate structures. For instance, consider the following sentences:

17.    A building will collapse in Philadelphia tomorrow, and a building will
       burn down in Boston the day after.
17d.   A building will collapse in Philadelphia tomorrow and will burn down in
       Boston the day after.[40]

Observe that what distinguishes (17) and (17d) is that in (17d) the subject, "a building," of the second verb phrase, "will burn down in Boston the day after," has been deleted. (Note that this is a case of syntactic ellipsis.) Granted this, (17) would be made true by one building $b1$ collapsing tomorrow in Philadelphia and another building $b2$ burning on the following day in Boston. Although, strictly speaking, (17) would also be made true if one and the same building collapsed in Philadelphia tomorrow and then burnt down in Boston the day after, this sequence of events is physically impossible. In contrast, the truth of (17d) requires precisely such an impossibility. In other words, the deletion of the subject of the second verb phrase in (17d) requires that the same building that collapses in Philadelphia burns down in Boston. Contrast this with the following sentences, which employ the bare plural count noun phrase "buildings":

18.    Buildings will collapse in Philadelphia tomorrow, and buildings will burn
       down in Boston the day after.
18d.   Buildings will collapse in Philadelphia tomorrow and will burn down in
       Boston the day after.

---

[40]  Cp. Delfitto (2006) 220.

Again in (18d), the subject noun phrase of the second verb phrase has been deleted. Yet the truth-condition of (18d) remains the same as that of (18). In particular, the truth-condition of (18d) requires no physical impossibility.

While the preceding examples have focused on bare plural count noun phrases, analogous examples can be generated using bare mass noun phrases. For example, consider the mass noun "beer" in the following sentence:

19.  Everyone drank beer.

There is no reading of (19) that requires that everyone drank the same beer or the same type of beer or beer from the same source. In other words, (19) does not require the following reading:

There is some beer that everyone drank.

Next consider:

20.  Toby did not see water on the floor.

Sentence (20) is equivalent to

Toby did not see any water on the floor.

In other words, (20) is not compatible with Toby seeing some body of water on the floor, but not another body of water on the floor.

Now consider the mass noun "gold":

21.  Katie is looking for gold.

Sentence (21) does not entail

There is some gold that Katie is looking for.

Next consider:

22.  Ronan sells gold and Gail wears it.

The truth of (22) does not require that Gail wear the very gold that Ronan sells.

Finally, consider the mass noun "hail":

23.  Hail will fall in Philadelphia tomorrow and will pummel Boston the day after.

The truth of (23) does not require the physical impossibility that the very same hail that falls in Philadelphia tomorrow pummel Boston the day after.

Having adverted to mass nouns, I propose now a fifth problem for the ambiguity theory. As examples (W1)–(W4) and (G1)–(G4) above illustrate, bare mass noun phrases are subject to the same array of readings as bare plural count noun phrases. Yet, as we also saw in the discussion of the grammatical properties that distinguish count and mass nouns in section 3.1 of chapter 6, mass nouns, including singular mass nouns, do not admit the indefinite article or individuating quantifier expressions of any kind. Consequently, even if, in the case of universal, generic, and existential readings of bare plural count nouns, unselective quantifiers were binding a covert variable corresponding to an indefinite article in the determiner position, a more general explanation for these readings, precisely the presence of the covert variable, would be required.

The final problem for the ambiguity theory that I will mention relates to the fact that a class of bare singular count noun phrases are subject to some or all of the readings associated with bare plural count noun phrases and bare mass noun phrases. These bare singular count noun phrases consist of certain time and date terms, precisely days of the week, months of the year, the four seasons, and holidays. I offer examples here using "Thursday," "February," "spring," and "Christmas." For convenience, I will hereafter refer to these terms as members of the class of "date-denoting" count nouns.[41]

First, I should note that while "Thursday," "February," and "Christmas" are standardly characterized as proper nouns and so capitalized, syntactic evidence supports the view that in fact they, along with "spring," either are count nouns or at least can occur as count nouns. For example, all four nouns can be pluralized and admit numerals:

This year there are five Thursdays in July.
During each of the last two Februaries, the team has used Winter Haven as its training site.
Two springs ago, we planted dandelions in the garden.
We have spent the last three Christmases with my in-laws.

In addition, the following sentences confirm that in the singular the nouns "Thursday," "February," "spring," and "Christmas" admit the individuating quantifier expressions "each," "every," and "a"; and that in the plural they

---

[41] I am unaware of any prior discussion of the syntax or semantics of bare singular date-denoting count nouns.

admit the individuating quantifier expressions "several," "few," "a few," "many":

> Each Thursday we meet for a drink.
> Every February I suffer from seasonal affective disorder.
> Every spring they plant marigolds in their garden.
> A Christmas without presents is like a Thanksgiving without turkey.

> Several Thursdays have passed since we last met for a drink.
> Few Februaries that I can remember have been this warm.
> Few springs can compare to the one that we are enjoying now.
> Many Christmases have been spent at your in-laws.

Note also that in the singular, the nouns "Thursday," "February," "spring," and "Christmas" do not admit the quantity expressions "much" and "little" that mass nouns do:

> * Much Thursday was spent doing household chores.
> * Much February was rainy this year.
> * Little spring was warm this year.
> * Little Christmas was spent with the family this year.

In addition, it should be noted that whereas the bearers of proper nouns need share nothing other than the fact that they bear the proper noun—for example, multiple individuals of various animal species may be named "Casey"—anything non-derivatively said to be "Thursday," "February," "spring," or "Christmas" is required to occur at particular times.

Having confirmed that "Thursday," "February," "spring," and "Christmas" are or at least can occur as count nouns, consider now the following sets of sentences which yield universal, generic, existential, and kind-denoting readings respectively:

> T1.   Thursday comes after Wednesday.
> T2.   Thursday is a busy shopping day.
> T3.   Thursday was uncharacteristically quiet at the supermarket.
> T4.   Thursday is one of the seven days of the week.

> F1.   February comes after January.
> F2.   February is the coldest month of the year in Pennsylvania.
> F3.   February was uncharacteristically warm.
> F4.   February is one of twelve months of the year.

S1.   Spring comes after winter.
S2.   Spring is rainier than summer.
S3.   Spring was uncharacteristically dry.
S4.   Spring is one of the four seasons.

C1.   Christmas occurs on December 25.
C2.   Christmas is more festive than Thanksgiving.
C3.   Christmas was uncharacteristically warm.
C4.   Christmas is a Christian holiday.[42]

The fact that these bare singular count noun phrases are subject to the same array of readings as bare plural count noun phrases and bare mass noun phrases further confirms that even if, in the case of universal, generic, and existential readings of bare plural count nouns, unselective quantifiers were binding a covert variable corresponding to a plural indefinite article in the determiner position, a more general explanation for these readings would be required. But the fact that "Saturday," "February," "spring," and "Christmas" are or at least can occur as count nouns and so admit the indefinite article more fundamentally problematizes the claim that the bare plural count noun phrases consist of a covert indefinite article. In fact, adding the indefinite article to the singular date-denoting count noun phrases not only alters the meanings of these sentences, but is semantically unacceptable in the sentences above. Consider, for instance, the "Christmas" sentences (C1)–(C3):

C1i.   # A Christmas occurs on December 25.
C2i.   # A Christmas is more festive than (a) Thanksgiving.
C3i.   # A Christmas was uncharacteristically warm this year.[43]

I do not claim that the preceding six difficulties present insurmountable obstacles for the ambiguity theory. Nonetheless, in light of them, I will at this point return to the kind-denoting theory. Precisely, I will conclude this

---

[42] I offer glosses of this last set of four sentences: "Christmas always occurs on December 25"; "Generally, Christmas is more festive than Thanksgiving"; "This Christmas was uncharacteristically warm"; and "The (holiday) Christmas is a Christian holiday."

[43] On behalf of the ambiguity theory, a possible rejoinder to the preceding account of bare singular date-denoting nouns is that in sentences such as (T1)–(T4), (F1)–(F4), (S1)–(S4), and (C1)–(C4), "Thursday," "February," "spring," and "Christmas" occur as mass nouns. Some evidence in support of this claim might be derived from certain event-denoting nouns—for example, "divorce," "marriage," "battle," and "war"—of which date-denoting nouns are arguably a subclass and which seem to easily convert from count to mass and vice versa. For example: "Divorce is painful; I've been through one"; "War is horrific; I've fought in many." On the other hand, as suggested above, "Thursday," "February," "spring," and "Christmas" appear to consistently fail diagnostics for mass nouns. The topic clearly deserves further consideration.

introduction to the problem of the ambiguity of bare noun phrases by adverting to Chierchia's more recent contribution to the kind-denoting theory.

## 4.  Chierchia's Neo-Carlsonian Kind-Denoting Theory

Chierchia's neo-Carlsonian theory of bare noun phrases appears in his seminal 1998 paper "Reference to Kinds across Languages." The governing aim of this paper is the development of a theory of cross-linguistic variation among noun phrases. Chierchia's central thesis is that there exists a so-called nominal mapping parameter within universal grammar. To clarify this idea, it is necessary to distinguish between principles and parameters in the theory of universal grammar.[44]

According to the theory of universal grammar, the language faculty that has evolved in *Homo sapiens* incorporates a set of grammatical principles. Accordingly, at a fundamental level of description, the grammars of all natural languages are the same; and in virtue of being endowed with a language faculty, any neurotypical human child may develop the grammar of any natural language to which she or he is appropriately exposed. On the other hand, the grammars of individual natural languages clearly exhibit considerable variation, and so aspects of universal grammar must also permit grammatical variation according to certain parameters. For example, all natural languages enable the formation of interrogative constructions. However, in some languages, such as English, interrogative constructions require that the interrogative term, called the "*wh*-expression*," be fronted, that is, move to the initial position in the interrogative clause. In other languages, such as Chinese, the interrogative occurs in its "natural" position, at the end of the clause, and so no *wh*-movement occurs:

How are you?[45]

*Ni    hao    ma?*
You   good   *wh?*

Consequently, among its interrogative principles, universal grammar encodes a binary *wh*-parameter, according to which interrogatives can be formed in one of two ways. In short, grammatical diversity among natural languages is explicable in terms of individual languages' various parametric settings.

Chierchia's paper proposes that universal grammar encodes a nominal parameter, that is, a parameter pertaining to nouns and nominal expressions.

---

[44] The summary in the following paragraph is informed by Radford (1997) 12–25.
[45] In English, the order of subject and predicate is also inverted.

According to this parameter, nouns may or may not occur as arguments and may or may not occur as predicates. Since the possibility of nouns occurring as neither arguments nor predicates would rule out their occurrence completely, the nominal parameter is in effect a ternary one:

Nouns may only occur as predicates.

Nouns may only occur as arguments.

Nouns may occur as both arguments and predicates.

For example, Chierchia argues that Chinese is a nominal-argument-only language; Italian is a nominal-predicate-only language; and English is a language in which nouns occur both as arguments and as predicates. While aspects of Chierchia's particular cross-linguistic results have been challenged, as Veneeta Dayal notes: "the impact of [Chierchia's] paper has been phenomenal and the response to it has transformed the empirical landscape, informing and deepening our understanding of the interpretive possibilities across languages."[46]

Hereafter, I will ignore Chierchia's cross-linguistic discussion and focus on his treatment of nouns in English, in particular his treatment of bare noun phrases. As noted, English admits nominal expressions in both argument and predicate positions. Since nominals in argument positions just are bare noun phrases, insofar as English admits nominals in argument positions, it admits bare noun phrases. Chierchia posits three universal grammatical operations for transforming a nominal expression with a predicative meaning—in extensional terms a function of type $\langle e,t \rangle$ and in intensional terms a function of type $\langle s, \langle e,t \rangle \rangle$[47]—into an argument—in extensional terms an individual $\langle e \rangle$ and in intensional terms a function from possible worlds to individuals $\langle s,e \rangle$. In English, only two of these operations are available.[48] And between these two, only one is relevant for our purposes here. The relevant operation consists of converting the noun, which is taken to have a predicative meaning, into a kind-denoting term. I will refer to this operation as "K-NOM," short for "kind-denoting nominalization."[49] I will offer an example momentarily. But first, I need to clarify Chierchia's conception of a kind.

---

[46] Veneeta Dayal, "On the Existential Force of Bare Plurals," in *From Grammar to Meaning: The Spontaneous Logicality of Language*, I. Caponigro and C. Cecchetto, eds., Cambridge University Press, 2013, 49–80, at 50.

[47] Recall that in type theoretic notation the symbol $s$ is used to stand for the semantic type of a possible world.

[48] Chierchia (1998) especially at 348–53.

[49] Cp. Dayal (2013) 50–55, who names the operation "*nom*." Chierchia originally introduced this operation in *Topics in the Syntax and Semantics of Infinitives and Gerunds*, University of Massachusetts, Amherst, dissertation in linguistics, 1984. Note that insofar as the ambiguity theory

Note that Carlson's original study of 1977 preceded Link's 1983 lattice theory of mass nouns and plural count nouns by six years. Chierchia's neo-Carlsonian theory incorporates Link's results into its conception of kinds. Chierchia understands a kind as an individual concept. An individual concept is a function from possible worlds to individuals (semantic type $\langle s,e \rangle$). The individual that a nominal expression functioning as a kind-denoting term refers to at a given world is the largest member of the extension, at that world, of the noun that heads the nominal expression.[50] For example, consider the plural count noun "dogs" in an argument position and so functioning as a kind-denoting term. Recall the following simple join semilattice diagram corresponding to the denotation of a plural count noun from section 3.3 of chapter 6:

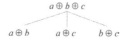

Assume now that this diagram represents the extension of a plural count noun at a given world. The largest member of the extension is the join $a \oplus b \oplus c$. Accordingly, a kind is, at a world, the so-called "plural individual" that comprises all of the atomic individuals (here, $a$, $b$, and $c$) that constitute the extension of the noun. Consequently, in the case of an assertion of (D4)—"Dogs are common"— "dogs" refers to the join, that is, the mereological sum comprising all individual dogs in the world indexed to the utterance. In the case of a mass noun such as "water" or a mass nominal expression such as "moral goodness," the kind term refers to all molecules of water or all instances of moral goodness in the world indexed to the utterance.

admits that at least in some contexts, such as those exemplified by (D4), bare noun phrases denote kinds, the ambiguity theory too must embrace K-NOM or some such type shifting principle.

[50] Chierchia defines this operation precisely as follows: "For any property [denoting term] P and world situation s, [the kind forming operation] $^\cap P = \lambda s\ \iota P_s$, if $\lambda s\ \iota P_s$ is in K, undefined otherwise, where $P_s$ is the extension of P in s and K is the set of kinds" (1998, 351). Note here that properties are identified as the denotations of predicate expressions, that is, expressions whose (extensional) semantic type is a function from individuals to truth-values. The symbol $^\cap$ is Chierchia's so-called down operator, which converts an expression with predicative meaning into an expression with individual meaning. $^\cap$ is called a "down" operator because it "lowers," that is, simplifies, the semantic type of the expression, in this case from $\langle e,t \rangle$ to $\langle e \rangle$ or, in intensional terms, from $\langle s,\langle e,t \rangle \rangle$ to $\langle s,e \rangle$. The expression $\lambda s\ \iota P_s$ should be read as a function ($\lambda$) from a situation (s) to the individual ($\iota$) consisting of all those atomic individuals of which the property denoted by P is true in s. Note that K-NOM is a partial function. That is, not all expressions with predicative meaning are admissible arguments of K-NOM. Kinds are limited to sets of individuals "with sufficiently regular function and/or behavior." "Moreover, kinds . . . will generally have a plurality of instances . . . Something that is necessarily instantiated by just one individual . . . would *not* qualify as a kind" (Chierchia, 1998, 350; cp. Dayal, 2013, 51).

Note that insofar as Chierchia maintains that kinds are plural individuals, he departs from Carlson's original theory according to which kinds are properties in the robust metaphysical sense of being spatiotemporally discontinuous and set unifying. The plural individual that is the extension of a kind-denoting term at a world consists of spatially discontinuous atomic individuals, but the set itself is not spatially, let alone temporally, discontinuous. Moreover, the plural individual that is the extension of a kind-denoting term is a set rather than an entity that is responsible for the unification of a set.[51]

I underscore here also the close semantic correspondence between nouns as arguments and nouns as predicates. Compare Chierchia's remark:

> the plural individual . . . can be taken as a representative of the [extension of the predicate expression] true of all its parts, which justifies viewing the kind[-denoting expression] as a "nominalization" of the corresponding [predicate expression] (and vice versa, viewing the [predicate expression] as a predicativization of the kind[-denoting expression]).[52]

Accordingly, Chierchia also recognizes an operation that is the converse of K-NOM, namely one that converts a kind-denoting nominal expression of type $\langle e \rangle$ or $\langle s,e \rangle$ into a predicate expression of semantic type $\langle e,t \rangle$ or $\langle s,\langle e,t \rangle \rangle$, call it "P-NOM," short for "predicative nominalization."[53]

With these points in mind, I turn to Chierchia's treatment of examples where the subject does not have a kind-denoting reading. This includes examples (D1)–(D3), (W1)–(W3), and (G1)–(G3). I underscore that, for expository convenience, my account here will simplify. Granted this, in all such cases, the subject of the sentence is a kind-denoting expression, but the predicate expression is not kind-level. For example, in (D1) and (D2)—"Dogs are mammals" and "Dogs bark"—the predicate expressions are individual-level; and in (D3)—"Dogs barked at the passing cyclist"—the predicate expression is stage-level. The semantic mismatch

---

[51] As such, Chierchia's neo-Carlsonian theory as well as the account of the denotation of mass nouns and gradable mass nouns such as "goodness" presented in chapter 6 is predominantly nominalistic. Cp. Moltmann's claim regarding the distinction between the ontologies of numerous traditional philosophical theories and the ontology reflected in natural language: "Natural language as such does not give support for [the sort of entities that philosophers have traditionally included in their ontologies such as universals . . . , at least not in a central role. Instead, it gives support for tropes of a great variety of sorts not as such discussed in contemporary philosophical ontology" (2013, 4).

[52] Chierchia (1998) 352.

[53] Chierchia symbolizes this operation using the so-called "up" operator symbol $^\cup$. The up or, as I am calling it, P-NOM operation is defined as follows. For a kind-denoting term k, $^\cup k = \{\lambda x \, [x \leq k_s]$ if $k_s$ is defined, $\lambda x \, [\text{FALSE}]$, otherwise$\}$ (Chierchia, 1998, 350; cp. Dayal, 2013, 52). In other words, the up or P-NOM operation $^\cup$ takes a kind-denoting term k and converts it to an expression whose semantic type is a function from individuals x to truth-values such that those individuals x of which k is true are constituents of the kind denoted by k in situation s.

triggers P-NOM. Accordingly, the subject expression, here "dogs," which was originally converted from its lexical predicative meaning, via K-NOM, into a kind-denoting term, is converted back, via P-NOM, into an expression with predicative meaning. Given this, since the semantic type of a predicate expression is a function from individuals to truth-values, the predicativized nominal expression now itself requires an individual argument. However, given the fact that the sentence already contains a predicate expression, the inclusion of an individual argument for the predicativized nominal expression would be syntactically unacceptable. Consequently, in all cases, the predicativized nominal expression is bound by a quantificational operator of some sort. The sort of operator that binds the predicativized nominal expression depends on the meaning of expression that is predicated of the originally kind-denoting, now predicativized, nominal expression, for example: "mammals" in (D1), "bark" in (D2), and "barked at the passing cyclist" in (D3). In (D1), the operator is universal; in (D2), it is generic; and in (D3), it is existential. For example, consider (D3): "Dogs barked at the passing cyclist." In virtue of appearing in an argument position, "dogs" must initially be converted, via K-NOM, into a kind-denoting term. Accordingly, "dogs" then refers to the maximal set consisting of individual dogs in the world indexed to the utterance. Granted this, the expression "barked at the passing cyclist" is not kind-level, but stage-level. Consequently, P-NOM is triggered; "dogs" is converted back into a predicate expression; finally, given that "barked at the passing cyclist" is stage-level predicate expression, the individual argument of the now predicativized nominal expression "dogs" is existentially bound. The result can be formally represented, as I represented (D3) earlier, namely as

$$\exists x \, (Dx \wedge Bx).[54]$$

In ordinary language, this formalization can be read as

There are individuals that are dogs and that barked at the passing cyclist.

or simply

Some dogs barked at the passing cyclist.

---

[54] In such cases as (D3), Chierchia more precisely invokes an operation that he calls "Derived Kind Predication," or "DKP" for short. According to DKP: If a predicate expression P applies to [stages of] objects, that is, ordinary individuals, and k denotes a kind, then $P(k) = \exists x[^{\cup}k(x) \wedge P(x)]$ (Chierchia, 1998, 364). Note the inclusion of the up, i.e. P-NOM, operation $^{\cup}$ within DKP. The formula $P(k) = \exists x[^{\cup}k(x) \wedge P(x)]$ is to be read as stating that a stage-level predication P of a kind-denoting term k is equal to an existential assertion according to which there are individuals x that are members of the plural individual that constitutes the kind, and the property denoted by P holds of those individuals.

Observe that according to Carlson's original theory, in a sentence such as "Dogs barked at the passing cyclist" the kind-denoting term undergoes no semantic type shift. Instead, the predicate expression simply applies to individuals or to stages of individuals associated with the kind or to kinds themselves, depending on whether the predicate expression is individual-, stage-, or kind-level. In contrast, in Chierchia's theory, the semantic type of the subject itself shifts from a kind-denoting expression to a predicate expression as a consequence of the semantic mismatch between the subject and predicate expression.[55]

Finally and importantly, the semantic type shift and, in this case, existential binding of the argument of the predicativized nominal expression are localized in such a way that the resulting existential quantificational force of the expression has obligatory narrow scope. The obligatory narrow scope of the expression thereby explains the difference in scopal properties between bare noun phrases and explicitly existentially quantified phrases such as "some dogs" or "a dog."[56]

In light of the preceding account, evidently Chierchia's theory shares with the ambiguity theory the view that in sentences such as (D1)–(D3) the nominal expression has a predicative meaning. What distinguishes the two theories is their views of how the nominal expression has or comes to have its predicative meaning. For the ambiguity theory, the predicative meaning of the nominal expression is the lexical meaning of the nominal expression; and the tokened nominal expression is able to retain this meaning because it is merely ostensibly, not actually bare; actually, it is the complement of a covert determiner. For Chierchia, the predicative meaning results from the operation of P-NOM (following prior conversion effected by K-NOM). In such cases, again the nominal

---

[55] Cp. Chierchia (1998) 364–65, remarking on DKP: "Whenever an object-level argument slot in a predicate is filled by a kind (in an episodic frame), the type of the predicate is automatically adjusted by introducing [an] . . . existential quantification over instances of the kind . . . Unlike what happens in Carlson's original proposal, DKP is not a lexical operation on predicate [expressions] but a [nominal] type shifter that applies on demand."

[56] Cp. Chierchia (1998) 368–70, 375–76. In Dayal's recent discussion of the existential force of bare plural noun phrases, she suggests modifying Chierchia's DKP in such a way so as to remove existential quantification from it. Precisely, Dayal proposes the following modification, which she calls "maximality": For a given predicate [expression] P, situation s, and kind[-denoting term] k, if P, indexed to s, applies to objects [that is, ordinary individuals, in contrast to kinds composed of ordinary individuals], then $P(s)(k) = P(s)(k_s)$, where [the extension of] $k_s$ is the extension of the kind[-denoting term k] at s (2013, 68). In other words, on Dayal's proposal, the nominal expression in argument, say subject, position is not type shifted to a predicate expression; it remains a kind-denoting term. However, the kind that it denotes is not the plural individual that comprises *all* of the atomic individuals that constitute the extension of the noun. Rather, it is the plural individual that comprises all of the atomic individuals that constitute the extension of the noun *in situation s*. More precisely, this is one of two modifications that Dayal proposes to DKP. In addition, she proposes to widen the domain of quantification for the bare noun phrase beyond situation s. On this point, cp. Dayal (2013) 67–77. My inclination is to think that at least Dayal's first proposed modification, maximality, is right. Moreover, I incline to think that the proposal might be applied to explain universal and generic as well as existential readings of bare noun phrases. Unfortunately, I am not in a position to attempt this application here.

expression is not actually bare since qua predicate expression it requires an argument and this argument is bound by a quantificational operator. Accordingly, Chierchia's theory also shares with the ambiguity theory the view that the universal, generic, and existential readings of bare nominal constructions derive from quantificational operators binding individual variables, which are associated with the bare nominals that are functioning predicatively.

Assuming that Chierchia's neo-Carlsonian theory is in fact tenable to this point, among many other things,[57] it remains to explain the felicity of the various readings of at least ostensibly bare date-denoting count noun phrases such as (T1)–(T4), (F1)–(F4), (S1)–(S4), and (C1)–(C4). Recall that it is Chierchia himself who claims that bare singular count noun phrases are "totally impossible" in English.[58]

Let me conclude the discussion now by clarifying the respects in which, according to the various theories, the nouns that head bare noun phrases are ambiguous. I've introduced Carlson's kind-denoting theory, a generic version of the ambiguity theory, and Chierchia's neo-Carlsonian kind-denoting theory. According to Carlson's theory, the nouns that head bare noun phrases are always kind-denoting expressions, and a kind is a property is some robust metaphysical sense. According to the ambiguity theory, the nouns that head ostensibly if not actually bare noun phrases are fundamentally two ways ambiguous between kind-denoting and predicative terms. I have said nothing about what, according to any ambiguity theorist, a kind is. Clearly, either Carlson's view or Chierchia's view is in principle possible. Likewise, according to Chierchia, the nouns that head ostensibly if not actually bare noun phrases are fundamentally two ways ambiguous: as kind-denoting terms and as predicative terms.

Crucially then, the question is whether there is any semantic difference between a kind-denoting nominal expression and a nominal expression with a predicative meaning. For Chierchia, a kind is a plural individual, precisely the maximal plural individual at a world and time. In contrast, the denotation of a predicative mass or plural count nominal expression has a join semilattice structure. As such, the meaning of the latter includes the former as a proper part. For example, "moral goodness" as a kind-denoting term refers to the maximal plural individual consisting of all instances of moral goodness at a world and time, whereas the lexical and so predicative meaning of "moral goodness" includes a

---

[57] For instance, it seems to me particularly important to consider what Dayal calls "partition-inducing bare plurals" (2013, 61–63) and "indexical bare plurals" (63–66).

[58] See footnote 11. Granted this, any adequate theory of bare noun phrases in English also has to explain why, as nominal heads of such phrases, plural count nouns and mass nouns are admissible, but not (the vast majority) of singular count nouns. The basic explanation may be that the denotations of mass nouns and plural count nouns include pluralities, which are requisite for the constitution of kinds. After all, a single individual cannot constitute a kind.

maximal plural individual, but also all sub-pluralities and individual instances qua individual instances of moral goodness. In this respect, "goodness" and other mass nouns as well as plural count nouns are ambiguous. The ambiguity is more precisely polysemy. In terms of the kinds of polysemy described in section 5 of chapter 2, we have here cognate words of distinct syntactic categories: a subject and a predicate respectively.

# Bibliography

Abbott, Barbara, "Definite and Indefinite," in *Encyclopedia of Language and Linguistics*, K. Brown, ed., Elsevier, 2006[2].

Alexiadou, Artemis, Haegeman, Liliane, Stavrou, Melita, *Noun Phrase in the Generative Perspective*, Mouton de Gruyter, 2007.

Algra, Kiempe, Barnes, Jonathan, Mansfeld, Jaap, Schofield, Malcolm, eds., *The Cambridge History of Hellenistic Philosophy*, Cambridge University Press, 1999.

Allott, Nicholas, Textor, Mark, "Lexical Pragmatics and the Nature of *Ad Hoc* Concepts," *International Review of Pragmatics* 4 (2012) 185–208.

Allott, Nicholas, Textor, Mark, "Lexical Modulation without Concepts," *Dialectica* 71 (2017) 399–424.

Anonymous, *Structural Notes and Corpus*, 1952.

Arnauld, Antoine, Nicole, Pierre, *Logic or the Art of Thinking*, J. V. Buroker, ed., Cambridge University Press, 1996.

Austin, J. L., *How to Do Things with Words*, Harvard University Press, 1962[2].

Bach, Kent, "Conversational Implicature," *Mind and Language* 9 (1994) 124–62.

Bach, Kent, "Semantic Slack: What Is Said and More," in *Foundations of Speech Act Theory*, S. Tsohatzidis, ed., Routledge, 1994, 267–91.

Bach, Kent, "Quantification, Qualification, and Context: A Reply to Stanley and Szabó," *Mind and Language* 15 (2000) 262–83.

Bach, Kent, "Context ex machina," in *Semantics and Pragmatics*, Z. Szabó, ed., Oxford University Press, 2005, 15–44.

Bach, Kent, "Context Dependence," in *The Bloomsbury Companion to the Philosophy of Language*, M. García-Carpintero and M. Kölbel, eds., Bloomsbury, 2014, 153–84.

Baglini, Rebekah, *Stative Predication and Semantic Ontology*, University of Chicago, dissertation in linguistics, 2015.

Bar-Hillel, Yehoshua, "Indexical Expressions," *Mind* 63 (1954) 359–79.

Barner, David, Snedecker, Jesse, "Compositionality and Statistics in Adjective Acquisition: 4-Year-Olds Interpret *Tall* and *Short* Based on the Size Distributions of Novel Noun Referents," *Child Development* 79 (2008) 594–608.

Barnes, Jonathan, *The Cambridge History of Hellenistic Philosophy*, K. Algra, J. Barnes, J. Mansfeld, and M. Schofield, eds., Cambridge University Press, 1999.

Barsalou, Lawrence, "Ad Hoc Categories," *Memory and Cognition* 11 (1983) 211–27.

Bartsch, Renate, Vennemann, Theo, "The Grammar of Relative Adjectives and Comparison," *Linguistische Berichte* 20 (1972) 19–32.

Baugh, Albert C., Cable, Thomas, *A History of the English Language*, Routledge, 2002[6].

Beck, Sigrid, "The Meaning of *Too, Enough,* and *So . . . That*," *Natural Language Semantics* 11 (2003) 69–107.

Belleri, Delia, *Semantic Under-determinacy and Communication*, Palgrave Macmillan, 2014.

Bhatt, Rajesh, Pancheva, Roumyana, "Implicit Arguments," in *Blackwell Companion to Syntax*, M. Everaert and H. Van Riemsdijk, eds., Blackwell, 2007, 558–88.

Bierwisch, Manfred, "The Semantics of Gradation," in *Dimensional Adjectives*, M. Bierwisch and E. Lang, eds., Springer, 1987, 71–262.

Blackburn, Simon, ed., *Oxford Dictionary of Philosophy*, Oxford University Press, 2008[2].

Bloomfield, Leonard, *Language*, Holt Reinhart and Wilson, 1933.

Bobaljik, Jonathan D., *Universals in Comparative Morphology*, MIT Press, 2012.

Boguslawski, Andrzej, "Measures Are Measures: In Defense of the Diversity of Comparatives and Positives," *Linguistiche Berichte* 36 (1975) 1–9.

Bolinger, Dwight, "Adjectives in English: Attribution and Predication," *Lingua* 18 (1967) 1–34.

Bolinger, Dwight, *Degree Words*, Mouton, 1972.

Börgjesson, Kristin, *The Semantics-Pragmatics Controversy*, de Gruyter, 2014.

Braun, David, "Indexicals," *Stanford Encyclopedia of Philosophy*, 2015.

Bresnan, Joan, Grimshaw, Jane, "The Syntax of Free Relatives in English," *Linguistic Inquiry* 9 (1978) 331–91.

Bruening, Benjamin, "Precede-and-Command Revisited," *Language* 90 (2014) 342–88.

Bühler, Karl, *Sprachtheorie*, Fischer, 1934.

Bunt, H. C., *The Formal Semantics of Mass Terms*, University of Amsterdam, dissertation, 1981.

Büring, Daniel, *Binding Theory*, Cambridge University Press, 2013.

Burnett, Heather, *Gradability in Natural Language*, Oxford University Press, 2017.

Bylinina, Lisa, Zadorozhny, Stas, "Evaluative Adjectives, Scale Structure, and Ways of Being Polite," in *Language, Logic, and Meaning*, M. Aloni et al., eds., The 18th Amsterdam Colloquium, 2012, 133–42.

Carlson, Gregory, "A Unified Analysis of the English Bare Plural," *Linguistics and Philosophy* 1 (1977) 413–57.

Carlson, Gregory, *Reference to Kinds in English*, University of Massachusetts, Amherst dissertation in linguistics, 1977 (published by Garland Press, 1980).

Carlson, Gregory, "No Lack of Determination," in *The Second Glot International State of the Article Book*, L. Cheng and R. Sybesma, eds., Mouton de Gruyter, 2003, 149–78.

Carnap, Rudolf, "Überwindung der Metaphysik durch logische Analyse der Sprache," *Erkenntnis* 2 (1932) 219–41; translated in A. J. Ayer, ed., *Logical Positivism*, Free Press, 1959, 60–81.

Carnie, Andrew, *Syntax: A Generative Introduction*, Blackwell, 2007[2].

Carston, Robyn, "Plurality of Mass Nouns and the Notion of a 'Semantic Parameter,'" in *Events and Grammar*, S. Rothstein, ed., Kluwer, 1998, 53–103.

Carston, Robyn, "Reference to Kinds across Languages," *Natural Language Semantics* 6 (1998) 339–405.

Carston, Robyn, *Thoughts and Utterances: The Pragmatics of Explicit Communication*, Blackwell, 2002.

Carston, Robyn, "Explicit Communication and 'Free' Pragmatic Enrichment," in *Explicit Communication: Robyn Carston's Pragmatics*, B. Soría and E. Romero, eds., Palgrave Macmillan, 2010, 217–85.

Carston, Robyn, "Mass Nouns, Vagueness and Semantic Variation," *Synthese* 174 (2010) 99–149.

Carston, Robyn, "Relevance Theory," in *Routledge Companion to Philosophy of Language*, G. Russell and D. G. Fara, eds., Routledge, 2012, 163–76.

Cheng, Lisa, Doetjes, Jenny, Sybesma, Rint, "How Universal Is the Universal Grinder?" *Linguistics in the Netherlands*, 2008, 50–62.

Chierchia, Gennaro, *Topics in the Syntax and Semantics of Infinitives and Gerunds*, University of Massachusetts, Amherst, dissertation in linguistics, 1984.

Chierchia, Gennaro, McConnell-Ginet, Sally, *Meaning and Grammar*, MIT Press, 2000.

Chomsky, Noam, *Aspects of the Theory of Syntax*, MIT Press, 1965.

Chomsky, Noam, "Questions of Form and Interpretation," *Linguistic Analysis* 1 (1975) 75–109.

Chomsky, Noam, *Lectures on Government and Binding*, Foris, 1981.

Clapp, Lenny, "Three Challenges for Indexicalism," *Mind and Language* 27 (2012) 435–65.

Clark, Billy, *Relevance Theory*, Cambridge University Press, 2013.

Cohen, Ariel, Erteschik-Shir, Nomi, "Are Bare Plurals Indefinites?," in *Empirical Studies in Formal Syntax and Semantics 2*, F. Corbin, C. Dobrovie-Sorin, and J. Marandin, eds., Thesus, 1999, 99–119.

Collins, John, "Syntax, More or Less," *Mind* 116 (2007) 805–50.

Collins, John, "The Syntax of Personal Taste," *Philosophical Perspectives* 27 (2013) 51–103.

Collins, John, "The Nature of Linguistic Variables," in *Oxford Handbooks Online*, 2014.

Collins, John, "On the Linguistic Status of Context Sensitivity," in *A Companion to the Philosophy of Language*, B. Hale, C. Wright, and A. Miller, eds., John Wiley & Sons, 2017, 151–73.

Condoravdi, Cleo, *Descriptions in Context*, Yale University, dissertation in linguistics, 1994.

Condoravdi, Cleo, Gawron, Jean Mark, "The Context-Dependency of Implicit Arguments," in *Quantifiers, Deduction, and Context*, M. Kanazawa, C. Piñón, and H. de Swart, eds., CSLI, 1996, 1–32.

Creswell, Max, "The Semantics of Degree," in *Montague Grammar*, B. Partee, ed., Academic Press, 1976, 261–92.

Crystal, David, *A Dictionary of Linguistics and Phonetics* Blackwell, 2011[6].

Dayal, Veneeta, "Free Relatives and Ever: Identity and Free Choice Readings," *SALT 7* (1997) 99–116.

Dayal, Veneeta, "Bare Noun Phrases," in *Semantics: An International Handbook of Natural Language Meaning*, vol. 3, C. Maienborn, K. von Heusinger, and P. Portner, eds., de Gruyter, 2011, 1088–109.

Dayal, Veneeta, "On the Existential Force of Bare Plurals," in *From Grammar to Meaning: The Spontaneous Logicality of Language*, I. Caponigro and C. Cecchetto, eds., Cambridge University Press, 2013, 49–80.

de Hoop, Helen, "Type Shifting," in *Semantics: An International Handbook of Natural Language Meaning*, vol. 3, C. Maienborn, K. von Heusinger, and P. Portner, eds., de Gruyter, 2011, 2259–71.

Delfitto, Denis, "Adverb Classes and Adverb Placement," in *Blackwell Companion to Syntax*, M. Everaert and H. van Riemsdijk, eds., Blackwell, 2007, 83–120.

Delfitto, Denis, "Bare Plurals," in *Blackwell Companion to Syntax*, M. Everaert and H. van Riemsdijk, eds., Blackwell, 2007, 214–59.

Depraetere, Ilse, Salkie, Raphael, eds., *Semantics and Pragmatics: Drawing a Line*, Springer, 2017.

de Swart, Henriëtte, Zwarts, Joost, "Less Form—More Meaning: Why Bare Singular Nouns Are Special," *Lingua* 119 (2009) 280–95.

Diesing, Molly, *Indefinites*, MIT Press, 1992.

Dobrovie-Sorin, Carmen, Beyssade, Claire, *Redefining Indefinites*, Spring, 2012.

Doetjes, Jenny, Constantinescu, Camelia, Souckova, Katerina, "A Neo-Kleinian Approach to Comparatives," *SALT 19* (2011) 124–43.

Dons, Ute, *Descriptive Adequacy of Early Modern English Grammars*, de Gruyter, 2012.

Elbourne, Paul, "The Argument from Binding," *Philosophical Perspectives* 22 (2008) 89–110.

Falkum, Ingrid Lossius, *The Semantics and Pragmatics of Polysemy: A Relevance-Theoretic Account*, University College London, dissertation in linguistics, 2011.

Fine, Kit, "Acts, Events, and Things," in *Language and Ontology*, W. Leinfellner and E. K. J. Schank, eds., Holder-Pichler-Tempsky, 1982, 97–105.

Finlay, Stephen, *Confusion of Tongues*, Oxford University Press, 2014.

Francez, Itamar, Koontz-Garboden, Andrew, *Semantics and Morphosyntactic Variation*, Oxford University Press, 2017.

Gaus, Gerald, *Value and Justification*, Cambridge University Press, 1990.

Geach, P. T., "Good and Evil," *Analysis* 17 (1956) 33–42.

Gillon, Brendan, "Bare Plurals as Plural Indefinite Noun Phrases," in *Knowledge Representation and Defeasible Reasoning*, H. E. Kyburg et al., eds., Kluwer, 1990, 119–66.

Gillon, Brendan, "Towards a Common Semantics for English Count and Mass Nouns," *Linguistics and Philosophy* 15 (1992) 597–639.

Gillon, Brendan, "Mass Terms," *Philosophy Compass* 7 (2012) 712–30.

Gillon, Brendan, "English Relational Words, Context Sensitivity, and Implicit Arguments," unpublished MS.

Gleason, Henry, *An Introduction to Descriptive Linguistics*, Holt, 1955.

Gotthelf, Allan, "The Place of the Good in Aristotle's Natural Teleology," *Proceedings of the Boston Area Colloquium in Ancient Philosophy* 4 (1988) 113–39.

Gough, James, "The Syntax-Based Semantics of the English Determiner Ø, A, The," *Papers in Linguistics* 1 (1969) 41–48.

Graff, Delia, "Shifting Sands: An Interest-Relative Theory of Vagueness," *Philosophical Topics* 20 (2000) 45–81.

Grano, Thomas, "Mandarin *Hen* and Universal Markedness in Gradable Adjectives," *Natural Language and Linguistic Theory* 30 (2012) 513–65.

Grice, Paul, "The Causal Theory of Perception," *Proceedings of the Aristotelian Society*, supp. vol. 35 (1961) 121–52.

Grice, Paul, "Logic and Conversation," in *Syntax and Semantics*, vol. 3: *Speech Acts*, P. Cole and J. Morgan, eds., Academic Press, 1975, 41–58.

Groos, Anneke, van Riemsdijk, Henk, "Matching Effects in Free Relatives: A Parameter of Core Grammar," in *Theory of Markedness in Generative Grammar*, A. Belletti et al., eds., Scuola Normale Superiore, 1981, 171–216.

Grosu, Alexander, *Three Studies in Locality and Case*, Routledge, 1994.

Hall, Allison, "Free Enrichment or Hidden Indexicals," *Mind and Language* 23 (2008) 426–56.

Hall, Allison, "Lexical Pragmatics, Explicature, and Ad Hoc Concepts," in *Semantics and Pragmatics: Drawing a Line*, I. Depraetere and R. Salkie, eds., Springer, 2017, 85–114.

Hamman, Cornelia, "Adjectivsemantik/Adjectival Semantics," in *Semantik/Semantics: Ein internationals Handbuch der zeitgenössischen Forschung*, A. von Stechow and D. Wunderlich, eds., de Gruyter, 1991, 657–73.

Hare, R. M., *The Language of Morals*, Clarendon Press, 1952.

Harman, Gilbert, "Deep Structure as Logical Form," *Synthese* 21 (1970) 275–97; reprinted in *Semantics of Natural Language*, D. Davidson and G. Harman, eds., Reidel, 1972, 25–47.

Heim, Irene, *The Semantics of Definite and Indefinite Noun Phrases*, University of Massachusetts, Amherst dissertation in linguistics, 1982.

Heim, Irene, "Degree Operators and Scope," in *Audiatur Vox Sapientiae*, C. Féry and W. Sternefeld, eds., *Studia Grammatica* 52 (2001) 214–39.

Heim, Irene, Kratzer, Angelika, *Semantics in Generative Grammar*, Blackwell, 1998.

Hellan, Lars, *Towards an Integrated Analysis of Comparatives*, Narr, 1981.

Hines, Carol, "Lexical Integrity: *Good, Great*, and *Well*," in *The Fifth LACUS Forum*, W. Wölck and P. L. Garvin, eds., Hornbeam, 1978, 134–41.

Hinterwimmer, Stefan, "A Comparison of Abstract and Concrete Mass Nouns in Terms of Their Interaction with Quantificational Determiners," forthcoming.

Hinzen, Wolfram, "Nothing Is Hidden: Contextualism and the Grammar of Meaning," *Mind and Language* 30 (2015) 259–91.

Hinzen, Wolfram, Sheehan, Michelle, *The Philosophy of Universal Grammar*, Oxford University Press, 2013.

Hofweber, Thomas, "Number Determiners, Numbers, and Arithmetic," *Philosophical Review* 114 (2005) 179–225.

Holton, Richard, *Willing, Wanting, Waiting*, Oxford University Press, 2009.

Horn, Lawrence, "Toward a New Taxonomy for Pragmatic Inference: Q- and R-Based Implicature," in *Meaning, Form, and Use in Context*, D. Shiffrin, ed., Georgetown University Press, 1984, 11–42.

Huang, Yan, *Pragmatics*, Oxford University Press, 2007.

Huang, Yan, *Pragmatics*, Oxford University Press, 2014[2].

Huddleston, Rodney, "More on the English Comparative," *Journal of Linguistics* 3 (1967) 91–102.

Huddleston, Rodney, Pullman, Geoffrey K., *The Cambridge Grammar of the English Language*, Cambridge University Press, 2002.

Jespersen, Otto, *A Modern English Grammar*, part II, *Syntax*, vol. 1, George Allen & Unwin, 1913.

Jespersen, Otto, *The Philosophy of Grammar*, George Allen & Unwin, 1924.

Kamp, Hans, "A Theory of Truth and Discourse Representation," in *Formal Methods in the Study of Language*, J. Groenendijk et al., eds., Mathematical Centre, 1981, 277–322.

Kaplan, David, "Demonstratives," in *Themes from Kaplan*, J. Almog, J. Perry and H. Wettstein, eds., Oxford University Press, 1989, 481–563.

Keenan, Edward, Faltz, Leonard M., *Logical Types for Natural Language*, UCLA Occasional Papers in Linguistics, no. 3, 1978.

Kempson, Ruth, *Semantic Theory*, Cambridge University Press, 1977.

Kennedy, Christopher, "Comparison and Polar Opposition," in *The Proceedings of Semantics and Linguistic Theory* 7, A. Lawson, ed., Cornell Linguistics Club Publications, 1997, 240–57.

Kennedy, Christopher, *Projecting the Adjective*, University of Southern California, dissertation in linguistics, 1997 (published by Garland Press, 1999).

Kennedy, Christopher, "Gradable Adjectives Denote Measure Functions, Not Partial Functions," *Studies in Linguistic Sciences* 29 (1999) 65–80.

Kennedy, Christopher, "Polar Opposition and the Ontology of 'Degrees,'" *Linguistics and Philosophy* 24 (2001) 33–70.

Kennedy, Christopher, "Vagueness and Grammar: The Semantics of Relative and Absolute Gradable Adjectives," *Linguistics and Philosophy* 30 (2007) 1–45.

Kennedy, Christopher, McNally, Louis, "Scale Structure, Degree Modification, and the Semantics of Gradable Predicates," *Language* 81 (2005) 345–81.

Kennedy, Christopher, Svenonius, Peter, "Northern Norwegian Degree Questions and the Syntax of Measurement," in *Phases of Interpretation*, M. Frascarelli, ed., Mouton de Gruyter, 2006, 129–57.

Klein, Ewan, "A Semantics for Positive and Comparative Adjectives," *Linguistics and Philosophy* 4 (1980) 1–45.

Klein, Ewan, "The Interpretation of Adjectival Comparatives," *Journal of Linguistics* 18 (1982) 113–36.

Korsgaard, Christine, "Two Distinctions in Goodness," *Philosophical Review* 92 (1983) 169–95.

Koslicki, Kathrin, "Nouns, Mass and Count," in *Encyclopedia of Philosophy*, D. M. Bouchert, ed., Macmillan, 2005.

Kratzer, Angelika, "What 'Must' and 'Can' Must and Can Mean," *Linguistics and Philosophy* 1 (1977) 337–55.

Kratzer, Angelika, "Die Analyse des bloßen Plural bei Gregory Carlson," *Linguistische Berichte* 70 (1980) 47–50.

Kratzer, Angelika, "Stage-Level and Individual-Level Predicates," in *The Generic Book*, G. Carlson and F. J. Pelletier, eds., University of Chicago Press, 1995, 125–74.

Krifka, Manfred, "Common Nouns: A Contrastive Analysis of Chinese and English," in *The Generic Book*, G. Carlson and F. J. Pelletier, eds., University of Chicago Press, 1995, 398–411.

Krifka, Manfred, "Bare NPs: Kind-Referring, Indefinites, Both, or Neither?" *SALT 13* (2003) 180–203.

Larson, Richard K., "Events and Modification in Nominals," *SALT* 8 (1998) 145–68.

Lasersohn, Peter, "Bare Plurals and Donkey Anaphora," *Natural Language Semantics* 5 (1997) 79–86.

Lasersohn, Peter, "Mass Nouns and Plurals," in *Semantics*, K. von Heusinger, C. Maeienborn, and P. Portner, eds., de Gruyter, 2001, 1131–53.

Lassiter, Daniel, Goodman, Noah, "Context, Scale Structure, and Statistics in the Interpretation of Positive-Form Adjectives," *SALT* 23 (2013) 587–610.

Laycock, Henry, "Mass Nouns, Count Nouns and Non-count Nouns: Philosophical Aspects," in *Encyclopedia of Language and Linguistics*, K. Brown, ed., Elsevier, 2006, 534–38.

Laycock, Henry, *Words without Objects*, Oxford University Press, 2006.

Le Bruyn, Bert, de Swart, Henriëtte, Zwarts, Joost, "Bare Nominals," in the *Oxford Research Encyclopedia of Linguistics*, 2017.

Lehrer, Adrienne, "Markedness and Antonymy," *Journal of Linguistics* 21 (1985) 397–429.

Lehrer, Adrienne, Lehrer, Keith, "Antonymy," *Linguistics and Philosophy* 5 (1982) 483–501.

Leslie, Sarah-Jane, "Generics: Cognition and Acquisition," *Philosophical Review* 117 (2008) 1–47.

Levinson, Stephen C., "Deixis," in *Handbook of Pragmatics*, L. Horn and G. Ward, eds., Wiley, 2007, 97–123.

Link, Godehard, "The Logical Analysis of Plural and Mass Terms," in *Meaning, Use, and Interpretation of Language*, R. Bäuerle, C. Schwarze, and A. von Stechow, eds., de Gruyter, 1983, 127–46.

Lyons, John, *Semantics*, vol. 2, Cambridge University Press, 1977.

MacInnis, Luke, "Agency and Attitude: Kant's Purposive Conception of Human Rights," *Philosophy and Social Criticism* 42 (2016) 289–319.

Maienborn, Claudia, Schäfer, Martin, "Adverbs and Adverbials," in *Semantics: An International Handbook of Natural Language Meaning*, vol. 3, Maienborn, K. von Heusinger, and P. Portner, eds., de Gruyter, 2011, 1390–420.

Mansoor, Jaleh, "Ed Ruscha's One-Way Street," *October Magazine* 111 (2005) 127–42.

Martí, Luisa, "Unarticulated Constituents Revisited," *Linguistics and Philosophy* 29 (2006) 135–66.

Matthews, P. H., *Oxford Concise Dictionary of Linguistics*, Oxford University Press, 2007[2].

McNally, Louise, "Modification," in *The Cambridge Handbook of Formal Semantics*, M. Aloni and P. Dekker, eds., Cambridge University Press, 2016, 442–64.

McNally, Louise, Kennedy, Christopher, "From Event Structure to Scale Structure: Degree Modification in Deverbal Adjectives," *Proceedings of SALT 9*, T. Matthews and D. Strolovitch, eds., CLC Publications, 1999, 163–80.

McNally, Louise, Kennedy, Christopher, "Degree v. Manner *Well*: A Case Study in Selective Binding," in *Advances in Generative Lexicon Theory*, J. Pustejovsky et al., eds. Spring, 2013, 247–62.

Milsark, Gary, *Existential Sentences in English*, MIT, dissertation in linguistics, 1974.

Moltmann, Frederike, "Properties and Kinds of Tropes: New Linguistic Facts and Old Philosophical Insights," *Mind* 113 (2004) 1–43.

Moltmann, Frederike, "Degree Structure as Trope Structure," *Linguistics and Philosophy* 32 (2009) 51–94.

Moltmann, Frederike, *Abstract Objects and the Semantics of Natural Language*, Oxford University Press, 2013.

Moore, G. E., *Principia Ethica*, Cambridge University Press, 1903.

Morzycki, Marcin, *Modification*, Cambridge University Press, 2016.

Mount, Allyson, "The Impurity of 'Pure' Indexicals," *Philosophical Studies* 138 (2008) 193–209.

Murphy, M. Lynne, *Lexical Meaning*, Cambridge University Press, 2010.

Neale, Stephen, "This, That, and the Other," in *Beyond Descriptions*, A. Bezuidenhout and M. Reimer, eds., Oxford University Press, 2004, 68–182.

Neale, Stephen, "On Location," in *Situating Semantics*, M. O'Rourke and C. Washington, eds., MIT Press, 2007, 251–393.

Neeleman, Ad, van de Koot, Hans, Doetjes, Jenny, "Degree Expressions," *Linguistic Review* 21 (2004) 1–66.

Nichols, David, "The Logic of Mass Expressions," *Stanford Encyclopedia of Philosophy*, 2013.

Nickel, Bernhard, "Dutchmen Are Good Sailors: Genericity and Gradability," in *Genericity*, Alda Mari et al., eds., Oxford University Press, 2013, 390–405.

Nunberg, Geoffrey, "Indexicality and Deixis," *Linguistics and Philosophy* 16 (1993) 1–43.

Ojeda, Almerindo E., "The Paradox of Mass Plurals," in *Polymorphous Linguistics: Jim McCawley's Legacy*, MIT Press, 2005, 389–410.

Partee, Barbara, "Noun Phrase Interpretation and Type Shifting Principles," in *Studies in Discourse Representation and the Theory of Generalized Quantifiers*, J. Groenendijk, D. de Jongh, and M. Stokhof, eds., Foris, 1987, 115–43.

Partee, Barbara, "Binding Implicit Variables in Quantified Contexts," *Papers from the 25th Regional Meeting of the Chicago Linguistic Society*, C. Wiltshire, R. Grazyte, and B. Music, eds., Chicago Linguistic Society, 1989, 342–56.

Peirce, C. S., "Logic as Semiotic: The Theory of the Sign," 1902; reprinted in *Philosophy Writings of Peirce*, Dover, 1955, 98–119.

Pelletier, F. Jeffrey, "Non-singular Reference: Some Preliminaries," *Philosophia* 5 (1975) 451–65.

Pelletier, F. J., Schubert, L. K., "Mass Expressions," in *Handbook of Philosophical Logic*, vol. 4, D. Gabbay and F. Guenther, eds., Reidel, 1989, 327–407.

Perry, John, "Indexicals, Contexts, and Unarticulated Constituents," in *Computing Natural Language*, A. Aliseda-Llera et al., eds., CSLI Publications, 1998, 1–11.

Perry, Ralph Barton, *General Theory of Value: Its Meaning and Basic Principles Construed in Terms of Interest*, Oxford University Press, 1926.

Pethö, Gergely, "What Is Polysemy?—a Survey of Current Research and Results," in *Pragmatics and Flexibility of Word Meaning*, E. T. Németh and K. Bibok, eds., Elsevier, 2001, 175–224.

Pethö, Gergely, "On Irregular Polysemy," in *The Cognitive Basis of Polysemy: New Sources of Evidence for Theories of Meaning*, M. Rakova, G. Pethö, and C. Rákosi, eds., Peter Lang, 2007, 123–56.

Pilch, Herbert, "Comparative Constructions in English," *Language* 41 (1965) 37–58.

Portner, Paul, *Modality*, Oxford University Press, 2009.

Pupa, Francesco, Troseth, Erika, "Syntax and Interpretation," *Mind and Language* 26 (2011) 185–209.

Pustejovsky, James, *The Generative Lexicon*, MIT Press, 1995.

Quine, Willard Van Orman, *Mathematical Logic*, Harvard University Press, 1940.

Quine, Willard Van Orman, *Word and Object*, MIT Press, 1960.

Radford, Andrew, *Syntactic Theory and the Structure of English*, Cambridge University Press, 1997.

Rappaport, Malka, Levin, Beth, "-er Nominals: Implications for the Theory of Argument Structure," in *Syntax and Semantics*, vol. 26, T. Stowell and E. Wehrli, eds., Academic Press, 1992, 127–53.

Rathert, Monika, "Adverbials," in *Oxford Handbook of Tense and Aspect*, R. I. Binnick, ed., Oxford University Press, 2012, 237–68.

Recanati, François, "The Pragmatics of What Is Said," *Mind and Language* 4 (1989) 296–329.

Recanati, François, "Unarticulated Constituents," *Linguistics and Philosophy* 25 (2002) 299–345.

Recanati, François, *Literal Meaning*, Cambridge University Press, 2004.

Recanati, François, "Pragmatics and Semantics," in *Handbook of Pragmatics*, L. R. Horn and G. Ward, eds., Blackwell, 2004, 442–62.

Recanati, François, *Truth-Conditional Pragmatics*, Oxford University Press, 2010.

Recanati, François, "Pragmatic Enrichment," in *Routledge Companion to Philosophy of Language*, G. Russell and D. G. Fara, eds., Routledge, 2012, 67–78.

Rett, Jessica, *The Semantics of Evaluativity*, Oxford University Press, 2015.

Reuland, Eric, "Binding Theory: Terms and Concepts," in *Blackwell Companion to Syntax*, M. Everaert and H. Van Riemsdijk, eds., Blackwell, 2007, 260–83.

Riddle, Elizabeth M., "A Historical Perspective on the Productivity of the Suffixes -ness and -ity," in *Historical Semantics: Historical Word Formation*, J. Fisiak, ed., de Gruyter Mouton, 1985, 435–62.

Rooryck, Johan, Vanden Wyngaerd, Guido, *Dissolving Binding Theory*, Oxford University Press, 2011.

Rothstein, Susan, "Counting, Measuring, and the Mass Count Distinction," *Journal of Semantics* 27 (2010) 343–97.

Rothstein, Susan, "Aspect," in *The Cambridge Handbook of Formal Semantics*, M. Aloni and P. Dekker, eds., Cambridge University Press, 2016, 342–68.

Rothstein, Susan, *Semantics for Counting and Measuring*, Cambridge University Press, 2017.

Rotstein, Carmen, Winter, Yoad, "Total Adjectives versus Partial Adjectives: Scale Structure and Higher-Order Modifiers," *Natural Language Semantics* 12 (2004) 259–88.

Russell, Bertrand, *Science and Religion*, Oxford University Press, 1935.

Saeed, John I., *Semantics*, Wiley Blackwell, 2009[3].

Safir, Ken, "Syntax, Binding, and Patterns of Anaphora," in *The Cambridge Handbook of Generative Grammar*, M. den Dikken, ed., Cambridge University Press, 2013, 515–76.

Sapir, Edward, "Grading: A Study in Semantics," *Philosophy of Science* 11 (1944) 93–116.

Sassoon, Galit W. "A Typology of Multidimensional Adjectives," *Journal of Semantics* 30 (2013) 335–80.

Schwarzschild, Roger, "Measure Phrases as Modifiers of Adjectives," *Recherches Linguistiques de Vincennes* 34 (2005) 207–28.

Schwarzschild, Roger, "The Role of Dimensions in the Syntax of Noun Phrases," *Syntax* 9 (2006) 67–110.

Sennet, Adam, "The Binding Argument and Pragmatic Enrichment, or, Why Philosophers Care Even More Than Weathermen about 'Raining,'" *Philosophy Compass* 3 (2008) 135–57.

Seppänen, Aimo, "Lexical Integrity or Semantic Diversity: *Good, Great,* and *Well*," *English Studies* 65 (1984) 534–49.

Seuren, Pieter A. M., "The Structure and Selection of Positive and Negative Gradable Adjectives," in *Papers from the Parasession on the Lexicon*, Chicago Linguistics Society, vol. 14, 1979, 336–46.

Shanklin, Robert, *On "Good" and Good*, University of Southern California, dissertation in philosophy, 2011.

Shields, Christopher, *Order in Multiplicity*, Oxford University Press, 1999.

Siegel, Muffy, *Capturing the Adjective*, University of Massachusetts, Amherst dissertation in linguistics, 1976 (published by Garland Press, 1980).

Simons, Mandy, et al., "What Projects and Why," *SALT* 20 (2011) 309–27.

Solt, Stephanie, "Notes on the Comparison Class," in *Vagueness in Communication: Lectures Notes in Computer Science*, R. Nouwen et al., eds., vol. 6517, Spring, 2011, 189–206.

Sperber, Dan, Wilson, Deirdre, *Relevance: Communication and Cognition*, Blackwell, 1995[2].

Sperber, Dan, Wilson, Deirdre, *Meaning and Relevance*, Cambridge University Press, 2012.

Stanley, Jason, "Context and Logical Form," *Linguistics and Philosophy* 23 (2000) 391–434.

Stanley, Jason, *Language in Context*, Oxford University Press, 2007.

Stassen, Leon, *Comparison and Universal Grammar*, Blackwell, 1985.

Stassen, Leon, "Comparative Constructions," in *World Atlas of Language Structures Online*, M. Haspelmath et al., eds., chap. 121, Max Planck Digital Library, 2008.

Stevenson, Charles Leslie, "The Emotive Meaning of Ethical Terms," *Mind* 46 (1937) 14–31.

Stvan, Laurel Smith, *The Semantics and Pragmatics of Bare Singular Noun Phrases*, Northwestern University, dissertation in linguistics, 1998.

Stvan, Laurel Smith, "The Functional Range of Bare Singular Count Nouns in English," in *Nominal Determination: Typology, Context, Constraints, and Historical Emergence*, E. Stark, E. Leiss, and W. Abraham, eds., John Benjamins, 2007, 171–87.

Suzuki, Seichi, "On the Origin and Development of the Action Noun Forming Suffix *-nis* in Old English," *Indogermanische Forschungen* 95 (1990) 184–207.

Szabó, Zoltán Gendler, "Adjectives in Context," in *Perspectives on Semantics, Pragmatics, and Discourse*, I. Kenesei and R. M. Harnish, eds., John Benjamins, 2001, 119–46.

Thomson, Judith J., "On Some Ways in Which a Thing Can Be Good," *Social and Political Policy* 9 (1992) 96–117.

Tovena, Lucia M., "Between Mass and Count," in *Proceedings of WCCFL*, K. Mergerdoomian and L. A. Bar-el, eds., Cascadilla Press, 2001, 565–78.

Travis, Charles, "On Constraints of Generality," *Proceedings of the Aristotelian Society* n.s. 44 (1994) 165–88.

Trips, Carola, *English Suffixes and Diachronic Morphology: The Development of -hood, -dom, and -ship in the History of English*, Max Niemeyer Verlag, 2009.

van Kuppevelt, Jan, "Inferring from Topics: Implicatures as Topic-Dependent Inferences," in *Linguistics and Philosophy* 19 (1996) 393–443.

van Riemsdijk, Henk, "Free Relatives," in *Blackwell Companion to Syntax*, M. Everaert and H. Van Riemsdijk, eds., Blackwell, 2007, 338–82.

van Rooij, Robert, "Vagueness and Linguistics," in *Vagueness: A Guide*, G. Ronzitti, ed., Springer, 2011, 123–70.

van Rooij, Robert, Sassoon, Galit, "The Semantics of *for* Phrases and Its Implications," unpublished MS.

von Stechow, Arnim, "Comparing Theories of Comparison," *Journal of Semantics* 3 (1984) 1–77.

Ward, Julia K., *Aristotle on Homonymy: Dialectic and Science*, Cambridge University Press, 2007.

Whorf, Benjamin, "The Relation of Habitual Thought and Behavior to Language," in *Language, Culture, and Personality*, L. Spier, ed., Sapir Memorial Fund, 1941, 75–93.

Wiggins, David, "On Sentence-Sense, Word-Sense, and Difference of Word-Sense: Towards a Philosophical Theory of Dictionaries," in *Semantics: An Interdisciplinary Reader in Philosophy, Linguistics, and Psychology*, D. Steinberg and L. Jakobovits, eds., Cambridge University Press, 1971, 14–34.

Wilkinson, Karina, *Studies in the Semantics of Generic Noun Phrases*, University of Massachusetts, Amherst, dissertation in linguistics, 1991.

Williams, Alexander, *Arguments in Syntax and Semantics*, Cambridge University Press, 2015.

Williams, Edwin, "Predication," *Linguistic Inquiry* 11 (1980) 203–238.

Wilson, Deirdre, Carston, Robyn, "A Unitary Approach to Lexical Pragmatics: Relevance, Inference, and Ad Hoc Concepts," in *Pragmatics*, N. Burton-Roberts, ed., Palgrave-Macmillan, 2007, 230–59.

Wilson, Deirdre, Sperber, Dan, "Relevance Theory," in *Handbook of Pragmatics*, L. Horn and G. Ward, eds., Blackwell, 2004, 607–32.

Wittgenstein, Ludwig, "I: A Lecture on Ethics," *Philosophical Review* 74 (1965) 1–12.

Ziff, Paul, *Semantic Analysis*, Cornell University Press, 1960.

Zwicky, Arnold, Sadock, Jerrold, "Ambiguity Tests and How to Fail Them," in *Syntax and Semantics*, vol. 4, J. Kimball, ed., Academic Press, 1975, 1–36.

# Index